A REASON FOR EVERYTHING

by the same author

DOPE GIRLS: THE BIRTH OF THE BRITISH DRUG UNDERGROUND
AS WE KNOW IT: COMING TO TERMS WITH AN EVOLVED MIND

A Reason for Everything

*Natural Selection
and the English Imagination*

MAREK KOHN

faber and faber

First published in 2004
by Faber and Faber Limited
3 Queen Square London WC1N 3AU

Typeset by Faber and Faber Limited
Printed in England by Mackays of Chatham, plc

The right of Marek Kohn to be identified as author of this work
has been asserted in accordance with Section 77 of the Copyright,
Designs and Patents Act 1988

A CIP record for this book
is available from the British Library

ISBN 0–571–22392–3

2 4 6 8 10 9 7 5 3 1

For Sue and Teo

Contents

REASONS FOR EVERYTHING

Aims and Acknowledgements

The idea for this book arose from the suggestion of my editor, Neil Belton, that biography might be a fruitful way to explore the history of evolutionary thought. Neil values biography as a means to take up wider stories about history and ideas; he has demonstrated its power in books that he has edited or written himself. He believes in books, in serious and passionate engagement with ideas, and in authors. Nothing gives me greater pride in my writing than Neil's editorial approval.

A Reason for Everything is centred upon the idea of adaptation by natural selection, which is what brings design to evolution, and what makes it challenging even for those who recognise that it not only can but must work. It is set in Britain, a country which has provided the idea of natural selection not only with its discoverers but also with an unusually congenial habitat. The story reflects upon the varied fortunes of one of the most momentous ideas ever introduced to human reason, and also upon the country which nurtured it.

There are half a dozen principal characters, all influential British evolutionary thinkers, and a common theme: how they have responded to the idea of natural selection. The book explores how they have understood the idea, how they have developed it, and how they have integrated it into their ideologies. All of them have been profoundly impressed by the power of natural selection; all have been deeply concerned with truths beyond science. Understanding better than anybody how it is possible for life, living creatures and living beings to evolve without the help of any intelligent power, they have faced the moral consequences of their insight. Their stories tell of how they pursued meaning in life.

The choice of thinkers was not the only one possible, as one or two evolutionary biologists were keen to point out to me. Nevertheless, it largely made itself. It is not an attempt to highlight the 'best' evolutionists, but rather to consider figures who have influenced evolutionary thought, who have influenced the public's understanding of evolution, and who have sought to understand evolution as more than just a mechanism. In this they are not typical of their discipline, which today is as sober and technical as any other, but they are telling. The story also includes cameos illustrating notable evolutionists at Oxford, where natural selection's most ardent admirers gathered, and the creatures they studied.

Darwin is not included because he is now a biographical science in his own right, archived and analysed more extensively than any other scientist. His hinterland has been minutely detailed both inside and outside the academic domain. On the other hand, Alfred Russel Wallace was an obligatory subject, since he not only discovered natural selection for himself, but in many respects embraced it more firmly than Darwin did, while the respects in which he recoiled from it are equally striking. The studies of the power of natural selection made by J. B. S. Haldane and R. A. Fisher, the former a pragmatic and the latter a true believer in 'adaptationism', are generally acknowledged to be fundamental to the 'modern synthesis' of Darwinism and genetics. W. D. Hamilton is widely regarded as the presiding genius of modern Darwinism, while John Maynard Smith is its senior British statesman and Richard Dawkins is its dashing public champion.

In each case, the main theme is the scientist's response to natural selection, and around it a cluster of biographical details that should illuminate it: his introduction to Darwinian ideas, his social and religious background, his education, his aptitudes, and the distinctive ways in which his scientific mind works. These are not intended to be full biographies in miniature, but selective explorations of each man's life and thought.

The treatments vary, however, in their approaches to this agenda and their deviations from it. Wallace is in a different league from the others as far as biographical attention is concerned. There are plenty of accounts, several of them recent; the intention here is to complement rather than to duplicate them. The account strays most from the path in the case of Haldane, whose life outside evolution is too arresting to ignore. Richard Dawkins's ideas are readily accessible, not just because of their scintillating expression but because his books are all in print and almost all aimed at general audiences. He has also been the subject of plenty of recent discussion; the treatment here is correspondingly briefer. Its main purpose is to set him in context, describing the scientific currents that shaped his view of natural selection.

Likewise, I have limited the discussion of some topics that have been widely aired already, such as the debates over sociobiology, or the contest over the public understanding of evolution between Stephen Jay Gould and those whom he labelled 'ultra-Darwinians', Dawkins and Maynard Smith among them. These themes have been explored by a number of authors, including Andrew Brown, Ullica Segerstråle and Kim Sterelny.

Richard Dawkins and John Maynard Smith both very kindly allowed me to conduct a series of interviews with them. In each case, the account is shaped by the stories they told and what they wished to disclose. Dawkins is both the most public and the most private of scientists.

They were not supposed to be the only living subjects. Originally there were to be three, each taking Darwinism forward into the new millennium in his own way. I wrote to Professor Hamilton in January 2000, asking for an interview. At that point he was on a field trip in Congo. Towards the end of it he fell ill; on his return to England he collapsed, and he died six weeks later without regaining consciousness. This has not been a good time for assessments. Those who cherished him – and they are many – have been mindful of their loss; those who had a less favourable opinion will have been inclined not to voice it. But there would be a gaping hole in this story without him, and I have tried to provide a discussion that is appropriate in the circumstances. I would like to express my deep appreciation and gratitude to his sisters Mary Bliss and Janet Hamilton, to his wife Christine Hamilton, and to his partner in the years preceding his death, Luisa Bozzi, for their time, their consideration and their readiness to talk about Bill Hamilton sooner than the natural course of bereavement would dictate. I'd also like to thank them for their hospitality, another facet of their generosity towards me and this project.

I'm also happy – and fortunate – to be able to say that I enjoyed talking to everybody else who was kind enough to discuss aspects of this book with me: my thanks are due to Brian and Deborah Charlesworth, Bryan Clarke, Patricia Clarke, Helena Cronin, Anthony Edwards, Adam Eyre-Walker, Alan Grafen, Alasdair Gray, John Hajnal, Paul Harvey, Peter Henderson, Jon Hodge, Edward Hooper, Jeff Joy, Alexey Kondrashov, John Krebs, Tim

Lenton, James Lovelock, Aubrey Manning, Julian Maynard Smith, Sheila Maynard Smith, Valerie Maynard Smith, Avrion Mitchison, Graeme Mitchison, Murdoch Mitchison, Desmond Morris, Sean Nee, Peter O'Donald, Andrew Pomiankowski, Andrew Read, Mark Ridley, Matt Ridley, Cedric Smith, Julian Tower and Mike Worobey. For advice and assistance of various kinds, I would like to thank Judith Adamson, Andrew Brown, Dieter Ebert, Hugh Ingram, Annamaria Talas, Robert Kruszynski, Jelena Mežnarić, Nigel Fisher of the Oxford University Land Agents, and staff in the Manuscripts section of the National Library of Scotland, as well as their counterparts at University College London and other libraries. I'd also like to acknowledge Ian Pitchford's rolling evolutionary news service at human-nature.com.

I am most grateful to those who have given permission to quote from correspondence and other material: John Maynard Smith, for his letters; Christine Hamilton, for letters written by her late husband Prof. Hamilton; Louie Burghes, for her grandmother Charlotte Haldane's letters; Lois Godrey, for her uncle J. B. S. Haldane's letters and other unpublished texts. My thanks are also due to the University of Adelaide and Professor J. H. Bennett, for permission to reproduce extracts from R. A. Fisher's writings.

I am extremely grateful for comments on drafts and parts of the text from Helena Cronin, Jon Hodge, Stephen Howe, Gill Scott, Colin Tudge and Henry Volans. And I am grateful above all for the love, support and patience of my wife, Sue Matthias Kohn.

John Maynard Smith died on 19 April 2004 as this book was being prepared for publication.

One day I visited the Sussex University campus to discuss the possibility of a 'Darwinian Left' with Richard Wilkinson, who studies the relationship between inequality and health. John Maynard Smith came into the café; we joined him and ventured on to the topic in hand. Before long, however, he was telling us about indignant greenfinches. Any bird rash enough to alight on campus, he explained, was liable to be ringed and pressed into experimental service. Having an interest in the evolution of animal communication, he had helped a colleague in a study of how various bird species use signals, such as the colour of their plumage, to settle contests. It appears that some male greenfinches are truly green, while others are drab. The green ones act with a confidence to match their plumage, while the drab ones are meeker. If, however, a drab finch starts to act like a bright one, it is punished with particular ferocity, as if its punishers were indignant that it had tried to pass for something it was not.

This example may have some bearing on Maynard Smith's thoughts about birdwatchers and their attitude to adaptation by natural selection – 'I never knew a birdwatcher who was not a naive adaptationist' – which are something of a keynote statement for this story. At the time, it reminded me of what I love about biology. To enjoy a constant curiosity about living organisms; to discern great processes in humble creatures; to speak about them simply, and with good humour: there is a grace and an art to this science. I first encountered it as an undergraduate in the School of Biological Sciences at Sussex University, and now realise that I owe John Maynard Smith thanks beyond that due to his unfailingly generous responses to my inquiries and the pleasure of conversing with him. He was the first Dean of 'Biols', and I must thank him for setting the tone.

His conversation is at once encouraging and enlightening – that is why its serene effects are cherished long after by those fortunate enough to have taken part in it – and so is his view of evolved life. I would be more than content if readers also find encouragement in this series of stories about understanding evolution and finding meaning in life designed by it, but I am only too aware of the obstacles. I have brought in humble and charming creatures where I can, but even these may raise hackles. Indignant greenfinches may smack of children's stories, not science (and would probably have provoked indignation in our Animal Behaviour lecturers when I was a student). Butterflies that respect property? Ideology passing as science, surely – even with the ironic use of the word 'bourgeois' to describe their behaviour. Then, below the creatures, there are the genes. Maynard Smith thinks it perfectly sensible to talk of a gene for tying one's shoelaces; but others may consider it absurd as well as juvenile. And whereas it may seem at worst silly to describe greenfinches as indignant, it may seem sinister to describe genes as selfish. Suspicions will be deepened by some of the lessons for society that certain of these evolutionists have drawn from their science. But as the exuberance of the metaphors shows, it is not a dismal science. It is an impassioned one, and we may be caught up by passions without sharing them.

7

Then, however, there is the maths. Even those reassured that science can be done by watching butterflies and garden birds may be vulnerable to panic when they see that what the bird is perched on is not foliage but a mass of knotted equations. At one glance evolution seems transcendentally simple, yet fiendishly complicated at the next. Neither view is deceptive. Ordinary observers stand to gain many insights into evolution, but it contains many problems that nobody has yet resolved. 'Maths panic' shouldn't daunt outsiders unduly. While John Maynard Smith thinks in equations, Richard Dawkins hums his way through them.

Another objection, apt to be made by foreign observers, is that British evolutionism lacks depth: with its collections of facts, metaphorical licence and its tendency to whimsy, it is vulnerable to the charge. Friedrich Nietzsche considered that Darwin's work on evolution exemplified what British thinking did well – a mechanistic natural process described through diligent, blinkered plodding. A more sympathetic view might be that the British have often shown a preference for empirical truths and for avoiding unnecessary complication. Darwin himself was 'especially indignant with Germans', according to his son Francis, 'because he was convinced that they could write simply if they chose'. He would have sympathised with the greenfinches.

And yet, if they have sometimes seemed to lack the will for grandeur that may be apparent in philosophy across the Channel, British evolutionists have always said more than they said on the surface. Perhaps the most obvious example is the much-noted similarity between Darwin's vision of natural selection and the competitive, capitalist Britain in which he lived: whatever view one takes of the relationship between the theory and its context, there is a sense in which the former speaks of the latter.

Even greenfinches or butterflies may have an allusive hinterland. Whimsy, shading into absurdity, is a style with a broad appeal to the British (and especially English) imagination. Part of its charm and its purpose is to represent, in tolerable form, features of a world that is hard to take straight; a world that may appear especially pitiless and indifferent, in Dawkins's words, to scientists studying natural selection. On the other hand, it expresses a delight in imagination, fired by the most fertile of ideas.

Mechanistic as the theory may be, it can support the richest and subtlest of meanings. I will outline parts of the mechanism, and pursue the meanings.

1

Senses of Purpose

Change is not so hard to accept, but life is intolerable without a sense of purpose. Living forms change as generations pass: once this is acknowledged, there are many ways to accommodate it within a belief that life has reason and direction. Change implies progress, after all. But what does progress mean if it takes place through chance events and their automatic consequences? It has no goal, no guidance and no predestined direction. Once the means of change is acknowledged to be natural selection, purpose loses its spirit.

Although natural selection does not exclude a role for spirit in the living world, it provides a full substitute for it. That is why, in the philosopher Daniel Dennett's phrase, it is 'Darwin's dangerous idea'. It shows that design may take place without a designer – and inevitably will if living organisms vary in traits that can be inherited. And that is prime among the reasons why, ever since it was first announced, natural selection has been denied, discounted, played down and contained. For anybody who does not insist on taking sacred texts literally, evolution can be an estate that respects the balance of philosophical power. But as selectionist currents gain influence within it, evolution threatens to become revolutionary.

Charles Darwin and Alfred Russel Wallace separately realised that organisms would increase or decline in numbers according to how well or poorly they were adapted to their conditions of existence. Their insight was publicly aired in 1858, at a meeting of the Linnean Society in London, where papers by the two naturalists were read. By that time, few if any of their peers believed that Genesis was a literal account of the origin of the world. It was clear to them that the earth must be millions of years old, rather than the few thousand which traditional interpretations of the Bible had suggested. After decades of research and debate, they understood fossils and strata for what they were. They were impressed by the sugges-tive pattern in the rocks, which showed fossil types appearing not at a stroke but in sequence. The possibility had been raised that one species might derive from another, but how this could happen was not yet explained.

One possible means had been proposed by the French scientist Jean Baptiste de Lamarck, who lodged the idea of evolution as a topic of debate in 1801 (and also introduced the word 'biology'). Lamarck argued that as organisms encountered changes in their environments, they would make greater use of some organs or body parts, and less of others. Structures that were used would grow; those that were disused would decline. These changes could be inherited, leading to adaptive evolution.

Lamarck's ideas secured little purchase in his lifetime, and the idea of evolution did not gain its bridgehead until 1859, when Darwin's *Origin of Species* was published. By the end of the century there was general accept-ance that living forms changed over time, and that species were descended from common ancestors, but Darwinism itself was widely held to be extinct. In 1932, J. B. S. Haldane prefaced his *Causes of Evolution* with the epigraph '"Darwinism is dead." – *Any sermon*'. Evolution was established on the basis of natural selection, but the process of establishing it entailed the replacement of natural selection by more wishful means. Some favoured a modified role for higher powers, gently guiding natural processes. Many, including Darwin himself, were drawn to the 'Lamarckian' idea that the inheritance of traits could be influenced by whether their possessors made use of them or not; many, but not includ-ing Darwin, took comfort from the sense of purpose in Lamarckian think-ing, which imagined that animals' wishes, not just their actions, influenced whether or not traits would be inherited. And when biologists became interested in mutations, some argued that evolution took place by mutant leaps rather than the iota of natural selection.

These represented different varieties of wishful thinking. Supernatural intervention implied the conscious wishes of the Creator or lesser immor-tals. Lamarckism was based on the belief that each new species was closer to perfection than the one before. Mutationism optimistically maintained that new forms, even species, could be created in one fell swoop, and would turn out to be adapted in every necessary way to the conditions they encountered – 'hopeful monsters', as their boldest advocate, the German-born biologist Richard Goldschmidt, called them. Darwin, however, had been sure from the start that nature did not make leaps.

For well over half a century, there were good reasons for wishful thinking. The Darwinians themselves seemed vainly ambitious to propose that such a slow and wasteful process, the epitome of inefficiency, was the force that had produced the variety of life. A basic problem they faced was the lack of a scheme for inheritance. Without the understanding that traits are passed on as discrete elements, Darwin was hard pressed to explain why a trait, once selected, was not then blended away in future generations. Ronald Fisher explained the problem in his own masterwork, *The Genetical Theory of Natural Selection*, which appeared in 1930. An individual inherited characters from each of its parents. In Darwin's time, there had been two theories of what happened to these characters when they were transmitted. One was blending inheritance, which proposed that each pair of character-transmitting units was transformed into a new unit. The other was particulate inheritance, which held that each unit remained an unchanged 'particle' in the offspring. Under particulate inheritance, then, the stock of variations in the population would be maintained, whereas under blending inheritance, individual variations would swiftly disappear. Fisher showed that under blending inheritance, the variance (his measure of variation) would be halved within a generation or two.

Darwin's theory of evolution required variation among organisms, for without diversity, nature would have nothing to select. As he supposed that inheritance was a blending process, he found it difficult to maintain the pre-eminent position he had given to natural selection in his original theory, and so was obliged to lay more weight on other possible mechanisms for evolutionary change. The problem had become a public one within ten years of the *Origin*'s appearance, when it was outlined by Fleeming Jenkin, a professor of engineering.

A particulate scheme had, however, been published two years before Jenkin's article by Gregor Mendel. He identified a number of traits in peas, such as yellow pods or wrinkliness, which did not blend, and showed how their transmission could be explained by the inheritance of units from each parent. Where there were alternative versions of a unit, a quarter of the offspring would have pairs of one version, another quarter would have pairs of the other, and the remaining half would have one of each. One form, the 'dominating' one, overrode the other, which he called 'recessive', so that individuals possessing the mixed pairs showed the character induced by the form which took precedence. The result was the ratio of three to one, now familiar in school textbooks, in the characters shown by the offspring.

Mendel was right, classically so, but his work made almost no impression until the end of the century. It was not just that he was a Moravian monk, counting peas in the seclusion of his monastery garden; he and his work were sufficiently known for his name to have been made during his lifetime, if the significance of his experiments had been grasped. Nor was it simply a question of putting two great insights together. Mendel's account of inheritance in peas was not initially understood to be a statement of fundamental principle, and then was not recognised as a solution to part of the Darwinians' difficulties. Instead, it was seen as the basis of an alternative means of change.

The reconciliation of Mendelism and Darwinism, and the building of what became known as the 'modern synthesis' of evolutionary and genetic theory, began at the end of the First World War and was largely complete by the Second. Three scientists are customarily acknowledged as the founders of the synthesis: Ronald Aylmer Fisher, J. B. S. Haldane and Sewall Wright. As the synthesis developed, Fisher and Wright increasingly found themselves at loggerheads over the question of chance. Fisher was confident that natural selection could handle all aspects of the evolutionary process. Wright believed that chance played an essential role in causing populations to diverge from each other, by changing the proportions of genes in small isolated groups.

Fisher had taken the first momentous step towards the synthesis in 1918, when he published a paper which reconciled two bodies of evidence that had previously been used against each other. Mendelians were interested in visibly discrete characters, such as the colour of peas or guinea pigs' fur. Recognising that inheritance of any particular trait operated not by blending both parents' qualities but by preferring one over the other, the Mendelians concentrated on traits that clearly indicated how the choice had fallen. Biometricians, on the other hand, were concerned with the inheritance of traits that varied continuously, such as human height or head size. They failed to see how their smoothly curving graphs could be produced by a mechanism that divided inheritance into particles. Fisher applied his imposing mathematical powers to show that particulate inheritance could operate at the finest of resolutions.

Haldane's contribution was also mathematical, generating a series of papers that helped to clarify what natural selection could do, and how quickly it might do it. Natural history had given rise to the insight. Mathematics confirmed that it was credible.

Adaptation could mean a number of things. It might mean that God had designed all the features of living things for the best. It might mean that organisms adapted themselves to their conditions of life by their behaviour or physiological responses, and that such adaptive changes were then inherited by their descendants. It might also mean that organisms could be shaped by internal forces which guided their evolution along adaptive lines. When Darwinism eventually prevailed, however, these possible meanings were discarded. The Darwinian concept of adaptation by natural selection was what remained.

An adaptation, in the Darwinian sense, is an inherited feature of an organism which tends to increase the number of its descendants, and which has arisen through that effect. That is selection, which may act to assist survival or to promote reproduction directly (the latter is known as sexual selection, but to modern Darwinians it is basically a variety of natural selection). There are no internal forces or goals that can produce adaptations; there is only selection: the exclusiveness of this power has impressed itself profoundly upon 'adaptationists'. Other evolutionists may look at an organism and see its structures as the products of internal logic, like patterns in inanimate nature, such as waves or crystals. They may suppose that some of its characters are of no adaptive value and therefore cannot be products of selection. But an adaptationist looks at a living thing and inclines to see, in all its characters, the work of unconscious design. An adaptationist will tend to assume a reason for everything.

That assumption has a venerable pedigree. In his essay 'On the Perfection of Animals', the Oxford biologist Arthur Cain treated those who rejected it as departures from a tradition maintained since classical antiquity. 'People from Aristotle on to the early nineteenth century were on the whole much nearer to being right than their successors,' he wrote in 1964. Aristotle had believed that most structures in living organisms were adapted to a purpose, and so could be explained if their function could be determined. This belief became orthodox, until it was placed in question in the middle of the nineteenth century, along with other fundamental propositions about the living world.

Cain, and Alfred Russel Wallace before him, were what the nineteenth-century evolutionist George Romanes had labelled 'ultra-Darwinians'. Unlike Darwin himself, they did not equivocate about selection and adaptation. Making a bid for the peak while keeping an eye on the paths back down, Darwin had declared in the first edition of the *Origin of Species* that 'Natural Selection has been the main but not exclusive means of modification'. This allowed him to fall back to more defensible positions in the face of scepticism about the power of natural selection, complaining in the final edition that his caveat had not been acknowledged: 'Great is the power of steady misrepresentation.' By that stage, as the historian of science Robert M. Young has observed, the book's title 'should have read *On the Origin of Species by Means of Natural Selection and All Sorts of Other Things*'.

Darwin also came to believe that he had failed to take proper account of traits that were neither helpful nor harmful. He attributed his misperception to the lingering influence of his former belief that species had been divinely created, which left him with the tacit assumption that each of their features must have some special purpose. His natural selection still bore traces of natural theology. But even as he recanted his error, he still maintained that the full power of natural selection had yet to be revealed. 'I am convinced,' he wrote in the *Descent of Man*, 'from the light gained during even the last few years, that very many structures which now appear to us useless, will hereafter be proved to be useful, and will therefore come within the range of natural selection.'

A century after Romanes, the American palaeontologist Stephen Jay Gould took up the term 'ultra-Darwinian' in his struggle against what he believed was an excessively zealous enthusiasm for adaptation, the 'British hang-up'. When Gould looked at an organism, he was more likely to detect compromise than assume adaptation. And he even had a soft spot for hopeful monsters.

Gould argued that, like the world in general, evolution is an untidy affair in which a lot of things just happen. He emphasised the role of chance events, like the asteroid that appears to have finished off the dinosaurs, and the importance of structural logic in determining the forms of organisms. Instead of emphasising the role of the world outside as the agent of the organism's design, he cast it in the role of capricious fate; meanwhile, he called upon the organism's inner laws to explain its form. He also called upon German design, or rather a German idea of design. Influenced by his reading of German biological texts, he introduced his public to the term *Bauplan* (ground plan), meaning a basic set of structural relations that shape an organism. Male mammals have nipples, he pointed out, but it is more sensible to assume that these are present because males and females are developed from a common plan, than that they are of any evolutionarily significant use to the males themselves.

Nor, as the Darwinian scholar Michael Ruse has noted, would Gould suppose that when female deer mount other females, they improve their reproductive chances. Evolutionary design finds uses for androgens and oestrogens – 'male' and 'female' hormones – in both sexes. High levels of androgens in females may induce 'male' behaviour, but that may be just a quirky side-effect of shared design arrangements. An adaptationist, however, will not write female mounting off so readily. Geoff Parker, a British evolutionary biologist, has suggested that females are most likely to behave like this when they are in heat. By acting like males, they attract the attention of dominant males, who approach them to investigate potential competitors, and instead discover potential mates. The implication is that when natural selection sees a quirk, it sees an opportunity.

In 1978, Gould and the geneticist Richard Lewontin issued a manifesto against adaptationism, which was read by Gould at a Royal Society meeting in London arranged by John Maynard Smith. For them this was taking the fight to the enemy stronghold. 'In very large part this has been a British pastime,' Lewontin had written in 1972, 'traceable to the fascination with birds and gardens, butterflies and snails that was characteristic of the pre-war upper middle class from which so many British scientists came.'

Arthur Cain, still nettled six years later, took the opportunity to proclaim his own humble origins in his concluding remarks.

Between them, Lewontin and Cain highlight a remarkable feature of British evolutionary thought. The idea of adaptation by natural selection not only originated in Britain but hung on and then flourished there, while struggling or failing to take elsewhere. Adaptationism receives a persistent and distinguishing emphasis among British evolutionists, from Darwin's time to the present, which runs counter to the current across the Channel. The British were willing to seek reasons in tangled and motley nature, whereas the French, according to the science historian Peter Bowler, were bound by formality: 'There were no real field naturalists because this approach violated the rationalist image of science as an activity that must take place in the carefully controlled environment of the laboratory or the dissecting room.'

Along the English Channel ran a line dividing those who were ready to see nature as the source of design in living organisms, and those who remained true to their belief that design arose from inner laws. In continental Europe, the understanding of nature was based on a belief in ideal forms. The historian of science David L. Hull observes that this tradition, whose founding father is Plato, reached its peak in France and Germany during the eighteenth and nineteenth centuries. French and German biologists were directed by idealist philosophy to see species as immutable, and they were more concerned with the relations within living structures than the possible effect of external influences. Holding ideal forms dear, they saw the variety of life as its imperfection. Each species had an ideal type, from which its individuals departed to various extents. Achieving perfection therefore depended on the ability of the organism to attain its inner ideal. Natural selection brushed such sentiments aside. Perfection was measured by reference to the outside world, not the inner essence; variation was not the weak flesh letting down the willing spirit, but the resource that made approaches to perfection possible.

As continental European scientists migrated to America from the nineteenth century to the middle of the twentieth, they extended the Anglo–Continental divide across the Atlantic. Continental idealism inspired the early resistance to natural selection in America, Peter Bowler argues, through the person of Louis Agassiz. A palaeontologist, a creationist, and a product of European learning in both French and German, Agassiz was professor of zoology at Harvard, where his museum hall became Stephen Jay Gould's office. American naturalists were persuaded of evolution by fossils, adds the historian Ronald L. Numbers, not by the living creatures that were their own objects of study. They accepted the record of change, but were not impressed by natural selection as a means of design. Even Darwin's most prominent American supporter, the botanist Asa Gray, would only admit to being a Darwinian 'in his own fashion'. Gray doubted that natural selection could fashion complex structures like organs, and gave God the credit for bringing humans into the world, as well as for leading variation 'along certain beneficial lines'.

As Bowler points out, the first Darwinians owed much of their success to their intimate position at the heart of intellectual and institutional power in London. Darwin and Wallace enjoyed the support of a coterie of influential scientists, of whom Thomas Henry Huxley, the great Victorian statesman of science, was first among equals. Public science education in Britain was instituted by Huxley to his own design; behind the scenes he pulled wires and smoothed paths, and he even founded his own convivial secret society, the X Club. The Darwinians also established a powerful editorial influence through their part in setting up the journal *Nature*, which was launched in 1870 and is now the world's premier scientific journal. And the Huxleys established themselves, as did the Darwins and the Haldanes, as one of the leading families in what the historian Noel Annan called the 'intellectual aristocracy'. This was a new formation, arising within the privileged classes, which capitalised upon the intellectual abilities that commanded increasing premiums as society restructured itself around science, knowledge and professions.

Agassiz was America's Huxley, a towering figure in the promotion of science and a Germanic idealist immigrant who found the American climate congenial. Born in Switzerland, from whose glaciers he deduced the previous existence of ice ages, he made a tour of German, Swiss and French centres of learning, before settling to his life's work with fossil fishes. Though he recognised progress in the fossil record, from simpler to more complex forms, he believed that it was the story of continuing divine creation. Each species was a 'thought of God'; as such, it was an ideal form.

Although his followers did not consider that his steadfast creationism was tenable, they turned his system of nature into a structure sufficiently sophisticated to withstand the initial challenge of natural selection. Agassiz saw the history of life as an ascent towards man, and saw a microscopic recapitulation of this journey in each individual journey through embryonic development. Lacking idealist conviction, the British had largely dismantled the ladder of life, and so it was not available as a support for British naturalists who wanted to uphold their sense of purpose. In the United States, however, Agassiz's students were able to reconfigure it. They abandoned the human species as the end point of all evolution and adopted a framework of branching lineages that resembled Darwin's, while retaining the idea of a predestined goal within each lineage. Evolution remained a process guided by inner order, 'laws of growth', not outer flux. They looked to the embryo rather than the environment; and when they began to contemplate the latter, it was within a Lamarckian frame.

In the end, by impeding the appreciation of the power of natural selection, their efforts to maintain order left more room for chance in America than in Britain. It was not that Americans were oblivious to adaptation and Britons obsessed with it. American geneticists, notably William Castle, Edward East and Thomas Morgan, prepared the ground for the 'modern synthesis' with experimental work which persuaded Mendelians that natural selection was a force to be reckoned with after all. In 1966, the American evolutionist George Williams presented arguments, in his book *Adaptation and Natural Selection*, which were as 'ultra-Darwinian' as anything on the other side of the Atlantic: they helped to define the new Darwinian orthodoxy by proposing that selection chooses between genes rather than groups of organisms. And the continental European emigrés Mayr and Dobzhansky were influential in what Stephen Jay Gould called the 'hardening' of the synthesis, a shift towards adaptationism that became evident in the late 1940s. (Gould began as an adaptationist too, under their influence at Columbia University, and Lewontin's formative teacher was Dobzhansky. Perhaps the two of them found it easier to fight their battles against the English rather than against their own mentors.)

Among the canonised founders of the 'modern synthesis', however, it was the American, Wright, who stood up for random drift against Fisher's all-pervading selectionism. 'Because of the accident that Wright is

American, whereas Fisher and Haldane were British,' observed John Maynard Smith, 'evolutionary biologists in America often place great emphasis on chance events, whereas we British know better.'

Maynard Smith knows better than anyone, though, that the British evolutionists' bias against chance is not an accident. As he points out, it has much to do with the British enthusiasm for natural history. 'I never met a bird watcher who was not a naive adaptationist,' he once remarked, 'but why? I think it may be that, if one watches an animal doing something, it is hard not to identify with it, and hence to ascribe a purpose to its behaviour.'

Purpose, for British naturalists, seems to have taken priority over type. Collection, the dominant activity of Victorian naturalists, is nothing without classification. Maynard Smith might also have suggested that it is hard not to sort the organisms that one sees into types, and so to see nature as an assemblage of species. That, after all, is how birdwatchers organise nature. They observe and often wonder about the behaviour of birds, but recording it is not their priority; their principal output is lists of species, with items ticked off. The highly influential evolutionist Ernst Mayr, who was raised in Germany and then settled in America, was truer to his bird-watching roots than his British counterparts. He limited his endorsement of the 'modern synthesis' on the grounds that it did little to illuminate the issue in the title of Darwin's book, the origin of species. His own account of the synthesis treats it as an international movement in which mathematical genetics, the anglophone speciality, was unimportant; he highlights his own role and that of other scientists from continental Europe, particularly Theodosius Dobzhansky, who ended up as a geneticist in America but started out classifying beetles in Russia.

Mayr appreciated the power of natural selection, and succeeded in impressing it upon his colleagues in America; but he wanted a synthesis that gave a fuller account of what Darwin, echoing the astronomer and chemist Sir John Herschel, had himself called the 'mystery of mysteries'. He gained his understanding of natural populations on hazardous expeditions in New Guinea (in the late 1920s, while searching for birds of paradise) and the Solomon Islands, and then went to the United States, where he developed the argument that species arise when populations become separated from each other and diverge in their evolution until they can no longer interbreed. For Mayr, adaptation was the means, and the origin of species was the end. He had been a German birdwatcher, not a British one, schooled in a *Gymnasium* and universities in a tradition where classification was not merely about lists but about ideal types. His achievement was to uphold that remnant of the Platonic tradition which remained tenable after Darwin had disposed of its foundation, by transcending it. Focusing his thought upon populations instead of types, Mayr maintained the importance of classes by insisting that species still matter, even if they do not have an essence.

British evolutionists were less concerned about classes of organisms, seeing them as one effect among many of adaptation's all-pervasive power. 'Theories of Evolution are of two kinds,' wrote Ronald Fisher, 'those that . . . "are explanations primarily of adaptation and only secondarily of the origin of species", and those which fail to account for adaptation.' The first kind included Lamarckian explanations and the theory of natural selection. 'For these two theories evolution *is* progressive evolution and consists of nothing else. The production of differences recognisable by systematists is a secondary by-product, produced incidentally in the process of becoming better adapted.' John Maynard Smith is just as categorical about the supremacy of adaptation: '. . . for me, it is *the* problem that a biologist has to explain. Go out there, look at anything. If you're a competent naturalist, the one thing that hits you in the face about everything you're seeing is adaptation.'

Maynard Smith was an engineer before he became a biologist, and Richard Lewontin might have had him in mind when he observed that what he called the 'adaptationist program' of evolutionary research, which assumed that all traits of organisms were not just adaptive but optimally so, was 'much more akin to engineering than . . . to physics', because 'the purpose of the investigator is to show *how* organisms solve problems optimally, not to test *if* they do'. And Lewontin might also have been thinking of Maynard Smith when he gave his potted class analysis of British adaptationism. John Maynard Smith was born into a family with considerable accumulated wealth and eminence; he grew up between the wars; he was schooled at Eton and educated at Cambridge; he was fascinated by birds and matured into a gardener of distinction. But British adaptationism had a broader class base, and a longer history, than Lewontin acknowledged in his condescending references to the 'genteel' fascination with snails and butterflies. The upper-middle-class cap also fitted Fisher (Harrow and

Cambridge) and Haldane (Eton and Oxford) – though nobody ever accused J. B. S. of being genteel. Others, like Cain and Wallace, did not conform to the stereotype.

The British love of nature, and the passion for domesticating it, has always been shared by all classes. From the rich man's rolling parkland to the backyard gardener's row of beans, the principle is the same. Natural history's constituency also crossed the classes, if not the sexes. 'All sorts of different people seem to watch birds,' observed the author of a Pelican paperback, writing during the Second World War, when all were in it together. 'Among those I know of are a late Prime Minister, a Secretary of State, a charwoman, two policemen, two kings, one ex-king, five communists, four Labour, one Liberal, and three Conservative Members of Parliament, the chairman of a County Council, several farm-labourers earning sixty shillings a week, a rich man who earns two or three times that amount in every hour of the day, at least forty-six schoolmasters, and an engine-driver.'

Although it was easier for members of the wealthier classes to translate their fascination into scientific studies, others played their part too. Darwin learned much about selection – the artificial kind – from the pigeon fanciers whose circles he frequented. Most were more respectable than the ones he rubbed shoulders with in a south London 'gin palace', but they were hardly out of the top drawer.

Darwin himself was the type-specimen of the gentleman naturalist, as secure in his squirish Kent house as the lawns around it were serene. He might well be the spirit presiding over Lewontin's image of bourgeois science with an English accent. Plenty of the props of English cliché are also present in Wallace's story, but they are arranged in a way that unpicks the package. There are flower shows, gardening magazines, beetle collections, and the Victorian mania for arranging the variety of life into dead rows. Alfred Russel Wallace was obliged to be a player rather than a gentleman, though. His family was chronically short of money, and it was in the doldrums of his apprenticeship to his brother, an underemployed surveyor, that he discovered and cultivated his love of natural history. He taught himself botany from cheap self-improvement texts, rambling across the Welsh countryside in the long periods when no work was to be had, and caught the odd tantalising glimpse of the tropics from the orchids admired by gardeners. When he travelled to the Amazon and the Malay Archipelago, he went as a working collector, hoping to finance himself by the sale of specimens.

Besides natural history there was natural theology, introduced in the late seventeenth century by the prominent scientists Robert Boyle and John Ray, the latter both a naturalist and an ordained Anglican priest. By proposing that the complexity of living things was the supreme material demonstration of God's wisdom and power, they offered a means to combine the methods of science with the aims of theology. Divine wisdom could now be affirmed by scientific observation as well as by studying scripture.

Evidence of design, of adaptation for purpose, was central to this project. Natural theologians came to regard living things as assemblages of adaptations, and they tended to see adaptation everywhere. Natural selectionists then adopted this perspective, so intuitive and rewarding, when they took over from the natural theologians. Darwin's personified nature, 'daily and hourly scrutinising, throughout the world, every variation, even the slightest; rejecting that which is bad, preserving and adding up all that is good; silently and insensibly working, *whenever and wherever opportunity offers*, at the improvement of each organic being', maintained a sense of purpose and omnipresence that was next to godliness.

This was an appropriation rather than a coup. Darwin himself felt 'most deeply that the whole subject is too profound for the human intellect. A dog might as well speculate on the mind of Newton.' He called himself an agnostic, using the term coined by Thomas Henry Huxley, who meant by it that knowing whether God exists is impossible in principle. Some of Darwin's successors have enjoyed greater confidence in the power of intellect, guided by science, and have become atheists. Others consider themselves agnostics, and some have kept their faith. Richard Dawkins is famously and fundamentally atheist; his intellectual forefather Ronald Fisher, who was a radical adaptationist before Dawkins was even a genotype, held to a conventional Anglicanism.

Bill Hamilton, another of Fisher's heirs, described himself as an agnostic, seeming to mean it in Huxley's sense rather than the uncertainty that Darwin felt. Haldane explicitly rejected the Huxleyan position, declaring that sufficient evidence was available to decide the question and placing himself in the atheist ranks. He was versed in both Christian scripture and Hindu mythology, but never seems to have felt the need to believe in any of it. Maynard Smith exchanged his Anglicanism for atheism in his teens. Wallace also rejected conventional religion as a young man, but in maturity became convinced of powers higher than nature. Paradoxically, his belief in the power of selection encouraged him to insist that supernatural intervention was necessary to account for the powers of the human mind. Since even 'savages' had mental capacities far in excess of what he considered they needed in order to survive, he denied that these faculties had been produced by natural selection. He therefore concluded that they had been bestowed by some form of higher intelligence.

Wallace's idiosyncratic contrivance of natural and supernatural selection was the most striking of the lengths he went to, throughout much of his life, to reconcile his belief in human progress with his understanding of the role of unconscious design in nature. He was not alone in his concern to integrate his evolutionary theory into a world view with broader philosophical and political dimensions. Fisher's evolutionary understanding was inseparable from the eugenic convictions he held all his adult life. Hamilton, for whom Fisher was an intellectual inspiration, was similarly persuaded. Haldane became a Marxist and one of the British Communist Party's leading public intellectuals; Maynard Smith was a communist before he became, under Haldane's wing, a biologist. Dawkins grew to love biology through treating it as philosophy: his evolutionism may be seen as his philosophical inclinations focused into a single theme.

The left commands a majority in this group. Wallace embraced socialism, of a characteristically quirky flavour, in his later years. Haldane was forced into a struggle between his Party loyalty and his scientific integrity when the Soviet Communist Party rejected genetics, or 'Mendel–Morganism', in the late 1940s; yet when he eventually detached himself from the Party, it was without ideological upheaval. Maynard Smith quit the CP, like many others, after the Soviet invasion of Hungary, but his sympathies remained undogmatically left-wing. Richard Dawkins is neatly, if fractionally, left of centre.

On the other side of the line, Fisher and Hamilton were right-wing in their instincts and held eugenic views that have been confined to the outer margins of acceptability for the past half century. Their views on human heredity are part of their Darwinism. But other eminent Darwinists – Haldane in his day, Maynard Smith and Dawkins in theirs – have practised the same science and have formed different views about what it means for society.

In their personalities they had their affinities and their differences, which played out in the relations between them. Haldane and Fisher professed their respect for each other in public, but it was mixed with rivalry that led to private irritation and a tendency to encourage separate followings. Both had legendary tempers, but inspired devotion as well as awe. Maynard Smith found Haldane's mind 'immediately sympathetic'. Nearly half a century after he became one of Haldane's students, he testified in the preface to a book that his teacher's influence was 'present on every page'; and present as he worked each day was a photo of Haldane, his office deity.

Hamilton belonged to the Fisherian current, though he was inspired by Fisher's writings rather than his brief encounters as a Cambridge undergraduate with the professor in his carpet-slippered twilight, 'the very image of Gorki's Tolstoy in his old age'. Some of Hamilton's most successful studies were undertaken in attempts to work out what Fisher had meant, an obligation which places considerable demands on Fisher's admirers.

Fisher was something of a prophet without honour in his own land. Neglected in Cambridge, he was a very significant influence in Oxford, through naturalists such as Edmund Brisco Ford, Philip Sheppard and Arthur Cain. They caught the butterflies and snails that he used as ammunition in his battles with Sewall Wright.

His calculations had shown him that even very small selective advantages could have decisive evolutionary effects. It was therefore difficult for a trait to be neutral: the fence it had to sit upon was narrow, and it would most likely fall on either the beneficial or the harmful side. A suitable case study presented itself in the form of *Cepaea*, a snail that comes in a variety of shades and has a varying number of bands. Despite detailed study, these variations at first seemed unconnected to the snails' conditions of existence. But when Cain and Sheppard analysed their distribution, they found that some varieties occurred more frequently in hedgerows, others in fields, and so on. One of the reasons turned out to be that thrushes found some varieties easier to spot than others. As Darwin had anticipated, structures that appeared useless had been brought within the range of natural selection.

In its turn, natural selection had been brought within the range of experimental procedure. Darwin had placed his faith in millennia, trusting that the earth had depth enough in time to let natural selection take life through its course. One of the reasons he drew back from selection was the challenge he faced from the physicist Lord Kelvin, who reckoned that the earth must be less than a hundred million years old. (Kelvin's calculations were based on the assumption that the earth must be cooling down from an initial state of incandescence. It was later realised that radioactivity, then unknown, could keep the primordial fire going.) Natural selection was referred to the unimaginable dimensions of geological time, not the manageable proportions of human lifespans. Seeing it in action was too much to expect.

The enthusiasm of the British adaptationists between the wars was fired not just by their love of their gardens and nature trails – though that was surely part of it – but by the exciting prospect that evolution could happen fast enough to be measured after all. Fisher demonstrated the power of 1 per cent in establishing selective change. In the field, the adaptationist naturalists found that selective advantages could reach 50 per cent or more. Natural selection now appeared salient and experimentally tractable. It could be used as the basis of a research programme; and so adaptation became a valuable working assumption.

The wildlife around Oxford readily yielded evidence of the power of selective forces, and by the early 1960s the Zoology Department of Oxford University had become a hive of adaptationism. It was in this atmosphere of presumed purpose that Richard Dawkins's evolutionary foundations were laid. Bill Hamilton's first papers also made an impression upon him that lasted ever afterwards. Fisher's current thus flowed down to Dawkins through the general influence of the Department, and the particular influence of Hamilton.

Hamilton reminded Dawkins of Eeyore, the lugubrious donkey in the Winnie-the-Pooh stories. Even when he had laurels in abundance to rest on, Bill Hamilton was never breezy. Before he began to receive the acclaim that eventually hailed him as the Darwin of the twentieth century, his defining characteristic was isolation. His thinking was overlooked, uncomprehended or regarded with suspicion. For many years he nurtured a bitter grievance against Maynard Smith over what he felt was unfair treatment at the outset of his career.

To a large extent, the failure in comprehension arose from a simple inability to cope with the ranks of equations that greeted raw biologists like festoons of barbed wire. Hamilton took a rather dim view of his own mathematical abilities, as Maynard Smith and Dawkins do of theirs. But those judgements go by the standards of mathematicians, not of biologists. As Haldane said of the calculations on which the 'modern synthesis' was founded, 'Our mathematics may impress zoologists but do not greatly impress mathematicians.' Although biologists need to be able to handle basic statistical tools – for which in large part they have Fisher to thank – to know a little maths is not to love it. Maynard Smith warns his students: 'if you can't stand algebra, stay out of evolutionary biology'.

Hamilton felt that it was not just a lack of sympathy for maths that inclined some people to steer clear of his work. They looked askance because they thought they heard sinister undertones in it. His first chosen theme was altruism, meaning behaviour which is against the interests of the individual that performs it and is in the interests of others. If one individual acts in such a way as to benefit others, to its own cost, it will increase the others' chances of reproduction, while diminishing its own. Any tendency it bears to behave in such a way will be eliminated along with it. Yet such behaviours are cornerstones of many species' ways of life.

The answer to this conundrum lay in kinship. What is good for others is good for the individual, to the extent that they are related. Haldane made the point in a popular essay, using an imaginary example of a gene that induced its bearer to leap into a river to save a drowning child. If the child was related to the bearer, it might also carry the gene. The more closely it was related, the greater the likelihood that, over a series of rescues, more copies of the gene would be saved than would be lost when their carriers drowned. A gene for altruism could spread, if its benefits accrued to its possessors. From the individual's point of view, it was altruism; from the gene's, it was selfishness.

Hamilton's first papers set this insight into a robust theoretical foundation. It could now serve as the basis for a new Darwinism, a tangled bank of calculations, conflicts, costs and benefits. Social behaviour was at the heart of the new project, and so was sex. Hamilton took up the latter as his second grand theme. The first act of his intellectual career was devoted to kinship; in the second, he addressed the greatest unsolved biological question of life: why sex evolved. He blamed parasites, which he had become convinced were the driving force behind much of evolution. Organisms had to continually throw up new variations in order to keep a step ahead of their parasites, which were themselves constantly in a flux that lent itself to rapid natural selection. Sex was a strategic asset in an arms race.

In a similar vein, Richard Dawkins saw communication between animals as an arms race between manipulators, seeking to deceive, and mind-readers, trying to tell whether they were being cheated. Before Hamilton, loosely Darwinian biologists had presumed that organisms would easily fall into arrangements that were to their mutual benefit. After Hamilton, Darwinism presumed genetic conflict; discoveries in recent years have revealed that it extends far beyond animal behaviour. Pregnancy was recast: rather than a harmonious process of nurture, it was presented as a contest for resources between mother and foetus, in which the latter struggles to maximise an investment that the former may prefer to ration for the benefit of other offspring. Advances in molecular biology opened up a submicroscopic world in which stretches of 'selfish' DNA pursued their own replication regardless of the organisms they occupied; conflicts were detected within individual genomes, between genes inherited from mothers and genes from fathers. 'When we look at the biological world, are we seeing the smiling faces of children furiously kicking one another under the table . . .?' wondered the biologists Linda Partridge and Laurence Hurst.

The more that conflict became apparent, though, the more interesting co-operation became, and biologists turned their attention to specifying conditions under which it could arise. Maynard Smith's most celebrated theoretical innovation was to address these problems by applying game theory to the evolution of behaviour and other biological processes. Later in his career, he and his Hungarian colleague Eörs Szathmáry told the story of 'major transitions in evolution', such as the emergence of chromosomes, sex and language. The most important feature these developments have in common is that in each case 'entities that were capable of independent replication before the transition can replicate only as part of a larger whole after it'. Understanding the complexity of life now meant understanding the resolution of conflicts.

Maynard Smith's games were set in the world of unconscious design by natural selection, not the human world of conscious intent. Humans could achieve arrangements, such as social contracts, that were not open to animals. For Hamilton and Dawkins, too, there was no question that humans were special. The more they understood of nature and its ways of selection, the more they cherished the fragile and precious instances in which humans seemed to rise above it.

ALFRED RUSSEL WALLACE

'We conceive it to be a most erroneous, a most contracted view of the organic world, to believe that every part of an animal or of a plant exists solely for some material and physical use to the individual, – to believe that all the beauty, all the infinite combinations and changes of form and structure should have the sole purpose and end of enabling each animal to support its existence . . .'
  Alfred Russel Wallace, 1856

'. . . I have endeavoured to show, that the known laws of variation, multiplication, and heredity, resulting in a "struggle for existence" and the "survival of the fittest," have probably sufficed to produce all the varieties of structure, all the wonderful adaptations, all the beauty of form and of colour, that we see in the animal and vegetable kingdoms.'
  Alfred Russel Wallace, 1870

2

Malthus, Malaria and the Malay Archipelago

Alfred Russel Wallace spent an afternoon as a pupa, and by evening had emerged as a butterfly. In the caterpillar phase of his life as a naturalist he had trooped through the forests of the Amazon, his appetite for natural variety boundless, and now he had set out to forage across the islands of the Malay Archipelago.

In February 1858, his expeditions were interrupted by a cycle of fevers, probably malarial. These are occupational hazards for naturalists in the tropics, and Wallace responded to the attack by accepting the routine it imposed. Each afternoon, he would take to his bed as the fits enveloped him, by turns cold and hot, for two or three hours. He was cocooned in a native hut, a chrysalis nestled deep within the mass of detail which natural historians need in order to flourish.

Outside were beetles, butterflies in multiple editions, shimmering birds and subfusc ones, uncountable insects of all kinds, a vegetable riot from mountains to shore. At further removes around the fragmented continent of the Archipelago there were birds of paradise, humans of varying forms, and orang-utans, the 'men of the forest', so suggestively close to humankind. As a collector, Wallace needed a natural cornucopia from which to acquire trophy specimens that he could sell for high prices. As a naturalist, he needed to be immersed in the details, in intimate contact with natural variety at its maximum. Wallace saw the variety of life not as a catalogue but as a system whose relationships it became his purpose to understand.

The relationships with which he had become preoccupied were those between varieties and species, for therein lay the answer to the question of how species arose in the first place. Pointing out that closely related species are found close together, he had already pronounced his 'Sarawak Law' in the Archipelago: that 'every species has come into existence coin-

31

cident both in time and space with a pre-existing closely allied species'. Darwin had realised the same thing when he reflected on the creatures, living and fossil, he had encountered during his voyage around South America on HMS *Beagle*: the implication was that it might be more than coincidence. Wallace had stated a circumstantial argument for evolution.

Now, as he lay shivering through the cold phase one afternoon, swaddled like a pupa in his blankets although the temperature around him approached ninety degrees, his thoughts turned again to the question of how one species might transform into another. Inside its cocoon a caterpillar dissolves in order to rise from the ground into the air as a butterfly. Fluid through fever, Wallace's thoughts were now able to reorganise themselves so as to achieve an equally exhilarating liberation. Something prompted the key to the answer to take shape in front of his mind's eye. He thought of Thomas Malthus's 'Principles of Population', which had impressed him when he read it in Leicester's town library about fourteen years earlier. The effect, he later remarked, was like 'friction upon the specially prepared match'.

Malthus argued that populations tend to increase faster than their food supplies, if they are not limited by 'positive checks'. Besides accidents, prominent 'checks' include war, famine and disease, elsewhere envisioned as horsemen. Suddenly it occurred to Wallace that such forces would act still more severely on wild animals. As animals tended to reproduce more quickly than humans, yet their populations tended to remain constant, 'there suddenly flashed upon me the idea of the survival of the fittest – that those individuals which every year are removed by these causes, – termed collectively the "struggle for existence" – must on the average and in the long run be inferior in some one or more ways to those which managed to survive'. This process 'would necessarily *improve the race*, because in every generation the inferior would inevitably be killed off and the superior would remain – that is, *the fittest would survive . . .*'

Wallace had grasped the principle of natural selection, and the conviction that comes with it. 'The more I thought of this the more certain it appeared to be; while the only alternative theory – that those who succumbed to enemies, or want of food, or disease, drought, or cold, were in every way and always as well constituted as those that survived – seemed to me impossible and unthinkable.' Once grasped, natural selection seemed obvious. On learning of it, Thomas Henry Huxley is said to have exclaimed, 'How extremely stupid not to have thought of that!'

Wallace certainly didn't think Huxley was stupid. His opinion remained in line with his first impression of the charismatic biologist, formed when he saw that wonder of the age lecture in 1852. Huxley displayed such acuity and erudition that Wallace assumed he must be many years his senior, although Huxley was actually a couple of years younger.

Looking back, Wallace thought he could see why it was that he and Darwin had succeeded where the 'greatest intellects' had failed. It was because of their inordinate fondness for beetles, to coin the phrase said to have been minted by J. B. S. Haldane, when asked what could be deduced about the Creator from a study of the variety of nature. Through beetle-hunting, they had learned the art of collection, which involved 'an intense interest in the variety of living things', and an eye for the fine distinctions between similar species. 'Now it is this superficial and almost child-like interest in the outward forms of living things which, though often despised as unscientific, happened to be *the only one* which would lead us towards a solution of the problem of species.'

Collectors were supposed to know their place, and there had been mutterings in entomological circles back in London when Wallace's Sarawak Law paper had appeared. Samuel Stevens, Wallace's agent, let him know that some people thought he should drop the theorising and stick to collecting. But those best able to perceive the variety of life were those best placed to grasp how it had arisen. Huxley and other interested parties 'had none of them the special turn of mind that makes the collector or the species-man'.

Huxley's intellectual shortcoming was not that the insight had eluded him, but that it failed to inspire him. Though he became 'Darwin's bulldog', his cause was evolution as a fact, not natural selection as a mechanism for it. There have always been those who see natural selection as obvious and insignificant: a circular argument, a trivial influence upon the forms of living organisms. Beneath the self-deprecation in what Huxley is supposed to have said, its note of irritation seems aroused by the idea itself. Whether or not the note was first sounded by Huxley, it has echoed among selection's sceptics ever since.

Others, however, see natural selection as obvious and fundamental; an axiom that transforms all understanding of living organisms and informs all thought about nature thereafter. Wallace immediately experienced this sense of transport – 'Then at once I seemed to see the whole effect of this . . .' That evening he stretched his new wings, writing notes on his idea. Over the next two evenings he developed his argument, on thin leaves of letter paper, and sent it to Charles Darwin.

Wallace's transcendent understanding was thus first communicated to almost the only other person who already possessed it. When the letter reached Darwin in Kent several months later, on 18 June 1858, he saw that the product of Wallace's fevered imagination was identical to the idea he had been nurturing privately for the past twenty years. He wrote immediately to his friend Charles Lyell: 'I never saw a more striking coincidence; if Wallace had my MS. sketch written out in 1842, he could not have made a better short abstract!' Wallace could not have made much more than an abstract, though. The senior naturalist had spent his twenty years building an edifice detail by detail. Wallace had an idea; Darwin had a theory.

In his autobiography, Darwin described how he had come to appreciate how selection by humans was the agent of improvement in domesticated animals, but he could not see how selection might work upon living things in the wild. Then, in 1838, he read Malthus's essay, and it 'at once struck' him that the struggle for existence would lead to the formation of new species. 'Here, then, I had at last a theory by which to work; but I was so anxious to avoid prejudice, that I determined not for some time to write even the briefest sketch of it.' He did not begin work on what was to be his definitive statement, a book to be called *Natural Selection*, until 1856. Only half of it had been written by the time Wallace caught up with him.

Now he was more alarmed by priority than prejudice – 'So all my originality, whatever it may amount to, will be smashed . . .' Within a fortnight, his theories were introduced to the public domain. He consulted his closest scientific intimates, the geologist Lyell and the botanist Joseph Hooker, who arranged a special meeting of the Linnean Society in London on 1 July. Two short texts by Darwin were read, followed by the paper Wallace had sent him. Later that month, Darwin began to prepare an 'abstract' of *Natural Selection* that could be issued quickly. This was published the following year as the *Origin of Species*.

Wallace did not know he had flushed Darwin from cover until several more months had passed. Had a request for his permission been sent out east across the seas, and his reply awaited, the reading could not have taken place for the best part of a year after he had written to Darwin. As history settled into place, Wallace was relegated to a supporting role as the stick that finally poked Darwin into standing up for his ideas. His account of natural selection was regarded as redundant, since Darwin's treatment was so much deeper. He was, in fact, the first to suggest this, and he 'gracefully resigned himself for a lifetime to being the moon to Darwin's sun'. In later years, his dogged belief in spiritualism cast a poor light on his reputation as a scientist, and his idealistic socialism added to the impression of erratic judgement.

Modern evolutionists often find that when they need to think about a major question, it is a good idea to go back and read what Darwin had to say on the matter. Bill Hamilton remarked that when looking for the earliest hint of any new evolutionary idea, a search of Darwin's writings usually 'reveals that he wrote and understood more about it than anyone has yet noticed'. He added that Wallace was worth checking too. But Darwin's theory is in a different league. Wallace acknowledged that time and again, most memorably when he gave the world the expression 'Darwinism'.

Nevertheless, when they differed, Darwin was not always right and Wallace always wrong. Darwin's timidity reasserted itself after the *Origin* appeared. Over successive editions, Darwin rowed back on natural selection, responding to critics by laying greater emphasis on other possible means of change. He leaned most heavily upon the idea of use and disuse: that the characters passed by an organism to its offspring might be influenced by the extent to which it made use of them. Darwin became his own deviationist.

Wallace grasped what Darwin ceded, and more besides. His original glimpse of natural selection – 'then at once I seemed to see the whole effect' – had not been as far-reaching as Darwin's. Darwin recognised more clearly the importance of competition between individuals. Wallace's vision was not as acute: he saw the wood but not the trees. When he wrote of 'varieties', it is often unclear whether he meant individuals or groups. But whether he thought that the targets of selection were singular or plural, he was second to none in his commitment to the principle of selection itself. In the years following the publication of the *Origin*, he became ever more convinced that 'Natural Selection is supreme'.

As Huxley became Darwin's bulldog, so Wallace became selection's terrier. The tone of satisfaction was unmistakable when Wallace sum-marised his contributions to evolutionary theory: 'some of my critics declare that I am more Darwinian than Darwin himself, and in this, I admit, they are not far wrong'.

Wallace regarded his eight years and fourteen thousand miles of 'wandering' in the Malay Archipelago as the 'central and controlling incident' of his life. Evolutionists do perhaps tend to think of things happening to individuals, rather than individuals causing things to happen. That is one of the reasons why their way of thinking causes such widespread discomfort. Things cer-tainly happened to Wallace: the story of his early life was one of the events beyond his control, mainly because they were also beyond his father's. But Wallace's Malay sojourn was the phase in which, through his discovery of natural selection, he decisively achieved control over his life's course. His story was aligned with the greatest biography of all, that of life itself.

He had been wandering almost from the start. Alfred Russel Wallace was born on 8 January 1823 at Usk in the Anglo–Welsh border county of Monmouthshire, into a precarious station of life that was petit bourgeois with peasant overtones. His father, Thomas, had qualified as a solicitor, but took the leisurely option of living off inherited money until his mar-riage, an economic challenge to which he failed to rise. The Wallaces relocated from London to Usk, far from the metropolis and correspondingly inexpensive. Here Thomas Wallace avoided the marketplace by teaching his eight children and growing the family's vegetables himself. Alfred, with his long flaxen hair, was known as 'the little Saxon' among the Welsh-speaking locals.

In 1828, the family moved to the county town of Hertford, about twenty miles north of London. Alfred enjoyed the benefit of a town library, whose librarian his father was for a time, and experienced more mixed emotions at the grammar school. In his last year there, though only just in his teens, he was obliged to earn his keep by giving lessons as well as receiving them. This he found humiliating, exposed as he was to his peers' antagonism, and it returned to him in nightmares for years afterwards.

His ordeal was brought to an end when he was sent to lodge with a London builder, to whom his brother John was apprenticed. Here Alfred mixed for the first time with working men, unpolished but skilled and fundamentally respectable; their speech, he later reflected, was less coarse than that of many wealthier and better educated young men. In the evenings he went out with John, sometimes to look at the shops, but most often to the Hall of Science, near Tottenham Court Road. This was a club for restless working-class thinkers who believed that knowledge was next to power, and a secular chapel devoted to the socialist gospel preached by Robert Owen. It was Alfred's university, convivial with coffee and dominoes, electric with lectures and books that urged freedom through inquiry.

Owen was Britain's first socialist leader; not a labour militant or a pamphleteering revolutionary, but a wealthy philanthropist who created the showpiece industrial community of New Lanark to demonstrate his vision. Wallace recalled him as, first of all, a thinker who believed that established wisdom had the truth about human nature upside-down. Once he saw the presiding spirit of the Hall, by then in his mid-sixties, materialise in person to give a short address. Alfred 'was struck by his tall spare figure, very lofty head, and highly benevolent countenance and mode of speaking'.

Owen was a radical determinist, who believed that 'the character of every individual is formed *for* and not *by* himself'. Heredity and environment were all; will power, the helm with which a Christian must steer towards the Lord, counted for nothing. It was futile to insist that people could behave well if they would only make the effort. But they could readily be induced to behave well if provided with a suitable environment. Owen was both a determinist and an optimist, who believed that goodwill could be the ether of human interaction. He embodied several philosophical tendencies that largely defined Wallace's own future orientation: scepticism about religion, a passion for the fundamentals of the human condition, a belief in progress and the conviction that marvellous advances could be achieved if established authority was left behind. These were the ingredients for the making of an evolutionist – though the final key ingredient was not to the taste of Owen, who maintained, *contra* Malthus, that there were sufficient riches in nature for all to live free from misery.

Wallace's radical schooling at the Hall of Science was sharpened by texts such as Thomas Paine's *Age of Reason* and a tract by one of Owen's sons against the doctrine of hellfire. The Wallaces had practised a vigorous Christianity that usually took in two helpings per Sunday, one in the morning and one in the evening at the Anglican church to which they owed their allegiance, with occasional visits to Dissenters' chapels and the Friends' Meeting House to vary the diet. With their custom of gathering together and waiting until one of their number was moved to speak, the Quakers offered a foretaste of eternity; endless wastes of silence interspersed by interminable wastes of breath, while the preachers promised their faithful that sinners risked torments that were truly endless and infinitely more excruciating. He was impressed by the simple integrity of the Quakers' manner of life and passingly carried along by 'the more picturesque and impassioned' of the Dissenters' hymns, but he was repelled by the doctrine of eternal damnation. 'I therefore thoroughly agreed with Mr Dale Owen's conclusion, that the orthodox religion of the day was degrading and hideous, and that the only true and wholly beneficial religion was that which inculcated the service of humanity, and whose only dogma was the brotherhood of man. Thus was laid the foundation of my religious scepticism.'

Alfred's education at the Hall of Science was formative but brief. In the summer of 1837, as his family had planned, he went with his brother William to Bedfordshire, where William began to train him as a surveyor. He wandered the flat acres and tramped the highways, sat in pubs and listened to the older men as they smoked their pipes and chewed the fat. He warmed to an itinerant way of life of fresh air, plain lodgings and making his way under his own steam. William took him west, across the border into Wales, to high moors and plunging waterfalls instead of the practical fields of London's hinterland. They made their way through Radnorshire, the Brecon Beacons, and in 1841 came to a halt for a couple of years at Neath.

Among the jobs they tackled was one of enclosure. Cottage-dwellers surrounding an area of moorland near Llandrindod Wells had the right to let animals graze upon it. This allowed each to keep a horse or a cow or a few sheep. Under the enclosure legislation they were deprived of these commons, and the land was parcelled out among private owners. Delineating private property required an attention to detail, every tree and every stream, which made the work interesting for Alfred. He thought that enclosing a wilderness was a shame, but supposed there was some good reason for it.

More than sixty years later, he obtained reports from a friend on what had become of the land. Almost none of the high moor had been improved. Some of the owners had, however, profited handsomely from building holiday homes, and the former commons had been turned into a golf course. The original commoners had been reduced from comfort to poverty or else been driven away to the towns in search of a living. Wallace came to regard enclosure as 'unjust, unwise, and cruel', in short, 'robbery', and campaigned for the nationalisation of the land. Robert Owen's political convictions seemed to lie latent in him through his early adulthood and middle age, and then found their voice in his later years. It was as if they had discreetly made room for strains of individualism, in particular the kind propounded by Herbert Spencer, which were more conducive to the study of evolution.

At Neath, Alfred found himself with time on his hands and only his own company. William spent much time looking for work, but did not find enough to keep them both occupied. Their living was always scraped and their circumstances humble, though William kept his constant money worries to himself. His limited resources led to his death less than five years after their arrival in Neath. Returning from London, where he had given evidence before a parliamentary committee on the South Wales Railway Bill, he fell fatally ill after a winter's night spent in a third-class railway carriage and a damp bed.

William suffered the effects of poverty despite his professional status and expert involvement with railways, the leading technological enterprise of the day. In the valleys, poverty spurred the ripple of insurgency known as the Rebecca riots. The campaign was triggered by road tolls but sustained by a wider range of grievances – including the rent charges introduced by a new system of payments for land use, a project which provided the Wallace brothers with plenty of surveying work. Bands of militants, often on horseback and dressed as women, descended upon toll gates at night and destroyed them. The leader of each band took the name 'Rebecca', from Genesis 24:60: 'And they blessed Rebekah, and said unto her, Thou art our sister, be thou the mother of thousands of millions, and let thy seed possess the gate of those which hate them.'

Despite its theatrical panache, the Rebecca campaign seems to have struck no chord with Alfred. Conflict never inspired him. He merely used the episode as a peg on which to hang an article he wrote about the hill farmers of Glamorganshire; however, it was rejected by the one magazine editor to whom he submitted it. The hill farmers themselves would not have thanked him for his efforts had they known of them. Alfred drew up an indictment, with an attention to detail he would later apply more constructively to his tropical specimens, of complacency in decrepitude. Doors gaped open, dung drained wastefully into ponds, fields suffered under inept and cruel regimes, crops were overrun by rioting weeds. This was the result of the same attitudes that had immobilised the once-dynamic civilisations of the East. 'The Welshman, when you recommend any improvement in his operations, will tell you, like the Chinaman, that it is an "old custom," and that what did for his forefathers is good enough for him.'

These obtuse rustics were the antipodes of the questing mechanics at the Hall of Science. Alfred had already been convinced that change was of the essence, and new knowledge was its key. In condemning the farmers for their inert adherence to traditional ideas, he was applying the principle that sent him on the road to evolution. But however far his mind was free to roam, his feet were stuck in the same clotted mud as theirs. 'The single window is a small and low one, and this is rendered almost useless by the dirtiness of the glass, some window drapery, a Bible, hymn book and some old newspapers on the sill, and a sickly-looking geranium or myrtle, which seems a miracle of vital tenacity in that dark and smoky atmosphere.' These are not the brisk notes of a passing journalist, but more likely an impression left by long exposure upon a sorry lodger's memory. Alfred and William had to live in intimate proximity to the farming folk who rented them rooms, and on occasion to the livestock as well. At one farm they were surprised to find an egg on the bed. They were told that it was thought lucky to let chickens lay eggs there – which also explained the fleas. Although at Neath their lodgings were of a somewhat better class, Alfred's anatomy of rural stagnation was also a measure of his own standard of living.

Alfred later recognised his time of underemployment in Neath as the turning point of his life. He reflected that if William had been able to keep him in work, he would probably have become completely absorbed in the profession, which would probably have satisfied all his intellectual wants. The family history of meagre income was also the making of him: 'Had my father been a moderately rich man and had he supplied me with a good wardrobe and ample pocket-money; had my brother obtained a partner-ship in some firm in a populous town or city, or had he established himself in his profession, I might never have turned to nature as the solace and enjoyment of my solitary hours, my whole life would have been differently shaped, and though I should, no doubt, have given some attention to sci-ence, it seems very unlikely that I should have ever undertaken what at that time seemed rather a wild scheme, a journey to the almost unknown forests of the Amazon in order to observe nature and make a living by collecting.'

His life as a surveyor's apprentice had stimulated an interest in science straight away. Having experienced the technical satisfaction of using 'that beautiful little instrument the pocket-sextant', he taught himself about subjects beyond the ken of his formal education, such as mechanics and optics, using cheap primers issued by the Society for the Diffusion of Useful Knowledge (SDUK). At Neath he applied this knowledge to astronomy, using a paper tube to make a telescope with which he could observe the moons of Jupiter.

Now, however, his attention shifted from what he had been doing to what was around him. His first solitary rambles in Bedfordshire had cast the initial shadows of an interest in nature, specifically a desire to know something about wild flowers. He had not pursued it since, but in 1841 obtained a shilling SDUK book on botany. This enabled his 'first intro-duction to the variety, the beauty, and the mystery of nature', which became his main interest and call upon his free time.

Diffidence as well as curiosity inclined him this way. Alfred always felt himself hobbled by shyness. Out of doors, though, the gangling figure ceased to seem out of place. When William was away, he would walk the hills or stream-banks, trying to identify the parts of plants and the taxo-nomic groups to which they belonged. Even when he was working, he spent his Sundays in the fields and woods, learning the forms of plants and the relationships between them, 'and as one after another the different orders were recognized, I began to realize for the first time the order that underlay all the variety of nature'.

He also began to hanker after varieties more exotic than anything he might find on his Sunday rambles. He thrilled at the sight of a tropical orchid at a Swansea flower show and was seduced further by the alluring phrases – 'too delicate and beautiful for a flower of earth' – that he saw applied to such a specimen in the *Gardener's Chronicle*. Orchids, he later reflected, played their part in drawing him to the tropics.

When he eventually got there, though, he decided there was no place like home. 'Our own weeds and wayside flowers are far prettier and more varied than those of the tropics,' he wrote to his sister Fanny. His spirits may have been fired by the specimens he pursued, but they were not lifted by the setting itself. The 'deep gloom of the forests and the mass of tangled vegetation . . . is certainly grand and interesting and in a certain sense beautiful,' he acknowledged. But 'a field of buttercups, a hill of gorse or of heather, a bank of foxgloves and a hedge of wild roses and purple vetches surpass in *beauty* anything I have ever seen in the tropics'. By then it was 1861 and he was off the map, giving his address as 'In the Mountains of Java'.

He got there by way of Leicester. Two things crucial for his fulfilment as an evolutionist took place during the year he spent in the city, a hundred miles north of London in the English Midlands. One was that he read Malthus's 'Principles of Population', and the other was that he met Henry Walter Bates.

The son of a local hosiery manufacturer, Bates was cut from similar cloth to Wallace and all the other young men of limited means and simmering intellectual ambitions. His university was the Mechanics' Institute; his philosophy was freed from tradition by an unconventional religious background: Bates's father was a Unitarian, believing in a single god rather than a trinity.

Henry Bates laboured thirteen hours a day as an apprentice to a hosiery firm and attended the Mechanics' Institute in the evenings. Here he learned Greek, Latin, French, drawing and composition, discovered natural history, and became an enthusiastic entomologist. Like Darwin and possibly the Creator, he had an inordinate fondness for beetles. Wallace was amazed to learn that such a passion could be gratified within an area ten miles around Leicester, where perhaps a thousand species were waiting to be found. But it could not be slaked, though, since the collector always leads himself on. 'Whenever I hear of the capture of rare beetles,' Darwin averred, 'I feel like an old war-horse at the sound of a trumpet.'

There had still been 'nothing doing at Neath' as Alfred neared his coming of age, in January 1844, so he departed for London. Staying with his brother John, he applied for a couple of posts as a schoolteacher. He failed to make the grade for the first, let down by his Latin and maths, but was hired as an assistant by the Reverend Abraham Hill, head of the Collegiate School in Leicester. Here he taught the three R's, as well as a little drawing and surveying, and struggled to expand his academic portfolio. His efforts met with limited success: he never quite grasped the secret of differential calculus, and integral calculus was 'an almost trackless labyrinth'. Characteristically, he doubted that he could have ascended to higher mathematics even with expert tuition, but he did not feel the lack of it in his subsequent researches. This was what separated Wallace and Darwin from their successors in the next century. Natural selection was based on natural history but established by mathematics.

Despite his academic limitations, he had a mesmerising effect on some of his pupils. A mesmerist came to town, demonstrating how to induce trances in volunteers from the audience. Back at the school, some of the boys succeeded in producing the effect on their fellows. Alfred, who had also been impressed by the lectures, found that he too had the knack. He embarked on a series of experiments in which he found that he could hang a chair upon a boy's outstretched arm for five minutes without provoking complaint, make him behave as if drunk by giving him a glass of water and telling him it was brandy, induce him to tear off his clothes by telling him his shirt was on fire, or cause him to forget his own name.

An element of showmanship is part of the teacher's art, but Wallace was impressed by its absence from the lectures and seemed unconcerned about his own audience. He took these experiments as seriously as he was to take his researches in natural history, and held to their lessons for the rest of his life. They were the other side of his philosophical coin. Before he believed in evolution, he believed in progress, and for much of his later life he struggled to reconcile the two. His spiritualism and his socialist autumn were necessary partners to his selectionism.

The most important aspect of mesmerism for Wallace was that it formed an extension to phrenology. He had read an influential popular account of phrenology, George Combe's *The Constitution of Man Considered in Relation to External Objects*, and had absorbed its message of human progress. Combe's phrenology was not just an account of mental anatomy, but a scheme of knowledge in which natural law included, and formed the basis for, moral law. His book was held to erode the concept of free will and to promote the idea of evolution.

Fortunately for Wallace, Reverend Hill did not feel as strongly about Combe's 'new bible of natural law' as some of his clerical colleagues. He took a keen interest in the experiments, which included ventures into 'phreno-mesmerism'. With the aid of a phrenological bust, indicating the position of the mental organs, Wallace satisfied himself that touching different places on the skull of an entranced subject would stimulate the appropriate emotion, as evidenced by the expression which appeared on the boy's face. 'When I touched the organ of Veneration in one of my boy patients . . . he fell upon his knees, closed his palms together, and gazed upwards, with the facial expression of a saint in the ecstasy of adoration.'

Stranger yet, trance states seemed to permit the telepathic transfer of sensations. If Wallace placed something in his mouth, his most suggestible subject tasted it as well; if somebody else secretly pinched or pricked Wallace, the boy felt the pain in the same part of the body. Wallace never entertained the notion that his findings revealed his own suggestibility. He believed that these phenomena were as real as those described by natural science, and as important. His experiences in Leicester left him on the threshold of a supernatural science, based on observation rather than revealed truth.

The year in Leicester also set him on the path to the genuine science that is his legacy. He read another visionary popular text, *Vestiges of the Natural History of Creation*. This was a kindred volume to Combe's *Constitution of Man*, its own message of progress based upon the argument that species might transmute into new species. In the act of praising the Creator's works, it prepared the ground for a history of life in which the Creator need not feature. *Vestiges* was the talk of the literary season, both for its own bold speculations and the speculation it excited about the identity of its anonymous author (revealed posthumously as Robert Chambers, Combe's publisher). It made a home for itself in Mechanics' Institute and palace alike: Prince Albert read it to Queen Victoria in the afternoons, finding in its exuberant prose a means to share his passion for science with his wife.

Scientists themselves regarded it as muddled, windy, credulous and amateurish. In Darwin's case, this judgement trailed in the wake of the dreadful shock of seeing a manifesto for evolution in print. When his *Origin of Species* finally appeared, he tartly remarked in its opening pages that the author of *Vestiges* failed to explain anything by proposing that one species might gave rise to another: the point was to account for adaptation. But in the mid-1840s, the point was that the reading public was spell-bound by a book which proclaimed the truth of transmutation.

Wallace's new friend Henry Bates shared the informed opinion of *Vestiges*, but the scientists' objections were largely immaterial to Wallace himself. At this stage he was a layman and an amateur. He was open to suggestion. 'I do not consider it a hasty generalization,' he wrote to Bates, 'but rather as an ingenious hypothesis strongly supported by some strik-ing facts and analogies . . . It furnishes a subject for every observer of nature to attend to; every fact he observes will make either for or against it, and thus serves both as an incitement to the collection of facts, and an object to which they can be applied when collected.' Though he did not know it, Wallace was defining his future research programme. And with-out being fully aware of it, he had become an evolutionist.

Darwin drew a similar conclusion to Wallace's, but for different rea-sons. The ire and scorn that *Vestiges* attracted was a preview of what lay in store for him. He could not avoid the ire, but he could guard against the scorn by means of what distinguished him from 'Mr Vestiges'. Darwin, veteran of the *Beagle* voyage, was an experienced naturalist. All *Vestiges* had, according to Thomas Huxley (his wrath undimmed nine years and ten editions after the book first appeared), was a 'spurious, glib elo-quence'. Darwin had observations, specimens, data and the skills to accu-mulate more. He applied himself to the acquisition of facts, upon which he would in due course hoist his banner.

For Wallace, on the other hand, *Vestiges* was not a threat but a promise. It was capable of improvement, certainly, and therein lay its appeal. *Vestiges* was evidently the work of an enthusiast but not an expert. It spoke of progress from the first spark of Creation to the human condition, and it spoke to the optimistic desire of the aspiring classes to make progress of their own. Wallace was nothing if not part of *Vestiges*' constituency, the army of artisans and clerks who yearned to better themselves through knowledge. The potential that he saw in *Vestiges*' thesis reflected the potential he saw in himself.

Having drifted into evolutionism and collecting, Wallace was on a meandering path to the tropics. Once again he was propelled across the country by an event beyond his control, the death of his brother William. This time, though, he was seizing an opportunity. A year as a teacher had convinced him that it was not his calling in life. Now he had the chance of taking over his brother's business, which now had the prospect of some railway surveying work.

Alfred would have realised just how bright the company's immediate prospects were had he ever looked at a newspaper. The railway boom was reaching a crescendo, but Wallace had not noticed. Now he found that surveyors were in demand, as were engineers and, most to the point, lawyers. Laying out imaginary railways became a major industry, albeit a largely sham one, in which profits were made by selling out to competitors rather than by constructing tracks. He and his brother John also branched out from surveying into architecture. Alfred designed the Mechanics' Institute in Neath, as well as lecturing on elementary science to the town's mechanics.

On a couple of occasions, he encountered individuals with a devious approach to settling bills. Although these are as inevitable in business as taxes, Wallace found the experience of dealing with them peculiarly distasteful. They were added to the ledger of reasons to leave the country.

In his free time, he returned to the open air, this time searching for beetles rather than botanical taxa. Bates joined him for a beetling holiday in 1847, and in the course of it they began to discuss a joint expedition. They read a glowing report of an Amazon journey, published that year, which persuaded them that this would be the ideal tropical destination for them. The jungle was magnificent, the people were friendly, the cost of living was moderate; all in all, the Amazon seemed to offer the best prospect of a tropical expedition that paid its way, through the sale of duplicate specimens.

The intellectual goals of the journey were also taking shape. In his last letter to Bates before they set off, Wallace referred to the 'overwhelming numbers' of beetles and butterflies he had been able to examine in the British Museum. 'I begin to feel rather dissatisfied with a mere local collection; little is to be learnt by it. I should like to take some one family to study thoroughly, principally with a view to the theory of the origin of species.'

Wallace and Bates set sail from Liverpool towards the end of April 1848, on a ship called the *Mischief*, and reached the mouth of the Amazon a month later. At Pará (now Belém), palms, pineapple plants and 'hot moist mouldy air' greeted the travellers, 'whose last country ramble . . . was over the bleak moors of Derbyshire on a sleety morning in April'.

Nevertheless, Wallace confessed to being disappointed at first. 'The weather was not so hot, the people were not so peculiar, the vegetation was not so striking, as the glowing picture I had conjured up in my imagination. . .' Even as he noted down his disappointment, though, a hint of the marvels in store fluttered past his head in the shape of a vampire bat with whom he was sharing his lodgings.

He soon realised that the forest was not the Zoological Gardens, with all its treasures on show for the visitor's delight. His eye needed to adapt to the tropical ambience. A naturalist is somebody who, surrounded by a living landscape, has the impulse to read it. Wallace now had to learn to read in a different language.

He had also to immerse himself in the forest, its air humming with the potential of terror, periodically discharged in the shrieks of stricken creatures. 'The few sounds of birds are of that pensive or mysterious character which intensifies the feeling of solitude rather than imparts a sense of life and cheerfulness,' wrote Bates, the more expressive writer of the pair. 'Sometimes, in the midst of the stillness, a sudden yell or scream will startle one; this comes from some defenceless fruit-eating animal, which is pounced upon by a tiger-cat or stealthy boa-constrictor. Morning and evening the howling monkeys make a most fearful and harrowing noise, under which it is difficult to keep up one's buoyancy of spirit. The feeling of inhospitable wildness, which the forest is calculated to inspire, is increased tenfold under this fearful uproar.

'Sometimes a sound is heard like the clang of an iron bar against a hard, hollow tree, or a piercing cry rends the air; these are not repeated, and the succeeding silence tends to heighten the unpleasant impression which they make on the mind. With the native it is always the Curupira, the wild man or spirit of the forest, which produces all noises they are unable to explain.'

Wallace, however, proved able to take Amazonia as he found it. The prizes were dazzling, from giant butterflies, beetles, toucans and parrots, to alligators and boa constrictors. Some were brought to him by locals, but the principal tool of his trade was his rifle. His sentiments towards his victims were abbreviated by practical considerations: 'The poor little animal was not quite dead, and its cries, its innocent-looking countenance, and delicate little hands were quite childlike. Having often heard how good monkey was, I took it home, and had it cut up and fried for breakfast . . .'

On one occasion, he was thrilled to see a black cat cross his path. It was a jaguar, 'the most powerful and dangerous animal inhabiting the American continent'. He raised his rifle, but realised that it was loaded with small shot, which would only have annoyed the beast; and so it got away. He could have taken that as an omen.

About a year after Alfred's arrival in Brazil, his younger brother Herbert came out to join him. Like the other brothers, Herbert had been given a meagre start in life. With little in the way of schooling, he spent an unhappy spell as a shop assistant, followed by a similarly unsatisfactory four years in a Neath foundry, at his brother William's instigation. For a time the Wallaces were with both Bates and two British botanists who had travelled out with Herbert, but they then went their separate ways, the brothers heading upriver without Bates.

Alfred not only coped with the wild, but also with the society he encountered along the great rivers of the Amazon system. Like many English people abroad, he seems to have left his social constraints behind him. Despite his shyness at home, he mixed comfortably with settlers of various stripes, and some of them very chequered too. For the first two years, all the natives he met were 'tame Indians', speaking Portuguese and wearing 'at least trousers and shirt'. Eventually he encountered 'absolute uncontaminated savages', so independent of civilisation that they ignored the white visitors altogether. He was thrilled and fascinated, his reaction contrasting with that of Darwin, who could 'hardly make oneself believe' that the natives he encountered in Tierra del Fuego were 'fellow-creatures' and felt that 'the difference, between savage and civilised man' was 'greater than between a wild and domesticated animal'.

Wallace experienced a romantic exhilaration in the company of 'savages'. At one village he was moved to verse, expressing his envy of the inhabi-

48

tants' unconfined freedom and his rosy view of what he believed were their simple and peaceful lives. (On Sundays they went to church, but he still counted them as savages.) Civilisation, with its wealth of knowledge and variety of stimuli, was preferable, but not if one's only goal is 'gold'. In that sense, Wallace was never a materialist.

By this time Alfred had parted company with his brother too. Herbert had not taken much more enthusiastically to birds and insects than to the trades he had tried earlier. Sadly, he had no further opportunity to drift through life. He returned down the Amazon from Barra (now Manaus) to Pará, intending to find a passage back to England. But Pará was in the grip of a yellow fever epidemic, and Herbert succumbed to the disease at the age of twenty-two. One of Alfred's sisters died at the same age; three others had died in childhood; and William was gone too. Three of the siblings survived to old age: John, whose own overseas adventure drew him into the Californian gold rush; Fanny, who spent some time in the United States more soberly employed as a teacher; and Alfred, who ventured farther into wilder regions than any of them and who outlived them all.

Alfred received news in Barra of Herbert's illness, but no confirmation of his fate. Bates had helped to nurse Herbert, sleeping by his side for four nights until the fever seized him too; his bout with it lasted ten days, but he prevailed. Alfred's own health suffered under the assaults of fevers – which may have been the first round of the illness he suffered later in the Malay Archipelago – and dysentery. He had planned to stay for five years, but decided to return home a year early, taking a collection of live animals in addition to his preserved specimens.

On reaching Pará, still beset by fits of fever, he found a cross-crowded cemetery, and also that many of his specimens had been held up by customs officials instead of being sent back to England ahead of him. All his eggs therefore went into one basket, the brig *Helen*, upon which he set sail in July 1852.

Three weeks later, after breakfast one morning, the captain interrupted his reading. 'I'm afraid the ship's on fire,' said Captain Turner, 'come and see what you think of it.' Much later, they realised that it probably started in a consignment of a substance called balsam-capivi, which was usually transported in wet sand because of its tendency to combust spontaneously when in motion. Ignorant of the risk, Captain Turner had it packed in flammable rice chaff. After unsuccessful attempts to reach the source of the smoke by throwing cargo out of one hatchway, a second hatch was opened. By fuelling the fire with more air this may have turned the crisis into a disaster.

The smoke became denser, and the men took to the boats. Wallace took a tin box containing some shirts and put in it some drawings he had made of palms and fishes, along with his watch and some sovereigns. The smoke in the cabin was too dense even for him to find the rest of his clothes. He did not return for them, or for a portfolio of sketches also in the berth, feeling 'a kind of apathy about saving anything'. Barely able to believe they could escape, he thought it 'almost foolish' to save even what was at hand.

Wallace and the sailors spent the afternoon in the boats, bailing them furiously – their timbers were dried and shrunk after long exposure to the sun – and watching the fire consume the *Helen*. Several of Wallace's animals clambered onto the bowsprit as the flames spread, but the men's attempts to coax them into the boats were fruitless. Some ran back into the fire when the flames reached the bowsprit. One parrot was clinging to a rope hanging from the bowsprit and fell into the sea when the rope burned above him: he was the only creature to be rescued.

During the night the men bailed and rowed to keep close to the ship. As it rolled in the swell, it 'presented its interior towards us filled with liquid flame'. In the morning they raised the boats' sails and left the burning wreck behind them. Their calculations showed them that the nearest land was Bermuda, seven hundred miles away.

After a few days in the boats, with the shock of emergency faded, Wallace's hopes began to rise. With them, though, came the realisation of his losses. Most of what he had sent back previously were duplicates, for sale. They would have covered little more than his costs. The profits would have come from the £500 or so that he could have made from the specimens that had been lost. Worse, however, was the loss of most of the collection he had intended to keep: everything acquired since he had left Pará, which he had hoped would make his 'cabinet' of American species one of the finest in Europe. By contrast, Bates's tally, when he finally returned after eleven years in the Amazon regions, was 14,712 specimens, of which 8,000 were new to science.

After ten days and nights, scorched by the sun and soaked by the spray, subsisting on raw pork and biscuits, the survivors of the *Helen* were still two hundred miles from Bermuda. Then they saw a sail. It belonged to a British ship, the *Jordeson*, bound for London. She was old, short of provisions, sluggish, and in places, rotten. One night, the captain slept with an axe at his side to cut away the masts if the ship capsized. Captain Turner confided to Wallace that he would rather be back in the boats. Nevertheless, the ship survived gales and storms to land them safely in England, eighty days after their departure from Pará.

Wallace reached London with only his tin box and a thin calico suit. His agent, Samuel Stevens, arranged to restore his wardrobe, and Stevens's mother restored his vigour with food and hospitality. Stevens had already taken more substantial action to protect his client's interests. A keen collector of butterflies and beetles himself, he had cannily insured Wallace's collections for £200.

Wallace ceded the Amazon territory to Bates, who was still in the field and effectively had a five-year start on him. For his next expedition he settled upon the Malay Archipelago, whose surface had barely been scratched by European scientists. He made a valuable contact in Sir James Brooke, who had been made Rajah of Sarawak by the Sultan of Brunei as a reward for suppressing a Dyak rebellion. This adroit move may seem out of character for Wallace, so prone to social unease. But he was democratically shy, awkward generally in company, and meritocratically so when in the company of individuals of high learning. He was not especially flustered by aristocracy, even a double English and Malayan dose.

Wallace enjoyed the Rajah's hospitality in the Archipelago, which he reached in 1854. He was impressed by Brooke's skill in ruling over 'two conflicting races – a superior and an inferior', and scorned the allegations of 'wholesale murder' that British critics had laid against the Rajah. When he discovered what he considered to be perhaps the most elegant butterfly in the world, he named it *Ornithoptera Brookeana*.

As he wrote to Bates in 1856, however, the Malayan islands were conspicuously lacking in magnificent butterflies compared with the Amazon region. Bates's dispatches from Brazil made Wallace long for the great river once again. But Wallace gained something far more important than a resplendent cabinet from his tour of the Archipelago. His field experience in two hemispheres broadened his understanding of the geographical distribution of species, which was the basis of his inquiry into the variety of life. Its epigrammatic expressions were a line and a law: 'Wallace's Line' – a name bestowed by Huxley – between the islands of Bali and Lombok, on one side of which the fauna were Asian and on the other Australasian; and the 'Sarawak Law' on the distribution of species.

Sitting out the wet season in a small house at the foot of a mountain and at the mouth of the Sarawak river, accompanied only by a Malay boy, his cook, Wallace reflected on his reading and on his own 'vivid impression' of the differences between the eastern and western tropics. It occurred to him that the facts at his disposal had never been properly used to address the question of the origin of species, and that the spatial dimension of geography could be combined with the temporal dimension given in Sir Charles Lyell's influential *Principles of Geology*. In concluding that 'every species has come into existence coincident both in time and space with a pre-existing closely allied species', Wallace was the first to promulgate evolution as a law.

Wallace sent Darwin a copy of his paper 'On the Law Which Has Regulated the Introduction of New Species'. Darwin showed it to Lyell, who took it to heart, making a hundred pages of notes towards a critique of it. Now Darwin explained to Lyell his own theory of natural selection. It was Wallace's paper, showing how near the wandering naturalist had come to the source of the river of life, which prompted Lyell to advise Darwin to commit himself to publication.

Nor was Wallace the only potential threat to Darwin's priority. Evolution was one of the themes of the time, and with such extensive attention being paid to the workings of nature, others might have hit upon an idea that in hindsight seems so obvious. In fact, one or two others had. Patrick Matthew, a Scottish naturalist, published the idea of natural selec-tion in 1831 but concealed it in the appendix to his book *Naval Timber and Arboriculture*. Still guided by his idiosyncratic sense of the proper place, he responded to Darwin's *Origin* by asserting his precedence in a letter to the *Gardener's Chronicle*, adding that he had also been the first to see the need for a navy of steam gun-boats. But Matthew failed to appreciate his own insight. Like many others since, he dismissed it as merely obvious.

Wallace, on the other hand, understood its significance for years before he grasped what it actually was. He had believed in evolution since he read

Vestiges of the History of Creation in 1845. He had disappeared into the Amazon forests to test his belief, and then lost nearly all the materials he had gathered there in the *Helen* fire. Despite that catastrophe, and his meagre financial resources, he started all over again in the Malay Archipelago. In Sarawak, he formulated a preliminary law of evolution. And, three years later, the pieces finally fell into place.

'One day something brought to my recollection Malthus's "Principles of Population" . . .' Thomas Malthus had reasoned that the human population of a region such as Britain, unchecked, will double in size every twenty-five years. The members of that population might succeed in doubling the quantity of food produced from the land in the first quarter century, but even their best efforts could not possibly match the increase in their numbers during the subsequent generation. 'And at the conclusion of the first century the population would be one hundred and twelve millions and the means of subsistence only equal to the support of thirty-five millions, which would leave a population of seventy-seven millions totally unprovided for.' A population will tend to increase geometrically, but its food supply can only increase arithmetically.

Against those imagined millions he marshalled an array of equally vivid checks. These burdens would weigh most heavily upon the lowest ranks of society. Among the North American Indians, the women were more completely enslaved to the men than were the poor to the rich in civilised countries. Their lot was 'the constant and unremitting drudgery of preparing every thing for the reception of their tyrannic lords', which would take its toll in miscarriages and the lives of all but the most robust infants. Not only did they have to suffer the deaths of their children, but they were obliged to occasion the deaths of their own parents, since custom dictated that the aged might be abandoned before their lives were spent. On top of these miseries the wretched native women of North America were tormented by 'the constant war that prevails among savages'. While the principal check on population among savages is misery, it is increasingly supplemented by war as savagery progresses into barbarism.

Wallace was as attentive to the patterns of humankind across the Archipelago as he was to the birds and insects. On a later visit to Gilolo he was disappointed by the fauna, meagre in the settled regions by comparison with the remote virgin forest, but delighted to find that the indigenous people resembled Papuans rather than Malays. This he discerned as an 'exact boundary-line' between human varieties, with an important bearing on the question of the diversity of life and the origin of species. For the science historian James Moore, Wallace's aptitude for drawing lines may be the key to his 'Malthusian moment'. Moore imagines Wallace on the island, surrounded by low hills topped by ruined colonial forts, like the castles of the Welsh marches. Having drawn a line between races, the surveyor-naturalist might then have fallen to speculating about their relations and their differing modes of survival, and then to have seen Wales in Gilolo, recalling his years of drawing lines across the lands where 'Saxons' dominated 'Celts'.

So race might have been the something that summoned the Malthusian vision of 'positive checks'. It came readily to the scientifically curious mind. The first author to anticipate Darwin with a clear statement of natural selection, Dr William Wells, applied the principle only to human varieties. In 1813 Wells read a paper to the Royal Society of London about an Englishwoman who had a dark-skinned arm. He observed that African ancestry seemed to confer immunity to some tropical diseases. 'Of the accidental varieties of man, which would occur among the first few and scattered inhabitants of the middle regions of Africa, some would be better fitted than others to bear the diseases of the country. This race would consequently multiply, while the others would decrease; not only from their inability to sustain the attacks of disease, but from their incapacity of contending with their more vigorous neighbours.'

In lighting upon disease resistance as a fundamental factor in evolution, Wells also anticipated Bill Hamilton; and in his suggestion about competition between racial groups, he prefigured an influential theme in evolutionary thought. Wallace foresaw a fundamental role for it in mankind's future, steering the course of human improvement.

There can be few moments in science sweeter than the first moment of realisation. They are private, pristine and pure, unlike the mixed pleasures of publication or the receipt of honours that have often been anticipated long before they are eventually bestowed. Wallace evidently treasured his, writing five different accounts of it. This was his mythical moment,

54

entering legend alongside the Oxford debate on Darwin's theory in which Thomas Huxley is said to have crushed Bishop Wilberforce – 'The Lord hath delivered him into mine hands' – with his reply to 'Soapy Sam' Wilberforce's sarcastic query about whether it was through his grandfather or his grandmother that Huxley claimed descent from a monkey. Huxley is said to have answered that he would not be ashamed to have a monkey for an ancestor, but would be ashamed to be connected with a man who used his gifts to obscure the truth.

The occasion was historic, without doubt, but the exact truth is itself obscure. No verbatim record of the exchanges exists, nor did the participants all reach the same verdict on Huxley's performance as history subsequently has. Wilberforce apparently came away with the impression that he had enjoyed the best of the encounter. Was Wallace's fevered 'eureka' moment also dramatised after the event?

The location certainly appears to have been shifted. According to Wallace's accounts, his epiphany took place on Ternate, one of the Molucca Isles on the east of the Archipelago. But his records indicate that during February 1858 he was on a neighbouring island, Gilolo, which is also known as Halmahera. Ternate was small but precious, one of the most celebrated of the Spice Islands; Gilolo was larger but obscure. Perhaps Wallace lost his way in his notes; or maybe he deliberately transferred the event to the more prestigious venue, as might an Oxford don inconveniently struck by a great insight while passing through Birmingham. Or perhaps, nearly half a century later, his memory allowed him a romantic indulgence without troubling his conscious judgement.

H. Lewis McKinney, one of Wallace's biographers, has argued that Wallace 'consciously manufactured' the legend over many years, covering his island trail even in his book *The Malay Archipelago*, which appeared in 1869. Even if he did, though, it would seem mean-spirited not to grant Wallace this small dramatic licence. In managing his reputation, his most consistent and visible gambit was his readiness to put Darwin first. He was equally generous in private, too. 'I do honestly believe that with however much patience I had worked up and experimented on the subject, I could never have *approached* the completeness of his book,' he wrote to Henry Bates, '– its vast accumulation of evidence, its overwhelming argument, and its admirable tone and spirit. I really feel thankful that it has not been left to me to give the theory to the public. Mr. Darwin has created a new science and a new philosophy . . .' For this gift to the world, he declared in a letter to a lifelong friend, 'his name should, in my opinion, stand above that of every philosopher of ancient or modern times. The force of admiration can no further go!!!'

It was not that Wallace was a man above ordinary human vanity. His problem was that he had raised himself out of the ordinary. Always burdened by his lack of academic baggage, he seemed convinced that he was not worthy of the company he kept. 'I have for many years felt almost ashamed of the amount of reputation and honour that has been awarded me,' he wrote in 1893, when urged to accept formal membership of the scientific élite at last by becoming a Fellow of the Royal Society. 'I can understand the general public thinking too highly of me, because I know that I have the power of clear exposition, and, I think, also, of logical reasoning. But all the work I have done is more or less amateurish and founded almost wholly on other men's observations; and I always feel myself dreadfully inferior to men like Sir J. Hooker, Huxley, Flower, and scores of younger men who have extensive knowledge of whole departments of biology of which I am totally ignorant.'

It would not have been difficult to feel inferior to a man like Huxley, with his encyclopaedic knowledge of natural history and his natural affinity for power. Although Huxley had arisen, like Wallace, from a middle-class family on its uppers – born over a butcher's shop, the son of a teacher – he had been an FRS for the best part of half a century, during which time he had marched through the institutions, advancing the cause of science on stage and behind the scenes. Yet it was Wallace the amateur, schooled among the mechanics in the Hall of Science, self-tutored in his hedgerow university, who discovered natural selection; and he understood it better than Huxley too. He had improved himself in exemplary fashion, but still felt ashamed of lacking the accepted foundations of status. A degree would have helped; an upbringing in a grander family would probably have prevented the questions from arising at all.

Those questions, however, arose from within. Huxley never earned a degree, though he did train as a doctor, and his family only reached eminence through his own achievements. But his was an insistent temper, and Wallace's a retiring one. Wallace felt that his weaknesses ran deeper than the circumstances of his upbringing. He judged himself to be delicate in bodily and nervous constitution, disinclined to physical or mental exertion, lacking in assertiveness and wanting in physical courage. His standards may be judged by his lifetime record of tramping highways, years spent on tropical expeditions, facing imminent death on at least three occasions, prolific writing on subjects ranging from natural selection to land nationalisation, and survival past his ninetieth birthday. However he appeared, though, this was how he felt. He judged that these qualities had caused his 'shyness, reticence, and love of solitude'.

Whether this inward tendency resulted from his qualities or from his unduly low opinion of them, it was the wellspring of his thought. Wallace believed that it had helped to give him 'those long periods, both at home and abroad, when, alone and surrounded only by wild nature and uncultured man, I could ponder at leisure on the various matters that interested me. Thus was induced a receptiveness of mind which enabled me at different times to utilize what appeared to me as sudden intuitions – flashes of light leading to a solution of some problem which was then before me . . .'

A retreat into solitude, and then a flash of light: this was Wallace's personal legend of redemption. From his weaknesses, his greatest achievements arose. The manner of the discovery was important to him, as well as the fact of it. If he set it on the wrong island, while stating with unlikely precision that the temperature in the room was 88 degrees Fahrenheit, this was because the scene deserved a suitable frame.

It was apt, though accidental, that the diffident naturalist was on the other side of the world when his discovery was unveiled at the Linnean Society. Darwin was also absent: his baby son Charles had died of scarlet fever three days before. Wallace provided the meeting with two texts he had already written, together with the hurried piece from the Archipelago, which he himself did not feel was ready to be published. Unanticipated and underpresented, the idea was lost on its audience. The President of the Society later observed that the year had not 'been marked by any of those striking discoveries which at once revolutionize, so to speak, the department of science on which they bear'.

The revolution did not start until the *Origin of Species* appeared the following year. Darwin's massed ranks of examples and reasoning at close quarters succeeded in impressing the momentousness of the theory upon his readers, including Wallace, who realised that he had only seemed to see the whole effect of selection that day in his Moluccan hut. He now became possessed with it.

His was the zeal of a convert. Even in 1856, after he had published his Sarawak Law, he was quite insouciant about adaptation. He unburdened himself of his views in a paper, 'On the Habits of the Orang-Utan of Borneo', in which he claimed that the large canine teeth of the male orang-utan would be useless to it in the event of attack by a tiger, which would spring from behind, or in any other circumstance. 'Do you mean to assert, then, some of my readers will indignantly ask, that this animal, or any animal, is provided with organs which are of no use to it? Yes, we reply, we do mean to assert that many animals are provided with organs and appendages which serve no material or physical purpose.'

The living world was full of such gratuitous extravagances, from birds' plumes to the kaleidoscope of flower petals. Flourishes such as these could not be explained, insisted Wallace, by assuming that they were of some use to their possessors. Moreover, 'the constant practice of imputing, right or wrong, some use to the individual, of every part of its structure, and even of inculcating the doctrine that every modification exists solely for some such use, is an error fatal to our complete appreciation of all the variety, the beauty, and the harmony of the organic world'.

This was fundamentally a spiritual argument. What would later be called adaptationism, 'a most erroneous, a most contracted' view of life, was an impoverishing perspective because it saw only the parts, not the divine whole. 'Naturalists are too apt to *imagine*, when they cannot *discover*, a use for everything in nature: they are not even content to let "beauty" be a sufficient use, but hunt after some purpose to which even *that* can be applied by the animal itself, as if one of the noblest and most refining parts of man's nature, the love of beauty for its own sake, would not be perceptible also in the works of Supreme Creator.'

Despite its vaulting leap off the habits of the orang-utan, Wallace's outburst did not bespeak a lack of interest in the great ape. His concluding remarks suggest that these primates, 'which at once resemble and mock the "human form divine"', were electrifying in their implications for an evolutionist. Referring to the lesson of the fossil record, that existing animals were represented in earlier epochs by forms which were similar but distinct, he ventured to suggest that fossil relatives of the orang-utan might one day be found, 'more or less human in their form and structure!' In his excitement he already dared what Darwin avoided for another fifteen years, unguardedly voicing the possibility that humans had evolved in the same way as other animals.

Unlike so many of his contemporaries, who felt they must choose between faith and evolution, Wallace was untroubled by fears of spiritual crisis. Having shed the doctrines of conventional Christianity, he worried little about what might stand in its stead. The musings of phrenology and the suggestions of mesmerism had provided him with an alternative current of belief in moral progress and had persuaded him that this was connected with phenomena beyond the grasp of science. These feelings were the germs of a faith that eventually flowered in Wallace's middle life, inducing him to declare that human evolution could not all have been the work of natural selection.

Wallace was able to adopt that position not because his belief in selection was shaky, but because it was strict. Having embraced the idea, he rejected all other possible evolutionary mechanisms. Once he had convinced himself that natural selection could not have produced the faculties of the human mind, his only possible conclusion was that it was the work of supernatural forces.

3

Natural and Supernatural Selection

After discovering natural selection, Wallace set out for New Guinea. He had a research strategy, and he needed evidence. Despite the fevers and other tropical miseries, the parasitic flushes as capricious and inevitable as the clouds in English skies, he was not ready to return. When his brother-in-law, Thomas Sims, entreated him to think of his health and come home, he responded with a firm statement of purpose: 'I am engaged in a wider and more general study – that of the relations of animals to space and time . . . I have set myself to work out this problem in the Indo–Australian Archipelago, and I must visit and explore the largest number of islands possible, and collect materials from the greatest number of localities . . . As to health and life, what are they compared with peace and happiness?' The best source of happiness was 'work with a purpose, and the nobler the purpose the greater the happiness'.

He added that the money was a consideration too. His plan was to live off investments made from the proceeds of specimen sales. This would allow him to continue to devote himself to natural history when he was back in his native land. (The strategy might have worked if Wallace had continued to rely upon the judgement of Samuel Stevens, who obtained £300 a year for his client by investing proceeds from sales in Indian railway stock, instead of listening to the advice of friends with exciting investment tips. After a less fortunate experience with foreign railway stocks, Wallace was tempted to invest in quarries and lead mines, thereby throwing much of his money into holes in the ground.)

Of all the specimens the region might yield, the greatest glories and highest premiums would be found in the birds of paradise. Wallace obtained some specimens on the island of Aru, and was determined to acquire more. They were the prize that drew him to New Guinea in 1858, but there he was frustrated and disappointed. He failed to buy any birds on sale at the port; the two Malay hunters he sent inland returned empty-handed. He and his four helpers were constantly sick and almost starved; one of the Malays died of dysentery.

Later that year, however, on the Moluccan island of Batchian, he discovered a bird of paradise hitherto unknown to science and also a new 'bird-winged' butterfly. On catching a specimen of the latter, he experienced a naturalist's rapture that matched and complemented the scientific epiphany of grasping natural selection: 'Fine specimens of the male are more than seven inches across the wings, which are velvety black and fiery orange, the latter colour replacing the green of the allied species. The beauty and brilliancy of this insect are indescribable, and none but a naturalist can understand the intense excitement I experienced when I at length captured it. On taking it out of my net and opening the glorious wings, my heart began to beat violently, the blood rushed to my head, and I felt much more like fainting than I have done when in apprehension of immediate death. I had a headache the rest of the day. . .' He named the butterfly *Ornithoptera croesus*, and the bird of paradise was named after him.

In 1860, he tried again. This time his mission was supplemented by the efforts of Charles Allen, a London carpenter's son whom Wallace had brought out east with him. Allen had proved more trouble than he was worth – he couldn't even do carpentry – and was replaced by a Malay boy, Ali, who accompanied Wallace on nearly all his Malayan travels from 1855 onwards. Allen had stayed in the region after leaving Wallace's employment, and now resumed an association with him as head of a separate collecting party.

Wallace bought a small boat, of local type, for the expedition. It was not a lucky vessel. 'My first crew ran away; two men were lost for a month on a desert island; we were ten times aground on coral reefs; we lost four anchors; the sails were devoured by rats; the small boat was lost astern; we were thirty-eight days on the voyage home, which should not have taken twelve; we were many times short of food and water;' and so on. In his accounts of the quest for the birds of paradise, he dwelt upon the difficulties and hardships, rather than dropping them with his usual insouciance along the trail of his narrative. He seemed to be getting tired. He and Bates compared notes on the *tædium vitæ* to which they found themselves vulnerable in the tropics. The islands' novelty had worn off, he admitted to his brother-in-law; his health was weakening; he was losing the 'elasticity and freshness which made the overcoming of difficulties a pleasure'. The Great Exhibition, due to take place at South Kensington in 1861, would induce him 'to cut short the period of my banishment'.

Allen, for whom Wallace had arranged a three-man military escort, raised local hackles on the island of Waigiou by proposing to go inland. Birds of paradise were an established item of commerce upon which the chiefs of the coastal villages enjoyed a monopoly. Allen threatened to disturb the trading equilibrium by going direct to the source, pushing a foreign wedge into a valuable market. Braving obstructions ranging from refusal to sell him supplies to an incident in which weapons were brandished, he spent a month in the interior, getting by with gestures and gifts. But his success in obtaining specimens was only a modest offset to Wallace's disappointing efforts. After five voyages and five years, Wallace withdrew from New Guinea with examples of only five out of thirteen known species. He blamed both the market and the habitat for erecting impassable barriers to outsiders.

Wallace did, however, succeed in bringing two male birds of paradise home alive. When he came across them in a Singapore market, he found them so irresistible that he buckled at the vendor's bluff and paid the stellar asking price of nearly £100. There then ensued weeks of anxiety as he strove to keep his purchases alive through the journey from the Far East to England in the early months of 1862. On the first leg of the voyage, to Bombay, he found that their preferred food was cockroaches, which he was permitted to brush into a biscuit tin each evening in the ship's storeroom. Provisioning became more difficult on the Mediterranean leg, as cockroaches were harder to find on the Peninsular & Oriental steamer, but a stop in Malta provided an opportunity to stock up on the insects at a local bakery. After a train journey across the wintry length of France, Wallace was at last able to pass his splendid responsibilities on to the Zoological Gardens in London, and ended with a profit of over 50 per cent.

He found accommodation for himself quite close by, in Westbourne Grove, with his sister Fanny and her husband. Soon he began, in his awkward way, to see about extending his reduced family by taking a wife. After two years of courtship, 'Miss L.' assented to betrothal, but some months later put the engagement out of its misery. Alfred was deeply hurt, but his persistence prevailed, and in 1865 he married Annie Mitten, the daughter of a botanist friend. She was eighteen and he past forty; they remained together until parted by his death nearly fifty years later. They had a son whom they lost, and a son and daughter who survived them.

Wallace's explorations were over, though his restlessness would persist for the rest of his life: he was never at a loss for a reason to move house. London was an ideal location in which to start this new phase of his life, since for the next five years he was among the colleagues whose respect he had earned. He could attend scientific meetings throughout the week, and on Sundays he could go round to the Huxleys' house in St John's Wood, where the pleasant domestic atmosphere put him at his ease. He was ready to shift from collection to interpretation, and his fellow scientists would learn that when it came to remarkable views there was nobody quite like Alfred Russel Wallace.

Henry Bates was also back in town, inspired by the *Origin* and keen to make his evolutionary mark. Though he said it himself, he had 'a most beautiful proof of the truth of the theory of natural selection'. Darwin and Wallace were inclined to agree. Even Huxley was impressed, though it was not the proof he demanded.

Bates had found the forest paths near Amazonian towns patrolled by hosts of Heliconid butterflies, sailing languidly on long black wings illuminated in red, blue, orange or yellow. In their 'bright dresses', they made up for the lack of flowers. These were insouciant insects, slow and fragile despite the swarms of insectivorous birds that surrounded them, yet they were conspicuous not just in appearance but for their abundance. And their example inspired imitation. Bates recorded dozens of species that bore close resemblances to Heliconids, although close examination showed that they belonged to distant groups; many of their relatives resembled cabbage whites, being part of the same family as the common European butterfly.

Mimicry was not confined to butterflies; it turned out to be a widespread tropical practice. One day Bates was startled by a sinuous form which uncoiled from the foliage of a tree he was examining. It was a caterpillar disguised as a poisonous snake, which alarmed everyone in the village when Bates took it back to where he was staying.

It was easy enough to see what advantage there might be for a caterpillar in resembling a venomous snake, and Bates recognised that mimicry in general must be advantageous. It had to be an adaptation, just like those of organs or instincts. The benefits of 'Heliconide dress' were not so transparent, but the multitudes of Heliconids attested to their evolutionary success. Bates had noticed that some specimens smelled peculiar when set out to dry and were avoided by the vermin that scavenged from his collections. Butterfly-eating predators also seemed to leave living Heliconids alone. He surmised, correctly, that Heliconids are unpalatable and that their mimics benefit by appearing to be inedible too.

Not only was mimicry an adaptation, but it was one which could only have been produced by natural selection, the selecting agents being insectivorous birds. There was no other way to explain the way in which mimics were tuned in not just to a species, but to the forms taken by its local varieties. This was the work not of sudden, massive transformations, but of 'many small steps of variation and selection'. Batesian mimicry, as it came to be known, exemplified the three great Darwinian themes of adaptation, selection and gradualism.

Mimicry became an important theme for two other great Darwinians, Wallace and Fisher. For Wallace, it was part of a broader preoccupation with the colours and markings of creatures. He was ahead of his time in realising that Batesian mimics relied upon their scarcity. Bates had observed that Heliconid models outnumbered their Leptalid mimics by a thousand to one. If it were the other way round, noted Wallace, mimicry would cease to work. As long as Heliconids maintained their predominance, there was little chance that Leptalids would be found out. A bird pecking a butterfly in Heliconid dress would be overwhelmingly likely to be left with an unpleasant taste. If mimics were common, birds would often come across them and learn that butterflies of that pattern could well be palatable. Wallace had anticipated 'frequency dependence', a familiar feature of modern evolutionary explanations.

It was hardly surprising that Wallace should have been impressed by colour and pattern in animals. The metallic finishes and iridescent highlights of beetles and birds were his bread and butter. The variety of life was to a large extent manifest as the variety of ornament; its importance was not just scientific and aesthetic but practical, since collectors like Wallace, lacking independent means, relied upon gorgeous specimens to pay their way. But Wallace was equally impressed by the opposite. To him, the cryptic female was as significant as the extravagant male. On this issue, he turned out to be more Darwinian than Darwin.

The differences between the two naturalists were elaborated in the correspondence between them, which was particularly active in the second half of the 1860s. These were differences arising from two distinctive understandings of adaptation. Wallace's was firmer, but Darwin's was broader.

Darwin had identified two basic selective processes: natural selection and sexual selection. From the start Wallace found it very difficult to take the latter seriously, and his doubts only hardened as the years went by. He could see that males competed for mates, and so the struggles between them could exert selective pressures for traits such as weapons and strength. These were much the same sort of characteristics that natural selection favoured in the struggle for existence. They were practical. Selection did not indulge in frivolities.

Wallace was thus left with the phenomena which he appreciated better than almost anyone, as he prepared his butterflies and his birds of paradise, holding them in his hands, picking out and recording every detail of tint, flourish and filigree. Darwin explained many of these ornaments as products of female choice. If females had a preference for particular ornaments, males who could display these ornaments impressively would tend to have more descendants as a result. Traits did not have to be sensible to be effective.

Nor was selection necessarily fatal. Nowadays, with sexual selection theory one of the most dynamic areas of evolutionary research, Darwinism is understood as a matter of 'differential reproductive success' rather than 'survival of the fittest'. The distinction between natural and sexual selection is eroded; the two are seen to be intimately linked and to be aspects of the same basic process. But sexual selection only really became established a hundred years after the debates between Wallace and Darwin. In her history of the scientific fortunes of sexual selection, *The Ant and the*

Peacock, Helena Cronin suggests that Wallace was largely to blame for its century of eclipse.

The blame must also lie with the broader resistance to the idea of female choice that prevailed throughout society until the successes of the women's movement in the later decades of the twentieth century. Wallace's own mid-Victorian attitudes were, however, usually tempered by his generous human sympathies. His doubts about female choice showed that he took females seriously.

Later on, after he had declared himself a socialist, he placed his faith in female choice as an alternative to eugenics. He looked forward to a serene future of public service and equal income, sustained by women's choices in marriage. The risk to such a society lay not in the Malthusian positive checks of war, pestilence and famine, but in their absence. Without them, the population would explode, outrunning its capacity to feed itself, and the curse of Malthus would return. Some other kind of checks would be needed to maintain the equilibrium. Wallace saw the answer in delayed marriage, based on female independence. Women would be able to take their time choosing husbands, as they would have as much money as men. Marrying later, they would have fewer children. Some would choose not to marry, but would still be 'fully occupied with public duties and intellectual or social enjoyments'. As well as stabilising society against Malthusian hazards, 'the cultivated minds and pure instincts of the Women of the Future' could improve the race. Women would be encouraged to choose their husbands with the greatest of care, both for their own sakes and society's, excluding selfish, idle, cruel and vicious men from fatherhood. Wallace certainly believed in human female choice, both instinctive and considered.

He did not expect them to choose according to looks, though, and in his debates with Darwin he had raised a number of objections to the idea that females of other species should exert any selective influence according to such criteria. It was not that he thought females were incapable of choice, but that he expected their choices to be sensible.

Even if females did have preferences concerning ornament, it was hard to see how these could be sustained or spread throughout a population. Without a good reason for their existence, they would not be supported by selection. From a selectionist point of view, traits are not expected to endure unless they are positively advantageous. If they have no adaptive value, they are likely to be replaced by characters that do, or by equally arbitrary ones.

They might be maintained, however, if they were linked to genuinely valuable traits. If peahens did prefer the most splendid peacocks, Wallace argued, it was because they were selecting the healthiest and most vigorous specimens. These would have the finest plumage, but it was their general fitness to which the females would attend. Although he realised that markings could be very useful as the means by which creatures could recognise members of their own species, he never grasped that the quality of decoration could serve as a reliable indication of fitness. Unable to see them as naturally valuable, he thought that potential mates would omit to see them as well.

Wallace was on surer ground with cryptic females. He emphasised that inconspicuous appearance needed explanation as well, and argued that females were under greater pressure to conceal themselves. Birds supported his case: it was easy to appreciate that females were vulnerable to predators as they sat on their nests. He was also able to point to exceptions that proved his rule. Brightly coloured females turned out to nest under cover, whereas female birds that nested in the open were invariably camouflaged.

His explanation, almost pedestrian in its Darwinian orthodoxy, made as stark a contrast to his explanation for striking plumage as that between the costumes of the two bird sexes themselves. Drabness, he argued, was the suppression of natural exuberance by natural selection. Inside the body, brightness was the rule. Blood, bile and vividly coloured organs showed that colour was a natural attribute of organic forms. Vividness flowed from vigour; superabundance of energy was channelled into colour. He suspended the great principle of adaptation that the evolutionists had appropriated from the natural theologians, that complexity is evidence of design. The appearance of design, in the elaborate patterns and forms that ornament took, was produced by physiological processes uninfluenced by selection.

He had held a King Bird of Paradise with plumes on its breast that it could spread at will into fans and tail feathers elongated into wires, spiralling into buttons at the end; he had been transported with delight at the uniqueness as well as the beauty of these features, and now he ascribed it all to the results of superabundant energy. Having failed to explain extravagant ornaments by natural selection, Wallace preferred to wave his hands in the direction of physiology rather than to endorse the selectionist alternative offered by Darwin. There had to be just one means to produce adaptive change, and if a structure was not produced by natural selection, plain and simple, it was not an adaptation.

Although his position, as on other matters, was distinctly idiosyncratic, Wallace was not the only person to suggest that colours and patterns might somehow arise from an animal's vigour. At least one commentator did, however, imply that Darwin had the better explanation for vividness, although Wallace made the stronger case on drabness. Remarking on a butterfly whose wings were dull underneath and bright above, he judged that 'We may give the under surface to Mr Wallace, but we must yield the upper surface to Mr Darwin.'

The two men were to remain on different sides of the issue, but the debates between them never led to acrimony. Their relations were warm, and they held each other in high regard. Despite his scientific seniority, it was the fretful Darwin who took their disagreements more to heart, and beyond. 'Heaven protect my stomach whenever I attempt following your argument,' he groaned. 'I grieve to differ from you,' he lamented six months later, 'and it actually terrifies me, and makes me constantly distrust myself. I fear we shall never quite understand each other.'

On at least one occasion, his children were forced to share his pain. Another issue on which the two men differed was that of whether natural selection could make species and varieties mutually sterile, or render hybrids sterile when they did occur. Darwin stewed in his doubts; Wallace struggled to allay them. After a couple of attempts to grapple with Wallace's nineteen-point thesis, Darwin complained that 'it has made my stomach feel as if it had been placed in a vice. Your paper has driven three of my children half mad.'

Wallace was confident that natural selection was capable of producing sterile hybrids, even though its methods were obscure. Thanks to Darwin and the *Origin*, his awe of natural selection had deepened since his Malayan epiphany. 'I am deeply interested in all that concerns the powers of Natural Selection,' he told Darwin, 'but though I admit there are a few things it cannot do I do not yet believe sterility to be one of them.'

Darwin was not so sure, partly because he appreciated better than Wallace that selection acted on individuals. He could not see how it helped an organism to be sterile, so he doubted that sterility was an adaptation. Primroses and cowslips sometimes interbreed, which is, of course, to the benefit of the parent plants. If any primroses or cowslips happened to be less mutually fertile than usual, Darwin pointed out to Wallace, that would hardly be likely to increase their numbers and enable them to replace the existing primroses and cowslips. Their sterility might be good for the species, in the sense that it would tend to maintain the species' integrity, but it would not be good for them.

Wallace did not distinguish between the common good and what was good for individuals. If sterility in crosses or hybrids was good for the species, it was within natural selection's remit. Naturalists and zoologists a hundred years later shared his confusion: modern Darwinism defined itself around demonstrations that natural selection had the interests of individuals, not species, at heart. Modern Darwinism is with Darwin, rather than Wallace, on individual and sexual selection. But it has affirmed the faith in natural selection to which Wallace held while Darwin wavered.

Darwin spent much of the 1860s beset by hybrids, first on one flank and then the other. Before Wallace, with his tortuous logic, had been Huxley, with his unbending standards of proof. Wallace was an enthusiast; Huxley an arbiter. To Wallace, natural selection was a fact and a force whose range was not yet measured. Sterility might turn out to be one of its blind spots, but nothing more than that. To Huxley, natural selection was a hypothesis that needed to be confirmed, like other scientific hypotheses, by observation. Never noticeably warm about the theory of natural selection, he made the sterility issue his condition of acceptance.

Huxley wanted to see experimental evidence that mutually sterile varieties could be bred from a common stock. This would demonstrate that selection could drive a process which, if extended long enough, could result in the origin of new species, isolated from each other by sterility. Artificial selection would prove the power of natural selection not just to produce adaptations but species. Until artificial selection was shown to produce sterility between varieties, Darwin's theory would be incomplete; and if it was shown to be incapable of doing so, he warned his audience of working men one night in 1863, the theory would be 'utterly shattered'.

As far as Darwin was concerned, Huxley was being overdramatic. Sterility need not be directly selected at all but might arise from the accumulation of differences that had been generated by natural selection. But he was unable to persuade Huxley, or provide the evidence that would satisfy him. Eventually he gave up trying to convince the 'Objector-General', who continued to await his required proof for the rest of his life.

By the end of 1868 he had agreed to differ with Wallace too, though with regret rather than exasperation. But their disagreements on sexual selection and sterility were about to pale in comparison with the gulf that Wallace opened between them the following year. At the same time that he had been asserting the powers of natural selection in his correspondence with Darwin, he had privately been seeking its limits. He was venturing out upon a new expedition, not to the tropics, but into another dimension.

'I must now tell you of the addition to my household of an orphan baby,' Wallace had written home in 1855, 'a curious little half-nigger baby, which I have nursed now more than a month . . . I am afraid you would call it an ugly baby, for it has a dark brown skin and red hair, a very large mouth, but very pretty little hands and feet. It has now cut its two lower front teeth, and the uppers are coming. At first it would not sleep alone at night, but cried very much; so I made it a pillow of an old stocking, which it likes to hug, and now sleeps very soundly.'

Then Wallace revealed how he came by his charge. 'I was out shooting in the jungle and saw something up a tree which I thought was a large monkey or orang-utan, so I fired at it, and down fell this little baby – in its mother's arms . . . I presume she was a wild "woman of the woods;" so I have preserved her skin and skeleton, and am trying to bring up her only daughter, and hope some day to introduce her to fashionable society at the Zoological Gardens.' His hopes were not realised; the infant orang-utan died after three months.

Wallace missed his 'dear little duck of a darling of a little brown hairy baby', for whom he had played nurse with gusto. But his references to its 'poor mother' are for the sake of the anthropomorphic conceit. The *frisson* of resemblance did not excite his sympathy so far as to make his finger pause on the trigger. Six to a dozen bullets were needed to kill an orang-utan, he noted in the 'Habits' paper, or to make it fall from a tree.

Nevertheless, as one of the first to blur the boundaries between simian and human, he played his part in stimulating the respect for great ape life that he and all his contemporaries lacked.

When he spoke of a 'woman of the woods', Wallace was playing on the translation of orang-utan, 'man of the forest'. He was toying archly with what he was preparing to discuss in earnest: comparisons between humans and other species, comparisons among human varieties, and what these all revealed about evolution. Like most of those who put their minds to the question of origins, Wallace was inclined to dwell upon his own species.

The exception was the man who proved the rule. Malthus had made a sharp impression on Darwin, as in their own ways had the indigenous people whom the young naturalist had encountered during his South American voyage on the *Beagle*. But in the two decades of gestation that preceded the *Origin*, Darwin secured himself a position in which human examples were pushed to the edge of the picture. He worked at home in Kent, classifying barnacles and breeding pigeons. Wallace's first papers were field dispatches, written during expeditions which constantly raised questions about the relationship between living varieties and geography, and about the distribution of human varieties.

As if hoping nobody would notice, Darwin hurried off stage at the end of the *Origin* with only the terse announcement, more of an admission than a declaration, that 'Light will be thrown on the origin of man and his history.' Of course, everybody noticed. Pigeons and barnacles were neither here nor there. Darwin's contemporaries understood that this was, above all, about humans and apes.

Thomas Huxley hung a collection of three essays, under the title *Man's Place in Nature*, upon this 'question of questions'. For all his panache and boldness, though, he had little to say about 'Whence our race has come; what are the limits of our power over nature, and of nature's power over us; to what goal we are tending. . .' Nor did he exactly raise the banner of Darwinism over the barricades. He gave a guarded endorsement of Darwin's theory, subject to proof that mutually infertile animals could arise by selective breeding from a common stock, but confined his own survey to comparisons of anatomy. An advocate for Darwin's view was the last thing he would want to be, insisted the circumspect bulldog, 'if by an

71

advocate is meant one whose business it is to smooth over real difficulties, and to persuade where he cannot convince'.

Wallace was made of plainer stuff. In 1864, at a meeting of the London Anthropological Society, he made the first public statement about how natural selection might have shaped humanity. He offered it as an intervention in a dispute among anthropologists over whether humans belonged to one species or several. The Anthropological Society was the stronghold of the faction that favoured multiple origins, and slavery; the rival Ethnological Society stood for emancipation and human unity. Behind them were the thunderous shadows of the American Confederacy and the Union states of the North, at war the past three years; and in the shadows of the Anthropological Society the Confederates were at work, injecting funds via an agent among its officers.

Huxley had quit the Anthropological Society after its journal ran a disdainful review of *Man's Place in Nature*, and he told Wallace he would not cross its threshold to hear him speak. Wallace took Huxley's point, but put in a word for the Society. Since the Ethnological Society had admitted ladies, hc noted, many important topics could not be aired there. Despite his experience of the world, his proprieties remained English.

The advocates of multiple origins held a strong card, Wallace told them, in the observation that racial differences seemed to have reached their current levels several thousand years ago. However, he believed that he could reconcile the two camps by the application of Darwin's theory. After outlining the mechanism of natural selection, he pointed out that man owes his survival to his mental faculties above all else. In a carnivorous animal natural selection might act upon the claws or canines; in man it would act upon the capacity to make a spear or a bow, or to combine his skills in a hunting party.

In man, therefore, nature had moved on from body to mind. The visible differences between races might simply be the legacy of selection exerted as ancestral humans diffused from a common stock to colonise different regions, but before they reached the threshold of full humanity. Once they were able to make their weapons and body coverings, rather than growing them, they would improve rapidly as selection built their intellects and characters. The suite of traits favoured by selection had a rosy moral glow, including sympathy, a sense of right, self-restraint and foresight.

All these would be selected because they were for the good of the community. Tribes rich in the higher virtues would enjoy an advantage in the struggle for existence over those less well endowed; the former would increase and the latter would dwindle to extinction. Racial competition was the motor of human evolutionary progress. Among its highest achievements was 'the wonderful intellect of the Germanic race'.

Like Darwin, Wallace saw this as an ongoing process: 'it must inevitably follow that the higher – the more intellectual and moral – must displace the lower and more degraded races'. Mankind would become what it had been at the beginning, a single homogeneous type, but universally finer than the 'noblest specimens of existing humanity'.

The process could certainly be seen going on, as the last full-blooded Tasmanian eked out her last years. But although Wallace regarded it as inevitable, he was appalled by those who pursued it actively. In his *Travels on the Amazon*, he had written warmly of the 'disgustingly coarse' but irresistibly delivered anecdotes told by Frei Jozé dos Santos Innocentos, a cleric 'prematurely worn out by every kind of debauchery'. Wallace admitted, however, that he could 'hardly help a shudder' at one of the friar's tales. Joseph of the Holy Innocents had boasted of saving the authorities in Bolivia the expense of a war with some Indian tribes by suggesting the cheaper alternative of letting them acquire clothes infected with smallpox. Four or five nations, the friar boasted, had been totally destroyed by this stratagem. Wallace consoled himself with the thought that 'it was probably one of the ingenious fabrications of Frei Jozé's fertile brain'.

Ten years later, he had seen much more of relations between colonists and natives; as a seasoned tropical hand, he was readier to face up to the rights and wrongs of them. Perhaps he also felt freer to speak his mind now that he was unconstrained by the commercial pressure to avoid trying his readers' consciences. In his essay 'How to Civilise Savages', published in 1865, he reported the friar's genocidal boast as an outrage. He added stories of an Australian colonist who demonstrated the accuracy of a rifle by shooting the baby from a passing aboriginal woman's back, and of a kindred spirit of Frei Jozé's, who disagreed with the policy of shooting any aborigines who approached a settlers' station on the grounds that poisoning them would be less trouble. 'The white men in our Colonies are too frequently the true savages,' he concluded.

One of the forms of domination he encountered in the tropics was slavery. In the Malay Archipelago, it occurred as a judicial measure, whereby debtors were bound over by magistrates to work for nothing until their debts were deemed to have been repaid. In Brazil it appeared in its frankest form, as chattel slavery. Wallace was morally perplexed by the benevolent proprietorship of Senhor Calistro, who every evening would bless each of his slaves and native workers as a father in those parts would bless his children. Some would beg favours such as a shirt or some coffee; always granted, Calistro assured Wallace, because the requests were always reasonable. On the other side of the patriarchal coin, he punished idleness with a 'moderate flogging'. 'In fact,' Wallace concluded, 'Senhor Calistro attends to his slaves just as he would to a large family of children.' It was a long way from New Lanark, but the principle of benign paternalism was similar.

Wallace considered that Calistro's slaves were better off than many free men. The problem was that they could not make their condition still better by their own efforts. 'Can it be right to keep a number of our fellow-creatures in a state of adult infancy, – of unthinking childhood?' he wondered. 'It is the responsibility and self-dependence of manhood that calls forth the highest powers and energies of our race. It is the struggle for existence, the "battle for life," which exercises the moral faculties and calls forth the latent sparks of genius. The hope of gain, the love of power, the desire of fame and approbation, excite to noble deeds, and call into action all those faculties which are the distinctive attributes of man.' These thoughts, first aired in 1853, show that Wallace recognised the 'struggle for existence' as vital and creative even before he realised it was the engine of the variety of life.

Wallace's faith in improvement qualified his evolutionary fatalism. Although in the long term the human species would be raised up by the disappearance of the 'lower' races and their replacement by the 'higher' ones, there was plenty of scope for improvement within many of the lower races themselves. Brazil had taught him that native peoples could be transformed by the influence of colonists, if not necessarily for the better. 'I could not have believed that there would be so much difference in the aspect of the same people in their native state and when living under European supervision,' he wrote of his first encounter with 'wild Indians'.

74

Willing as he was to see good in paternal domination, he would find it easy to take an optimistic view of the potential for improvement under European influence.

Wallace did not believe that 'savages' were capable of appreciating the natural wonders around them, such aesthetic faculties being the product of civilisation. He assumed that birds of paradise were wasted on the indigenous people of New Guinea, yet reflected on the irony that if 'civilised man' opened up the forest, he would so disturb it 'as to cause the disappearance, and finally the extinction of these very beings whose wonderful structure and beauty he alone is fitted to appreciate and enjoy'. (A similar fate awaited the Papuans: 'A warlike and energetic people, who will not submit to national slavery or to domestic servitude, must disappear before the white man as surely as do the wolf and the tiger.')

Yet in their social relations, tropical peoples seemed to approach closer to an ideal of harmony than did the great mass of people living in civilised society. At the end of his *Malay Archipelago*, Wallace affirmed the themes he had aired in verse in the Amazon village nearly twenty years before. Having contrasted the physical, intellectual and moral qualities of the Malays, Papuans and miscellaneous races of the Archipelago, he turned to the subject of human progress. An ideal state of society would be one in which individuals knew what was right and had an unerring urge to do it, so that laws and punishments would be unnecessary. The achievement of such a state would result from proper development of, and balance between, the physical, intellectual and moral dimensions of human nature. Wallace believed that conditions approaching such a state of affairs obtained in some of the Amazonian and Malayan communities he had visited, where a natural sense of justice and of neighbours' rights prevailed. As he had remarked, writing home in 1855, 'The more I see of uncivilised people, the better I think of human nature on the whole . . .'

These qualities also flourished in the more privileged strata of civilised societies, but the lives of the masses were blighted by moral deficiency. Civilised societies needed to develop the sympathetic and moral faculties, and allow these to exert their proper influence upon laws, commerce and social organisation. Only then would civilised peoples truly have attained superiority over savages.

*

75

Although Wallace did not believe that Papuans could properly appreciate birds of paradise, he had a degree of respect for their intelligence, being inclined to think that it might be greater than that of Malays. He was in general impressed by the mental capacities of 'savages', many of whom seemed to have 'as much brains as average Europeans'.

He was not, however, impressed with the uses to which they put these faculties. Savages produced little better than a cacophony by way of music; they often could not even count up to the number of fingers on their hands; many had barely a scruple in respect of truth and falsehood. The occasional exceptions, such as the Santals of India, who had 'as pure a love of truth as the most moral among civilised men', showed that higher capacities were universal but latent among uncivilised peoples. Lofty sentiments and abstractions would interfere with the animal reflexes on which savages depended in their struggles with unsentimental nature.

As far as Wallace could see, writing in 1869, a savage could manage with a brain slightly larger than that of a gorilla. The implication of this overwhelmed the account of human evolution he had given in his 1864 paper. Since natural selection addressed present needs, not future ones, it 'could only have endowed savage man with a brain a little superior to that of an ape, whereas he actually possesses one very little inferior to that of a philosopher'. Some other force must have endowed savages with minds prepared in advance for civilisation.

Wallace adduced human hairlessness to this proposition, arguing that humans could not have evolved from simian hairiness through the action of natural selection. Loss of hair would be harmful even in the tropics, where living savages often covered their backs to protect themselves from wind or rain; and it would be restored, by reversion to ancestral type, when humans spread into cold regions. The human hand and foot also seemed to Wallace to be overdesigned for savage applications.

As he consolidated his thesis, he dropped these physical traits from it, deciding that natural selection could be responsible for them after all. He was as steadfast on the central argument in 1889, though, as when he first advanced it twenty years earlier. The Greeks produced greater works of art than the Romans, he observed, but their statues did not protect them from Roman domination. And mathematical skills might have helped the Romans build their empire, but they did not save it from falling to the barbarians.

He also proposed humour as a higher faculty, almost absent in savages. Even in civilised societies wit was like a talent for music, confined to a small percentage of a population. (Wallace was sure that he possessed neither gift himself.) The rareness and extreme variability of such faculties were, he argued, inconsistent with the way natural selection works. Survival of the fittest was a 'rigid law, which acts by the life or death of the individuals submitted to its action'. It eliminated harmful traits and kept useful ones up to standard. The traits it developed would therefore be present in all members of the population and would not vary greatly. A genius for maths or music could not therefore be an adaptation, but it might be a gift.

By drawing a line between the Bali of the body and the Lombok of the mind, Wallace revealed the grandness of his design. Beyond the limits of natural selection, he had detected the effects of powers from another dimension. In 1864, Wallace had told a story of human evolution in which selection shifted smoothly from body to mind, continuing to shape Man after taking him across the threshold of humanity. Man could rise above natural selection by exercising his mental faculties, but his power to do so had been conferred by natural selection itself. Now, Wallace warned Darwin, he was ready to pronounce the limits to natural selection. 'I hope you have not murdered too completely your own and my child,' Darwin replied apprehensively.

On reading the paper, Darwin sprayed it with exclamation marks, and branded it with an outraged 'No', underlined three times. 'I differ grievously from you, and I am very sorry for it,' he wrote to its author. 'I can see no necessity for calling in an additional and proximate cause in regard to Man.'

'I can quite comprehend your feelings with regard to my "unscientific" opinions as to Man,' replied Wallace, 'because a few years back I should myself have looked at them as equally uncalled for.' He explained that 'my opinions on the subject have been modified solely by the consideration of a series of remarkable phenomena, physical and mental, which I have now had every opportunity of testing, and which demonstrate the existence of forces and influences not yet recognised by science. This will, I know, seem to you like some mental hallucination . . .'

It was an admission that the argument of his paper concealed the processes of his thought. He presented his case as though he had devel-

77

oped it by subjecting natural selection to closer scrutiny, thereby revealing the need for an additional cause. But the explanation he gave Darwin implies that he became convinced of the extra-scientific forces first and then felt impelled to pick large enough holes in natural selection to give them the influence they demanded. For these phenomena were not merely complementary to those already recognised by science, but represented a higher power altogether. He reordered his view of human evolution so as to place the supernatural above the natural. Since his lecture to the Anthropological Society, Wallace had become a spiritualist.

Ever since his mesmeric experiments in Leicester, he had accepted that forces might exist which could not yet be explained by science. By the end of the 1860s, he believed supernatural phenomena to be as real as natural ones and did not always distinguish between them. In *The Malay Archipelago*, he recorded a local report that ghosts were very rare in Lombok, offering the intelligence as a 'contribution to the natural history of the island'. (He added – and it should be remembered that irony was another higher faculty with which he was not burdened – that as the evidence was negative, to accept it fully would show a lack of scientific caution.)

While he was writing up his experiences in the Archipelago, he became convinced that he had access to the other dimension in his own home, not by inference from ethnological comparisons but through the ritual of the séance. With the conviction that comes of spending too long with suggestible people in darkened rooms, he believed that spirit forces existed in a sort of proximity to the material world and could impinge on it under certain circumstances. If the souls of the dead were in hailing distance of ordinary Victorian parlours, perhaps more powerful spiritual forces might have made more momentous interventions in the history of life.

He first took his place at a séance table in July 1865, at the house of a lawyer friend. The group, mostly members of the friend's family, placed their hands on the table and waited. Duly there came tapping sounds, jerks and vibrations. The effects developed in subsequent sessions, until the table went zigzagging around the room. In his notes he recorded an 'unknown power developed from the bodies of a number of persons' connected by their hands on the table. Next he began to visit a medium, under whose influence he saw a table rise a foot from the floor and a chair raised in the air while a woman was seated upon it. He was inspired to try it at home. The results were unspectacular at first, but then a woman with a talent as a medium became involved. A small table regularly hovered, and on one occasion an armchair wheeled up to her.

Spiritualism, a faith he shared with his sister Fanny, was a natural destination for him. The movement had arisen from that of mesmerism, which practised clairvoyance and engendered the idea that the trance state was an antechamber to the spirit world. Like the kindred belief system of phrenology, spiritualism offered a vision of progress and a guide to earthly behaviour as preparation for the next world. It spoke to Wallace's deepest beliefs, and much about it was very familiar. Like a Quaker meeting, a séance was a gathering in which a group of lay people hoped to make contact with the supernatural realm, though when the spirits moved them, the pronouncements were briefer and warmer than those which Alfred had sat through as a boy at the Friends' House.

The voices were domestic, not philosophical. Innocent of snobbery, Wallace thought none the worse of them for that. For Huxley, though, they were voices from below rather than beyond. 'It may be all true, for anything I know to the contrary,' he wrote to Wallace, declining to join him in one of the Wallace circle's regular Friday evening table-rapping sessions, 'but really I cannot get up any interest in the subject. I never cared for gossip in my life, and disembodied gossip, such as these worthy ghosts supply their friends with, is not more interesting to me than any other.'

If tactful to Wallace – Huxley had damned spiritualists far more vehemently in print, along with the rest of the mesmerising, clairvoyant 'Witch Sabbat' casting their spells over the public – his irony was insensitive to the reason of reasons that people sought news from the spirit world. Above all, they hoped for news of their loved ones. The first ghostly words addressed to Alfred referred to his dead brother Herbert; he was later offered solace from the other side after the death of his young son, who bore Herbert's name. Mediums have frequently been mocked for the banality of their messages, whose effect derives from what their recipients project onto them. Huxley's point, however, was that the messages were trivial; and they were trivial because they were nothing to do with science.

Having gone through so much to achieve his scientific status, Wallace was particularly sensitive on this score. As so many advocates of the paranormal feel obliged to do, he insisted that his methods were scientific. He took pains to emphasise the precautions he and his fellow participants had taken against fraud during the séances; he noted when they had been conducted in daylight. To these assurances he added another familiar device of paranormalist rhetoric, attesting that for the twenty-five years preceding his encounters around the animated tables he had been an 'utter sceptic' about 'preter- or super-human intelligences'. His scepticism may not have been quite as absolute as he made out, but even so, what he underwent was a conversion. As he acknowledged, his theory required 'the intervention of some distinct individual intelligence, to aid in the production of what we can hardly avoid considering as the ultimate aim and outcome of all organized existence – intellectual, ever-advancing, spiritual man'. His theory of change now had a sense of purpose.

The light of the Creator shone through the holes he had torn in the theory of evolution, as if bursting through the shell of the celestial sphere to the heavens beyond, and he was dazzled. But his arguments smacked more of contortion than revelation. Throughout the rest of his writings on evolution, when his purpose was to affirm that natural selection was the sole means of adaptive change, he emphasised that nature always provided a great stock of variations upon which selection could act. Here he had to downplay the extent of variation, in order to depict the extremes as anomalies.

He also had to turn his back on everything else he had written about 'savages' – including an article, 'On Instinct in Man and Animals', which appeared in the same collection of essays as 'The Limits of Natural Selection as Applied to Man'. Nearly twenty years after he had first travelled beyond Europe, he suddenly adopted a tone that echoed Darwin's dismay on first meeting uncivilised people rather than the sympathetic curiosity that he brought to such encounters himself. Never mind apes; wolves and foxes showed as much sophistication in hunting and storing food as did savages. 'What is there in the life of the savage, but the satisfying of the cravings of appetite in the simplest and easiest way?' he demanded.

As Huxley was quick to point out, Wallace answered his own question in his essay on instinct. Refuting the popular assumption that savages found their way by brute instinct, Wallace described how painstakingly forest people accumulated topographical knowledge, first-hand and shared around the campfire, finer-grained and subtler than any map. Huxley added that savages needed comparably extensive knowledge of plants and animals, that their languages were often complex to a degree that made them difficult for Europeans to master, and that 'even an Australian can make excellent baskets and nets'. Pointedly, he observed that 'every time a savage tracks his game he employs a minuteness of observation, and an accuracy of inductive and deductive reasoning which, applied to other matters, would assure some reputation to a man of science. . .'

He might also have asked why, if savages did nothing that could not be managed with ape-sized brains and natural selection did not confer surplus capacities, gorillas were not observed swapping travel notes around campfires and weaving baskets. Wallace had abandoned his naturalist's sense of detail, discarding close observation and careful reasoning for a fervent, and slightly hysterical, sketch of a revelation.

When Wallace 'seemed to see the whole effect' of natural selection in his Malayan hut, he saw selection bringing about the origin of species. Unlike the universal Darwinians of the later twentieth century, he never imagined that selective processes could have anything to do with the origin of life itself. Hoping for insight into that question, Wallace and Bates went to see Herbert Spencer, the railway engineer turned philosopher to whom the world owes the phrase 'survival of the fittest'. Wallace urged it upon Darwin in order to avoid the misunderstanding that nature was somehow conscious in its selection. He had never shared Darwin's belief that the breeding of domestic animals could usefully be compared with natural processes and felt that it had led Darwin down an unfortunate metaphorical path.

Spencer was another of those thinkers who happened upon natural selection without appreciating what they had within their reach. By 1852, he had worked out that those who did not die prematurely 'must be the select of their generation', but did not see the whole effect until the *Origin* showed it to him seven years later. Thereafter he incorporated Darwinism into his philosophy, while remaining a Lamarckian at heart. His lasting contribution to evolutionary thought was to give it a bad name: Social Darwinism. Detesting the influence of the collective over the individual, he took up natural selection as a stick to beat the state, which had a pernicious inclination to alleviate the misery of the poor. *Laissez-faire* was a law of nature and a cornerstone of morality. 'If left to operate in all its sternness, the principle of the survival of the fittest, which, ethically considered, we have seen to imply that each individual shall be left to experience the effects of his own nature and consequent conduct, would quickly clear away the degraded.'

On this occasion, however, he offered none of his usual certainties. How life had arisen was too deep a question to be addressed for a long time yet, though it had probably been some kind of development of matter. Wallace was deeply impressed by Spencer but not by matter. Having dealt with the mind and consciousness, he ended his paper on the limits of natural selection with some reflections about the nature of matter and the universe. Matter, he considered, was nothing in itself; in fact, as popularly understood, it did not exist. Matter was force, and force was will, and the universe was the will of higher intelligences or a single supreme one. The universe did not just have purpose; it *was* purpose.

For Benjamin Disraeli, the Victorian statesman, the question posed by the Darwinists was that of whether man was an ape or an angel. 'I am on the side of the angels,' he declared. Wallace contrived to be on both sides at once. His first statement on evolution had been based on the recognition that earthly species came in series, often with gaps only a naturalist's eye would notice. This, he believed, was one aspect of a universal law of 'continuity'. It could hardly be chinks all the way up to man and then a chasm between him and God. There were surely beings in between, and these might have been the guiding intelligences that had intervened in human evolution. Angels had taken apes and turned them into men.

Wallace was prepared to believe a lot of things that his peers saw through, but his fringe interests were confined to the supernatural dimension. When challenged by somebody who insisted that the Earth was flat, he took it as an opportunity to educate the public and make a profit into the bargain. John Hampden offered £500 to anybody who could demonstrate convexity on lakes or courses of water. Wallace employed a six-inch telescope and his old surveying skills to show the Earth's curvature from measurements made along a stretch of an East Anglian canal.

However, it soon appeared that the reason Hampden was prepared to offer such an extravagant stake was that he was incapable of accepting that he could lose it. He was not a gambler but a crusader, certain that the Earth was flat because his Bible told him so, on an all-consuming mission to scourge the infidels who argued for the globe. The umpire ruled in Wallace's favour but did not pass the stake to Wallace straight away. This enabled Hampden to exploit a loophole in the law governing wagers, which holds them to be null and void, and forced Wallace to return the money five years later.

That was not the end of the matter, though. Hampden's campaign went on for over fifteen years in all. He defamed Wallace in letters, postcards and pamphlets to acquaintances, strangers, neighbours, newspapers and societies, his mania only temporarily muted by several spells of imprisonment. Wallace had to meet the legal costs of defending himself against Hampden's persecution, but he felt that he deserved some punishment for accepting the wager in the first place. As a man of science, he must have felt as sure as Hampden that the prize money was his. Mixing science and gambling was an ethical lapse.

Wallace failed to appreciate the episode as a lesson in the folly of seeing only what one wants to see. During a visit to the United States in 1886, he attended a séance in the company of the eminent psychologist William James. Wallace showed himself willing to be led by the nose, almost literally. James noted that at the beginning of the séance a 'spirit' appeared and took Wallace out of the room. Anybody seeing this, James remarked, would suspect that this manoeuvre was intended to allow people to move around out of Wallace's sight – anybody except Wallace, it turned out. He added that a female spirit was noticed at one point to be wearing black trousers, identical to those worn by the male spirits who preceded and followed her.

James recounted his experience after the couple presenting the spectacle were exposed in mid-séance and found to have crammed four children, representing beings from the other side, into a cabinet with a hidden door. Wallace defended the bogus mediums publicly, ignoring what others had seen and insisting upon the truth of his own observations, just as Hampden refused to accept what Wallace's telescope showed. He knew his strengths as an observer of natural phenomena, surveying land or comparing beetles, but did not understand his weakness in perceiving the nuances of human behaviour. When he sensed deception, during his brief exposure to ordinary business dealings as a young man, he was disturbed and repelled. He did not understand what the other parties were up to, and so his impulse was to flee – into the Amazon jungle, as it turned out. But he took the supernatural literally, seeing it as a higher dimension of nature, and so he was confident that it could be investigated by the methods at which he had proved so adept in the field.

If his peers in Britain detected a touch of poetic justice in the sorry spectacle of Wallace's persecution from a region of the fringe remote even from that which he had occupied, they did not show it. But at least one felt that he had blotted his copybook by accepting the wager. In 1864, Darwin had helped to secure Henry Bates's future by favouring his application for the post of assistant secretary of the Royal Geographical Society. Wallace had applied and failed to get the job the previous year. Nearly twenty years later, Wallace still lacked the financial security to match his scientific status. Darwin had the idea of trying to get his friend a government pension and consulted Joseph Hooker about it. Hooker was derisive, referring among other things to Wallace's lack of honour in taking Hampden's wager and to his spiritualism. Wallace had 'lost caste terribly', Hooker loftily remarked, implicitly acknowledging how much prestige Wallace had amassed by his endeavours in natural history.

Hooker was mollified, however, by Wallace's book *Island Life*, which he admired and which was dedicated to him. Guided by Huxley, Darwin sent a petition, bearing a dozen distinguished names, to William Gladstone, the Prime Minister. Gladstone recommended a Civil List pension of £200 a year. At the age of fifty-eight, Wallace's material dimension was finally placed on a solid footing.

At the end of the 1880s, Wallace began to call himself a socialist, his Owenite roots finally prevailing over the individualism he had imbibed from Herbert Spencer. He spent much of the rest of his life, nearly a quarter of a century, happily tending the bees in his bonnet. He advocated the nationalisation of the land and the railways, at pains in each case to assure proper compensation for the private owners; he opposed strikes, militarism and vaccination.

His views on eugenics, an ideology on the rise during his later years, were ahead of their time. Other scientifically minded intellectuals took it up enthusiastically, but he abhorred the idea that they should decide who should and should not be encouraged to reproduce. 'Give the people good conditions, improve their environment, and all will tend towards the highest type,' he declared. 'Eugenics is simply the meddlesome interference of an arrogant, scientific priestcraft.' For Wallace, science was knowledge, not power.

He was still ever ready with an essay or a letter to the editor by the time the golden jubilees of natural selection came around, in 1908 and 1909, commemorating first the Linnean Society meeting at which Darwin's and Wallace's papers had been read, and then the publication of the *Origin of Species*. By then he was bathed in the glow of a grand old man, 'the last of the great Victorians', but not one who would live long enough to see the rest of the world come round to his way of thinking. Darwinism was widely assumed to have been consigned to the dustbin of the nineteenth century; right to the end, Wallace had to stand up for the simple truth of natural selection.

He died peacefully at his home in Dorset on 7 November 1913, aged ninety. By then the young men who were to confirm the power of natural selection had set down their markers. Ronald Fisher and J. B. S. Haldane published their first scientific papers in 1912, as did the American member of the future triumvirate, Sewall Wright. In the nineteenth century, Wallace had discovered natural selection by intuition. In the twentieth, Fisher and Haldane established it by calculation.

RONALD AYLMER FISHER

'Natural selection is a mechanism for generating an exceedingly high degree of improbability.'
  R. A. Fisher

4

Natural Nobility

The lectures that Ronald Aylmer Fisher gave to his fellow undergraduate eugenicists were like peas in a pod. They were strikingly compact and their internal structure was a challenge to discern. They were the full-grown plant and the harvest of Fisher's thought in miniature. Like Mendel's peas, to which the first of them referred, they were nuclei whose complexities would not be appreciated in their own time. By his early twenties, while still in the youthful flush of Nietzsche and Nordic fantasies, Fisher had revealed to himself a vision of natural selection that would not be widely shared until the other end of the century.

In his first talk, 'Mendelism and Biometry', he revealed himself to have a vision broader than those of his seniors. One was William Bateson, the leading geneticist. Bateson is said to have discovered Mendel while on a train in 1900, reading about his experiments of the 1860s and immediately rewriting the speech he was travelling to London to give. He soon began to call himself a Mendelian, and in 1905 introduced the word 'genetics'. Another was Karl Pearson, the pioneer of biometry, and he and Bateson were at loggerheads.

Mendelians saw inheritance as a system of boxes to be checked or left empty; green or yellow, wrinkled or smooth. Biometricians were preoccupied with traits, like height, that formed curves on a graph. They imagined natural selection subjecting these traits to a scrutiny even closer than their own, continuously acting on continuous variation. While they kept the lamp of selection lit through the 'eclipse of Darwinism', as Julian Huxley called it, the Mendelians regarded natural selection as a footnote to an evolutionary process handled largely by mutation. They did not see adaptation as an issue.

Pearson and his biometrical colleagues drew their inspiration from Francis Galton, the cousin of Darwin who invented eugenics. Galton was

89

captivated by genius and awed by its scarcity. Only one man in 4,000 was eminent, Fisher told his audience, yet to this élite 'all advances in thought are due, they produce all the best literature, give us leading scientists, doctors, lawyers and administrators'. Galton had shown that intellectual and moral characters were inherited as strongly as physical traits such as height and likewise followed the 'normal curve' – the 'bell curve' that inflamed public controversy a hundred years later. Biometrics, a statistical practice, would permit the improvement of the population. It required careful examination of children's mental powers and the allocation of special facilities to children found to have high ability.

Here, however, Fisher saw a grave difficulty, which would dominate his ideas on social policy beyond his youth and into his middle age. Able individuals rose 'inevitably to comfortable position', but their eugenic potential was thus vitiated, for 'the most valuable classes' produced fewer children than the average and markedly fewer than 'the lowest mental and moral class of the population'. Enabling clever children to rise up the social scale was 'worse than useless' in these circumstances.

Fisher also saw a profound eugenic potential in Mendelism, for once it was known how mental characters were inherited, then every boy could be born a Shakespeare or a Darwin: 'the thought of a race of men combining the illustrious qualities of these giants, and breeding true to them, is almost too overwhelming, but such a race will inevitably arise in whatever country first sees the inheritance of mental characters elucidated'.

Mendelism and biometry thus had to be reconciled. He was right that this could be done, and within a few years he would in fact do it. But he was not unique in welcoming both strains of science. In that respect, as the historian Pauline Mazumdar points out, he was following the line of the Eugenics Society, whose Cambridge University branch he founded, chaired and sustained. It petered out after his departure, despite having recruited a troop of senior dons, a brace of Lords, four of Darwin's sons, and John Maynard Keynes as treasurer. His talk, delivered at the society's second meeting, was something of a keynote address.

In the course of the quarter hour for which he spoke, he showed the level of detail he had already attained. He drew attention to the suspicious neatness of Mendel's data, suggesting that the monk had unconsciously interpreted ambiguous results so as to conform to his theory. Fisher confirmed his suspicions and published them twenty-five years later, taking the opportunity to blame 'Bateson's eagerness to exploit Mendel's discovery in his feud with the theory of Natural Selection' for the canards that Mendel thought his work contradicted Darwin's theories, and that Darwin's influence suppressed Mendel's. He reflected on why no one had previously looked at Mendel's experiments closely enough to notice that they were demonstrations rather than tests, or to understand what they were really saying. 'Each generation, perhaps, found in Mendel's paper only what it expected to find; in the first period a repetition of the hybridization results commonly reported, in the second a discovery in inheritance supposedly difficult to reconcile with continuous evolution. Each generation, therefore, ignored what did not confirm its own expectations.'

Talking to his own generation, in 1911, he gave a hint of what science meant to him, though the significance of his words would not be clear except in retrospect. They would certainly have left little impression upon the circle of students gathered round in one of their number's Trinity College rooms for whom Fisher felt obliged to provide an elementary sketch of Mendelian inheritance. 'One of the great beauties of biometrical work,' he went on to say, 'is the certainty of the results obtained; biometricians . . . appear to be able to squeeze the truth out of the most inferior data.' Their power over truth arose from the properties of statistics, which allowed them to overcome the noise of swarming errors. 'I was recently impressed by the potency of the theory of probabilities in this respect; if you put a kettle over a fire it will probably boil, but it is not a certainty; it may freeze; it is true that the odds against such an event are very large; but it remains a possibility, or so my "theory of gases" tells me.'

The theory of probabilities was thus a means to deal with the confusion of the world. Even though certainty was impossible in theory, it was attainable in effect. Orderly patterns would emerge from the countless individual impulses of molecules, even though at any given moment any given molecule might go this way or that. And this, for Fisher, was how natural selection worked too. A given individual might pass or fail nature's tests at any given moment, but from countless individual tests, adaptive design would emerge. What appeared at first glance to be chaos was in fact the basis of order.

Seeing the same processes at work in physics and biology, Fisher recognised that selection was not confined to nature. He opened his second talk, on 13 March 1912, with the observation that 'the same process is in progress with respect to languages, religions, habits, and customs, rocks, beliefs, chemical elements, nations, and everything else to which the terms stable and unstable can be applied'. Selection is, in Daniel Dennett's words, substrate-independent; in short, Darwinism is universal. Though Fisher changed his mind subsequently, coming to see living processes as different in kind from those of inanimate matter, his precocious vision shows an extraordinarily intense ability to imagine the power of selection.

Sixty-odd years before Richard Dawkins devised the word 'meme', Fisher was airing the idea that elements of cultural information might replicate as elements of biological information do. He mused about how an entity might induce a different entity to help it replicate, seventy years before Dawkins developed the idea in his book *The Extended Phenotype*. A parasitic worm tickles a parrot's throat and makes it cough over its food, spreading the worm to other parrots; the game of bridge spreads in a similar way, by driving the habitual player 'to infect others with a similar passion'. Cultural and social entities could act as hosts for behavioural parasites, such as smoking or prayers. But when Fisher spoke of prayers as parasites, his words carried none of the moral tension with which Dawkins charges his depiction of religions as 'mind viruses'. Fisher grew up in the Church of England and remained there, partly from a very personal sense of tradition, but also because he upheld his faith through his synthesis of mathematics and biology.

He had been like that from the start. In his high chair, three years old, Ronald had asked his nurse what a half of a half was. And what, he asked when told the answer, was half of a quarter? Nurse told him that it was an eighth; he pondered this for some time, and asked what half of an eighth was. A sixteenth, Nurse informed him. After a long silence, he announced his conclusion: 'Then I suppose that a half of a sixteenth must be a thirty-toof.' Joan Fisher Box, his daughter and biographer, observed that the mode of thought and expression attributed to the toddler was characteristic of the man. She also thought that the story might actually be true.

His father was good with numbers too. George Fisher had prospered as half of Robinson & Fisher, a prestigious art auction house. By the end of the century, he had established his family in a mansion and five acres of parkland on top of Hampstead Hill, in north London. The children grew up with country houses, 'horses, tennis courts, and boats' at their disposal.

Among them, too, Ronnie enjoyed a special degree of privilege. It was not just that he was born a prodigy but that he came into the world at all. On 17 February 1890, his mother Katie was delivered of a son, stillborn. All believed that this tragedy had ended the episode, but then, a quarter of an hour later, a second son was born, tiny, alive and perfectly unexpected. He was christened Ronald Aylmer. Katie had previously lost another son, Alan, while her children Geoffrey and Evelyn had survived: she took care that each subsequent child had a 'y' in their name.

Ron was Katie's darling, but they were not altogether close. Katie seemed 'cold and insensitive' to outsiders, observes Box. To her children she was a brief and regal manifestation in the nursery, descending from the adult world over which she presided and in which 'her husband's devotion made her something of a goddess'. Box suggests that Ronald might have got his difficulties with personal relationships from his mother. 'Their communication at an emotional level . . . was stilted and unconvincing, and they were curiously oblivious of the feelings of others.' Katie's place in her household and her husband's affections minimised the costs she incurred through her insensitivity. Ronald, however, paid a high price for his lack of sympathy and his consequent temper, both personally and professionally. It made him a solitary genius and a lonely one.

He 'scattered her memorials through his life', says Box, in his gallantry towards women and his fondness for 'plump little' ones; in the names of his eldest daughters and the long hair like hers that he directed them to grow. Another memorial was his 'unquestioning adherence' to the Church of England. His mother's faith became the foundation of his understanding of evolution.

And so, in a sense, did her science. Mother and son achieved communication – 'their love made an *intellectual* hothouse,' according to Box – through the medium of ideas. 'When he was five she opened the heavens to his contemplation as she lay on the sofa reading Sir Robert Ball's astronomy to him and he sat enthralled beside her on a velvet cushion on the floor.'

It came to an end suddenly when he was fourteen and the winner of an outstanding maths scholarship to Harrow; Katie fell ill with peritonitis and died within two days. Responding more like an adult than a child, he wrapped himself up in his schoolwork, winning a medal during his second year in a mathematics competition open to pupils of all ages. But he was not absorbed exclusively in abstractions. At prep school (short for preparatory, as junior private schools are known in Britain) he had chosen books on natural history as maths prizes, and he continued the practice of taking his mathematical winnings in biological currency at Harrow.

His single handicap was his poor eyesight, but even that was turned to advantage. The doctor advised that he should avoid reading by artificial light, so his evening maths tuition was conducted by discussion alone. Excused from conforming to algebraic convention, he was free to examine mathematical relationships in his mind's eye. This honed his ability to tackle problems in his head and promoted an unusual faculty for treating them geometrically. In a number of cases, he was able through geometry to solve problems which other workers had failed to crack using algebra. Box attributes his colleagues' frequent complaints about his inadequate proofs to their lack of similar geometrical insight.

He found it hard to choose between biology and mathematics as the subject for his higher education. What settled the matter, he later claimed, was the sight of a cod's skull in a museum, its bones all labelled. It was all too true a representation of what his life as a zoology undergraduate would have been. University biology in those days was a stupefying diet of facts, for which Fisher's talents were not required.

From Harrow he won a mathematical scholarship to Cambridge. He needed it now: his mother's death had been followed within eighteen months by his father's financial ruin. With him he took a set of thirteen volumes that he had chosen as his final school prize. Once again he had opted for biology; this time his selection was controversial. After some hesitation on his masters' part, they presented him with the collected works of Darwin.

*

Precocious in childhood and professorially serious as soon as he became an undergraduate, Ron Fisher was nevertheless young once. His friends at Cambridge called him Piggy, a nickname he had carried with him since prep school. Yet even his youthful fantasies were about being ancient. Piggy became part of a small circle of romantics who called themselves the We Frees and coined their own argot from Icelandic sagas.

They included a medical student or two, a poet, a motorcycle enthusiast who became a man of the cloth, and, despite Piggy's initial misgivings, a woman, whom they named Gudruna and accepted. She was married to one of the medics and tied to the household; the men enjoyed the freedom of bicycle excursions, picnics and drinking sessions in which they self-consciously carolled their fellowship with the songs of Hilaire Belloc, a Catholic reactionary who loved the English countryside for its social order rather than its natural history. Piggy added a couple of zoological verses to 'His Hide Is Covered with Hair', whose chorus thanks God that 'I was born in the West and not in the East'. Gudruna remembered him as 'top-heavy' in appearance, 'due to his great head . . . The poet made for me a caricature of Ron as a Norse savage, short, phenomenally broad, with a noble head, a naked pink skin and a mace. He had captured the characteristic pugnacity of his stance.'

The We Frees mixed their Bellocian stout and old Icelandic ale with a fulminating German brew, which induced them to attempt to converse in the idiom of *Also Sprach Zarathustra*. It was their way of joining in a vogue for Nietzsche that had latterly arisen among English intellectual and artistic circles. Fisher incorporated Zarathustra into a speech he gave to the Eugenics Education Society in 1913: '"What man is to the ape," says Zarathustra, "a joke and a sore shame: so shall man be to beyond-man, a joke and a sore shame". We can set no limit to human potentialities; all that is best in man can be bettered . . .'

Fisher did not let the message of God's death interfere with his Anglicanism, so Nietzsche's influence upon him cannot be said to have been radical. This was no more than Nietzsche would have expected, for the philosopher had regarded with contempt the way that the English held on to Christian ethics after ceasing to believe in their basis. But Fisher was not a man to treat Nietzsche as merely a source of inspirational quotes. Zarathustra's value to him may be discernible in the following passage, in which Fisher displays an understanding of Darwinism that is remarkable in its theoretical precocity:

> From the moment that we grasp, firmly and completely, Darwin's theory of evolution, we begin to realise that we have obtained not merely a description of the past, or an explanation of the present, but a veritable key to the future; and this consideration becomes the more forcibly impressed on us the more thoroughly we apply the doctrine; the more clearly we see that not only the organisation and structure of the body, and the cruder physical impulses, but that the whole constitution of our ethical and aesthetic nature, all the refinements of beauty, all the delicacy of our sense of beauty, our moral instincts of obedience and compassion, pity or indignation, our moments of religious awe, or mystical penetration – all have their biological significance, all (from the biological point of view) exist in virtue of their biological significance.

Fisher recognised that, although evolution did not exclude the possibility of a Creator, it took responsibility for all aspects of human being. Higher sentiments did not float fairylike above man's animal organism: they were subject to, and products of, the same evolutionary rules. His elders generally regarded natural selection as incapable of doing much at all, beyond perhaps a little tweaking and polishing, but already he had embraced a universal Darwinism and the idea of a psychology shaped by natural selection at all levels. It was impossible for him to treat nature as the enemy of morality, like Thomas Huxley before him, or to rewrite the doctrine of separation between body and mind, as did Stephen Jay Gould after him, by asserting that much of what makes us human is a side-effect of evolution rather than its design.

He needed a philosophy in which nature was not considered inferior, and in Nietzsche he found one. Nietzsche had reflected upon Darwin and concluded that natural selection threatened ethics only in so far as they were based on the principle that nature was base. By his own sulphurous extremity the German seer absolved those who warmed to him from following in his path: Fisher was thus at liberty to appreciate Nietzsche according to his own lights, as one of the few who had seen as deeply into Darwinism as he himself had.

Like the communists whom Cambridge nurtured a generation later, Fisher had found something which was a philosophy, a movement and a way of ethical life. Like communism and Christianity, it found virtue in simplicity. 'From the individual point of view our duty is, I think, clear; like all healthy philosophies, eugenics urges us to simplify our lives, and to simplify our needs; the only luxury worth having is that of a healthy human environment. We must be ready to sacrifice human success, at the call of nobler instincts. And, even as regards happiness, has any better way of life been found than to combine high endeavour with good fellowship?'

He had learned the value of fellowship perforce, being ineligible for many Cambridge coteries because of his family's reduced circumstances, and had joined a circle whose members had to make a virtue of their lack of money. But his father's mansion in Hampstead and its surrounding parkland were no loss. After all, he had received his true inheritance at conception and he had every reason to believe that it was exceptionally rich.

'We require a new pride of birth,' he went on, '. . . and a new confidence in our instinctive judgments of human worth. As the Dean of St. Paul's says, "We need a new tradition of nobility".' This would be established by the eugenists, who would become its exemplars:

We do not dub ourselves knights of a new order. But necessarily, inevitably, it might be unconsciously, we are the agents of a new phase of evolution. Eugenists will, on the whole, marry better than other people, have higher ability, richer health, greater beauty. They will, on the whole, have more children than other people. Their biological type, characterised by their solicitude for human betterment, their scientific insight, above all their intense appreciation of human excellence, has a strong tendency to improve and survive. Many will fail; many will forget; that is how we shall become more steadfast and more successful. And those that remain, an ever increasing number, absorbing more and more the best qualities of our race, will become fitted to spread abroad, not by precept only, but by example, the doctrine of a new, natural nobility of worth and birth.

The promise of historical inevitability matches that of Marxism, the vanguard role echoes that of Leninism, and the choice of qualities – scientific insight, intense appreciation of excellence – reflects Fisher's own narcissism. Nor does it take Fisher's advanced understanding of sexual selection to appreciate that, in order to marry better, one must oneself be better than the competition: Fisher was flattering his fellows, as well as foretelling their descendants' qualities.

Confident in his own natural nobility, he displayed a vanity unmixed with venom. He was concerned with the promotion of genius, not with the eradication of imbeciles. Most of his fellow eugenists, by contrast, seemed far more exercised by the threat they perceived from the classes far below them. 'I am afraid that the urban proletariat may cripple our civilization as it destroyed that of ancient Rome,' warned the Dean of St Paul's, William Inge. 'These degenerates, who have no qualities that confer survival value, will probably live as long as they can by "robbing hen roosts", as Mr Lloyd George truthfully describes modern taxation, and will then disappear.'

Although his comrades widely shared his horror of the lower classes, the vision that haunted them was of a social system in which the degenerates not only failed to disappear but increased faster than their betters. Fisher, however, was not much exercised about the factors that encouraged the poor to multiply. What seized his attention, and held it throughout his life, were the factors militating against fertility in the higher social strata. Social status and fertility were natural antagonists. The fewer children that a man had, the more wealth he would probably accumulate. And with the social status it brought came more pressure to invest in goods rather than offspring. Outlay on luxuries was money well spent, Fisher admitted, for it secured the pleasant company that a person of means enjoyed. But the pressure to 'keep up' added to the forces which united high quality with low fertility.

This was the dilemma that faced the committed eugenist. His duty was, of course, to maximise the quantity and quality of his children. This would entail considerable material sacrifice, but here eugenics as a movement would support him. Enlightened by their understanding of what was truly valuable, eugenists would create for themselves an enclave in which fellowship replaced luxury. Their central political demand, Fisher argued, should be for subsidies to counteract the effects of extra mouths upon standards of living. Family allowances should be paid proportionally to income, so that those of higher ability should not be discouraged from multiplying. J. B. S. Haldane liked to point out that another way to address the problem would be to abolish the inheritance of wealth, since the rich were encouraged to limit their families in order to maximise each child's endowment. If he were to be persuaded by Fisher, Dean Inge and Major Darwin, he should have to become 'a rather extreme kind of Socialist', which in due course he did.

The eugenist would approach closest to the truth of nature as he approached reproduction itself. 'Judgements of human excellence' were, according to Fisher, entwined with sexual nature: 'It is only under the influence, and during the growth of sexual attraction, that we can hope that these judgements will fully reveal themselves. Only the strongest passion could possibly free us from the bias of aesthetic and moral ideals, which accident and inappropriate teaching and surroundings may have ingrained in the character.' In sexual passion we are closest to nature, and in nature lies truth. Yet at present 'too many have not sufficient depth and power of abstraction': only the naturally noble will understand that the sense of beauty is a higher faculty. 'In the deepest minds the idea of beauty links itself with one of altogether higher significance . . . Here is the highest plane, and the source from which all our valuations in the lower categories take their value.' Here 'we pass, like Nietzsche, beyond Good and Evil', and morality becomes a 'formulation of the requirements of the Highest Man'.

This was a lover's Darwinism, its poet ecstatically convinced of his supremacy. Gudruna, as he continued to call his friend Geraldine Heath, introduced him to her younger sister, Eileen Guinness, whom he dubbed Nicolette, after the heroine of the medieval French troubadour's tale *Aucassin and Nicolette*. He regaled her with Belloc's 'Song of the Pelagian Heresy' and took her collecting celandine flowers – to measure the variation in the numbers of petals, selection in mind. They wed in 1917, just after her seventeenth birthday. 'She . . . felt the need to give her life to some worthy cause,' Joan Fisher Box wrote, 'to serve some ideal, as she had seen her parents serve God. As a girl she could find no proof of the existence of God and could not center her life upon Him. Then Ron presented himself, an idealist with very real and worthwhile ambitions, and she found her life's work in him . . .'

She had her work cut out for her. As well as bearing him eight children and raising them with little of the assistance that a woman of her class could usually command, she was obliged to minister to her husband, who in the 1930s expected her to play medicine ball with him daily before a leisurely breakfast, over which she read him *The Times*. She also acted as secretary, taking down his entire masterwork, *The Genetical Theory of Natural Selection*, at his dictation, and sounding board. Her role as housekeeper merged with that of lab technician, in the course of which she prepared specimens and cleaned out the mouse cages.

Nor did she enjoy much of a honeymoon. After graduating with a First and spending a postgraduate year studying physics, Fisher came down to earth with a job as a statistician for a City of London investment company, but he failed to fit in. Then the war began, but each time he tried to join up, he was rejected for military service because of his weak eyesight. The Army's selective criteria were tighter than those Fisher envisaged for his new nobility. Denied uniform and the opportunity to realise his heroic ideals, he faced the personal challenge of what to do in the war and the dilemma that the war posed for a eugenist.

Fisher's understanding of sexual selection led him to see eugenic advantages in war. Nothing revealed men's moral and physical excellence better than the heroism that they displayed in combat; the fair would be able to pick out the brave, heroes would be preferred as husbands, and heroic traits would increase within the population. Once the war was over, he suggested, heroes with the medals to prove their bravery should be encouraged to have large families. Measures like these, however, would be elements of a programme of 'racial repair' that would be required to overcome the war's dysgenic effects. With every hero that fell, the nation's stock of heroic virtues diminished: the next generation might be unfit to fight the next great war. This was the terrible dysgenic consequence of martial selection, which took its victims from a 'great body of men, selected from every part of the nation for three precious gifts, of health, courage and patriotism'. Ronald was excluded from this eugenic body; his brother Alwyn had been included, and killed.

Denied permission to trade his part-timer's Territorial Army uniform for a regular one, Ronald spent much of the war in a series of miserable engagements as a teacher. Seeking genuine purpose, he grew convinced that he could find it in nature, or as close to it as could be reconciled with civilised life. Subsistence farming was an authentic living. Like soldiering, it was valuable to the nation and a true test of a man's mettle. And it was suited to the eugenist, making good use of the labour available in a large family. It should be the foundation of a eugenic way of life, meeting needs instead of pursuing luxuries. Fisher's vision had much in common with Belloc's 'Distributist' ideal of one man, three acres and a cow.

In practice, as is usual in subsistence farming, most of the work was done by women. A few months after his marriage, Fisher got a teaching job at Bradfield College, near Reading in Berkshire, where he leased the game-keeper's cottage and some land. The cell of intellectual peasantry in Great House Cottage was a ménage comprising Ron, Nicolette and Gudruna, who was now separated from her husband and had a baby daughter. Nicolette looked after the chickens, which were named after legendary Greek women with absent menfolk such as Clytemnestra and Persephone; Gudruna bred pigs and milked the cow. In the evenings the women read aloud, working their way through Norse sagas, the twelve volumes of mythology in Sir James Frazer's *Golden Bough*, Edward Gibbons's *Decline and Fall of the Roman Empire*, and much to do with Arabia, including Sir Richard Burton's unexpurgated accounts. From these various angles they contemplated the question that history posed for eugenists: that of why civilisations rise and fall.

5

In the Sixth Day

Fisher's attempt to reconcile Mendelism and biometry succeeded in uniting the geneticist Reginald Punnett and the biometrician Karl Pearson. Refereeing his paper for the Royal Society's journal, in 1916, each recommended that it should be rejected. Fisher's friend Leonard Darwin eventually got it published by the Royal Society of Edinburgh, which required Fisher to meet some of the costs.

'I suspect that the rejection of my paper was the only point in two long lives on which they were ever heartily at one,' Fisher later remarked to his friend C. S. Stock. By then, however, he was in a position to crow. 'Lest this sad story seem depressing, it has the point that the author of the paper was chosen to succeed each pundit in turn.' Fisher replaced Pearson as Galton Professor of Eugenics and Genetics at University College, London, in 1933, and ten years later succeeded Punnett as Arthur Balfour Professor of Genetics at Cambridge. The antagonism he provoked with his reconciliatory paper would prove typical of his relations with his academic colleagues. It was untypical in having an ultimate outcome that was satisfactory to him and that was not largely of his own making.

In the earlier part of his career, though, he had a Darwin to watch over him. Major Leonard Darwin, third son of Charles, was as passionate a eugenist as Fisher. He was childless, and Fisher's relationship to him has been regarded as filial – which would make Fisher the moral equivalent of a grandson to Charles Darwin. But while Leonard Darwin gave fatherly advice about Fisher's career and his relationships with his colleagues, he had to look up to follow the younger man's ideas, a Boswell to a Johnson.

Pearson, too, quickly found that he could learn from Fisher. When he read a statistical paper Fisher published in 1915, he set his staff to work on a study making use of Fisher's innovation. But he did not consult Fisher, who was all too obviously a threat. In explaining the correlation between relatives within a Mendelian framework, Fisher's subsequent paper reached a conclusion that Pearson had previously rejected. Yet Pearson had inspired it positively as well as negatively, for Fisher's interest in applying mathematics to evolution had been kindled by a paper by Pearson on the subject.

In the course of reconciling genetics and biometry, Fisher introduced a new measure of variability, which he called 'variance'. It allowed variation to be parcelled according to cause, and Fisher was confident that it would show the effects of environment to be trifling in comparison with those of heredity. His successors employ it to argue that intelligence and personality traits are largely inherited, and far outside such controversies it is a routine tool for the analysis of data. The practising eugenist had two great lines of intellectual descent: he was a founding father both of modern evolutionary biology and of modern statistics.

He was of greater immediate interest as a statistician. Pearson offered him a job at the Galton Laboratory, but Fisher preferred not to place himself under Pearson's control. When he went to the Galton, it was to take over Pearson's department – except for a section of it which was hived off as a Pearsonian enclave, headed by Pearson's son. In 1919, he had a better offer from the Agricultural Research Station at Rothamsted, thirty miles to the north.

Broadbalk Field, Rothamsted's experimental plot, looked like the work of uncannily enlightened peasants. Since the 1850s, it had been divided into strips of scrupulously equal size, and these had been used to compare the effects of different fertiliser treatments. As well as going back over the records, applying to them his analysis of variance and the rest of his battery of techniques, he devised new experimental methods and made new patterns on the land – squares rather than strips, commemorated, at Anthony Edwards's instigation, in stained glass above the hall of Gonville and Caius College, Cambridge.

Meanwhile, he continued his genetical studies in his spare time, using poultry and snails which the Station accommodated, and mice which he kept at home. He used the fowl to develop his theory of dominance. Genes are classed as either dominant or recessive, the dominants always achieving expression and the recessives hidden unless combined in pairs. Fisher believed that recessiveness was produced by natural selection, acting on other genes which had an influence over whether a harmful gene was expressed or not.

Over the course of the 1920s, he developed his vision of evolution. It beheld large populations, single genes and low rates of mutation, these being the conditions for efficient natural selection. A mutation was 'a leap in the dark', and so a system which got by with the minimum of such random events would be preferable. In a large population recombining genes through sexual reproduction, the effect of a mutation could be tested across a range of genetic combinations. Mutation was necessary, but the larger the population, the less of it was needed. Sex was a better source of variation.

And the smaller the mutations were, the better. Mutationists envisaged that with one mighty leap an organism might land itself in a happier situation, but Fisher saw that a leap was much likelier to send it into an abyss. He offered the metaphor of a microscope's focus. An organism's level of adaptation can be compared to a microscope lens positioned so as to give a clear image but not perfect focus. A small adjustment has a reasonable chance of improving the focus, but a large one will almost certainly wreck the instrument's purchase on the image.

Even the smallest of adjustments is likely to have some sort of effect upon the focus. According to Fisher's calculations, the neutral zone was 'extremely minute'. A mutation would almost always turn out good or bad, not indifferent. But its value might not become immediately apparent or might vary, being sometimes positive and sometimes negative. Perfect adaptation was impossible because the environment was always changing – and therefore always deteriorating, from the point of view of an organism whose adaptive tuning was constantly spoiled. Fisher anticipated what is nowadays known as the Red Queen view of evolution, in which organisms are constantly striving to keep up with the flux. He accepted that much variation might be effectively neutral when it arose, but argued that it would be turned one way or another by the restless environment. These indifferent iota would form much of the material available for selection, because it would take longer to deal with them. 'The fate of those powerfully selected is quickly settled; they do not long contribute to the variance. It is the idlers that make the crowd, and very slight attractions may determine their drift.'

These attractions would usually amount to selective pressures of between 0.1 and 1 per cent per generation, which were all that were needed for natural selection to do its work. A mutation with an advantage of 1 per cent would have almost a 2 per cent chance of establishing itself: it would only have to occur about a hundred times to be a racing certainty. And Fisher considered it reasonable to assume that even the tiniest of selective advantages would eventually make its mark. If one selective intensity was a fifty-thousandth that of another, it would just take fifty thousand times longer to produce the same effect. The larger the population, the larger would be the pool of minutely graded variations that formed selection's working capital. The larger the pool, Fisher argued in *The Genetical Theory of Natural Selection*, the faster the fitness would increase.

He dictated his great statement to his wife between October 1928 and June 1929; it was published in 1930. Beginning with a demonstration that Mendelian inheritance preserves the variation that Darwinian evolution needs, it went on to discuss the relationship between mutation and selection, and the relationships between genes, in the form of the modifying genes which Fisher believed were responsible for whether a gene is dominant or recessive.

It took Darwin's theme of sexual selection, which had lapsed into disuse, and offered two ideas about it that would have to wait another few decades for their usefulness to be understood. One – which he had already introduced fifteen years earlier – was that sexual selection could cause traits to get carried away with themselves. Once upon a time, before peacocks became the sight they are today, a peahen might have chosen for a mate a peacock with a slightly longer tail than his fellows and been rewarded with a larger number of surviving peachicks. Longer tails would become hereditarily entwined with the female preference for them, which would drive them past the point at which they were functionally optimal, and on to spectacular exaggeration.

The other was that the ratio of males to females will always tend to equal itself out. Bill Hamilton called the passage in which Fisher indicated the process 'a good example of what may be called his slit-trench style – short and deep'. Fisher posed the problem in terms of the reproductive value of the two sexes, which must be equal, since each sex contributes half the ancestry to future generations. As Hamilton explained, 'Fisher's principle' 'states that the sex ratio is in equilibrium when . . . the totals of effort spent producing the two sexes are equal'. If not, individuals gain an advantage by producing more of the sex that is receiving less investment. If fewer males are born than females, a newborn male's prospects of offspring are better than a newborn female's, and so parents who tend to produce males will tend to have more grandchildren than average. These descendants also tend to produce males, and the disparity between male and female births decreases. As it does so, the advantage of producing males declines, and the ratio stabilises at 1:1.

Hamilton was more proud of his own paper on sex-ratio theory than of 'almost any I have written'. This was, above all, because 'it helped sex-ratio theory well on its way to becoming the section of evolutionary theory that best proves the power and accuracy of the Neodarwinian theory as a whole'. It had achieved a predictive power up to the standards of chemistry or physics.

By the time he gave that judgement, sex-ratio practice had also set up a vast spontaneous test of the theory among the largest population groups on the planet. In India and China, prospective parents employ ultrasound scans to identify female foetuses, which they then have aborted. Fisher would not have worried about the eugenic implications, since his theory predicts that females will acquire scarcity value to set against the dowry costs, or loss as a resource for parents through marriage, that tip the balance towards their destruction. But he would not have expected it, for he thought that peoples exposed longest to civilisation would have undergone strong selection against feticidal tendencies. The selective agent would be private property, which would increase the temptation to destroy newborns: once people could accumulate surpluses instead of living hand to mouth, they might choose to kill babies so as to save the resources that the children might otherwise consume. In doing so, 'those who are most willing to murder their offspring, for the sake of an easier or freer life' would eliminate their own selfish genes; the population would increase correspondingly in numbers. Fisher anticipated that contraception would go the same way. Addressing an audience which included Marie Stopes and Margaret Sanger, the founding mothers of family planning, he suggested that societies which practised contraception would evolve a moral revulsion against it.

Conscience, in other words, evolved under natural selection. Surveying attitudes to feticide in the classical era, he saw early Greek acquiescence yield inexorably to later Roman condemnation. Christianity did not determine moral sentiments; it cut with the grain of a morality that had already evolved as an instinct. The effects of the process could be seen by comparing Jews with Catholics and Protestants. The Jews had been civilised longest and had the highest reproductive rates; the Catholics were next, being mostly Mediterranean and thus descended from Roman stock, while the Protestants, with their northern barbarian roots, had been modified least by civilisation and consequently had the lowest rates of increase. Private property, the material foundation of a civilised race, generated the selective forces which could both make a civilisation and break it. The greater the wealth a people generated, 'the more severe will be the selection, and the more fiercely and clearly will their new morality be branded on their conscience'. But the more severe the selection, the more slowly would the eugenically desirable classes increase, and the more quickly they would diminish as a proportion of the whole. The contradiction between wealth and fertility underlay the last third of the *Genetical Theory*, which was devoted to the human species.

The keystone of the *Genetical Theory* was what Fisher proudly named the Fundamental Theorem of Natural Selection:

> The rate of increase in fitness of any organism at any time is equal to its genetic variance in fitness at that time.

It came to him as he paced his living room dictating Chapter 2, his wife taking it down in longhand as he formulated it. Loosely speaking, it says that the more raw material natural selection has to work on, the faster it works. But Fisher spoke hermetically, not loosely. What he meant by it, and what it meant to him, have subsequently become the subjects of long and profound reflection.

He himself compared it with the Second Law of Thermodynamics; he was well placed to do so, having studied physics in Cambridge for a year after graduation with Sir James Jeans, who made his mark as a researcher studying gases. Fisher saw similar processes at work in gases and in populations undergoing natural selection. The Second Law, like his theorem, stood out among the laws of nature by being statistical. It described the results of processes acting upon countless individual elements, and it dealt in probabilities.

It also stood out, according to one description that Fisher noted, as the supreme law of nature; he proclaimed that his theorem likewise occupied 'the supreme position among the biological sciences'. And Fisher's theorem spoke of progress where its counterpart in physics promised degeneration. The Second Law states that heat will not pass of its own accord from a cold body to a hot one. Energy will tend to become evenly distributed, until eventually it is homogenised. The universe must proceed in the direction of disorder, meaning absolute inert uniformity. Life superficially appears to be an elaborate attempt to defy this law, by producing the most highly ordered arrangements of matter that we know. In Fisher's universe there are two directions, according to the science historian Jonathan Hodge. There is the way down, the inexorable entropic settling into states of higher probability and greater disorder; and there is life's unique drive to generate less probable, more ordered states, which is the way up. As the engine of life, natural selection is a fundamental force for order in the universe. John Turner, an evolutionary geneticist with an interest in his subject's history, has argued that, for Fisher, this made natural selection divine.

Fisher's Anglicanism may have been a memorial to his mother, as his daughter suggests, and it was certainly rooted in his conservative affinity for tradition. Whatever its basis, though, it was not just an observance but a faith. He believed in an ultimate Creator and that natural selection was the creative force that shaped life: the latter must be the way by which the former worked, and Creation must still be in progress: 'In the language of Genesis we are living in the sixth day, probably rather early in the morning . . .' he observed in a radio talk in 1947. The Divine Artist, he suggested, might only stand back and declare his work 'very good' when humans had become more competent to take over the running of the planet. 'Instead of being shocked at the thought of the human race being a produce of evolutionary agencies . . . we might pray to be made more worthy of our high responsibilities. Instead of being a soulless creed, the possibility of evolution might well be the very centre of our faith and hope.'

Some, perhaps many, of Fisher's listeners may have construed his remarks as a wish for divine intervention. It is hard, after all, to construe a call to prayer any other way. He dabbled privately in speculation to the effect that 'the primary elements of indeterminacy in development and choice are fortuitous only in the physical sense, being in reality divinely guided'. His correspondent, the neurophysiologist Charles Sherrington, thanked him for writing, 'although your letter by its conundrums adds to the puzzlement of life'.

Whatever Fisher may have imagined was going on at the quantum level, which he seemed to see as the plane through which divine influence might be injected, his sense of the importance of choice in natural selection was clear. Humans had free will; other organisms also did one thing rather than another. In his vision of ongoing Creation, 'where the organism meets its environment, where it succeeds or fails in its endeavours . . . there it is that the doctrine of natural selection locates the creative process'. The endeavours of the organism resonated with the Christian ideal of striving towards moral perfection; and Fisher's reflections upon them echoed the sentiments that had in earlier times attached themselves to Lamarckian ideas.

A creative process was one that made a difference and so was only possible in a world in which events were not determined from the start. Fisher argued that science now understood that the world was not deterministic. Although the patterns of behaviour shown by large masses were predictable, they were the statistical product of the uncountable numbers of particles that comprised them. Causation was 'like the result of a game of chance; we can imagine ourselves able to foresee all its possible forms, and to state in advance the probability that each will occur. We can no longer imagine ourselves capable of foreseeing just which of them will occur.' Fisher the evolutionist, the believer in creativity and free will, was sustained by Fisher the statistician.

For Fisher, uncertainty thus had two faces (both of which have been studied in depth by Jonathan Hodge). There was good uncertainty, the basis of creativity and progress, and bad uncertainty, for which he had little use. Mutations were necessary to produce the variation on which selection acted, but Fisher would not allow them any opportunity for creative expression. Bold ones that took flying leaps would almost certainly damage their bearers; the only ones likely to be valuable were modest ones that took but a single step. Nor were assemblies of genes likely to get anywhere by random drift. There was a world of difference between the indeterminacy of natural selection, which had a sense of purpose, and the arbitrariness of mutation and drift, which were meaningless.

The Fundamental Theorem itself has been surrounded by a third kind of uncertainty. 'Many authors have maintained that the theorem holds only under very special conditions,' wrote one of its exegetes, George Price, in the early 1970s, 'while only a few . . . have thought that Fisher may have been correct – if only we could understand what he meant!' Forty years after Fisher pronounced it, Price realised that the Fundamental Theorem had been fundamentally misunderstood. Nearly everybody had taken Fisher to have been referring to fitness as a whole. Since variances in over-all fitness are always positive, the theorem would imply that the fitness of populations could never decrease.

Though Fisher certainly believed in evolutionary progress, he did not believe that fitness was one long boom. Since a population's numbers could not increase or decrease indefinitely, they would stabilise sooner or later, and so its fitness would stay roughly the same. Price realised that Fisher had been referring only to that component of fitness which is passed on in the genes from one organism to its offspring. Environmental effects, and interactions between genes, are excluded. Once this was realised, the theorem was proved to be true and exact. What the theorem said, Price concluded, was that natural selection, in Fisher's restricted sense, 'at all times acts to increase the fitness of the species to live under the conditions that existed an instant earlier'. But the total average fitness of a population, as distinct from the part of the fitness to which the theorem referred, could go down as well as up.

So, inevitably, would the rate of natural selection. Fisher's formulation said that the more genetic variation there was in a population, the faster natural selection would speed up; but this implied that as selection did its work, removing less fit variants and thereby reducing the variation, it would slow itself down.

Despite the efforts of Price and other analysts, controversy continued over how fundamental the theorem was. Even among Fisher's greatest admirers, hardly any seemed to share his opinion of its importance. In less sympathetic quarters it was regarded as a red herring; 'either false or trivial', as John Maynard Smith put it. Or perhaps it was the best that could be done. 'However regrettable and unfortunate it may be,' observed the Cambridge geneticist Peter O'Donald, 'it does seem that Fisher's fundamental theorem is the only general statement that can be made about natural selection.' O'Donald took the theorem to Fair Isle, a dot in the middle of the archipelagos to the north-east of the Scottish mainland, where he applied it to the variation in breeding dates of the Arctic skuas which lived there.

Although O'Donald found that the theorem offered insights into the selective processes acting on the skuas, Fisher's successors by and large are left wondering what to do with it. That, however, was not its author's criterion of its value. General statements and fundamental laws were his goal. And the Fundamental Theorem was fundamental to his struggle against disorder. As he pointed out, he had stated it in such a way as to counter the objection that 'the principle of Natural Selection depends on a succession of favourable chances'. One could say the same about a casino proprietor's income, he added, 'although the phrase contains a suggestion of improbability more appropriate to the hopes of the patrons of his establishment'. Natural selection does not play dice.

After six chapters on genetical theory, and before the five chapters on humans, there is a central chapter devoted to mimicry. This was Fisher's counter to a mutationist challenge by Reginald Punnett, who had argued that mimicry defied selectionist explanation. Punnett went to Ceylon, where he studied a swallowtail butterfly whose females came in three forms, two of which mimicked swallowtails of other species. Crossing experiments showed that a single gene was responsible for the production of each form. Punnett believed that each form had arisen in a single exuberant mutation. His view, that 'the function of natural selection is selection and not creation', was the reverse of Fisher's. Improbable as they were, mutations did the creative work of evolution.

Fisher's response was that the single genes were merely switches. The different forms were the products of long evolutionary processes involving many genes, but it only took a single gene to choose one option or another.

While he was on the subject, he anticipated Bill Hamilton's notion of inclusive fitness with an idea about how insects could have evolved to taste unpleasant. The obvious difficulty was that a butterfly was unlikely to survive being tasted and so would not derive any benefit from the lesson it taught its predator. But it might, suggested Fisher, have tasted unpleasant when it was a caterpillar. Before they get their wings, insect larvae are limited in their mobility and so are often found in large groups of closely related individuals. If a bird pecked one of them and found it distasteful, the victim's kin would benefit from the deterrent effect.

Having broken the swallowtail spell by showing that the mimetic hole in one might be an illusion, Fisher found himself increasingly embroiled on another front of his war against chance. Over the years it would deteriorate from a collegial disagreement between like minds into a legendary feud. Accentuating the differences between evolutionists either side of the Atlantic, it helped to kindle the fire in the hearth of adaptationism at Oxford.

The Fundamental Theorem stimulated in Sewall Wright a vision of landscapes. Increasing in fitness was like climbing a mountain. Since each step natural selection takes is an improvement, each step on the slope must be upwards, towards a peak representing a combination of genes which could not be further improved upon. There might well be other peaks in the 'adaptive landscape' representing other highly fit combinations, but these would be inaccessible by selective steps, for reaching them would require crossing valleys of lower fitness.

Wright believed that random drift could take a population across terrain natural selection could not traverse. In a small population, gene frequencies might be markedly influenced by random events – the death of a family in a landslide, for instance – which would take the population down a fitness slope and leave it in a position nearer to a different peak. Random processes, acting counter to natural selection, might nevertheless provide natural selection with opportunities it could not have gained on its own.

Fisher, gifted in his ability to comprehend multidimensional spaces, was unimpressed with 'picturesquely' named landscapes. Wright's exposition of 'adaptive topography' was indeed ambiguous, and the way that his landscapes became part of the currency of biology tended to confirm the prejudices of the mathematical minority within it. Their popularity certainly gained from their intuitive appeal. But they also expressed an understanding of nature that was shared by many biologists and differed in a basic way from Fisher's. Wright believed that species were not like gases. They were denser in some regions than others. He thought that a species would usually be divided into local populations, isolated from each other to greater or lesser degrees. The ideal would be a large population, containing local populations small enough for random effects to alter gene frequencies.

Fisher doubted that isolation could have this creative effect. If a group was so small and isolated that random processes could make an impact, it was probably either on the way to becoming a new species or to extinction. If local groups were interconnected, then the effective population size was normally the 'total population on the planet'. To Fisher, the peculiarities of small populations were a sampling error; to Wright, they were life's rich tapestry.

After the *Genetical Theory*, Fisher discontinued his efforts to formalise Darwin's theory and turned towards human heredity. One of his initiatives at the Galton Laboratory was a project to investigate blood groups, whose distribution he supposed must be due to balances between different selective forces. These forces proved elusive – and remain so, offering adaptationists a substantial humility check – but he and his colleagues did manage to clarify the genetics underlying the rhesus system.

His eugenic proposals left no such legacy. The Eugenics Society's campaign for voluntary sterilisation, in which he was involved, failed to make the statute books between the wars. Family allowances were brought in after the Second World War, but without the eugenic weighting which for Fisher was the point of them. Eugenics itself was anathematised along with Nazism, but Fisher did not change his views, though he gave up arguing for them.

Nor did he let the lessons of the war get in the way of his previous collegial friendships. Once hostilities ended, he swiftly got back in touch with Corrado Gini, who before the war had acted as a demographic adviser to the Italian dictator Mussolini, and with Otmar von Verschuer, whom Fisher 'was able to befriend', according to Joan Fisher Box, '. . . when, in the aftermath of war, he was unemployed and almost destitute'. If it had been up to the team that first investigated him during that period, Baron von Verschuer would have remained out of academic work for good. They branded him 'one of the most dangerous Nazi activists of the Third Reich' and urged that he be prevented from coming into contact with German youth. Before the war, he had acted as an expert witness in cases of disputed racial classification or prosecutions for racial pollution. By 1944, he felt able to declare that the 'dangers' posed by Jews and Gypsies to the German people had been 'eliminated through the racial–political measures of recent years', but insisted that further efforts, across the whole of Europe, would be needed in order to purify Germany of 'foreign racial elements'. The terminus of those racial–political measures, at Auschwitz, became for him a source of research material: blood, children's organs, pairs of eyes, dispatched to his institute by his protégé and twin-studies colleague, Josef Mengele.

Von Verschuer's embarrassment, however, was brief. The German academic establishment was as keen as Fisher to rescue him from his reduced circumstances and as ready to accept his protestations of ignorance as his defence. When a colleague affirmed that von Verschuer was the innocent scientist he claimed to be, the geneticist thanked him for the *Persilschein* – the 'Persil shine' promised in washing-powder advertisements. This was a 'very good term', in von Verschuer's opinion, and it was certainly clever, for *Schein* also means 'certificate'. In 1949, a second investigation reversed the earlier verdict, declaring that von Verschuer embodied all the qualities desirable in a teacher of academic youth. He soon had a professorial chair from which, in the 1950s, he was able to collaborate on twin studies with his English colleague. Fisher sought his assistance in a rearguard action against the devastating new epidemiological evidence of the dangers of smoking, and also obtained financial assistance from the tobacco industry.

When Fisher first reached out to his destitute friend, he can scarcely have been expected to be familiar with the German's wartime publications. He may have been unaware of von Verschuer's Auschwitz connection, which was exposed by a German newspaper in 1946. Yet he would have known subsequently that he was collaborating on twin studies with a man who had collaborated on twin studies with Mengele. In doing so, he implicitly asserted not just that von Verschuer's work had been conducted without knowledge of its context, but that genetics could proceed as though Auschwitz had nothing to do with it.

If that were true, his own story would be meaningless. Eugenics and evolution combined as a single current in the fount that had carried him into professional science. The point was not merely to interpret the world, but to change it by improving the population. Although he wanted this to be done by the promotion of genius, he formed his eugenic fellowship with comrades whose priority was to reduce the numbers of those they deemed substandard. Fisher's own involvement in the Eugenics Society declined as governments in various countries implemented their own versions of the negative eugenic project, but this seems to have resulted from his distaste for politicking rather than from any reservations about the way the broader eugenic movement was going. In Gini and von Verschuer he chose as friends men who were intimately involved, as scientists, in the totalitarian projects of Fascism and Nazism. They worked their way into their roles when the regimes took power, long before the war: Fisher could not have been oblivious to the way they applied their science.

Eugenics was not the only theme present in Fisher's early chapters that was also taken up in Germany. In hindsight, his enthusiasm for playing at Vikings and poring over Nietzsche cannot help but prompt the question of whether Fisher's youthful enthusiasms sent him travelling along the same path that the Nazis took. It seems unlikely, though. Fisher was too conservative to be a Nazi or a Fascist. He may have come under suspicion at one stage: Joan Fisher Box wondered whether his association with von Verschuer was the reason that the authorities denied him an exit visa to the US in 1941. On the other hand, she also hazarded that it might have been because of all the communists in his department. J. B. S. Haldane got along tolerably well with him, considering that Haldane was an irascible Marxist and an intellectual rival. Haldane would certainly not have maintained collegial relations with Fisher if he had held him to be complicit in the Nazi project, and would doubtless have treated him with the contempt that he expressed for a Eugenics Society activist whom he did accuse of promoting the Nazi cause.

Fisher's opaque exterior and scholarly absorption leant themselves to the generous interpretation that sympathisers took of his post-war friendship and collaboration with the former Nazi: that he was oblivious to the world beyond the towers of Oxbridge, loyal to his colleagues and devoted to his pipe. He was 'slight, bearded, eloquent, reactionary, and quirkish', according to the summary adjectives of his *Dictionary of Scientific Biography* entry. Eugenics was a reactionary ideology, based as it was on the premise that contemporary social processes were undermining civilisation, as were Fisher's King and Country conservatism and the folkloric fantasies of his youth. The knighthood he received in 1952 was a fitting honour for a man who saw the future through the past, even if it did not represent the natural nobility of which he had once dreamed.

His views were not entirely of a backwoods piece, though. In the mid-1950s, his colleague E. B. Ford organised a scientific memorandum to the Wolfenden Committee, whose report to Parliament recommended that homosexual acts by consenting adults in private should cease to be criminal offences. While the Committee was unpersuaded by medical and psychiatric opinion, which regarded homosexuality as a disease or a disorder, it seemed to have been influenced by the biologists' view of it as perhaps 'no more than a natural biological variation comparable with variations in stature, hair pigmentation and so on'. The doctors sat in judgement; the evolutionists accepted diversity – appreciating as they did that without it evolution cannot proceed. Fisher's name was on the memorandum, as were those of Julian Huxley and the geneticist Cyril Darlington. According to E. B. Ford, Fisher said that he would sign the report 'because Jesus Christ would have signed it'.

By contrast, Fisher's counterblast in favour of tobacco was reactionary in the strictest sense. He reacted, often explosively, and the effects were often irreversible. Once he clenched his fist in rage at a subordinate and crushed to death the mouse he was holding in his hand. 'See what you made me do,' he thundered at his assistant, throwing the corpse out of the window.

The assistant pulled a face at him; he saw her, and his countenance admitted a grin; that was that. But in the long run, his reactions rebounded upon him. During the war his wife Eileen finally rebelled against his tyranny, finding the strength she needed through an evangelical conversion by her brother, who had formerly been a missionary in China. 'He felt that he had been dethroned,' his daughter Joan observed, 'and replaced by some mirage his wife called God.' The spirit also descended upon his children, who now conducted Bible readings at home. Fisher had prophesied natural nobility but had not foreseen the possibility of revolt. When he went to Cambridge, he was offered a house but no departmental buildings. He chose to devote the house to genetics and left his family behind. A year later he lost his firstborn child, George, killed in a plane crash while serving in the Royal Air Force.

The eugenic triumph of his family, scarred by loss, was rendered hollow by his insistence on lordship. Having spent much of his life as a scientist working in a family home, with children all around, he passed the latter years of his career as a bachelor don. He could discourse at dinner *ad libitum* – a favourite sparring partner was the Marxist sinologist Joseph Needham – but he was lonely. If a student of his had a baby, he loved to see it and give it his benediction.

In his daughter's words, 'He needed friends imperiously,' and sometimes his authority received its due. Those whom he did not alienate developed a fierce loyalty towards him. Among them were some of his undergraduates, whom he looked after, taking care not to repeat the mistakes he had made with colleagues. His sense of isolation was accentuated by the resentment he felt towards the university, which he blamed for not supporting its genetics department properly, and by the widespread readiness among his peers – both in genetics and statistics – to consign his work to history.

After retirement, he left Cambridge for Australia, spending three years at the University of Adelaide, until his death in 1962. His archive remains there in exile. Even today, with Fisher presiding in his rightful place throughout a host of evolutionary biology papers, he defies casual admiration. The Oxford evolutionist Mark Ridley observes that Fisherians are like Wagnerians, and the comparison may be savoured. Both cults are aloof, exacting, devoted and impressed by grand designs; there is also, of course, Nietzsche and all that. The true keepers of the flame are an exclusive few, those who, through years of contemplation and scrutiny, can say they know what Fisher really meant.

Throughout his Cambridge years he used to visit a holiday home, which he had discovered round about the time that he lost his family. Often he would take one or other of his children with him. It was not a roof over his head but a rural locality where he felt himself to be immersed in an older and truer England. At Sparkford, in the south-western county of Somerset, there was a colony of primroses that added a third form to the two usual ones, pin and thrum, whose differing reproductive apparatuses Darwin had identified as a means of arranging cross-fertilisation between them.

Though the selective processes remained mysterious, Fisher's trips represented the culmination of his evolutionary career, in which mathematics, natural history and experiment were synthesised. His eyesight limited his own ability to take his theory into the field, but there were others eager to test Fisherian predictions against nature. They gathered at Oxford and sallied out into the surrounding countryside to look for evolution in action. Where others had assumed indifference, they identified adaptation; where Fisher had assumed advantages of 1 per cent or less, they measured selective pressures an order of magnitude greater.

THE OXFORD SCHOOL

6

Mounting Pressures

Scarlet Tigers

Julian Huxley, on the lookout for ways to advance the selectionist cause at Oxford and beyond, could see that Fisher needed a lieutenant. In 1923, he told him about an undergraduate named Edmund Brisco Ford, with whom Huxley worked on the genetics of the development of a crustacean called *Gammarus chevreuxi*. Ford later recalled how he returned to his rooms one day to find 'a smallish man with red hair, a rather fierce, pointed red beard, and very white face', with eyes 'hard and glittering like a snake's', wreathed in pipe smoke. Fisher had descended upon him from Cambridge and out of the blue.

According to Ford, Huxley conducted the *Gammarus* research with him as an equal. The way Ford described his relationship with his father, a vicar, had a similar ring to it. On 27 July 1912, aged eleven, he began to collect butterflies: Ford senior was 'delighted to join me, and we gradually developed our entomological studies together'. To take E. B. Ford at his own estimate would occupy a whole book. One of his own books, *Taking Genetics into the Countryside*, began with a reference to 'my friend Dr A. L. Rowse' and ended with a folk tale (of how a white moth flutters from a man's mouth at the moment of his death) that 'Thomas Hardy told me'.

Ford grew up in Cumberland, went to Oxford and never left. In his wake he left an intensely selectionist atmosphere that enveloped Oxford zoology and a legend upon which he had worked as meticulously as on his lepidoptera. The anecdote which defines him is that of how Henry, as he was known, arrived to give a lecture and happened to see only women in the audience: 'Nobody present,' he declared, and walked off. There are a number of versions of the story, possibly corresponding to different occasions on which he played out the stunt.

Ford never ceased to advertise his attitude to 'female women', though he made exceptions for a select few. One of them, the naturalist Miriam Rothschild, used her influence to help him secure a retreat perfectly suited to his exquisite sensibilities at All Souls College, where his sense of etiquette and his knowledge of heraldry were properly appreciated. He lobbied as hard behind the scenes to deny women rights at All Souls as he had worked to secure rights for homosexuals in private. At one stage, as if to ensure that the stereotype was complete, he acquired a well-built 'ward' named Kevin.

For Richard Dawkins, choosing his words considerately, Ford was a 'fastidious old bachelor'; for the American author Judith Hooper, Ford serves as a wicked queen. In her book *Of Moths and Men*, an unsympathetic treatment of English selectionism, his vanities and absurdities create a background against which she casts him as an ultra-Darwinian villain who would not let even the truth stand in his way. Bryan Clarke, Ford's biographer for the Royal Society, found himself playing Fisher to Ford's Mendel when he analysed Ford's *Gammarus* data. Like Mendel's peas, they were too neat to be natural: Clarke suggests that they might have been 'conditioned by his expectations' rather than consciously faked.

Ford certainly made himself easy to dislike and was sectarian in his Darwinism – he refused to speak to John Maynard Smith because the latter was a follower of Haldane, not Fisher. But he cultivated a style that was designed neither to confirm nor deny by hovering divertingly in between. It included self-mockery and the odd touch of innuendo. He spoke of 'my friend the Pope', and on visiting the home of his colleague Bernard Kettlewell would raise his bowler to the nanny and inquire, 'How is your pussy?' It was the comic style that made the actor Kenneth Williams a national treasure and a taste as peculiarly British as butterfly-collecting or adaptationism.

In combining science and camp, Ford was an exotic specimen; in his general eccentricity he was a more familiar scientific type. He ate moths, ostensibly checking for protective distastefulness; he talked to himself; and he affected a limping 'wounded partridge' walk when he did not want to be disturbed. But he could also be companionable and, in his way,

down to earth. During the annual summer fortnight of scarlet tiger recording, he would end the day by leading the researchers on a pub crawl. The
goal was to try every beer in Oxford, an exercise which required him to
'clean his palate' with a gin each time. His poise remained undisturbed.

The house in which Edmund Ford spent his first ten years was built on the
site of a Roman fort. His intellectual curiosity began at home, making him
an archaeologist first and a naturalist second. Consequently, he later
observed, he was never a true butterfly-collector. Archaeology taught him
to value data as material with which to interpret the past, not as its own
reward. 'So even as a child I collected natural history specimens only to
learn about them. . .' When he embarked on his studies with his father,
they 'always avoided the aimless amassing of varieties, and kept the problems set by the biology of these insects constantly before our minds'.

They maintained a watch on a colony of marsh fritillary butterflies,
confined to a few swampy fields on the edge of a Cumberland wood, for
nineteen years. Comparing their data with records and specimens accumulated by an earlier generation of amateur lepidopterists, they were able
to see how the colony had gone from abundance to near extinction and
then abundance again. By 1924, the air was a 'dancing haze' of fritillaries,
and within it 'a great outburst of variability was apparent'.

Ford interpreted this in the light of Fisher's prediction that large populations would contain more variety than small isolated ones. In due course
the variety dwindled and the butterflies settled upon a constant form,
which was different from the kind preserved in the old collections. The
variation that had come with the swarms had allowed natural selection to
pick a new configuration better suited to current conditions. During the
1920s, he and Fisher collaborated on a study of variation in moths, which
also upheld Fisher's expectation. Their major joint venture did not begin
until 1939, though it was Fisher's discussion of polymorphism in his 1927
paper on mimicry that showed Ford how to take 'genetics into the field'.

If a butterfly or a snail occurs in more than one form, there are two
possible evolutionary explanations. One, which Darwin accepted and his
successors shared until the 1940s, is that the differences are not adaptive.
The other, which Fisher proposed, is that the different forms are maintained within the population by a balance of selective forces. In the decade

following the Second World War, Fisher and his associates managed to replace the general assumption of neutrality with the presumption of adaptation.

Over seven years, in a small marsh five miles from Oxford, Fisher and Ford gathered the data with which they hoped to slay Sewall Wright's theory that random drift in small populations was a wellspring of evolution. Their subject was a handsome species of moth known as the scarlet tiger, *Panaxia dominula*, which is found over marshes or river banks and lives on the herb comfrey. At Dry Sandford Marsh, a colony of *Panaxia* was confined by unwelcoming territory, like the Cumberland fritillaries, and had given rise to two unique variants. One was quite abundant, up to a fifth of the population, and manifested itself in alterations to the moth's bold patterns of black, white and red; the second was much rarer and blacker. Breeding experiments established that the first kind arose in insects carrying one copy of a particular gene variant, and the second in individuals that had inherited two copies of it.

In the field, Fisher and Ford assessed the size of the population by capturing scarlet tigers, marking them with dots of paint, releasing them, and recording how often they were recaptured. (They also ate them, and found them not unpleasant.) The incidence of the variant gene changed markedly: 4 per cent in one year, 11 in another, a degree of fluctuation that would only occur by chance once in a hundred times. Here was a small, isolated population, and it was being swept by genetic squalls much too intense to be random. There was only one other possibility: the gene was being blown by winds of selective change.

Fisher and Ford proclaimed that they had demonstrated a fact 'fatal' to theories of evolution by random drift. Together with other workers' studies of wild populations, their data showed that selective forces would produce fluctuations of similar kind and scale in the largest and the smallest populations alike. There was nothing special about small populations, except that they went extinct far quicker than large ones.

Wright rebutted the claim of fatal wounding vigorously. He argued that large populations could themselves be affected by random drift and presented calculations to show how this could arise from changing rates of migration and fluctuating selective pressures. Wright felt that his English adversaries were attacking a caricature of his theory, which proposed a 'shifting balance' between random effects and selective ones. But he himself was shifting the balance within it towards selection – of groups rather than individuals – a score on which Fisher had already taken him to task, accusing him of treating evolution as though it worked for the 'general good'.

The result of the controversy was a kind of balanced polymorphism, maintained by powerful forces. According to the historian of science William Provine, the vehemence of each side left most evolutionary biologists feeling that the matter was unresolved. The next round was the 'Great Snail Debate'.

A Million Snails

Philip Sheppard arrived at Oxford with an RAF greatcoat and a diploma, third class, in cottage gardening, earned through a correspondence course in Stalag Luft III. He spent three years there, after his bomber was hit by a German minesweeper on his twenty-first birthday, and took part in the famous escape scheme that used a wooden vaulting horse to conceal a tunnel: he helped dispose of the excavated soil.

At Oxford he proved his intellectual mettle by fulfilling a vacation assignment to read and comprehend Fisher's *Genetical Theory*. After graduating he went on to study scarlet tigers for a doctorate, under E. B. Ford, from whom he took over the Dry Sandford Marsh surveys. One day he was complaining to his friend Arthur Cain, another ex-officer zoologist, about the lack of variation in scarlet tigers. Cain's route to Oxford, like Sheppard's, had begun with boyhood natural history. He had also been a juvenile Darwinian, an adaptationist who was shocked to reach university and find his textbook shrugging off the possibility that this trait or that might possibly be of some use. Cain regarded this as complacency. 'They didn't even dream of doing any actual work or directed observation on the subject,' he told Provine, '– because *they* could see no sense in it, therefore the phenomenon was random, or non-adaptive, or neutral. . .' Adaptationists were converging on Oxford, even though it was not entirely ready for them.

Cain produced a collection of snail shells and poured it onto his table. For the best part of a century, snails of one kind or another had been held up as examples of variation without evolutionary significance. The ones on the table belonged to the latest such negative example, a common European land snail called *Cepaea nemoralis*. The snails had been studied extensively by Captain Cyril Diver, who had pursued his researches into ecology and genetics while serving as a Civil Service clerk to a series of House of Commons committees. Despite collaborating with Fisher, Diver had found himself leaning towards Wright's random drift model as an explanation for the variety of colouring and pattern that the species encompasses. The shells can be yellow, pink or brown; they can have five dark bands following the spirals of their shells, or one, or none. Gazing at the variety, Cain and Sheppard 'decided then and there' that it could not possibly be 'wholly neutral' and that they would work on it.

They surveyed snails at twenty-five spots within fifty miles of Oxford and found that shells of the various types tended to occur where they were least conspicuous. Yellow morphs turned out to be commoner on grassland, banded ones could be expected against variegated backgrounds, and brown ones survived upon the leaf litter in the woods. In early spring, against a predominantly brown background, the brown morphs were safer, but their fortunes reversed as the season grew greener; conversely, the yellow shells, which may appear greenish when snails are inside, figured less in June's debris than in April's. In Wytham Woods, an estate bequeathed to the university in 1943, there was forensic as well as circumstantial evidence. Song thrushes, one of a range of birds and animals that eat the snails, left debris around the anvil stones on which they cracked the shells open.

Cain and Sheppard's first study convinced them not only that their initial hunch had been right but that they had pulled the rug from under the prevailing assumption that polymorphisms were indifferent to natural selection. Now, they declared, 'all situations supposedly caused by drift should be reinvestigated'. They were riding an adaptationist wave. Julian Huxley, leading with his antennae, spoke of 'the all-pervading influence of natural selection, and the consequent omnipresence of adaptation'.

Across the Channel, however, a biologist called Maxime Lamotte was reviewing data from field studies he had begun during the war, when France was occupied and he was in the Resistance, as an attempt to test Wright's ideas about random effects in small populations. After surveying over nine hundred French *Cepaea* populations, he concluded that whether or not a snail had bands was decided by random drift. The English selectionists prevailed in the ensuing debate. Positions were not exclusive: Cain acknowledged that random processes, such as flooding, might shape some populations, while Lamotte found that bandless snails seemed to do better where summer temperatures were higher and yellow ones where winters were colder. Climate is now recognised as an additional selective force – darker shells absorb more solar energy, making their occupants more vulnerable to heat – and the roles of other factors, such as population density, have been explored. In some regions, changes in the frequency of different shell forms may mark where previously isolated populations have met, each bringing genotypes shaped by vanished historical conditions.

By the 1970s, the geneticist Steve Jones and his colleagues were able to review literature based on data from ten thousand populations, amounting to a million snails; they noted that this represented 'a body of information on populations in their natural habitats greater than that which exists for any other animal except man'. They suggested that *Cepaea* polymorphism might be 'a problem with too many solutions'. Whether this was nature's fault or its interpreters', the solutions were overwhelmingly adaptive.

Peppered Moths

The peppered moths' public début was more memorable than planned. Bernard Kettlewell had brought hundreds of the insects from Oxford to a grand occasion at the Royal Society. He stepped outside briefly, leaving them in E. B. Ford's care. When he came back, he found Ford 'pointing at the chandeliers whilst entirely surrounded by VIPs, explaining that Dr Kettlewell's exhibit had, unfortunately, transferred itself to the various lights . . .' *Biston betularia* had demonstrated that it could steal a scene and that its investigators could find themselves facing unexpected complications.

It had been noted as a curiosity for more than a century. In 1848, a Manchester calico-maker and lepidopterist caught a specimen that was black instead of the typical speckled ivory colouring. The moth emphatically blended with its surroundings in a city described by the regional military commander as 'the chimney of the world'. By the end of the century, almost all peppered moths in the Manchester area were black. J. W. Tutt, an entomologist, suggested that this was an example of natural selection in action. A typical peppered moth was camouflaged against the background of lichen that normally encrusted tree trunks and branches, concealing it from birds. Air pollution poisoned the lichen, as well as darkening trees with soot: against the new industrial background, black variants would be at an advantage.

A quarter of a century later, J. B. S. Haldane showed that the advantage must amount to 30, or even 50, per cent. He then found himself in dispute with J. W. Heslop Harrison, who fed caterpillars chemicals containing lead and manganese, and announced that he had thereby induced blackness ('melanism') not only in the larvae but also in their descendants. Heslop Harrison's results failed to be replicated, and now languish under the cloud seeded by suspicions that he planted exotic species on the Scottish island of Rum and claimed them as rare discoveries.

Ford later remarked that the melanic peppered moth 'looks as if dipped in ink', but he never believed that chemicals caused industrial melanism directly. He was also initially sceptical about the idea that the advantage of melanism lay in concealment. Following Fisher's ideas about the evolution of dominance, he suggested that melanic heterozygotes – individuals that had inherited a copy of the melanism gene from one parent rather than both – might be physiologically superior to the typical form. In rural areas, this advantage was overridden by their visibility but came into its own in the smoke. His priority was the scarlet tiger, though; he eventually delegated the peppered moth to Kettlewell, whom he first met that year pursuing lepidoptera in a Scottish pine forest called the Black Wood of Rannoch.

Kettlewell reached Oxford in 1951, via Cape Town, where he had gone to practise medicine. He sent his wife and children by sea, while he drove from the Cape to Cairo. At first the family was housed in a caravan at Wytham Woods, where he husbanded caterpillars in preparation for his experiments. These took place further afield, though, outside Birmingham and in Dorset. Kettlewell adapted the technique of marking, releasing and recapturing insects that Fisher and Ford had applied to the scarlet tigers. He found that in the industrial hinterland he recaptured more of the melanic moths, while in the Dorset woods it was the other way round.

This was evidence that natural selection was taking place off-stage. To catch it in the act, Kettlewell invited Niko Tinbergen down to Dorset with his cine camera. The Dutch zoologist had come to Oxford in 1947, drawn by the prospect of research and the presence of colleagues like E. B. Ford and the ornithologist David Lack. Like Philip Sheppard, Tinbergen had been imprisoned by the Nazis, spending two years in a hostage camp. Like Ford, he had invented a new form of natural history, together with his German kindred spirit, Konrad Lorenz. Ford's new natural history took 'genetics into the countryside'; Tinbergen's took animal psychology back into the wild where it belonged.

Ethology, the field study of animal behaviour, also belonged in homes and classrooms. Intuitive and accessible, it offered explanations for amateur naturalists who assumed there must be a reason for whatever they saw an animal doing. And, just in time for television, it was a visual science. Although today that might seem unremarkable in itself, even in the mid-1960s Tinbergen was unusual among Oxford lecturers in using slides.

Tinbergen's camera recorded what Kettlewell had observed through his binoculars: birds swooping onto tree trunks and taking the more conspicuous forms first. The resulting film was entitled *Evolution in Progress*. It did far more than answer the reviewer of Ford's *Moths* whose scepticism had needled Kettlewell into securing the footage. Kettlewell and his moths became natural history celebrities. The peppered moth had the great advantage of clarity. It was black and white – as was television, upon which any variation more subtle would have been lost – and it had topical significance as a striking example of nature's response to industrial pollution.

Kettlewell activated a network of amateur lepidopterists to obtain information about the incidence of melanism around the country. The picture was broadly consistent: black peppered moths were commoner around industrial areas, and pale ones in unpolluted countryside. Sheppard and his colleague Cyril Clarke calculated that, around Liverpool, pale peppered moths were at a selective disadvantage of about 60 per cent: the odds were even higher than those J. B. S. Haldane had calculated in the early 1920s. And as clean-air acts went onto the statute books and smoky industries declined, the dark moths began to yield ground to the pale ones once more. In Manchester, the place where the first dark specimen was caught, the proportion of melanics fell from 98 per cent at the start of the twentieth century to less than 10 per cent at the end of it.

As Ford had suspected, though, the case of the peppered moth was more complex than the simple story that became enshrined in the textbooks. Dark moths flourished in unpolluted East Anglia. Pale moths began to reappear before the lichens that were supposed to conceal them, while dark moths had risen and fallen in the United States while the lichens there stayed the same. Doubts grew about Kettlewell's experiments, which looked to many researchers like selection out of doors but not in nature. Kettlewell had released his nocturnal moths onto tree trunks in daylight, where the torpid insects dotted the bark like decorations on a cake. But field observers saw peppered moths on tree trunks in daytime just twice in forty years. Some of them concluded that moths generally rested underneath branches, where dark moths had the advantage in the shadows.

One of these researchers was Michael Majerus, who bought Ford's *Moths* at the age of ten, in May 1964, caught his first melanic peppered moth four weeks later, and never looked back. In 1998, he published a book entitled *Melanism: Evolution in Action*. It was reviewed in *Nature* by the American evolutionist Jerry Coyne, who devoted almost all his attention to the chapters reviewing the case of the peppered moth. Majerus remained confident that birds were the major selective agents acting on peppered moth melanism in Britain. Local currents of migration could explain anomalies like the dark moths in East Anglia. Coyne, however, thought that Majerus had shown that 'the prize horse in our stable of examples' was in 'bad shape'. His own reaction resembled 'the dismay attending my discovery, at the age of six, that it was my father and not Santa who brought the presents on Christmas Eve'.

Creationists seized on the quote like children snatching a Christmas present. They were not so taken with his statement that '*B. betularia* shows the footprint of natural selection, but we have not yet seen the feet'. Views among American moth researchers ranged from that of Bruce Grant, who spoke of 'fine tuning the peppered moth paradigm', to the heterodox Theodore Sargent, who thought that Heslop Harrison might have been on to something with his induction hypothesis after all. But even Sargent was 'certain' that selection had produced industrial melanism. As Coyne later testified, rebutting the use of his review by creationists, 'all of us in the peppered moth debate agree that the moth story is a sound example of evolution produced by natural selection'.

Michael Majerus put it more strongly than that. On a public platform, unrestrained by the conventions of scientific prose, he declared what he really thought. He invoked his forty-odd years of collecting moths, man and boy: 'I have caught literally millions of moths in moth traps. And I have found in the wild more peppered moths than any other person alive or dead.' As a scientist he had read hundreds of papers on the subject; as a naturalist he had acquired a 'feeling for the organism' that gave him certainty – 'I know I'm right, I know Kettlewell was right, I know Tutt was right.'

As a scientist, however, he had to acknowledge that the evidence identifying birds as the selective agents remained circumstantial. And so he had embarked on a laborious five-year study that would show for certain what happens to peppered moths in nature. But 'if I get that proof, and splash it over every front page I can get', and the moth-bothering Darwin-baiters read it, 'will they be convinced?'. He fell silent. Whatever the science finally said, it would not be the end of the peppered moth story.

Wings and Prayer

On a day of precious spring brilliance in May 1941, David Lack sat above the seacliffs of Hoy, looking southwards across the Pentland Firth, which separates the Orkney islands from the north-eastern tip of mainland Scotland. He would come here on his days off from his duties with a heavy anti-aircraft battery, a posting he regarded as a wonderful birdwatching holiday. But this time the dot in the sky was a plane, a German marauder, which dived at a British convoy that was steaming through the channel as slowly as an hour hand.

Lack's comrades opened up at the attacker, gulls mobbing a skua. And in answer to the gunfire, a migrant robin began to sing. In the radiance and the song a pulse of exaltation passed through Lack. It was not the first time and it would not be the last, but it was the last time natural rapture intimated to him that God is in everything and everything is God. At this stage he was a passionate birdwatcher with a keen interest in Darwinism, but neither his understanding of evolution nor his beliefs about ultimate causes were fully shaped.

In the years after the war, his natural philosophy was resolved into two distinct vectors. He replaced his undefined pantheism with conventional Anglicanism, and his early inclination towards random drift with an adaptationism that became steadily stronger as the years went by.

Before the war, he had travelled to the Galapágos Islands, where he studied the finches that had steered Darwin's course to natural selection. In 1835, voyaging on HMS *Beagle*, Darwin had collected specimens of small birds, apparently the small change of a group of islands upon which crawled giant tortoises and marine iguanas. On his return he passed them on to the ornithologist John Gould, who determined that they represented different species of finch. They differed in their bills, which came in different sizes and shapes. Darwin remarked, daring and disingenuous in the same breath, that it was almost as if 'one species had been taken and modified for different ends'. He revealed the mechanism later, in the *Origin of Species*, but did not elaborate on why one unremarkable species might become thirteen. It fell to Lack, more than a hundred years later, to provide the textbooks with their explanation.

Fearing that the expedition's bedraggled collection of live finches would not survive the passage home, Lack made landfall in the United States on his way back. Here he came under local influence and interpreted his observations in the light of Sewall Wright's ideas. After some years back in his native land, however, he concluded that the finches were better explained by adaptation. Natural selection was the spine of his field research and his popular writings alike; inevitably, he gravitated to Oxford, where he commanded not only respect and influence but great affection too. John Maynard Smith considers that Lack 'more than anybody introduced clean, clear Darwinian ideas into ethology' through his influence on Niko Tinbergen.

He was born in 1910, the son of an eminent surgeon, and spent his early years surrounded by servants in a splendid London home. In due course he was sent to Gresham's School, in Norfolk, the least illiberal of the established public (that is, private senior) schools. Its products were remarkable, though unpredictable. Among his contemporaries were the poet W. H. Auden, the composer Benjamin Britten, Christopher Cockerell, who went on to invent the hovercraft, Alan Hodgkin, who won a Nobel prize for physiology, and Donald Maclean, who transferred from the Foreign

Office in London to its counterpart in Moscow when faced with arrest as a Soviet spy.

Whatever effect Gresham's had on the others, it turned Lack into a birdwatcher. This was the great discovery of his teenage years: he pursued it on Sundays, striding across the chilly north Norfolk flats in the Gresham Sunday uniform of black suit, stiff collar, and most impractically in that landscape, straw hat. It was the substance of his teenage rebellion too. He had a basic competence in maths, and his parents envisaged that he would use the skill to earn his living, probably as a chartered accountant. Instead, he announced that he was going to be a zoologist.

There are nice echoes here of John Maynard Smith's early life. Ten years Lack's junior, Maynard Smith was also the son of a distinguished surgeon and spent his early childhood in a house down the road from the Lacks' establishment in Devonshire Place; he was expected to go into the family stockbroking firm, on the strength of his maths, but in his mid-teens declared that he would not. Unaware that there were careers to be made from natural history, he opted for engineering, retraining as a biologist after the war. He did not become a field worker, however, because his eyesight was limited; Lack's, on the other hand, was excellent. They became collegial friends in later life, and complemented each other. Lack respected Maynard Smith's superior mathematical skills and understood enough maths to communicate with him; Maynard Smith admired Lack's outstanding abilities as a naturalist and had the necessary grounding to appreciate them.

Both of them, however, had an antipathy to the anatomy and morphology that dominated traditional zoology courses. In Lack's day, there was little else to the degree: he was not taught evolution, ecology or genetics. But outside the curriculum he read Haldane's *Causes of Evolution* and Fisher's paper 'On the Evolution of Dominance', the first works which excited his 'zoological imagination' that were not about birds. As a naturalist, the question that sprang to his mind when he looked at a living creature was not 'what?' or 'how?' – the most that traditional zoology would ask – but 'why?'. He found these questions in the field, and the beginnings of answers in evolutionary theory.

Lack was fortunate to acquire as a patron Julian Huxley, who had inherited his grandfather's gift for influence and arrangements. Huxley had connections with Dartington Hall, in Devon, which had opened a radically liberal school in 1926. He suggested that the school should hire an ecologist as a biology teacher and mentioned Lack's name. (Meanwhile, at Eton, John Maynard Smith did not have the option of studying biology at all, let alone with an ecologist.) It was an inspired suggestion. Lack was overwhelmed by the children's happiness, a condition for which no traditional public school could have prepared him. Dartington encouraged him to take the children out into the fields and folds of the Devon landscape in which it had raised the banner of educational freedom. His lecturing style was honed, too, by market forces not usually encountered in British educational institutions at the time: the children were free to choose whether or not they attended classes, and so teachers had to earn their attention.

It was while helping a class of eleven- and twelve-year-olds, in 1935, that he began one of his most celebrated studies. Having caught and ringed a number of robins, he began to study them himself, and continued until the eve of the war. As well as watching wild birds, he built large aviaries, in which hatched the first British robins to be bred in captivity. His observations became a book, *The Life of the Robin*, which was published in 1943.

Its wrapper, in the abrupt utility style that made everything look like government issue, belied its contents. Lack displayed a happy fluency and breadth of perspective, interweaving scientific insight and practical craft with strands of literature, history and folklore. The first chapter was prefaced by quotes from Sir Thomas Browne on 'the debt of our reason we owe unto God' to study and contemplate the world, from Thomas Love Peacock on how the scientist 'suffices to himself, makes all around him happy', and from Anita Loos, in *Gentlemen Prefer Blondes*: 'I finally told him I thought, after all, that bird life was the highest form of civilization . . . Gerry says he has never seen a girl of my personal appearance with so many brains.'

Perhaps the most remarkable thing about *The Life of the Robin* is the density of quotes Lack achieved without looking as though he was showing off. The accumulation of epigraphs in archaic English developed a folkloric and historical theme, affirming not just England's favourite bird but her heritage too. When he quoted Chaucer, Lack was doing what the film-makers Pressburger and Powell did in *A Canterbury Tale*. He conjured up a vision of what the British were fighting for.

Lack also had a knack for striking up alliances between science and other traditions of knowledge. To illustrate the intimidatory power of robin song, he referred to H. G. Wells's account of how the last papal crusade against the Hussites collapsed in 1431, when the Germans camped before Domažlice fled at the sound of the approaching Bohemians' song. Although his literary and naturalist perspectives placed him squarely in the English neo-Romantic movement of the time, his scientific eye was shrewd. He had no illusions that animals acted for the good of the species. And he was also ahead of his time on sexual selection, entertaining not only the notion itself but also the idea that the process might operate by female choice.

Like a young Victorian naturalist, he needed to make an expedition. Once again, Huxley fixed it for him, securing grants for his journey to the Galápagos Islands in 1938. The rewards of the trip were entirely scientific, 'offset by an enervating climate, monotonous scenery, dense thorn scrub, cactus spines, loose sharp lava, food deficiencies, water shortage, black rats, fleas, jiggers, ants, mosquitoes, scorpions, Ecuadorean Indians of doubtful honesty, and dejected, disillusioned European settlers'. The finches brought little cheer to the scene, for they were dull both in plumage and song, but they provided Lack with the data that made him an influential evolutionary naturalist. In California, he began to draw his conclusions, interpreting the differences in bill sizes as means by which the various finch species maintained their separate identities. He had been impressed by their reluctance to interbreed, having failed to repeat his aviary success with robins. At the same time, he had failed to see what practical difference the variations in bill size made. The finches shared a common diet and dining room, eating seeds off the ground. There was 'no evidence whatever . . . that their differences have adaptive significance'.

Like many of his contemporaries, Lack became a pacifist; and unlike many of them, he remained one when the war broke out. His conviction did not survive contact with his fellow anti-combatants, though. He spent a trial night in the East End of London with a unit of volunteers undertaking civil defence duty in the air raids, 'but was so put off by the pacifists' earnest attitudes, and so excited by the flashes and bangs, that I was immediately converted from pacifism'.

Despite his protestations of ignorance, the military authorities took his biological training to be a suitable basis for work on the secret new technology of radio direction finding, or radar. His logical and mathematical abilities evidently did prove adequate, for he worked on radar for much of the war. The posting to the Orkneys was a practical application of his efforts. Later on, he helped to identify 'angels'. These tenuous apparitions showed up on radar screens even though no aircraft were aloft, and it was said that many RAF officers, men after Alfred Russel Wallace's heart, more than half believed that the miraculous devices had indeed detected angelic beings. They were actually flocks of migrating birds. Later in his career, Lack used radar to track migrant flocks.

At the end of the war, Lack took stock of his finch material and saw a new explanation for the differences in the finches' bills. He thought about his findings in the light of the argument made by Georgyi Gause, a Russian biologist, that two species with the same ecology cannot share the same region. The finches seemed to illustrate this principle, for similar species did not occur together, and in species which did share an island, the differences were accentuated. It looked as though members of each population were under pressure to develop adaptations, principally in the size and shape of their bills, which helped them avoid competing for the same resources as members of the other species. Some adopted ways of life like those of warblers, others filled the role taken elsewhere by titmice, and still others reinvented themselves as woodpeckers.

Lack published his selectionist interpretation in his book *Darwin's Finches*, which appeared in 1947. At that stage he still accepted that many of the differences between subspecies and closely related species might have no adaptive significance. By 1960, the book had helped to shift the balance of opinion towards the presumption that nearly all differences between species and subspecies were adaptive. And the birds had come to be known as Lack's finches too.

He went on to demonstrate a similar division of habitats among more familiar species, the cormorant and the lesser cormorant, or shag. Although they were similar enough in appearance to confuse inexperienced birdwatchers, Lack demonstrated that their habitats were quite distinct. Cormorants nested on flat ledges, whereas shags preferred hollows; cormorants scooped flatfish from the silt of estuaries and coastal waters, while shags caught free-swimming fish in open sea. Having identified the phenomenon on the ground and in the water, he also reported something similar high in the air. Above 1,000 metres, he said, the common swift was replaced by Hardy's swift, *Apus durus*, which exploited the 'aerial plankton' of high-altitude insects. Though this was a joke in honour of his friend Alister Hardy, some of his ornithological colleagues took it as seriously as the RAF officers had taken the angels.

Around the same time that Lack saw how selection might press species to cleave to different feeding niches, another Darwinian insight came to him in a flash. He realised that selective pressure might determine the average number of eggs laid in a clutch. The more eggs a bird laid, the less it would be able to invest in each of its offspring; the best number to lay would be the highest number it could successfully raise. This number would vary according to the region and the season. Birds would cut their cloth according to their means.

As he pointed out in a memoir, his insights about Darwin's finches and clutch size 'essentially depended on the full acceptance of natural selection'. He gave credit for this not to Fisher or Haldane but William Pycraft, whose bird books he had treasured as a youth. Lack was proud to have followed the English tradition of amateur naturalism and noted that he might have been one of the last Fellows of the Royal Society to have been elected on the strength of work done while an amateur.

He became unarguably professional in 1945, when he was appointed director of the Edward Grey Institute of Field Ornithology at Oxford. One of his first projects was a study of great tits in Wytham Woods, launched in 1947. It became a local tradition, maintained by other workers; it survived his death in 1973 and continued into the next century. As the seasons turn, the great tits of Wytham are watched and counted still.

The tits broadly upheld his hypothesis about clutch size, which experimenters could manipulate by adding eggs to nests. But they did not conform to his predictions, producing fewer eggs than expected. George Williams, the American counterpart of Bill Hamilton and John Maynard Smith, suggested that this was because Lack had not taken into account the persisting effects of parenthood. Lack had assumed that the costs of rearing a brood were incurred entirely during the year that the effort was made, but it was possible that parents would still be suffering the effects in the subsequent breeding season, impairing their ability to raise the next generation.

Things crystallised fast for Lack in the years that followed the war. After his embrace of natural selection and his institutional establishment came, in 1948, his conversion to Christianity. He wrote a book in which he attempted to harmonise Darwinism with his Anglicanism, leaving his colleagues bemused, and touched lightly on the theme to pleasing literary effect in his popular book *Swifts in a Tower*. It begins in 1855 with 'a group of bearded and reverend scientists' singing at the dedication of the foundation stone for the University Museum in Oxford. 'And as they sang "O, all ye fowls of the air, bless ye the Lord" there came, it may be supposed, an answering scream from the circling swifts . . .'

A tower arose upon the site, the museum galleries to either side. In 1860, Thomas Huxley and Bishop Wilberforce debated evolution in the museum's reading room. A century later, Lack and his wife Elizabeth Silva would ascend past the scene of the debate and climb up inside the tower to study the swifts nesting inside. The birds' clutch sizes supported Lack's hypothesis; their screams answered Huxley's echo, but Lack brought his story back to reverend science. 'Could . . . man have evolved from beasts by natural selection and yet apprehend truth and goodness through a supernatural gift?' The difficulties inherent in this view were no greater than those of alternative views. Agnostic biologists had attempted to show how natural selection could have produced the human sense of goodness, but if it had, why should any value be attached to it? Lack left his readers with a reminder that the tower had been built 'by those who held that the study of nature should lead us . . . to a fuller worship of the Creator. . .' Within the tower, he implied, Darwinism was contained.

J. B. S. HALDANE

'Fitness is a bugger.'
J. B. S. Haldane to John Maynard Smith.

7

Loose Cannon

The summer of 1913, in North Oxford, on the meadows by the river Cherwell. Two young men share the stage of the Dragon School with a number of guinea pigs. The youths are playing the parts of geneticists. They bat the subject of eugenics to and fro: unfair to the poor, a boon to the Empire. *Exeunt*, and enter a strapping undergraduate, built to row for one ancient English university or the other, and strikingly great in head as well as frame. He is dressed in Mayan style as Cahu Halpa, a dignitary in an imaginary Andean realm. 'Twins, my god, twins!' he bellows. Jack Haldane's opening salvo causes several casualties in the audience, the blow to their sensibilities propelling them from the hall altogether.

A couple of minutes' walk from the Dragon School stands Cherwell, a new and voluminous riverside pile, incorporating a laboratory indoors and a dairy farm outside. On its lawn graze three hundred guinea pigs. Naomi Haldane, author of the play and Jack's kid sister, knows many of them by their individual voices. She has named two of them after Bateson and Punnett, the leading British geneticists of the day.

Jack and Naomi cast their net across Oxford in search of varieties of guinea pigs and mice. Once, at St Giles's Fair, they pick up two pink specimens, but these turn out to be dyed albinos.

The spring of 1915, in France, on the Western Front. Jack is now a lieutenant in the Black Watch and to his delight has been placed in charge of his brigade's grenades and trench mortars. He is known to his men as the 'Rajah of Bomb', among other things. Lt Haldane busies himself with sorties into no-man's-land, mortar bombardments and a bomb-making workshop.

Even so, he finds time while in the trenches to finish writing up the genetic project that he and Naomi had husbanded on the Cherwell lawn. Their paper, 'Reduplication in Mice', is the first report of linkage between genes in mammals, meaning that genes (for pink eyes and for true albinism) tend to be inherited together, being close to each other on the same chromosome. They had embarked on the study after Jack read a genetics paper and spotted evidence of linkage that the author had missed. It is published in the *Journal of Genetics* later in the year.

By then Naomi is studying science at the university, Jack is an incipient legend, and their co-author A. D. Sprunt is dead, killed in action before the final draft. By the end of the year, several members of Naomi's school-hall cast have also fallen. One, Thomas Huxley's grandson Trev, took his own life during the first month of the war, but his brother Aldous has been saved by an illness that left him nearly blind. It is no longer clear, as it had been to the Victorians, that the fittest survive.

In May 1915, J. B. S. Haldane was wounded during the battle of Aubers Ridge. The incident left his memory blank, though he remembered being given a lift to a dressing station afterwards by the Prince of Wales. 'Oh, it's you,' said His Royal Highness when Haldane got into the vehicle.

Forty-six years later, Haldane remarked on his interlude with fate to the writer Robert Graves. 'It has always seemed to me plausible that I did not buy a return ticket over the irremeable stream, but have imagined events since 1915. They are now becoming rather outrageous, so perhaps I shall wake up.' His own circumstances had settled into a relatively calm emeritus eccentricity, in which he had adopted both Indian domicile and dress. But in general his life continued after the Western Front as it had started, powered by his immense heads of intellectual, physical and dramatic steam.

'How you propose to make sense of my career beats me,' he told a would-be biographer around the same time. He gave a list of what he regarded as his main achievements, a dozen of them, to illustrate his point. Number one was neutralising half the bicarbonate in his body by drinking ammonium chloride and calcium chloride; number twelve was his recent calculation of the cost of natural selection. In between came first reports of genetic linkage in various species, including the one published in 1915, advances in statistical techniques, the identification of the enzyme cytochrome oxidase in higher plants, moths and cats, the invention of methods to help divers avoid the 'bends' on their return to the surface, along with the elucidation of how newts regulate their own ascents from under water; and the discovery that at five or six times normal atmospheric pressure oxygen tastes like 'dilute ginger beer with some ink in it'.

And there were his evolutionary firsts, beginning with the first calculation of natural selection's intensity, the 50 per cent gradient upon which the peppered moth seemed to find itself. He also claimed the first measurement, with Lionel Penrose, of mutation rates in humans and of rates of evolutionary change in quantitative characters in horses. Evolution was a process rather than a principle for him. He got plenty of philosophy from traditional sources, without resorting to Darwinism. J. B. S. was more inclined to ask evolution the kind of questions that an engineer would appreciate.

Many of his other achievements also fell within family tradition, in that they were applications of what his father taught him. John Scott Haldane's science was applied extensively to mines and the safety of the men who worked in them. He dealt in gases, pressures and explosions; heroic phenomena that demanded heroic investigation. After he had been summoned to investigate a mine disaster, the family would receive a succession of messages by telegram that he was safe. This was not because he felt he needed to reassure his loved ones but because his memory had been stifled by carbon monoxide poisoning.

The animals on the lawn were apt. Jack was raised by Uffer, as he and Naomi called their father, to be a human guinea pig. In his teens, off the Scottish coast aboard a gunboat named HMS *Spanker*, his father let him clamber into a diving suit and take part in a project to establish decompression procedures, a natural extension of Uffer's studies of physiology at depth. Big as Jack was, though, he did not fill the suit, which consequently leaked. He managed to keep the water at chest height until the time set for his return to the surface. During the Great War, he and his father gassed themselves repeatedly with chlorine as they tried to develop effective gas masks for the soldiers in the trenches.

J. B. S. took great pride in being, as he put it in one of his essays, his own rabbit. He continued to practice what his father had taught him during the

Second World War, working for the Admiralty on diving experiments. The taste of oxygen came at the price of injuries sustained during the convulsions these exercises induced. In all this he was upholding another family tradition, for the motto on the Haldane coat of arms is 'Suffer'. But perhaps that is stretching the point. Murdoch Mitchison, Naomi's son and J. B. S.'s nephew, observes drily that on the family silver the watchword has worn down to 'Supper'.

Once, in a North Staffordshire mine, Uffer told Boy (as Jack, for his part, was known) to stand up and recite from *Julius Caesar*, beginning 'Friends, Romans, countrymen . . .' Boy soon found himself panting, and round about 'the noble Brutus' he collapsed. On the floor he found he could breathe again, which taught him that methane, known to miners as firedamp, is lighter than air and not toxic. The incident illustrates more about J. B. S.'s scientific thought than just the legacy of his principal tutor's robust methods in practical chemistry. All his life, J. B. S. excelled in reciting classical literature from memory. As youngsters he and Naomi, whose family diminutive was Nou, used to play verse capping, in which each had to produce a line of verse containing the last word of the other's line. He seemed to contain volumes inside that cranium which impressed everyone so much (the palaeontologist Arthur Keith was said to have laid claim to it in the event that Haldane should predecease him).

This capacity, combined with an analytical engine to match, may be what made his career the account-confounding chimera that it seems at first to be. John Maynard Smith has observed that 'the kind of scientist who is good at developing clear theories often finds it difficult to remember facts, whereas those who know the facts tend to jib at the algebra. It seems to me that there is no single idea in biology which is hard to understand, in the way that ideas in physics can be hard. If biology is difficult, it is because of the bewildering number and variety of things one must hold in one's head.' Haldane had ample room in his head for any number of things and tackled mathematics with the relentless determination of a tank crossing trenches.

As Maynard Smith also points out, Haldane was a puzzle-solver, and he had the cognitive resources to make a model for each one that came along. Unlike Fisher, for example, he did not need a general theory that could be applied to all cases, and so he was not obliged to build a system to contain all his thought. At one stage he pursued evolution; at another decompression. Along would come the problem; out would come the notebook, and the epic verses of algebra would unfold.

'Haldane's characteristic style was to set up a problem,' observed the geneticist James F. Crow, 'grind out the results as fast as possible, and publish them with no further polishing.' To purists, they are not a pretty sight. 'There's no elegance in them at all,' Anthony Edwards says of the papers on selection which Haldane published in the 1920s, 'whereas Fisher hits the nail on the head immediately.' In Edwards's opinion Fisher was a 'mathematician's mathematician', Haldane a 'plodding algebraist'. But as Crow went on to note, Fisher's aesthetics exacted a price. 'Elegance took precedence over clarity, with the consequence that much of his writing is impossible to understand.'

J. B. S. started at Oxford as he would continue thereafter. During his first year, he made his début as a scientific author, handling the mathematical analysis in a landmark study of respiratory physiology conducted by his father. For his second year, he switched from mathematics and zoology to 'Greats', a course in classical history and philosophy. Although he left New College with Firsts in both maths and classics, J. B. S. became one of Britain's foremost scientists without ever taking a science degree.

John Burdon Sanderson followed in John Scott's footsteps because he spent much of his childhood at his father's heels. Other Victorian scientists, notably Darwin and Huxley, knew the distractions and sweetness of working with their children around them, for they did much of their science in their studies at home. John Scott Haldane demonstrated his love of his son's company more actively, though it is safe to assume that he did not put his feelings into words. 'What's the formula for soda-lime?' demanded Uffer; the twelve-year-old Boy's correct answer earned him a working trip in a submarine. Uffer was frequently abstracted and oblivious to those around him; on one celebrated occasion, he absent-mindedly put himself to bed when he was supposed to be dressing for dinner.

Boy was born on 5 November 1892, Bonfire Night, and his adventures underground with Uffer began when he was four: he found himself on the Metropolitan Line in London, watching his father take samples of the smoky air using a tube held out of the carriage window. At the age of five, according to family legend, he was taught to read out the *Times* reports of the doings of the British Association for the Advancement of Science. 'I was bottle-washing for my father from a very early age, from about eight,' he recalled towards the end of his life, 'and in my opinion if you have really learnt to wash bottles, chemically clean, bacteriologically clean, you've learned about a third of science.'

His apprenticeship nearly came to an end about that time. He was at Uffer's heels again, perched behind him as Haldane senior's bicycle-clipped legs pedalled the pair of them towards home. Boy fell off the bicycle and fractured his skull on the kerb of Parks Road. At first the doctors feared he would not survive, but after ten days, he had recovered sufficiently to reprimand the surgeon who ventured to prescribe him medicine. 'But you are the mechanical chap,' he protested. 'Leave that to the chemical chap.'

He never spoke a truer word, as far as his distinguishing traits of precocity and arrogance were concerned. It was also characteristic of the man, as well as of the boy, to be correct in theory but wrong about how the world works in practice. And it was the true voice of a boy born into a family that took both knowledge and power for granted. He liked to claim descent from Pedro the Cruel, a king of Castile and Leon in the fourteenth century, and he portrayed the Haldanes as a Scottish military clan employed to protect lowlanders' cattle against highland raiders. By Jack's time they were an intellectual and a political force as well as a martial one. The relative after whom he was named, his great-uncle John Burdon Sanderson, was the first Waynflete Professor of Physiology at Oxford. His uncle Richard Burdon Haldane served in a Liberal administration as Secretary of State for War for seven years, and then as Lord Chancellor for three; he resumed the post in the 1924 Labour government. Naomi's first portent of the Great War's horror came when she caught a glimpse of the Foreign Secretary's ashen face in the hall at Uncle Richard's house.

Viscount Haldane was not permitted to continue as Lord Chancellor in Herbert Asquith's coalition government of 1915 because he was suspected of German sympathies. Though the suspicions were unfounded politically, the Haldanes certainly leaned towards Germany rather than France on matters of culture and knowledge. John Scott Haldane 'had few French colleagues', recalled Naomi, 'and on the rare occasions when he met them, he tended to address them as *"Ach, mein liebe Kollege!"'* He was a philosopher as well as a physiologist; both he and Richard were heavily influenced by Hegel. As a scion of a Hegelian family, J. B. S. was facing in the direction of Marxism long before it presented itself, in the 1930s, as an urgent political choice.

J. B. S.'s political heritage was a mixture of paternal liberalism and maternal conservatism. Louisa Kathleen Haldane, known to the children as Maya, was both a feminist and a passionate imperialist. She also came from a Scottish family, the Trotters, which took pride in the gold braid that its menfolk had accumulated in the service of Crown and Empire. Naomi observed that in the discussion about eugenics between the geneticists in her play, the remark about its benefits for the Empire echoed her mother, while the suggestion of unfairness to the poor sounded more like her brother. While Uffer took Boy down mines, Maya swept him along to imperialist meetings, recruiting for the Children of the Empire with the aid of exhibited native artefacts. He was a faithful gosling to Maya's imperial mother goose. 'My mater and I are very sorry to hear of Mr Chamberlain's resignation,' he told his diary on 18 September 1903, referring to the Conservative Colonial Secretary, 'but hope he will get into office again soon.'

Eton seems to have made a Liberal of him, or at least to have sent him in the direction of his father's side of the family. After the Dragon School, unconventional enough to admit both him and his sister, he found himself on the receiving end of the sustained juvenile persecution for which English public schools were a byword. At one stage this included beating on the soles of his feet, though there was a glimmer of humanity in the shape of Julian Huxley, who broke with tradition by giving Haldane an apple during Jack's service as a 'fag', a menial for whom punishment was normal and reward almost unknown. As John Maynard Smith learned to his own distaste, thirty years later, Eton boys were able to maintain their autonomous little tyrannies with little regard to higher authority. When the Lord Chancellor made an official visit to the school, Haldane was prevented from meeting his uncle by means of a table weighed down with sandbags.

J. B. S. aired his contempt for Eton in a draft autobiography, written in the 1930s. Referring to Pop, the prefects' society, he scurrilously reported that the 'shapely youths who were alleged to assuage the desires of this august body, often in return for presents, were known as "Pop bitches".' He cast himself as insider and outsider at the same time, revealing the sordid secret while implying that his information went no further than allegation. Yet if anybody was in a position to know what went on behind the scenes of the Eton Society, as Pop is properly known, it was Haldane. Not only was he a member of it, sporting the Pop carnation in the buttonhole of his top-coat, but by the time he finished he was Captain of the School too. He was hugely proud of belonging to this élite, hanging its rules in the schoolroom at Cherwell, and around them canes decorated with blue ribbons.

Academically, he gave the school its due: 'From an intellectual point of view the education available at Eton in 1905–11 was good.' He had the advantage of being a Colleger, having won a scholarship, rather than one of the Oppidans, boys whose presence at Eton had little to do with scholarship and who were keen to keep it that way. 'It was possible to escape being educated at all, and any Oppidan who made the attempt' – to be educated, not to escape it – 'was liable to bullying which in some cases left him a nervous wreck for life. On the other hand a Colleger could learn a good deal, and I did.' He went back to Oxford on a maths scholarship. Here too there were gangs of thuggish philistines, known as Bloods, who burned books and harassed studious undergraduates. But they posed little threat to a student who weighed in at fifteen stone and had been alpha male at England's alpha school.

Haldane felt comfortable in the role of outsider at the top. At New College he joined the Liberal Club, but also showed the first signs of left-wing sympathies. He served behind the Co-operative Society counter and was impressed by a fellow student who advocated syndicalism, a socialist ideology which urged workers to seize control of their industries and the state by militant action.

In 1913, Oxford's students got an opportunity to show their solidarity with the workers when the city's horse tram drivers went on strike and were replaced by blacklegs. On the first three evenings, strikers and their supporters tried to unharness the horses and were dispersed by police baton charges. Haldane was unable to take part, he later explained, because he was training for a race. On the fourth night, though, he walked up and down Cornmarket Street chanting the Athanasian Creed and the psalm *Eructavit cor meum*. The trams were blocked by the crowd that collected around him, allowing the strikers to loose the horses. He was fined two guineas by the university authorities, 'the first case for over three centuries,' he boasted, 'when a man was punished in Oxford for publicly professing the principles of the Church of England'. A scene-stealing cameo role, a feat of memory, a lengthy canonical Latin quotation, a snook cocked at authority and an Oxonian irony: with this piece of street theatre, J. B. S. established his *modus operandi*.

Meanwhile, Naomi's education plodded on in second class. After leaving the Dragon School, she was taught at home by a governess whose skills as a teacher were patchy at best. Women did not gain the right to obtain full degrees from Oxford until 1920, but Naomi was allowed a peripheral association with the university as a 'home student'. She took some science courses, but they petered out. It was not the drive but the direction: she wrote more than seventy novels, volumes of poetry and other books in the course of a lifetime that lasted to the age of 101. Naomi also involved herself in politics as she grew older, less demonstratively than her brother; she joined the Labour Party, one of whose peers her husband Dick Mitchison eventually became.

Would Naomi have built a career upon her early interest in science had she enjoyed a fairer share of the educational resources and expectations that were invested so disproportionately in her brother? Naomi herself was doubtful. She believed that she could have gone to boarding school if she had made a fuss about it; and her mother would have been delighted if she had become a doctor, as Maya would have liked to have done herself. But Nou had no interest in medicine and a 'love–hate' relationship with science.

That ambivalence may have had much to do with the intense and overwhelming feelings she had for her brother and with the daunting shadow that his gifts cast over her. Naomi had none of Jack's aptitude for numbers, yet was aware from her father's work, and her own collaboration with Jack, how important maths now were for a working scientist. She suspected that she had enjoyed a degree of privilege, getting through her science prelims because the examiners dared not fail a Haldane.

Her mixed feelings also had their roots in her parents' expectations. Although her father did once take her down a mine, it was never anticipated that she might do that kind of thing for a living, whereas her brother had become her father's colleague and fellow scientist by the time he was ten. As adulthood approached, marriage was a certainty; a professional career was merely a vague possibility. And in the corner of her eye she sometimes glimpsed things that had haunted her childhood, mocking her attempts to apply herself to the rational. As late as 1937, on the way home from the Labour Party conference, she 'happened to notice a hobyah type of fairy just going away'.

Cherwell was luminous with minds gifted in both sciences and arts. The physicist Nils Bohr came to visit; young John Gielgud appeared in one of Naomi's plays. She remembered her girlhood in a golden auroral light, like many of her class and age, a time when youth was touched by divinity. Her generation became mortal on 5 August 1914, the day Jack Haldane learned that he had graduated with a First.

After the pinstriped trousers and the high Eton collar, and the gown and mortarboard, came the kilt and the Highland glengarry cap. Boy joined the Black Watch, one of the most famous Scottish regiments, and one of the fiercest too. Their kilts proved suitable for the trenches, once the tartan was camouflaged by khaki aprons, being less prone to rot in the mud than putteed trousers. In the warmth of spring they would go bare-chested and so naked but for their kilts and boots; Lieutenant Haldane enhanced his resemblance to an ancient Celtic warrior with a moustache grown out to form an intimidatory battle crest.

Inside he was a warrior scientist, however, observing men and munitions with detachment. Describing in a letter to Naomi how he had been illuminated by an enemy flare and targeted, he remarked that the Germans' use of pink flares might be 'swank' to show that if their copper supplies were running low, they nonetheless had plenty of strontium. Perhaps, having grown up in a family impressed by German thought, he supposed that Germans thought like him.

'I am enjoying life here very much,' he wrote to his father in February 1915. 'I have got a most ripping job as a bomb officer.' He went on to note that two kinds of men made his best pupils: reckless ones 'who are always breaking rules and things in peace time', and NCOs with sufficient education to 'have faith in the uniformity of Nature'. In other words, the required qualities were those he embodied himself: a love of risk and an appreciation of scientific laws. 'The average man certainly does not like it.' He asked his father to send him the journal *Nature* and tables of sines, cosines and tangents for calculating ranges.

This was where his apprenticeship paid off. He admitted in a letter to his mother that his pupils' nerves would be rubbing off on him had he not taken to smoking a pipe and affecting bored contempt. 'However,' he added, 'I have had too much to do with Uffer for that sort of thing to be likely to frighten me much.'

Haldane quickly cornered the market in small bomb operations. He became a raider, as near to freelance as the Army permitted, venturing up to the German lines and throwing bombs at them; or roving up and down the British front line with a trench mortar crew, firing rounds from one spot and then another. His enthusiasm for the trench mortar was not widely shared. In its primitive state of development, it was a weapon with casualties at each end, and it attracted retaliation. 'I can always start an artillery battle if I like, which is interesting,' he remarked. Other interested parties, the troops who had to withstand the retaliatory fire after Haldane's crew had scrambled away, took a dimmer view. Once he was pushed into a ditch by gunners to prevent him firing a mortar he had placed close to their battery. He was, in fact, and not for the last time, a loose cannon.

'Bombo' Haldane was effectively fearless but realised that this was due to his situation as well as his temperament. 'I find this sort of fighting very enjoyable, also reconnoitring etc.,' he observed to Maya, 'but then this demands coolness rather than dash, and I don't know if I shall like attacking so well.' Night raids demanded cognitive skills, particularly in forming an accurate mental map of the route. The initiative he showed in this 'subaltern's war' allowed him to calculate many of the risks he ran. Once he cycled across a gap in full view of the Germans, calculating that they would be too surprised to react in time and that he would thus improve his standing with his 'less intellectual subordinates', because they would be convinced that he had luck on his side. Exhibitions of voluntary courage also dispelled any suspicions of 'funking', or cowardice.

His faculties of cognition and reason would not help him if he had to go over the top as part of a massed assault. Most of his fellow officers were killed in such an attack during the battle of Aubers Ridge; he was wounded trying to catch up with them after duties elsewhere. 'I seem to remember remarking to an uncomprehending guardsman "The real is rational," a saying of Hegel's which appeared to me to be refuted by the existing circumstances.' At that stage he had not embraced the Marxist dictum that quantity turns into quality.

By contrast, the following period, April 1915, was 'one of the happiest months of my life'. The Rajah of Bomb was awarded the official title of Brigade bomb, trench mortar and rifle grenade officer – 'the best job ever,' he told Uffer. Among his own men, he was popular. They were, however, a select group. He ran a bomb-making workshop in which he made smoking compulsory. This was his heroic idea of a confidence-building measure. 'The chaps who didn't like it resigned, you see, and then we had the right sort of chaps.' As well as selecting out nervousness, it presumably concentrated the minds of those who remained upon the need for care when making bombs.

He was pulled out of the line by his father, who needed his help once again. Richard Haldane, still Lord Chancellor, consulted his brother about how to meet the challenge of chemical warfare, which the Germans had begun to wage with chlorine gas attacks around Ypres. John Scott Haldane immediately left for France, rendezvousing with his son and his Oxford colleague C. G. Douglas. Several years previously, the trio had investigated how carbon monoxide combines with haemoglobin, the resulting paper being J. B. S.'s first scientific publication. Now they spent a week in an improvised gas chamber at a school in St Omer, breathing chlorine with and without various types of respirator. As physiologists, they knew how to avoid killing themselves or the other guinea pigs, but Haldane senior was left with lasting effects, and his son was short of breath for some time after.

His slow rate of progress may have saved his life by delaying his return to his unit. As it was, he was wounded twice while trying to rejoin them for Aubers Ridge. His wounds amounted to a 'Blighty', injury serious enough to warrant evacuation to the home country. As well as pain, he knew fear; he 'jumped like a shot rabbit at any explosion'. Not that it moved him to sympathy for other rabbits of war: this, he judged, was genuine shell-shock, not the 'war neurosis which was usually dignified by that name'.

Soon, however, he was up to his old tricks again. He was posted to Scotland, where he taught soldiers how to use grenades. Although known as 'Safety Catch', for the assiduous way he drew his men's attention to this feature of their weapons, he made a habit of carrying powder, detonators and loose matches around with him in his pockets. In one letter home to Maya, he drew a little diagram of a stick grenade he had accidentally left behind on a recent visit. If she would cut through the fuse and take the detonator off, he instructed her, it would be quite safe for her to send on to him by post. Most sons in uniform would be content with warm socks and handkerchiefs in their parcels from home, but Boy's mother was of steelier mettle.

In October 1916, he was sent out to the Mesopotamian front, where he commanded snipers along a stretch of the river Tigris. A couple of months later, he was injured in an explosion while tackling a fire in a bomb depot. He spent the rest of the war in convalescence, bomb training and India.

Haldane returned to New College, where he had a fellowship lined up, and taught physiology. While continuing to publish papers on genetic linkage, he resumed his experimental purgatories in attempts to build upon his father's great discovery: that breathing is controlled by levels of carbon dioxide in the blood. Early attempts to acidify his blood by drinking dilute hydrochloric acid were unsuccessful, but he achieved the desired effect with ammonium chloride – imbibing more, proportionally, than had proved fatal to a dog. One of these experiments went on for almost two uncomfortable, painful and disturbed weeks. Explaining these ordeals, he pointed out that a rabbit could not tell the experimenter if it had a headache or had lost its sense of smell. He noted with interest the effect of these laboratory staples upon his mood and state of mind: hydrochloric acid provoked exhilaration and irritability; chlorides induced hallucinations.

Throughout his life, J. B. S. also took a passing interest in the effects of organic chemicals upon his consciousness. In his youth, he and Naomi dabbled with chloroform; in his later years, relocated in India, he swallowed *bhang*, a cannabis preparation. If he had to drive a long distance, he would take Benzedrine; his second wife, Helen Spurway, let on that it was used for all-night working sessions when lecture materials had to be completed. 'We must have a shot at cocaine some day,' an earlier lover remarked to him, apropos of nothing, in a letter of November 1923, though what cocaine could add to that mind and ego is hard to imagine.

In 1922, Haldane accepted an offer from Frederick Gowland Hopkins to become Reader in Biochemistry, and in effect Hopkins's deputy, at Cambridge. It was not such a departure as the title might suggest; biochemistry had until recently been known as chemical physiology, and Hopkins recruited Haldane as part of his project to establish it as an independent discipline.

While developing his new theme, J. B. S. continued his physiology experiments and his linkage studies. And, over the ten years he spent at Cambridge, he published all but the last of a series of nine papers that are the core of his contribution to evolutionary science. He set down the principles of the project, 'A Mathematical Theory of Natural and Artificial Selection', in the opening lines of Part I, which appeared in 1924:

> A satisfactory theory of natural selection must be quantitative. In order to establish the view that natural selection is capable for accounting for the known facts of evolution we must show not only that it can cause a species to change, but that it can cause it to change at a rate which will account for present and past transmutations.

In any given case, he continued, we must specify the mode by which the character is inherited, the system of breeding among the organisms, the intensity of selection and its targets, and the rate at which the proportion of organisms showing the character rises or falls. With this information, it should be possible to obtain an equation connecting the intensity of selection with the incidence of the character.

He proceeded to work through different types of selection, ending up with a table showing how many thousands of generations would have to pass for changes to spread through populations. These were theoretical situations, with a slow pressure of one part in a thousand, but in one case he considered an example from nature. This was the peppered moth, whose pale version had by then been replaced in Britain's industrial areas by the dark variant. He calculated that the selective pressure on it must be at least 33 per cent, and perhaps 50. This was a glimpse of a selective power that had not yet appeared in Fisher's papers (which Haldane did not cite) and that would have to wait thirty years for support from field-work. But J. B. S. described it as 'not very intense'. He took natural selection in his stride.

Though the series formally ended in 1932, the year in which his book *The Causes of Evolution* appeared, it continued informally for the rest of his life. In his last year, he noted that he was 'still publishing what could have been sections of it'. He maintained a perennial interest in the power of Darwinian selection. In 1942, he analysed data on the proportion of silver pelts among the fox skins brought to market in Canada over the course of a century. Like the peppered moth, this was a case of artificial selection in the wild: silver fur was more valuable, and so silver foxes were sought out by hunters. Haldane calculated that the recessive gene for silver fur was at a selective disadvantage of 3 per cent a year. In 1954, he calculated a selective intensity of 2.4 per cent from figures on birth weight and mortality among British babies.

Like Fisher, he generally worked with models that disregarded the effects of chance. But he acknowledged the latter and calculated, in Part V of the 'Mathematical Theory', the likelihood that a mutation would survive the vagaries of accident. If it was a dominant gene, its chances were twice its selective advantage. A recessive gene's chances were far more slender, amounting only to the square root of what remained after the advantage was divided by the population size.

Having demonstrated that selective pressure might be torrentially strong, as in the case of the peppered moth, or negligibly weak, as in the case of a recessive gene in a large population, he showed that as far as the fitness of a population was concerned, it might be quite irrelevant. One of his most notable findings, published in 1937, was that if a mutation was harmful enough to keep it rare, the particular degree of harm had no effect on the population's fitness, which was determined solely by the mutation rate. In *Drosophila*, it appeared to be about 3 or 4 per cent, while humans were taxed at 10 per cent.

'Haldane's principle', as it was sometimes known, was the beginning of a train of evolutionary thought from which emerged the idea of 'genetic load', the degree to which the average genotype of a population falls short of the optimum. To Hermann Muller, who developed these ideas independently, it had implications for humans that required eugenic solutions. To researchers in the nuclear age, it promised answers to ominous questions about radiation damage. To Bill Hamilton, who became convinced that humankind was at mortal risk from the mutations that it was accumulating thanks to medical indulgence, it posed natural selection as an imperative for human survival.

It never became such a burden for Haldane, but he did develop it into an argument that posed a fundamental question about how evolution worked. In 1957, he published a paper called 'The Cost of Natural Selection'. He noted that in Kettlewell's recently published experiments on the peppered moth – in which he naturally took an interest, having predicted the results thirty years before – the frequency of the more conspicuous form could be halved in a day. What if selection had been acting with such force on ten independent characters instead of one? Only one in a thousand would have survived. If natural selection was too intense, the species would be wiped out.

Haldane described a situation similar to that in the 1937 paper: the cost of natural selection had little or nothing to do with its intensity. Since mutations balanced out – severer ones were eliminated more quickly, milder ones lasted longer – the loss of fitness depended on how fast they occurred, not how damaging they were. They went sooner or later through the deaths of their bearers. Assuming that the process of elimination required deaths on top of those which would occur anyway, Haldane calculated that to replace one gene with another, at least ten or twenty times the number of individuals in a generation would have to die. Sometimes the multiple might be as high as 100; thirty was a reasonable average, and the process might take 300 generations.

These calculations provided the stimulus for the 'neutral theory' of evolution, whose adherents suspect that most evolutionary change confers neither advantage nor disadvantage. Their lenses are focused, however, at the molecular level rather than that of organs or of behaviour. The first data on the sequences of amino acids that make up proteins such as haemoglobin began to appear in the 1960s. Motoo Kimura, a Japanese geneticist whose idol as a youth was Sewall Wright, realised that these varied too much to be squared with Haldane's terms. He concluded that most of them are caused by random processes, not natural selection. Neo-Darwinian orthodoxy challenged the theory at first, then decided it was beside the point. 'As far as we are then concerned,' wrote Richard Dawkins, speaking of adaptation, 'a neutral mutation might as well not exist because neither we, nor natural selection, can see it.' The dish would taste the same even if some of the words in the recipe had changed to a different font.

One of the first critics was John Maynard Smith, who challenged Kimura by questioning the assumptions of his own mentor, Haldane. They were, he argued, true only in exceptional circumstances. One of the assumptions was that the fitnesses of individual genes must be multiplied together. But as Maynard Smith pointed out, selection could take a bundle of genes as its target: if a bird's survival through the winter depended on its position in a pecking order, selection might act upon genes affecting a range of characters, such as behaviour, strength and disease resistance. Three hundred generations might not be needed to replace one gene with another; it could happen ten times as fast, or a hundred. 'Haldane's Dilemma' had been answered by his vicar on Earth, solving the puzzle in favour of adaptation.

While warming to his new scientific themes in the mid-1920s, Haldane discovered that he liked the taste of publicity. Asked to give a talk to the Heretics Society, he dusted off and revised an essay he had written as an undergraduate in 1912. A scout for the publisher Kegan Paul was in the audience; a smart pocket volume ensued, in 1923, under the title *Daedalus, or Science and the Future*. Bertrand Russell responded with *Icarus, or the Future of Science*; other titles ran the gamut of prophecy from *Thrasymachus, the Future of Morals* to *Nuntius, or Advertising and its Future*.

Daedalus opened with a cinematic image from the Great War. 'Through a blur of dust and fumes there appear, quite suddenly, great black and yellow masses of smoke which seem to be tearing up the surface of the earth and disintegrating the works of man with an almost visible hatred. These form the chief part of the picture, but somewhere in the middle distance one can see a few irrelevant looking human figures, and soon there are fewer.' The 'huge substantive oily black masses' seem to be the actors; the men merely 'their servants, and playing an inglorious, subordinate, and fatal part in the combat'. Science, materialised as machinery and chemicals, seemed to be the future.

Classical physics and chemistry, wantonly applied, were only the fanfare. The ensuing movements would be conducted by relativistic physics and achieve their profoundest effects through biology, 'the centre of scientific interest'. Science would enter an era of Kantian idealism; the prophet of this higher understanding was Einstein, 'the greatest Jew since Jesus'. Haldane was beginning to reveal his gift for speaking in quotes.

Einstein, he believed, 'has told us that space, time, and matter are shadows of the fifth dimension, and the heavens have declared his glory . . . We may not call ourselves materialists, but we do interpret the activities of the moon, the Thames, influenza, and aeroplanes in terms of matter. Our ancestors did not, nor, in all probability, will our descendants.' As the immediate descendant of an idealist, he was honouring his father. By associating the science of the future with the magic of the past, he hinted at the irrational streak that his sister knew he shared with her. He affirmed it by raising the possibility that science might one day uphold spiritualism's claims.

J. B. S. retained these occult sympathies after he had decisively rejected idealism in favour of dialectical materialism. In 1943, he told a correspondent – Frank Allaun, later a Labour MP – that he was inclined to think that people could make telepathic contact with each other using planchette boards. Scientists did tend to take an indulgent view of the paranormal in the early to middle decades of the twentieth century, though. Confident in their public standing, they saw it as a diversion rather than a threatening ideology. 'I dare say it does happen,' said Haldane of telepathy, 'but it's still a damned intrusion on one's privacy.'

Daedalus did not neglect the nuts and bolts of futurology – wind farms, new drugs to enhance everyday performance, and so on. Its centrepiece, though, was a vision of a world transformed by genetic engineering. Haldane presented extracts from a fictional essay written by a 'rather stupid' undergraduate in his first term at Cambridge, 150 years hence.

It opened with an account of the 'so-called eugenic movement' of the twentieth century. 'A number of earnest persons, having discovered the existence of biology, attempted to apply it in its then very crude condition to the production of a race of super-men. . .' Haldane also intimated his disdain for eugenicists later on in *Daedalus*, observing that the 'eugenic official' favoured by some enthusiasts would be 'a compound . . . of the policeman, the priest and the procurer'. But his aversion was like that of a mainstream Anglican for evangelical missionaries. He accepted that eugenics would work in principle. His plodding undergraduate recalls that the twentieth-century eugenists succeeded in preventing much heritable illness. Although they earned the hatred of 'the classes they somewhat gratuitously regarded as undesirable parents', the idea that their prejudice was gratuitous is cast into doubt by the student's subsequent declaration that, had it not been for advanced reproductive technologies, civilisation would have collapsed because of 'the greater fertility of the less desirable members of the population'.

Instead, the cream of each generation was selected to provide the genetic material for the next, which was produced industrially from extracted ovaries. Each generation was an improvement on the one before, producing more first-class music while committing fewer thefts. Meanwhile, the sea had turned purple, thanks to a genetically engineered alga which had, by happy accident, colonised the oceans and nurtured a cornucopia of fish to feed humankind.

Closing his imaginary student's book, Haldane observed that, if sex were indeed to be detached from reproduction, 'mankind will be free in an altogether new sense'. Although his predictions were comprehensively unfulfilled, he anticipated some of the concerns that would preoccupy his successors at the turn of the next century as they faced new prospects for the manipulation of human genotypes. Culture might no longer outpace heredity: national character might be altered by selective breeding as quickly as institutions could be altered by political methods.

The technologies described by his student fell into the category of 'biological inventions', in which new biological relationships were created among humans or between them and other species. These, Haldane emphasised, were different in kind from physical or chemical inventions. Their effect upon humanity was more fundamental and intimate; the reactions they provoked were correspondingly stronger. 'There is no great invention, from fire to flying, which has not been hailed as an insult to some god. But if every physical and chemical invention is a blasphemy, every biological invention is a perversion.' Milking a cow, allowing its secretions to rot and then eating them: there was a 'radical indecency' in our relation to cattle, yet these practices had come to seem entirely natural and were now embedded in ritual. The same went for the sexual act, which he believed had been the subject of the most fundamental biological invention of all, one which 'altered the path of sexual selection . . . and changed our idea of beauty from the steatapygous Hottentot to the modern European, from the Venus of Brassempouy to the Venus of Milo'. He added that some races had yet to discover the innovation.

Although even Haldane drew the line at referring to face-to-face intercourse explicitly, the effect was to enhance the impression that he was a man with an outstanding suite of endowments. It suggested a virility to match the heroism that his opening reference to a battle scene had recalled, as well as his muscular intellect. And, as a biologist, he was 'the most romantic figure on earth'. The modern biologist might seem to be 'a poor little scrubby underpaid man', as vulnerable and insignificant as the creatures that filled his life of study, but he was driven on by a higher power.

He was an iconoclast too. Thomas Huxley had ruled that evolution and ethics were separate; the latter were not to be worked out on the basis of the former. (His lukewarm attitude to natural selection may have owed much to the need he felt to keep evolution under control.) That view was no longer tenable. Scientific progress inevitably changed morality. Passive resignation in the face of epidemic disease might once have been virtuous, but modern knowledge of hygiene rendered it an offence. Patriotism might once have been a simple virtue, but with the monstrous power of modern weaponry, it became a menace. Good and evil were essentially matters of degree. 'We must learn not to take traditional morals too seriously,' he opined. And because all religions insisted that morality was fixed, 'there can be no truce between science and religion'.

In this Haldane demonstrated how he had won the war. He had witnessed, taken part in and nearly become part of mass slaughter on an unprecedented scale. Many of his contemporaries were dead or broken. The Aftermath was filled with a nervous and hysterical brittleness. Values that had seemed eternal now appeared hollow, placing the very idea of values in question. But Haldane's sense of self was robust enough to withstand the onslaught and thus to continue to support the complex structure of his world view. He also had the benefit of an upbringing in which religion had played little part and philosophy had loomed large. His values were obtained by reason, not revelation. When the sky of Europe fell on their heads, lesser men were left in despair, perceiving only emptiness beyond. Jack Haldane did not feel let down by God, and he did not take it personally.

Aldous Huxley made a name for himself with his Aftermath novels, indicting the emptiness of fashionable society and dragging unwieldy philosophical discussions in to fill the void. Haldane had no time for his family friend's hand-wringing. 'It took a staphylococcus to make the man who most perfectly voices the spiritual muddle of the English middle class intellectuals,' he wrote in his draft autobiography, referring acidly to the infection which had left Huxley almost blind. 'He can only repeat "*Oh, comme j'ai souffert*"...', attributing his unhappiness to his deceitful heart. It was as if he was so wicked that he deserved his blindness, jeered Haldane, enjoying the clarity of vision of the 1930s leftist, 'or his generation so much wickeder than that which came before them as to deserve fascism'.

It was below the belt, but then so had been Haldane's involuntary appearance as the basis of a character in Huxley's novel *Antic Hay*. Shearwater was a scientist as imagined by a jealous novelist, wrapped up in his physiological investigations and unaware that his wife is conducting her own physiological experiments with his friends. Although he shared no traits of character with J. B. S., he was recognisable by his immense head. (A similar figure also appeared in *The Flying Draper*, by Ronald Fraser.) Huxley was a house guest who helped himself to his hosts' lives rather than their spoons. He turned John Scott Haldane into a figure of fun too, using him as the prototype for the abstracted scientist Lord Tantamount in *Point Counter Point*. And he appropriated *Daedalus*'s idea of industrialised breeding for his most famous novel, *Brave New World*.

Daedalus became the talk of Oxford, to the mortification of John Scott Haldane. Jack's mother wrote to Julian Huxley, asking him not to poke fun at the Senior Partner, as she used to call her husband, about it. 'I knew he'd object,' she told Huxley, 'but had no idea till to-day how really unhappy he is – odd people these Liberals and no accounting for them!'

The author himself had his taste for public controversy whetted, and he returned to the 'To-day and Tomorrow' lists in 1925 with *Callinicus: A Defence of Chemical Warfare*. Callinicus, J. B. S. explained, was the eighth-century Syrian inventor of the incendiary substance called Greek fire, and his name means 'he who conquers in a noble or beautiful manner'. Gas attacks on the Western Front had inspired a peculiar terror – which persists to the present day – and moves were afoot to prohibit the use of chemical weapons. Writing before these initiatives succeeded, under the Geneva Convention of 1925, Haldane argued that to discriminate between chemical and other weapons was irrational. The terror of gas arose from wartime propaganda, its effect on 'uneducated' soldiers and a grotesque interpretation of sporting conduct.

He made full use of his ability to speak both as an expert and from experience. 'Besides being wounded, I have been buried alive, and on several occasions I have been asphyxiated to the point of unconsciousness. The pain and discomfort arising from the other experiences were utterly negligible compared with those produced by a good septic shell-wound.' And the latter was far more deadly. Mustard gas killed one soldier for every forty it put out of action; shells killed one in three.

It was also a weapon to which a colonial power had a ready defence. American Army investigations had reported that 80 per cent of black soldiers were immune to it, as were 20 per cent of whites. This was unsurprising, Haldane considered, as the blistering caused by the substance resembled sunburn, to which dark-skinned people were resistant. He foresaw a new balance of forces, between German chemical industries and French colonial manpower, and a new scene on the battlefield: 'Suddenly, behind the usual barrage of high explosive shells appears a line of tanks supported by negroes in gas masks . . .' There would be sufficient immune white officers to command them.

Haldane's assumption here was entirely conventional; but whether he believed that colonised peoples were innately incapable of commanding themselves, in war or in government, is unclear. Later on, in the light of Nazism, he began to write against racism. His position on the eve of the Second World War was still equivocal. Like many other scientists of liberal or left-wing dispositions, he rested comfortably upon the amply overlapping test scores of different groups and the undecided question of whether the differences were caused by nature or nurture. This resulted in a posture that was elliptical at best, and tended to convolution. 'If I stated that race A is superior to race B . . . I might mean that the least musical negro was more musical than the most musical Europeans, or that the cleverest negro was stupider than the stupidest Europeans. I think it will be generally conceded that no examples of that kind are to be found.'

Underneath the circumlocution, he was still guided by the assumption, revealed in his remark about sexual intercourse in *Daedalus*, that different psychological traits had evolved in different races. He acknowledged his view that slight innate differences in intelligence-test scores would be apparent even if the subjects' environment was the same, 'but I should hesitate to say in which direction they should be found, except to suggest that as the intelligence tests have all been devised by whites, they would be likely to show a certain superiority of whites over negroes'. Despite his reputation for trenchancy, Haldane had a well-developed gift for having it both ways.

As he negotiated the treacherous racial terrain, he threw out an argument that echoed his path-breaking first paper on the mathematics of natural selection. In some American tests, he noted, blacks in the north had done better than whites. Perhaps this was innate, but if so, it showed that selection for intelligence could act extremely swiftly. This was a contentious claim, and the only precedent for such swift selection was the example he had published in 1924. The analogy must have been irresistible, though Haldane understandably refrained from drawing his readers' attention to it. Like the peppered moth in England, the melanic forms might be undergoing intense selection pressure in the industrial north.

Whereas *Daedalus* had highlighted Haldane's iconoclasm, *Callinicus* illustrated his conventional views on a number of issues besides race. Having a bombproof ego, he had no difficulty in contemplating more of what he had just undergone, and felt no need to reconsider the ideology that had brought it about. There would be another war in due course; 'I prefer that my country should be on the winning side'. The fantastic predictions of *Daedalus* were replaced by a doggedly conservative view of the future of war. Chemistry was not far from its limits, in both gas and explosives; neither would become much more powerful. The power of the atom would remain untapped even when 'some successor of mine is lecturing to a party spending a holiday on the moon'.

That remark had originally been directed to the summer holidaymakers at a Swiss resort who were the first to hear *Callinicus*, thanks to a lecture programme instigated by the holiday entrepreneur Sir Henry Lunn. It was not exactly deckchair material, but at least Haldane spared the vacationers the demonstration he inflicted upon an audience in a Scottish village. Telling them that a chemical agent used in the war had been extracted from cayenne pepper, he vaporised a spoonful of the spice over a spirit lamp, giving them first-hand experience of pepper gas. Nobody ever popularised science quite like J. B. S. Haldane.

Charlotte Burghes was not altogether sorry to be wandering around Cambridge on a Saturday afternoon in 1924, transported by the college lawns and the river banks, dazzling in the emerald green of exquisite privilege. She had taken to working seven days a week, as a reporter for the *Express* newspapers, to get away from the debacle of her marriage. Charlotte had imagination, drive, intelligence and sensual beauty. She also had a dissolute husband, a young son and a lifestyle beyond her means. In a word, she was exciting.

Charlotte was killing time while she waited for the man for whom she had made the journey from London. She had been too impatient to wait any longer for a reply to the letter she had sent him a couple of weeks earlier; not because he was hot news – though she had easily persuaded her editor that he was a story – but because she was anxious to get her novel going. She had hit upon the question that Fisher was to raise in the *Genetical Theory*: what would happen if parents could choose the sex of their offspring? The title, *Man's World*, came to her as well, but when she began to explore the theme, she found herself stymied by her lack of scientific education. She needed a guide, she realised. Then she read *Daedalus* and decided, 'This is my man!'

Eventually, hot and footsore, she was shown to Haldane's rooms in Trinity College. He received her courteously, weighed her down with a pile of textbooks, and took her eventual admission that she was a journalist as well as an aspiring novelist in good part. The Reader in Biochemistry informed her that, if she got her facts right, he would call at the *Express* building in Fleet Street at one o'clock on Monday to take her to lunch.

They dined on lobsters and hock, and talked of poetry, mostly Racine's. Charlotte found herself in the awesome presence of everything she had always believed she should be. She had been born into a prosperous bourgeois family that had steadily lost its means of support as her father's fur-trading business ran into mounting difficulties. Instead of going to Bedford College, which provided women with higher education, she learnt shorthand and typing. A job at a concert agency gave her an entrée to culture, and she became friendly with the ballet dancer Anna Pavlova, but a secretary she remained.

The final blow to the family finances had been the wartime seizure of her father Joseph Franken's remaining assets on the grounds that, as a German Jew, he was an enemy alien. He and his wife departed for the United States; back in Britain, his daughter was barred from war work. She ended the war as a press officer for a music publisher, ghostwriting copy which appeared in women's magazines under the bylines of the company's star performers. Although she saw redeeming social value in journalism – once she had graduated from the *Daily Express* gossip column to the leader page – she believed that her proper place was in a world of culture from which financial exigencies had removed her.

Her circumstances thus suited both of them, for 'teaching was J. B. S.'s supreme hobby, as learning was mine'. They quickly became lovers and discovered a mutual desire for children, which was to become the deepest bond between them. She expressed it as a symbol in one of her letters to him, signing herself as a drawing of a circle with a cross at its lower pole and a foetus within. Almost from the start of the affair, he was urging her to marry him for the sake of 'that little devil of an Unborn', as Charlotte put it. His sister Naomi warned her that he wanted a child far more than a wife.

In the summer of 1924, Charlotte asked her husband for a divorce. He refused and insisted on keeping their son, Ronnie. The lovers were therefore obliged to have their adultery witnessed. The arrangements proved tricky – 'Could you manage 4 o'clock on Monday?' their legal representative inquired – and required the hiring of a private detective, a standard procedure in those days. Charlotte did not care for the first hotel they chose, Haldane recalled, so they asked the investigator to follow them to the next, and gave him one of their suitcases to carry. He duly appeared in the bedroom the next morning, but there was a complication: in their replies to the divorce petition, both denied that their stay had been adulterous.

The arrangements were the stuff of farce, and as Peter Medawar observed, a chaste adultery added a touch of comic opera. Haldane's declaration also led to a posthumous indignity being visited upon him. His biographer Ronald Clark suggested that his sexual boasts were a 'charade' to compensate for his failure to father a child and his underlying shyness with women. Medawar and the poet Stephen Spender both gleefully related Julian Huxley's claim that Haldane's penis was diminutive. Charlotte herself claimed that Haldane was impotent, according to her biographer Judith Adamson. It was a canard, assisted inadvertently by Naomi, who placed the archive file containing Charlotte's letters to her brother under embargo until 2000. After the millennium it could be revealed that the ex-wife who made slighting remarks about his potency and his truss was once the ardent lover who hailed him as 'My pink pillar . . .'

At the time, however, the couple's denial served as part of Haldane's defence against the *Sex Viri*, a committee of six senior university figures who sought his dismissal on the grounds of 'gross and habitual immorality'. (After the episode, in which Haldane inevitably followed the convention of pronouncing a Latin 'v' as 'w', a seventh member was added.) He lost, but won his appeal, having called as witnesses his professor, his father and his sister.

Charlotte and Jack married in 1926. She had her man, 'Big, fat, bald, sensual, funny, grumpy, canine, pontifical', and for a while the two of them were happy. They moved into Roebuck House, in a suburb of Cambridge. Charlotte reinvented the former Roebuck Inn as an intellectual hostelry, where talented but unstable young men would drink whisky and pick out jazz tunes on her Bechstein piano. In due course she flirted or had affairs with one or two of them, including Martin Case, who remained a friend and colleague of her husband's, and the future novelist Malcolm Lowry. She was prepared to allow Jack similar licence, but whether or how he exercised it is not on record.

Although Charlotte's first husband was given custody of their son in the divorce settlement, Ronnie Burghes came to live with his mother. J. B. S.'s desire for a son did not translate into an empathy with children in general. He wrote a number of acclaimed children's stories, but even in these he could sometimes sound like a professor bending stiffly down to improve unformed minds: 'Bind him in chains of brass, or better of tungsten, which hath a higher melting point . . .' Nor did he manage to form much of a bond with Ronnie. The boy enjoyed being taken for walks, upon which he was fed the names of plants, but soon came to feel that he could not keep up. Where Haldane did not appear to find him inadequate, he treated him as a rival. His children's stories began when Ronnie, aged twelve, wrote one for his mother. 'Well, if he is writing fairy-tales I suppose I had better do so too,' harrumphed J. B. S.

At first Charlotte and Jack worked well together. She used the skills she had acquired in journalism and promotion to sell his articles abroad; he did not especially need the money, but he was proud of the fees he could command in the marketplace. Politically they were of similar mind. Charlotte had grown up under the shadow of anti-Semitism, and it had steered her to the left. Both were keenly interested in the young Soviet experiment, and when the Russian plant geneticist Nikolai Vavilov invited J. B. S. to visit the Soviet Union, in the summer of 1928, they jumped at the chance.

Under the Red Star they saw things somewhat differently. Their tour included some of the lavish entertainment that the Soviet authorities would routinely apply to divert their foreign guests' attention from the lot of ordinary Soviet citizens. Vavilov, in Charlotte's words 'a handsome man in his early forties with little dark twinkling Tatar eyes – rather like Lenin's – a great love of life, women and wine, and a sense of humour', threw a spectacular party for them at his Moscow institute. But they also experienced life without such privileges, staying in a modest flat in the Arbat district and queuing along with everybody else for exit visas. Charlotte departed with a sense of relief, but J. B. S. was immensely impressed. 'To him,' according to her, 'its outstanding characteristic was the Soviet attitude to science and scientists.' He was also impressed by the scientists themselves and their leading role in the measurement of natural selection. Had it not been for the language barrier, the familiar founding trinity of the modern synthesis might well have been a quartet including the Russian geneticist Sergei Chetverikov.

Despite Charlotte's mixed feelings – which were accentuated in print, for she aired them in the course of recanting communism twenty years later – she and Jack were being drawn into the Soviet orbit. They became part of a broader movement among western intellectuals in general and Cambridge ones in particular. The Dunn Laboratory, where Haldane was based, became a hotbed of leftism among the university's science establishments, as did the Cavendish physics laboratory. Haldane was not yet a comrade, though. In 1933, he left Cambridge to take the chair of genetics at University College in London. He was soon complaining that UC was 'as full of bloody Communists as Cambridge'.

Haldane had already extended his academic reach beyond Cambridge. He had become a part-time genetics researcher at the John Innes Horticultural Institution, in the south London suburb of Wimbledon, and professor of physiology at the Royal Institution. By the time he left Cambridge – and within a few years of the scandal that almost ended his career – not only was his academic foundation secure, but he had also been accepted as a Fellow of the Royal Society. 'Prof', as he came to like being known, was also an established public intellectual, a rising celebrity and, as his biographer Ronald Clark points out, a 'character'. The British generally have a soft spot for characters, and will tolerate in them behaviour or views that they would ordinarily consider unacceptable. A character pays a price for that tolerance, however, in credibility.

When the Spanish Civil War broke out, the Haldanes rallied to the cause, but each in separate ways. Jack kitted himself out in motorcycle leathers, from cap to trousers, and made for Madrid. He experienced modern aerial bombing and narrowly escaped death by it; the elderly woman who had been sharing a park bench with him did not. Charlotte's son Ronnie, sixteen years old, volunteered for the International Brigade; Jack insisted that he should take a gas mask. Charlotte herself went to Paris, where she worked as a clandestine *responsable* for International Brigade volunteers, looking after them as they prepared to make their way to Spain. When Ronnie was wounded, she made a Blighty of it, using her Communist Party contacts to get him home.

It was not surprising that the Party obliged, for she had proved herself to be just the kind of person they were looking for: a sympathiser with talents for both conspiracy and publicity, ideal for leading front organisations. She had been working for the Communist International in Paris, and in 1937 the Comintern sent her on a propaganda mission to China.

During that year, her husband became a Marxist. They had always shared political sympathies, and now their sentiments were being hardened into a common party line. But their marriage was decaying: within a few years, Party discipline was the only thing that kept them together.

She probably did not realise it, but Charlotte had displaced the most passionate of the women who loved Jack Haldane. His sister Naomi affirmed that he was 'the love of her life'. She hinted at an erotic undercurrent in this passion, recalling an incident on a walking holiday in France where they lay down in an old quarry to sleep off food and wine, and 'turned dizzily towards one another. And suddenly Jack was shocked to his respectable Haldane soul. I wasn't. But that was all.' Jack was notorious for his urge to *épater les bourgeois*, but that time he was the *bourgeois épaté*. A point to Naomi, who liked to boast of sexual daring as much as her brother, but was more subtle about it.

When Naomi's son Geoff died of meningitis, aged nine, she went straight to her brother. But Jack denied her his sympathy and blamed her for her child's death. Charlotte had recently published a book, *Motherhood and its Enemies*, which condemned modern women who put their careers before their traditional duties. Naomi was devastated. Driving home from Cambridge in darkness, her son Denny next to her, she ran the car into a wall. She pulled herself together, took Denny to rejoin her other children in Oxford, and turned her back on her brother.

Parenthood, of course, was the one thing that Jack wanted desperately and never experienced; and the one event in which Naomi had won the competition between the two of them. He was callous and perhaps cruel, but not contemptible like Aldous Huxley, who saw fit to avail himself of the tragedy of Geoff's death for an episode in *Point Counter Point*.

Like so many others, J. B. S. was quick to appreciate the power of Marxism as a language of moral denunciation. In 1936, when John Scott Haldane faced the final reckoning for his gas-corroded lungs and his seventy-five years, Naomi told the press that he was ill. Jack made an ideological issue out of the ensuing quarrel, but the conflict ran deeper than class and was more primitively expressed. As their father lay dying upstairs, Naomi and Jack fought like children in the dining room: 'I bit his arm; he twisted my wrist,' remembered Naomi. After the cremation of the Senior

Partner, Jack was entrusted with taking the ashes to be scattered at Cloan, the family seat in Scotland. He insisted on travelling third class on the train, as the workers would, with the package up on the luggage rack.

The final straw for Naomi came when she received a legacy from an aunt and shared it with Jack as an attempt at conciliation. Unearned wealth was perhaps not the ideal olive branch: he gave it to the Party. Many years later the rift was bridged, according to Naomi, when Helen Spurway 'with great courage knocked our stupid heads together and restored some of what had been lost'.

Spurway came into Jack's life in the mid-1930s, as his distance from his wife and his sister grew. Like Charlotte, she was bold and passionate, leaving an impression in her wake of an appetite for neat gin and messy affairs. Unlike Charlotte, however, she was a scientist, with aptitudes that complemented Prof's. And she found throughout her life that her scientific and her erotic passions were inseparable. Perhaps she implicitly acknowledged this when, as a University College undergraduate, she announced her intention to marry Professor Haldane.

8

Comrade Prof

'In the application of Marxism to science, we must proceed with the very greatest caution,' Haldane warned in 1938, showing the opposite of a convert's zeal. 'At best Marxism will only tell a scientist what to look for. It will rarely, if ever, tell him what he is going to find, and if it is going to be made a dogma, it is worse than useless.' These were the words of a Marxist who was not yet a communist, or at least not one carrying a Party card.

With hindsight, the most egregious – and damning – thing about the red recruits of the 1930s is that they went over to Moscow during the period when Soviet terror reached its most monstrous extremes. They were not, however, walking into turpitude with their eyes open. On the contrary, they believed that the communist cause was a higher one. The purges, the show trials and the liquidations were reported in the West, but the West had lost credibility in the eyes of many of its citizens. Europe was steadily filling with dictatorships, and the surviving democracies appeared morally and politically bankrupt before them. And the prevalence of economic bankruptcy, in the years of Depression and mass destitution, completed the indictment. While the intellectuals swung left as they saw the Fascist right tighten its grip on Europe, the broken men and the hungry children of the industrial districts stiffened the resolve of the working-class militants who officered and led the Party. Capitalism had yet to show that it could keep the people secure from want; communism had yet to show that it could not.

The converts of the 1930s thus did not flock to the red banner in a spirit of revolutionary optimism, but were driven to it by a sense of crisis and of duty. In a time of emergency measures, they found it easy to believe that reports of the Terror were distorted accounts of the Soviet Union's response to genuine threats. If they retained doubts, they gave Stalin the benefit of them.

Haldane presented his own conversion as the result of negative political and positive scientific influence: 'Till 1933 I tried to keep out of politics, but the support given by the British Government to Hitler and Mussolini forced me to enter the political field . . . Mr Chamberlain's policy, and recent developments in physics and biology, combined to convince me of the truth of the Marxist philosophy.' Haldane considered that dialectical materialism, which sees contradictions and oppositions as the cause of change in the world, helped make sense of quantum theory and relativity. He added that Soviet biologists were finding Marxism to be a valuable guide, as he was himself. But although he offered his evolutionary knowledge as a tribute to his new universal philosophy – arranging a dialectical sequence in which natural selection 'negates' mutation, for example – he gave no instances of how Marxism had actually helped him do his science. Sixty years on, a historical study by Arthur M. Shapiro did not detect any increased Marxist influence after Haldane's conversion in the late 1930s. Shapiro did, however, find that Haldane's series of papers on selection became increasingly dialectical through the 1920s. Haldane's guide was not Marx but his father, from whom he had learned about Hegel and dialectical thought. (He did not get dialectical materialism from Marx either: it stemmed from Engels and was developed by Lenin.)

Marxism was also a beacon for those in the West who rejected the spiritual self-pity of Aldous Huxley or the political submissiveness of Neville Chamberlain. Speaking in commemoration of his uncle, Richard Haldane, he presented Marxism as the upholder and rightful inheritor of values abandoned by the bourgeoisie. Marxists, he said, were the only intelligent people who preserved their grandparents' belief in progress. Theirs, however, was a 'grimmer optimism'.

Even at the start, confidently affirming science's independence from Marxism, J. B. S. felt obliged to deny that Soviet biologists were suffering for their ideas. In the 'violent discussions' on Darwinism that had taken place in the USSR, some geneticists had been called anti-Darwinian because they had discarded the idea, entertained by Darwin for want of a mechanism of heredity, that use or disuse could influence the inheritance of characters. But, so far as Haldane knew, none of them had lost their jobs as a result.

His information may well have been inadequate. The American geneticist Hermann Muller had been reluctant to say too much when he visited the Haldanes in the late 1930s, having got out of the Soviet Union, after several years' service in the Academy of Science's Institute of Genetics, by volunteering for a medical unit in Spain. Muller delayed talking to J. B. S. at all, judging from Haldane's letters that the newly Marxist professor was 'at present having his political opinions impressed upon him with a rubber stamp', and anticipated that Haldane would simply think he had become a reactionary. The American was also unwilling to speak out in public for fear that his disillusionment would be appropriated by the Soviet Union's enemies. But he told the Haldanes of the creeping Party assault on Nikolai Vavilov, who had brought him to the Institute of Genetics and who had hosted the Haldanes on the visit in which Jack had been so impressed by the way the Soviets treated their scientists.

Vavilov's chief tormentor was Trofim Lysenko, a Ukrainian agronomist who rose to power by turning his scientific ignorance into a weapon of ideological struggle. Lysenko understood that the regime wanted the same things from biology that it wanted from every other sector of Soviet activity: ideological conformity and increased output. He presented it with an irresistible combination of practical and ideological boasts, claiming to have devised a number of techniques for getting higher yields from crops on the basis of a theoretical analysis that subjected neo-Darwinism to Marxist scrutiny and found it wanting. Lysenko's message was that acquired characteristics most certainly could be inherited, enabling agricultural progress to reach the heroic rates that the central plans required.

He conducted his campaign like any other communist factional struggle, with labels, denunciations and claims to doctrinal authority. Raking the embers of the dispute between the early Mendelians and the surviving Darwinists, Lysenko and his colleagues dubbed their opponents 'Mendel–Morganists', the second part of the term referring to the American geneticist Thomas Morgan. With this label, they dismissed the emerging evolutionary synthesis in which Soviet geneticists were involved. Mendelism was still the enemy of Darwinism, whose value Marxism recognised. They also came up with the denunciatory compound 'Morgano-Weismannite', adding to the cast of villains the German biologist August Weismann, who had undialectically insisted that the cells from which new organisms formed were isolated from changes affecting other cells, making Lamarckian inheritance impossible. The Lysenko camp called itself Michurinist, after a cranky fruit horticulturist with Lamarckian leanings.

In several respects, the Lysenkoites harked back to views prevalent among Russian evolutionists in the nineteenth century, who saw Darwin through Lamarckian eyes, mistrusted the influence of Malthus upon him and were inclined to emphasise co-operation rather than competition, especially within species. Though these thinkers had opposed the Tsar, they embraced ideologies equally unacceptable to the Soviet regime, such as the co-operative anarchism promoted by Prince Peter Kropotkin, whose thesis on evolution was called *Mutual Aid*.

Haldane's initial stance towards the dispute was detached, with a touch of condescension. There was no evidence for the 'rather mechanical' Lamarckian views that had become popular in the Soviet Union, where scientists were not yet thinking as dialectically as they might. Just because a hypothesis was dialectical did not mean it was true, though. Ronald Fisher argued that selection would favour a gene which dampened the effects of a common mutation, rendering dominant mutants recessive and encouraging the accumulation of modifier genes. This was a 'beautifully dialectical theory', resting upon the antagonism between mutation and selection, but it was contradicted by the facts.

Haldane mentioned this, he said, to refute the prevalent belief 'that acceptance of Marxism is an emotional cataclysm which completely ruins one's judgement'. As a Marxist, he observed, he hoped that Fisher's argument would prove to have a wider validity than currently seemed likely. As a British Marxist, he had yet to realise that there was more at stake than an opportunity to exercise his scientific wit at his reactionary colleague's expense.

First-hand information from the Soviet Union became harder to obtain as the authorities closed off contact between Soviet geneticists and their western colleagues. The International Congress of Genetics was due to be held in Moscow in 1937, but was cancelled; the Soviets declined to send a delegation to its replacement, held in Edinburgh in 1939. It fell to Vavilov to communicate the prevarications and excuses to his friends in the West. At the height of the Terror, in 1937, Vavilov and several colleagues also signed a letter to Haldane denying that he or other scientists had been arrested, assuring Haldane that 'arrests on the ground of scientific opinions are quite impossible'. So that, as far as Haldane was concerned, was all right then.

Haldane remained confident that Soviet ideology was compatible with his own understanding of biology. In *The Inequality of Man*, written in the early 1930s, he had predicted that the 'test of the devotion of the Union of Socialist Soviet Republics to science will, I think, come when the accumulation of the results of human genetics, demonstrating what I believe to be the fact of innate human inequality, becomes important'. He was wrong: the test was that which the Lysenkoites were already beginning to apply.

Like Julian Huxley and other scientists, he felt an increasingly pressing obligation to comment on claims about human inequality as the Nazi regime developed its racial project. In the centre and on the left, a new sense of responsibility about race was developing. Before the Third Reich, neither Huxley nor Haldane had bothered to conceal their contempt for black Americans. In 1924, Huxley had argued that white admixture was making black Americans more capable and therefore more discontented: 'The American negro is making trouble because of the American white blood that is in him.' Haldane likewise saw America's race question as one of how to contain the 'negro' rather than how to liberate 'him'. 'So if you keep the negro out of cars, factories, and so forth, or frighten him away from contact with whites by an occasional lynching,' he wrote in *The Inequality of Man*, 'you drive him back to the cotton fields where he lives healthily and breeds rapidly, thus creating a negro problem for future generations.'

There had always been a sharp dissonance between the principles of the American Constitution and the rules applied to its black minority. As far as Haldane was concerned, however, the fundamental flaw lay in the Constitution itself. He was never greatly concerned with race in itself, but his belief in heritable inequality was fundamental to his understanding of society. In 1938, he opened his book *Heredity and Politics* with a comparison of the American and Soviet positions on human equality. Thomas Jefferson considered it self-evident that all men were created equal, but Haldane found 'little positive evidence' in support. The Soviet communists, by contrast, made no presumption of equality.

Nor had Marx, who recognised that 'one man is superior to another physically, or mentally', and proclaimed communism as the only way to reconcile the imbalance. 'The formula of Communism, "From each according to his abilities, to each according to his needs", would be nonsense if abilities and needs were equal,' Haldane pointed out, rebutting a late-1940s attempt to drive a wedge between himself and Moscow. Like him, Stalin recognised human inequality, 'and also recognises that different nations have different contributions to make to human culture. I agree with him.'

The British Communist Party leadership was wrong-footed by the outbreak of war, which it initially hailed as anti-fascist. This, the Comintern in Moscow informed it, was no longer correct; the war was an imperialist one. Its pro-war General Secretary, Harry Pollitt, was ousted in the ensuing struggle and had to sit it out until Germany invaded the USSR, whereupon the line changed and he was restored. Meanwhile, Haldane carried on regardless, serving the Admiralty as well as the *Daily Worker*, the Communist Party newspaper for which he wrote a weekly science column.

He was brought to the Navy through the electrical and engineering trade unions. In the spring of 1939, the submarine HMS *Thetis* had sunk during sea trials. A large number of those lost were civilian workers, and their unions asked Haldane to investigate the disaster. At Siebe Gorman, an engineering company with which he had enjoyed a long association, he repeated his father's experiments in breathing carbon dioxide – and politicised them by using four International Brigade veterans as volunteers. The Admiralty asked for details of the experiments, which he provided. In sum, Haldane had responded to a request from reformist trade unions by assembling a team from a communist organisation, obtaining facilities from a private company and supplying the results to a military element of the bourgeois state.

The old familiar hull was visible below his shiny new Marxist superstructure. He had sought out his volunteers for the same qualities of resolve that he had demanded from the volunteers in his Western Front bombing unit; he had shown a similar paternal sense of responsibility for the safety of workers to that which he had shown the soldiers under his command. His relations with industry and Whitehall also ran along the lines familiar within his class. At the same time, his ability to deal with mutually antagonistic bodies was an expression of his ability to separate his activities into compartments. His intellectual capacity allowed him to work on genetics, biochemistry and physiology concurrently; a similar division of mental labour proved useful politically as well.

In January 1940, the Admiralty asked him to undertake further research into the problems of escape from submarines. His volunteers this time included Elizabeth Jermyn, his secretary, Helen Spurway, Hans Kalmus, an exiled Czechoslovak scientist, Martin Case, the onetime guest at Charlotte's Roebuck salon, and Juan Negrín, the former prime minister of Spain. They were locked inside a metal chamber, in which they were subjected to the extremes of temperature and pressure that would be encountered in a sunken submarine, breathing gas mixtures that simulated a dwindling air supply. Sometimes they became elated, sometimes belligerent; sometimes they were sure they were going to die. After more than half an hour in melting ice, breathing a mixture heavy with carbon dioxide at up to ten times normal atmospheric pressure, Haldane lost consciousness. Convulsions and decompression created further hazards, and he was left with permanent spinal damage. Nevertheless, he and several of his colleagues undertook further trials for the Admiralty, including experiments conducted to help develop miniature submarines.

While he pushed himself beyond the limits of his endurance in the war effort, he encouraged ordinary people to object to the working conditions imposed on them in the emergency. Eventually the authorities' patience with the *Daily Worker*'s campaign of querulous obstruction ran out. In January 1941, on the orders of the Home Secretary, the police closed it down. Haldane, who six months previously had been made chairman of the paper's new editorial board, may well have taken it personally. He detested the minister with a vehemence that went beyond politics. Long afterwards, in 1954, he told Naomi that he didn't mind missing a wedding because 'that nasty little lecher Herbert Morrison might be at the reception and start pawing Helen...'

The suppression of the *Daily Worker* came soon after Haldane had finally conceded another struggle, this time with the University College authorities, which had been running since they revealed their evacuation plans in 1939. Like Fisher, Haldane stayed put while the college was gradually removed to North Wales. He hung on for more than a year, through the Blitz. That may have taken more courage than the diving experiments.

When he escaped death on a park bench during an air raid in Madrid, he knew a terror he had never met in Flanders. Hans Kalmus recalled that he took Haldane's pulse during a raid and found it to be 'hard, small and very irregular'. There was more than political point-scoring behind Haldane's insistent public calls for air-raid precautions.

In November 1940, Haldane agreed to move, along with the rump of his department, to Rothamsted. (This, incidentally, disposes of the allegation made by the spy writer Rupert Allason, aka 'Nigel West', that Haldane was a Soviet military intelligence agent. About the only checkable detail in Allason's tenuous speculations is the statement that the agent known as 'Intelligentsia' lived 'in the provinces'. It appears in an intercepted message sent in September 1940, when Haldane was still in London.)

Spurway moved in with him at Rothamsted. He was still married to Charlotte, at the Party's insistence. A divorce between two prominent sympathisers would have been bad for its image, playing badly with its morally conservative working-class supporters and fellow travellers. That was Charlotte's account of the matter, anyway. But her recollections, written after their eventual divorce and his marriage to Helen in 1945, were coloured by Cold War penitence.

In 1941, she persuaded the editor of the *Daily Sketch* to send her to Russia, thus becoming Britain's first female war reporter. Jack asked her to find out what had become of Vavilov, but she met only with evasions. Scientists in general did not enjoy the high status that the Haldanes had observed in 1928, though performing artists 'were cossetted and privileged to an absurd degree'. Bureaucrats and NKVD security personnel filled the new élite. The oppressive manifestations of inequality finally became unbearable for her in the city of Kuibyshev. On the way to a shop stocked with food, from bread to caviar, exclusively for foreigners, she saw a young woman carrying in a cardboard box the body of her young child, starved to death.

When she returned home in November, she asked Jack to meet her and spent three hours giving him an account of her experiences. These caused him 'surprise and mental uneasiness', she recalled, but 'he was intellectually and emotionally incapable of assessing their objective value'. Charlotte left the Communist Party; Jack finally joined it, in the middle of 1942.

He was now bound by rule-book and order-paper, in harness to motions and delegate conferences. The intellectual aristocrat placed himself under workers' control, enlisting in a movement dominated by men like Harry Pollitt, once a boilermaker in the London docks and now the Party's leader, and Willie Gallacher, a former engineering worker from Red Clydeside, who was now the communists' lone Member of Parliament. Two years later, at Shoreditch Town Hall in east London, Haldane was elected to the Party's executive committee. He came fourth in the ballot, within a dozen votes of the poll-toppers Pollitt and Gallacher. The reds had a soft spot for a star.

Haldane had been forced to retreat a little on the matter of Soviet genetics. By 1940, he had to acknowledge that 'one or two' geneticists had lost their jobs. He compensated for the concession with assertions of equivalence, the first resort of the Soviet apologist. British geneticists had also lost their jobs for political reasons, he asserted. S. C. Harland, 'our finest plant geneticist, was dismissed from his post, among other things, for marrying a "coloured" wife, and is now in Peru'.

Whatever the circumstances were that had steered Harland's career, though, they certainly did not direct him into the arms of Lysenko, with whom he had spent several frustrating hours during a visit to Odessa in 1933. 'You simply couldn't talk to Lysenko – it was like discussing the differential calculus with a man who did not know his 12-times table,' he recalled. Nor was his practice any less inept than his theory. Harland noted that some of his assistants were trying to grow plants in pots without drainage holes.

Haldane never saw the fruits of Lysenko's methods for himself, but enthusiastically passed on to his *Daily Worker* readers the academician's report of 'very remarkable examples' demonstrating 'vegetative hybridisation', whereby grafting apparently induced heritable changes in tomatoes. 'On the other hand,' he added, 'I think Lysenko went too far in several respects.' One of these was his antipathy to chromosomes, which led him to claim that any hereditary trait could be passed on without them. 'This would be very serious if he were dictator of Soviet genetics. But, so far from being dictator, here is what he says to his Mendelian colleagues: 'The important thing is not to dispute; let us work in a friendly manner on a plan elaborated scientifically ...'

Lysenko was not yet the dictator of Soviet genetics, but he was getting there. By this time, he had secured the positions from which Vavilov had been ousted, as head of the Institute of Genetics and of the Lenin Academy of Agricultural Sciences. Vavilov was arrested some time during 1940, his connections with western scientists trumped up into charges that he was a British agent. He was sentenced to death, but after Hitler's invasion was sent to work at Magadan, a penal city on the Siberian coast through which thousands of prisoners entered the Kolyma *Gulag* camps. There he died, probably in 1942, though he was denied the dignity of a recorded fate. In its absence, Haldane remained free to cast aspersions west instead of east. 'Vavilov was shot about once a year in the American press,' he wrote in a wartime article, 'though he continued to communicate papers to the Academy at least up to 1942.'

At the close of the war, Eric Ashby, a botanist in Moscow on a diplomatic assignment, attempted to study the research on which Lysenko based his vaulting claims. Julian Huxley also visited the USSR and met Lysenko. Finding shambolic experimental procedures, bizarre theoretical postures and open contempt for statistical analysis, Ashby and Huxley came to the same conclusions as Harland.

Haldane made an attempt to apply due scrutiny too. When Lysenko told him that he had arranged for his book *New Paths in Genetics* to be translated into Russian, Haldane entered the modest reservation that if he was writing it at the moment, his views might end up closer to Lysenko's. Could his Soviet colleague send him reprints giving the facts in question? In science, J. B. S. always stayed true to the facts. He considered that his job as a *Daily Worker* columnist was to 'refute false views on scientific grounds' rather than to explain the political or economic grounds on which such views were held. Science was in a separate compartment, outside which different rules applied. He was not obliged to adhere to scientific standards of evidence when speaking outside his field of expertise, and so was free to serve the communist cause.

As for the poor standards of argument brought to bear against the 'Mendel–Morganists' in the Soviet Union, this was the inevitable result of popular interest in science. 'Interventions of this kind,' he wrote in response to a newspaper article by the philosopher Bertrand Russell, 'are part of the price which is paid for the type of democracy prevalent in the Soviet Union, of which public discussions are a prominent feature.' Even Lenin might have felt this was going beyond the willing dupe's call of duty.

Among his own people, Haldane found the popular interest in science trying. His demeanour on public platforms left much to be desired, though some were amused by the sight of Professor Haldane carrying on as if he were in his office, or asleep. He felt greatly put upon by his correspondents, who would seek his opinions on subjects from telepathy to cat breeding. They would send him their pet theories, their medical histories and, on one occasion, a dead weevil found in a tin of spaghetti by a supporter of the People's Press Fighting Fund. Some asked about chemical hazards in their workplaces, some about flaws in their families' chromosomes. J. B. S. had encouraging advice for an Indian man living in Wimbledon who had anglicised his name and could 'pass for white', but was worried that his children might have dark skin. Haldane told him that 'from the Eugenics point of view, a little infiltration of genes from talented Asiatic races would probably be an excellent thing for England'.

He was overtaken by events in the summer of 1948. In June, he wrote to the Provost of University College, outlining his desire to give a series of lectures in Prague. In Czechoslovakia, he noted, there was now a tendency to reject certain genetical ideas, partly in reaction to Nazi racial theory. 'Recent controversies in the Soviet Union have reinforced this tendency. It seems to me important to combat it. And I am well qualified to do so. As you are aware, I am a Marxist, and hope to be able to show that while the ideas in question are incompatible with the extreme egalitarian principles embodied in the American constitution, they are quite compatible with Marxism, as they are with various philosophical views more generally held in this country. If I can achieve this, I shall have done something for the unity of science which is threatened at the present time.'

This intriguing proposition was an attempt to serve science and play Cold War politics too. The point of the contrast between Jefferson's view of equality and Stalin's, which Haldane had made ten years previously, was now clearer. The United States and the Soviet Union were not just ideological poles between which philosophical positions could be explored but the dominant global powers between which the peoples of Europe must choose. Haldane implied that British and Soviet philosophies had more in common with each other than with the 'extreme' positions held across the Atlantic.

181

His bid to act as a double agent for Marxism and science was flawed because of his failure to accept what was happening in the East. Four months earlier, the Czechoslovak communists had mounted a successful coup against the democratic government. The gloves were off. During the second half of the 1940s, the communists methodically eliminated their coalition partners in governments throughout the zone now dominated by the Soviet Union, creating a string of satellite regimes.

Soviet biology followed a somewhat similar course. The Michurinists had not achieved total hegemony by the end of the war: the Mendelians had sufficient friends in the Soviet Academy of Sciences that plans were mooted to create a separate new institution for them to compensate for the loss of the Institute of Genetics to the Michurinists. For several years the Academy's premier journal, *Doklady*, continued to publish orthodox biological papers, while Michurinism was conspicuous by its absence from *Doklady*'s pages. Then, in 1948, the Michurinists staged their final putsch. In what Hermann Muller described as a 'carefully laid trap', the Mendelians were invited to state their case in the press. The ensuing controversy provided a cue for another conference on genetics, held at the beginning of August.

At the close of the proceedings, Lysenko revealed that the Central Committee of the Communist Party had approved his report. Later that month, the Academy of Sciences resolved to remove 'Morgano–Weismannite' geneticists from institutes and editorial boards, and to replace them with 'progressive' Michurinists. It pledged to 'further Michurin's biology and to root out unpatriotic, idealist, Weismannite-Morganist ideology'. The science of genetics was liquidated.

Towards the end of the year, the Soviet moves were reported favourably in the *Daily Worker*. A botanist, A. G. Morton, emerged to parrot the Michurinists' harangues in a document produced by the newspaper as an 'Educational Commentary'. Like his models in Moscow, he treated the controversy as entirely ideological: 'The struggle against Mendel–Morganism waged by the Communist Party of the Soviet Union, and with Comrade Stalin's direct guidance, is the struggle against a bourgeois theory which would retard the progress of science and of socialist agriculture,' and so on.

Haldane was outraged, declaring his 'absolute disagreement' with the document and protesting 'in the very strongest manner' that it had been produced without any discussion involving communist geneticists. He also threatened to resign if it went any further, but that was the least convincing of his expressions of indignation. J. B. S. was casting around for a way out of the Party. He drafted a resignation letter, giving as his grounds his loss of confidence in comrades whose recommendations about American publishers and British solicitors had proved unreliable. Later he tried to extricate himself from his *Daily Worker* commitments by claiming, on the strength of a couple of critical letters, that he no longer commanded enough support among the paper's readers. Underneath the pretexts, his heart wasn't in it any more.

He wrote and circulated a statement rebutting the Commentary. It was a blustery text, at one point supporting the contention that August Weismann's views were out of date with the observation that the German evolutionist had been a contemporary of Gladstone's. So, his readers may have noted, were Darwin and Marx. But his opposition could not be ignored.

Maurice Cornforth, the communist philosopher leading the moves to endorse Michurinism, organised a meeting with about a dozen Party geneticists. To his dismay, they roundly endorsed genetics and trenchantly criticised Lysenko. They deplored his lack of statistical analysis or experimental controls, and rejected his claim that the idea of competition between individuals of the same species was 'bourgeois'. Lysenko had raised the stakes again, and he was not going to let elementary Darwinian logic stand in his way. He had grasped the power of grand claims from the start: they were the Michurinists' only real weapon in their struggle to wrest official favour away from the orthodox scientists, whose strength was expertise and whose weakness was the time that scientific expertise took to achieve results. Academic biology did not offer to tame the ice and the steppe and the threat of famine in a season or two. But Lysenko understood the Bolshevik spirit, which had seized power and held it against similarly titanic challenges. And he was a son of the Soviet soil, from which foreign invaders had been expelled at unimaginable cost, leading a Soviet movement against the foreign influences entailed in orthodox science.

Now, he proposed to transform the climate of the great Soviet land mass by sending the peasants out in swarms to plant acorns. The steppes would be sheltered by belts of forest and become meadows behind them. And the trees would begin to contribute to the project even as saplings by sparing their planters the trouble of thinning them out. Planted the easiest way, in clusters, they would decide among themselves which should wither and which should grow into a pillar of socialism. Weaker specimens would succumb not to competition but co-operatively, for the good of the species. His methods were applied – as were conventional ones – in the 'Great Stalin Plan for the Transformation of Nature', to the accompaniment of Shostakovich's 'Song of the Forests'. By the time that Stalin was denounced, in 1956, 95 per cent of the trees planted in Lysenko's clusters were dead or nearly so.

Haldane himself had given the idea of intraspecific competition a dialectical spin long before it became a bone of ideological contention. In *The Marxist Philosophy and the Sciences*, which was based on lectures he had given shortly after adopting Marxism, he indicated the limits to the role that natural selection could now play in his philosophy. Marx and Engels had regarded Darwin's theory as valuable but incomplete; dialectical materialism expected all theories to contain within themselves their own negation. Haldane had never felt in natural selection the fundamental power that so impressed Fisher, and so was quite content to see it contained within a framework of dialectical materialism.

Placing Marxism first, as it demanded, he now looked to evolutionary theory for signs that affirmed Marxist theory: 'A good Marxist will expect that the Darwinian theory of natural selection should contain its own internal contradictions.' It ought to negate itself, and competition within species was one way in which it did so. As he had observed in *The Causes of Evolution*, such competition was inevitable as soon as a species became fairly dense – a point that Lysenko, who had *Causes of Evolution* translated into Russian, failed royally to apply in his pronouncements on forestry. In species among which males fought for mates, sexual selection would favour adaptations for combat, such as antlers or claws. This would shift the population away from the suite of characters that were optimal for the struggle against the rest of the environment and so reduce the fitness of the species.

Haldane had also brought the fact of intraspecific competition to the notice of the communist rank and file in one of his early *Daily Worker* columns. Noting that contests between males over mates selected for increases in size, he added that the fossil record showed that steady growth usually led to extinction. Competition within species was thus widespread, he implicitly acknowledged, though inadvisable. United they stood, divided they fell.

When push came to shove in 1948, though, Haldane lined up with Lysenko on the question. He now told his *Daily Worker* readers that Lysenko's view was right, though overstated. Several Soviet geneticists had declared not only that competition within species was normal but that 'without it . . . natural selection is nothing but a fiction'. Far from it, said Haldane; 'Natural selection can and usually does occur without conflict between members of the same species.' This was a profound denial of the power of natural selection. He managed it by saying that natural selection was often conceived as a Malthusian process in which numbers outstrip resources and the weakest perish, which 'happens very rarely'. Admittedly, Lysenko had disregarded sexual selection, involving fights between males. But these were 'a perversion of the normal course of evolution', which could even lead to the extinction of the species. Haldane left his communist readers in no doubt that evolution ought to be looking after the interests of the collective. Long after the dust had settled, he felt able to praise Lysenko while accepting that intraspecific competition was part of the ordinary currency of evolution. But during the present crisis, it was class struggle all the way down to the Cambrian.

Concessions like this, however sweeping, were not enough. Michurinism, now officially incorporated into Communist Party ideology, was part of the conformity being imposed across the Soviet zone. It was not a question of reconciling Mendelism and Michurinism, but of choosing one or the other. The nadir of Haldane's career as a public commentator was the broadcast about Lysenko that he made on BBC radio in November 1948. Four scientists each stated their views, which were then published in *The Listener*. J. B. S. was the odd man out.

S. C. Harland offered a homage to Vavilov – 'a mind that never slept . . . entirely selfless . . . one of the great scientists of all time' – which showed Stalinist hagiographers a thing or two. Cyril Darlington, a prominent geneticist, mocked Lysenko's denial of competition within species – 'Even pigs and potatoes, it seems, have the right communist attitude; even cannibals co-operate in a friendly way with their victims' – and denied that his practical contributions to agriculture amounted to anything more than cutting up seed potatoes to make them go further, as English farm workers had been doing for a hundred years.

Expressing his curiosity about what made Lysenko tick, Ronald Fisher used the academician's statement at the summer conference to determine what kind of man the President of the Agricultural Academy might be, and found that it ruled out two of three possibilities. Lysenko could not be dismissed as an ignorant peasant, although many in the West did just that, or as a fringe scientist deluded by vanity. That left the third explanation: Lysenko was 'an ambitious politician of a type likely to become prevalent in a system avowedly guided by a rigid ideology'. His goal was power, 'power to threaten, power to torture, power to kill'. In the climate of the Cold War, Fisher was not obliged to bring his moral clarity to bear upon the Axis-era roles of his friends von Verschuer and Gini. When he wrote of the power to torture and kill, did the image of von Verschuer's protégé Mengele, in Auschwitz, come to mind?

Out on the left, though, Haldane was caught in the open. This time he did not come out fighting, instead producing reedy complaints about not being properly informed. He refused to comment on the summer's events until the reports documenting them had been translated into English; his resort to equivalence was feeble even by the standards of the genre: a genetics laboratory in Moscow might have been closed by decree, but we had no business telling Moscow what to do when there was no regular practical course in plant genetics for botany students in London.

Much of Haldane's talk was an attempt to accord Lysenko scientific credibility without making a mockery of his own. He endorsed Lysenko's claim to have produced changes in plants by grafting, which were then inherited in non-Mendelian ways. He also noted that there were other means to alter organisms in heritable ways, such as exposure to X-rays or a chemical called colchicine. And he was inclined, he said, to believe that Lysenko had succeeded in changing the inherited tolerance of wheat to cold by manipulating the temperatures to which seedlings were exposed. Many of Lysenko's views were 'seriously exaggerated', but there was something in them.

What would not have been clear to much of his audience was that he was giving Lysenkoist claims a Mendelian blessing. X-rays and colchicine were understood to produce mutations in genes and chromosomes, a process that did not challenge Mendelian tenets at all. His comments on the cold tolerance induced in wheat, suggesting that the changes had occurred in the plants' germ cells, also implicated genes and chromosomes. Even the non-Mendelian changes supposedly achieved through grafting might be explained by the transmission of viruses or similar agents, as he had suggested in a previous commentary; such a mechanism avoided confronting Mendelism directly. Haldane was trying to minimise the contradictions between Lysenko's claims and the orthodox genetic paradigm. He stood up in due course to be counted as a 'Mendel–Morganist', in a Party journal, but he still had a good word to say for Lysenko even at the end of his life, round about the time that Lysenko's political credit finally ran out.

Haldane's position, politically evasive and scientifically neither one thing nor the other, left him exposed to public flak and internal Party antagonism. 'We geneticists are not going to stand an indefinitely frequent repetition of these slanders against us,' he warned Maurice Cornforth in February 1949, but he was unique among the small band of Mendelian Marxists in the weight of dialectical contradictions he bore and failed to resolve. Even his position as a Party member became cloudy. In 1950, he refused to confirm or deny reports that he had resigned. Writing to a friend in 1963, he claimed that he had quit about fifteen years before, 'because of Stalin's interference in science'. But when it was reported, after Stalin's death in 1953, that he had resigned because he could not accept that external authorities could pronounce infallibly upon scientific problems, he had said that this was 'not entirely correct'. And he signed a letter of condolence for the late dictator.

According to one account, Haldane remained a member until the spring of 1956, when the Soviet Communist Party denounced the man who had ruled it for thirty years. In February that year, Nikita Khrushchev made a secret speech condemning Stalin; its contents began to filter out to foreign comrades over the following weeks. On 2 April, the authorities ordered the republication of Vavilov's works, and a week later Lysenko resigned the presidency of the Lenin Academy of Agricultural Sciences. That month, Haldane 'quit the Party and began the trickle of resignations by intellectuals that would become a flood'.

*

He slipped out of the Communist Party through a side door, but he quit his country with a more characteristic performance. 'I want to live in a free country where there are no foreign troops based all over the place,' he declared on the apron at Heathrow Airport, in July 1957, as he and Helen Spurway prepared to board their flight to India.

The previous November, the British government had presented him with an irresistible opportunity when it staged its attempt, together with France, to repossess the Suez Canal by force. He tendered his resignation from University College, informing the Provost of his 'wish no longer to be a subject of a state which has been found guilty of aggression by the overwhelming verdict of the human race'. Helen, meanwhile, was undergoing a brief spell of incarceration by the 'criminal state' after refusing to pay a fine for being drunk and disorderly: the conviction ensued from an incident in which she trod on a police dog's tail on the way back to UC from the Marlborough Arms. Her resignation was required as a result. Haldane had already secured their future by accepting a post at the Indian Statistical Institute. Though he presented his decision as a response to the military adventure, it was the conclusion of approaches that he had been making for several years.

There were plenty of reasons for the Haldanes to emigrate, such as climate, culture and the opportunity for the two of them to continue research together. The one he usually gave was the wildlife. What biologist wouldn't like to live in a country, he asked by way of explanation, where one can find chameleons in the garden? But closest to the point, perhaps, is his nephew Murdoch Mitchison's suggestion: that Haldane went there because the Indians are used to dealing with cross holy men.

Even so, he fell out in due course with the ISI, and with the government agency which took him on next. In the end, the state government of Orissa gave him a 'one-storied "ivory tower"' of his own. The Haldanes moved south from Calcutta to their new Genetics and Biometry Laboratory at Bhubaneswar in the summer of 1962.

One institutional relationship in Haldane's life endured the test of time. Among all the questions of his loyalties, the greatest conundrum of all is how he managed to remain married to Helen for nearly twenty years until his death parted them in 1964. As a union of two impossibles, the marriage was improbably successful.

Several years after his death, John and Sheila Maynard Smith encouraged their younger son Julian to go and stay with Helen in India after leaving school. John Maynard Smith's motive was that 'I was afraid Helen was going to kill herself, because she said she would. She'd said, 'I don't want to live after Haldane dies."

Maynard Smith's fear was not realised. Helen lived on in a state of ceaseless melodrama – thus maintaining her emotional continuity, although the Haldanes' double act was over. Writing in 1968, she suggested that the main impact of bereavement had been upon her work. 'The most important and so far lasting reaction to Haldane's death was to make me lazy. It was quite a discrete and abrupt sensation which I recognised at the time as a spring breaking inside me.'

Helen understood this as more than the depressive effect of loss. For her, sex and work were synergistically linked. 'Because so much of my work is bound up with sexual love I probably as Haldane pointed out get more hap[p]iness out of both than most people.' All her successful love affairs had been 'accompanied at the beginning with a great burst of intellectual work which may or may not be in collaboration with the man in question'. Often, when affairs turned sour, 'work becomes nauseating too'.

These were handwritten and highly strung pages, in which her emotions were glimpsed but not resolved. She hoped that she was not the only person who felt the same way. Perhaps the main purpose of the manuscript, she observed, was to air the question of sexual sublimation in scientific activity. This, she thought, might be commoner than usually supposed.

She even ventured the idea that scientific papers might, despite appearances, be able to sustain erotic or emotional subtexts: 'Emotional unhappiness can be expressed in coherent scientific ideas which by their nature have a manifest content quite remote from their stimulus.' From outside science, commentators have argued that scientific writing is influenced by its social context, and here is a scientist suggesting that it contains secret personal narratives. If abstracts and references could talk, what would they say about Professor and Doctor Haldane's singular marriage?

The manuscript itself was costively discreet about her late husband but suggestive in its tenses. She may have been referring to relationships in early adulthood and in widowhood, but she writes as though her affairs continued throughout her life, with Haldane looking sympathetically on. He certainly does not seem to have required sexual fidelity in his first marriage: he surely cannot have helped but notice Charlotte's affairs, and she sanctioned casual flings for him. But she was playing with the juniors. Instead of the intense young men that Charlotte went for, Helen obliged her husband to contend with a lover in his own league.

In 1954, Desmond Morris, then a young ethologist and later a famous science populariser, observed a curious spectacle in a Paris hotel lobby. One distinguished scientific celebrity and his wife were trying to hide from another such couple, the Haldanes; which sounds like a vain effort, for any space that contained the Haldanes was a confined one. The tension between the couples became so awkward that, over dinner with the Haldanes one evening, Morris asked what the matter was. 'I'll tell you what it is,' answered Helen, 'I've been fucked by Konrad Lorenz!'

So, it seems, she had; correspondence between Spurway and Lorenz is said to confirm the affair. It is not hard to see what she saw in him. Lorenz had a leonine presence, a charismatic personality, and genius. Whereas Haldane's interest in animals was largely the product of Helen's influence, Lorenz shared the passion for observing animals that had been alive in her since she was four years old. His distinguishing feature is symbolised by his famous demonstration of imprinting, in which young geese filed dutifully in his wake, taking him for their parent. Whereas Niko Tinbergen watched birds, Lorenz got his birds to follow him. Animals and humans alike recognised his dominance.

He differed from Haldane in another fundamental respect, too. While Haldane was gravitating towards communism in the late 1930s, in Austria Lorenz was warming to Nazism. He joined the Nazi party in 1938, and over the next few years offered a number of public commentaries in which he related his own social and biological concerns to Nazi ideology. Lorenz saw the great eugenist question, 'What causes the decline of civilisations?', through the prism of animal behaviour. He argued that civilisation domesticated humans in the same way that humans domesticated animals, which led to the genetic decay of the human race and enabled 'socially inferior human material' to 'annihilate the healthy nation'. By 1940, however, he felt confident that the 'racial idea as the basis of our state' had done much to stem the degenerative tide.

Choosing Lorenz as a lover might seem, from an ideological point of view, to border on the perverse. But it was not a matter of party loyalty. Helen saw the communists and the *Daily Worker* as her rivals for Haldane's commitment rather than comrades. And the course she took in her intimate relations was in line with the attitude of her scientific seniors, including her husband, towards collegial relations with Lorenz. Haldane occupied the left of the political spectrum in a coalition of scientists, including David Lack and the omnipresent Julian Huxley, who tried to bring Lorenz to England in 1950. The Britons were taking an opportunity created by the disinclination of the Austrian authorities, with whom his Nazi past had put him out of favour, to grant him a position in his home-land.

As with Fisher and von Verschuer, there is the question of how much news and how many journals had filtered through the occupation zones. Likewise, there is the question of why the British scientists were so uncon-cerned about what their colleague might have done in the war.

In this case, however, they had a compelling example of forgiveness. Tinbergen had spent two years interned as a hostage by the Nazi occupa-tion forces in Holland, threatened with execution in reprisal for Dutch acts of resistance. Lorenz had written to Tinbergen's wife, offering to use his influence to obtain Tinbergen's release; she replied that her husband wanted nothing more to do with him. Four years after the war, however, Tinbergen met Lorenz at a scientific meeting in England. He declared the resumption of their friendship – with the ambiguous words 'We have won!' – and forgave him in the presence of their peers.

The British also knew that Lorenz had himself been interned during the war, in the Soviet Union, having served as a military doctor; his record as a German in uniform therefore seemed relatively innocuous. At Oxford, questions about his ideological activities did not arise until 1953, when the American ethologist Daniel Lehrman published a critique of Lorenz's the-ories of instinctive behaviour. This project had entailed the translation of all Lorenz's writings, thus letting the Nazi cats out of the bag.

Had he been challenged about his readiness to help von Verschuer, Fisher might have responded that it was no different in kind from the efforts made by his fellow British biologists to help Lorenz, and he might have pointed out that one of these colleagues, Haldane, belonged to the political movement most implacably opposed to Nazism. Lorenz was not in von Verschuer's league. He did not work with Mengele. But the generosity he was shown from England – including financial help from the writer J. B. Priestley – bespeaks a presumption of scientific innocence, shared across all shades of political opinion, in the early post-war period. It took some time before this presumption was reversed. In Lorenz's case, the criticism did not really gather force until he won the Nobel Prize in Physiology or Medicine, together with Tinbergen and Karl von Frisch, in 1973.

If Tinbergen was prepared to resume the friendship, any reservations among his British colleagues might have seemed precious. But there seems to have been little or no resistance to overcome. For scientifically progressive British biologists and naturalists, the important thing was to get ethology going in the English shires. It was part of the Darwinising of British nature.

At length, addressing the Royal Anthropological Institute in 1956, Haldane did point out that Lorenz's insistence on 'scientifically-based race politics' as the only thing that could save civilised peoples from extinction – published not in a Nazi newspaper but in the *Zeitschrift für Tierpsychologie* (*Journal for Animal Psychology*) – was based on the tenets of National Socialism. It was, however, a brief and passing jibe. (Haldane was more interested in tweaking the anthropologists' tails by using Hindu terms such as *dharma* and *moksha* to classify human cultural traits, on the grounds that cultural anthropology was a product of colonialism and so required corrective influences from colonised cultures.)

Spurway also aired the Aryan theme in a review of Lorenz's book *King Solomon's Ring*, but the nearest she came to an explicit reference was in her title, 'Behold, My Child, the Nordic Dog'. She presented a catalogue of complaint and trenchant criticism, her central objection being that Lorenz failed to appreciate 'the ubiquity and speed of evolutionary processes'. When he looked at dogs, he saw breeds which varied according to their degree of wolf ancestry. Spurway briskly dispelled his murky visions of ancient wolf blood by pointing out that the degree to which different dog breeds resemble wolves could be explained by the selection pressures upon them. Then, by way of conclusion, she hinted at a mysterious and ominous vision of her own. The study of natural selection, she observed, was the contemplation of death; it was a better way to promote a sense of community with other forms of life than the study of behaviour, which, because it relied on 'the observation of inappropriate actions, either apparently accidental or provoked, may be described as the contemplation of sin'. Was it inappropriate, or accidental, or provoked, that in this contemplation her last word on Lorenz was 'sin'? The manifest content, to use her later phrase about the secret life of scientific texts, was hardly remote from its stimulus, but her secrets were safe within it nonetheless.

The Haldanes were united on the Lorenz question, as they were united in the arguments they would conduct at full volume, bathing in the ripples they stirred among companions and innocent bystanders, and in their love of making scenes. Helen's affair with Lorenz had been a grander drama and one whose electricity she and her husband were unable to discharge in their usual fashion – by making it public – but the Haldanes were the winners. In the group photograph taken at the Paris conference, the leonine Lorenz hangs uncharacteristically in the back row, while the bearish Haldane is to the fore. Prof and Helen have put themselves right in the middle of the front row. She is beaming broadly and they are holding hands, like teenagers on a trip to the seaside.

Ernst Mayr came to visit Haldane in Bhubaneswar, and they spent three weeks discussing the differences in their views of how to study genetics. Mayr's approach tended to the holistic. He was concerned with the interactions between genes and the systems that developed from these interactions. 'To consider genes as independent units is meaningless from the physiological as well as the evolutionary viewpoint,' he wrote. Mendelians had liked to compare gene pools to bags of coloured beans. A mutation replaced a bean of one colour with a bean of another. This was 'beanbag genetics'.

It was also a discipline to which Haldane had contributed over ninety papers. Haldane's response, 'A Defense of Beanbag Genetics', appeared in 1964. He did not directly challenge Mayr's central objection. Instead, he argued that beanbag genetics was imperfect but practical. Verbal arguments were imprecise and therefore misleading. In mathematical models, however, the imprecisions were specified. Although simplifying assumptions were necessary, they had to be stated. 'In the consideration of evolution, a mathematical theory may be regarded as a kind of scaffolding within which a reasonably secure theory expressible in words may be built up.'

John Maynard Smith, whose *modus operandi* this was too, continued the defence in the 1980s. He sidelined Mayr's objection – that selection acts on individuals rather than genes and that genes adapt to one other – as 'both true and largely irrelevant'. Another way to look at it was to say that a gene had to be a 'good mixer' to succeed, interacting effectively with its fellows. Just because the beans are not loose in the bag, that is no reason not to consider them one at a time.

Within population genetics, he went on, there were differences across the Atlantic. The British view sprang from Fisher, who thought that one gene replaced another because it was beneficial on its own. Chance had little to do beyond causing mutations in the first place. The American view was guided by Wright, who thought that it would often be advantageous for several genes to be replaced at the same time, even though each replacement would be harmful on its own. For that to happen, chance was vital and would require small populations in which to act. 'In effect, the English think that evolution is a hill-climbing process, and the Americans that it also involves jumping across valleys.

'As a student of Haldane's, I take an impartial view. However, both views are essentially reductionist, and both were first formulated mathematically. There *is* only bean-bag genetics.'

Haldane's defence of beanbag genetics was also an *apologia pro vita sua*, with an eye on the horizon of posterity. He hoped that he would have many years ahead of him, but knew that he might not.

Late in 1963, Haldane attended a conference in Florida at which he met Alexander Oparin, a Russian biologist with whom he shared the title of a hypothesis. The Oparin–Haldane theory – the order was correct, for the Russian had thought of it first and published in 1924 – had taken a step demanded by the theory of evolution. It addressed the question of how life evolved in the first place.

The key was not the presence of oxygen but its absence. Lightning bolts and ultraviolet light could supply energy for the synthesis of organic compounds from which living systems might be built, but if oxygen were present, they would rapidly end up as carbon dioxide. Without oxygen,

Haldane suggested, organic molecules might have accumulated 'until the primitive oceans reached the consistency of hot, dilute soup'. His phrase was modified and caught on as the expression 'primordial soup', and the fluid itself was simulated in a famous experiment conducted in 1953. Electrical discharges were sent through a mixture of water, methane and ammonia; the hypothesis was rewarded by a profusion of organic molecules.

Having finally rendezvoused with Oparin to discuss the origin of life, Haldane received the first intimations of how his own life would conclude. He suffered bleeding and was warned that he might have cancer. On his arrival in London, in November 1963, he went into University College Hospital, where the diagnosis was confirmed.

While he was there, a BBC producer wrote to him, suggesting with inspired insensitivity that he might like to take the opportunity to record his own obituary. Haldane agreed that this was an excellent idea, while stipulating that the BBC must wait until he was indeed dead before broadcasting it. There was, however, the possibility that he might not survive his imminent operation for rectal carcinoma. As he was readied for the theatre, he turned to John Maynard Smith and delivered the last words he had prepared in case: 'Well, Smith, just had me last shit!'

He survived to write verse on the subject, 'Cancer's a Funny Thing', which duly gave offence to *New Statesman* readers, and to deliver his 'auto-obituary'. The address was recorded in his old room at University College, which Maynard Smith had now inherited. Haldane was dressed in the Indian clothes that he had taken to wearing, especially when not in India, and smoked a pipe with a bowl shaped like a diver's helmet, a token of appreciation from the Siebe Gorman engineering firm.

'I am going to begin with a boast. I believe that I am one of the most influential people living today, though I haven't got a scrap of power.' He was the first person, he went on to say, to measure the mutation rate of a human gene. His voice seems to affirm what his written words imply but never admit. There is an overtone of questioning in it, an audible uncertainty – and perhaps even, at the upper limits of emotional pitch, a bat-squeak of humility. He resumes his scientific achievements and puts in a good word for Lysenko: the affair was still on his mind. But posterity, he realises, will make its reckoning without regard to his own. What he considers valuable may be discarded; and he may be best remembered for some footnote that he has forgotten himself.

He had begun by calling fate's bluff, with the hope that the recording would not be shown until 1975, when he would be eighty-two. It was, however, aired at the end of 1964. In September, he learned that his cancer had spread. His doctors had concealed it from him, but one passed the news on to a colleague of his. 'I am not appreciably upset by the prospect of dying fairly soon,' he wrote to Maynard Smith. 'But I am very angry.' He had taken on scientific commitments without realising he might not be able to fulfil them: as a result, he would have to work almost to the point of death.

The telegraphic address at the top of the letter was 'Elah', the name of the brook from which David took the stone that he used to slay Goliath. Huge as he seemed to those around him, Haldane identified himself not with the giant but with the underdog. Helen and Prof had visited Elah, and he kept a stone from it with him like an amulet. It fell from his hand when he died.

JOHN MAYNARD SMITH

'I think I was always an adaptationist, even when I was reading Kipling as a boy.'
John Maynard Smith

9
Better Do the Sums

On 12 May 1937, King George VI was crowned, and the boys at Eton put out the flags. They hung the jostling crosses of the Union from every window – except for one, which flew an improvised banner emblazoned with the Bolshevik hammer and sickle. John Maynard Smith had raised his standard.

He was aged seventeen and in the throes of a personal revolution. His school career had hitherto been one of social isolation, relieved by the camaraderie of the playing fields and the private revelations of solving problems in maths. Around the age of fifteen or sixteen, his suspended judgement gave way to a hostile verdict. He decided he hated Eton and did not believe in God; he developed pacifist leanings and an interest in evolution. And he decided that he would not become a stockbroker, as his family had expected: he would be an engineer instead. In this period of upheaval Maynard Smith discovered the elements that would make him what he later became, although another fifteen years or more would pass before his path became clear.

He was born on 6 January 1920 and spent his early years in Wimpole Street, part of the quarter of London where wealth and the medical profession consummate their union. His father, Sidney Maynard Smith, had been a military surgeon in the Boer War, caught tuberculosis, and then travelled round the world as a ship's surgeon, influenced by the contemporary idea that fresh air was good for TB sufferers. He returned to military duties during the First World War, and it was while working at an army hospital in Ypres that he met Isobel Pitman, who was serving as a volunteer nurse. They married in 1917.

Sidney Maynard Smith's war service, in which he became Surgeon-General to the Fifth Army Corps, earned him honours including the

French *Croix de Guerre* and a Companionship of the Order of Bath. Afterwards he went back to St Mary's Hospital, in Paddington, where he had trained as a doctor. He was from modestly middle-class stock: his father had been a Clerk of Works, and his mother, who lived in the south London suburb of Streatham, had a trace of the local accent to remind the other side of the family that there were a number of rungs on the ladder between them. 'The Pitmans speak – to practically nobody,' a nineteenth-century observer of Edinburgh society had noted in verse, alluding to the Lowells of Boston, who were said to speak 'only to God'. They were pillars of the Edinburgh financial establishment; Isobel's father, Frederick, had migrated south and built up a successful stockbroking firm, Rowe & Pitman, in London. He occupied a house of Georgian substance called Scarletts, off the Bath Road a few miles short of Reading, which became the family's centre of gravity.

John was brought up through his early childhood by his nanny, who doted upon him. Apart from reading bedtime stories to him and his sister Valerie, who was a year older, their mother had little contact with them. She and her husband took their holidays separately, visiting another sizeable property of her father's on Exmoor, while the children would be taken to stay with their nanny's sister. John saw his father once a week, at Sunday lunch.

He was denied the possibility of closer acquaintance. In February 1928, his father became ill, almost certainly from a recurrence of tuberculosis, and died a month later. His passing was as removed from the children as his life had been. They were not informed of it until he had been laid to rest. On the day of the funeral, Valerie and John were told they were to spend the day with the sister of one of the servants. Looking out of the window, they saw the cortège pass by. The next day, they were summoned from the Scarletts schoolroom to an upstairs sitting room, where their mother took John on her knee and told them, 'Daddy's gone to live with Jesus.'

John's life was transformed upon this loss. The house in Wimpole Street was sold; Isobel took the children to live not far from Scarletts; and John, aged eight, was sent to a boarding school in Kent. He thus lost both his father and his nanny, who had played the role of a mother to him. At both his prep school and at Eton he was an isolated boy; not despised or bullied, but not accepted either. He was saved from complete ostracism by his enthusiasm for games, especially football – which, unlike cricket, was played with a ball large enough for him to see properly. His isolation was not the result of his temperament but of his early upbringing. Once his schools were behind him, he revealed a natural confidence and ease in company that enabled him to make friends and fit in effortlessly wherever he found himself.

Although his mathematical abilities became apparent early on and were cultivated by a discerning teacher, John was not regarded as a prodigy nor even as especially bright. He did not begin to get high marks for essays until the later stages of his school career, when marks were awarded for reasoning rather than imagination. In music he was all at sea: like Haldane, he just could not hear it. He did, however, have some talent for drawing, an artistic theme which he did not develop, though two of his children did: his daughter Carol became a theatrical designer, and his son Julian a performance artist.

His unhappy experience at prep school turned out to be a suitable preparation for an unhappy sojourn at Eton, which he entered in 1933. Although his circumstances and intelligence might have suggested a scholarship, his grandfather was keen that he should live in an ordinary house and offered help with the fees to make this possible. Frederick Pitman, who had been part of the victorious Cambridge rowing team in three successive Boat Races against Oxford, failed to appreciate that John's intellectual temperament was better suited to the company of scholars. As Haldane had observed, the division between Collegers, who had won their scholarships by academic performance, and Oppidans, whose qualifications were financial, promoted a hostility among the latter to intellectual exercise. John found himself in a society whose values, formed by the boys at the masters' discretion, he came to loathe.

The house was effectively run by four or five boys who were said to be 'in the library', meaning that they were permitted to use the library, unlike the others. Another privilege they enjoyed was that of beating other boys. Beatings were also administered by senior boys to their 'fags', junior boys who were forced to do their bidding. Maynard Smith did his duty and duly received his beatings, but these he shrugged off. What he came to find repulsive was the atmosphere of snobbery, exclusiveness and prejudice.

His isolation was not quite complete. There was one other boy of like mind, Julian Tower, who defied the prevailing contempt for ideas. The two dissidents formed a friendship that got them through Eton and would last into the next century. (A third pupil distanced himself sufficiently from conformity to enjoy a measure of sympathy with them. This was Maurice Macmillan, son of the future Prime Minister Harold Macmillan.) Both became pacifists and dabbled in the left. Julian took the Labour-supporting *Daily Herald*; John got the school to give him the theoretical basis of Marxism. Unlike Fisher, Maynard Smith did not choose Darwin when he won a book as a school prize. He walked off with a copy of Marx's *Capital*, inscribed in Latin by the headmaster: '*Honoris causa dedit* Claudius Aurelius Elliott'. And, in due course, he read it.

That rare volume speaks of the subtlety of the Eton regime. Maynard Smith was allowed to tweak its tail and to opt out of the school's traditional culture – though his pacifist sympathies did not propel him so far as to quit the Officer Training Corps. The school took note and continued to educate him.

Its emphasis was on Latin and Greek. Biology was not taught; chemistry was, but by a notably dull man, so Maynard Smith avoided the subject. The teaching that he remembered with gratitude and affection was in mathematics. There are moments in learning maths when the student feels completely stuck and inadequate to the problem. Guidance at such junctures is especially precious, Maynard Smith observes, for it imparts a special self-confidence. On one such occasion, when he was having difficulty with imaginary numbers, his teacher showed him how to think of them geometrically. He had seen that although his pupil was not fluent in algebra, he had a geometrical imagination.

Maynard Smith also rose to the challenge of the problems that were set each week for him and two other boys who excelled at maths. The competition provided extra incentive, and he would spend eight or ten hours a week solving them. It was 'marvellous training' for science: unlike biologists in general, he became used to the idea that answers can be worked out as well as looked up. 'What I am as a scientist is a good puzzle-solver ... and I learnt that at Eton, so I mustn't be wholly critical.'

He was also able to give himself a grounding in biology and physics, making use of the library's popular science books and the ample spare time left in the school routine. The library also provided support for his ideological revolution in the school library, where he read Haldane's essay collection *Possible Worlds*. Having noted the hatred Haldane provoked among the masters as an apostate Old Etonian who had discarded religion and sympathised with socialism, Maynard Smith made sure to seek out his works.

He was particularly affected by the title essay, which discussed the limitations of trying to understand the universe using sensory systems evolved to address more practical exigencies. Haldane imagined a species of intelligent barnacle-like creatures, with eyes and the equivalent of arms. They considered objects that they could touch to be real, whereas objects that they saw were regarded as visions, and they believed that 'no good will come of mixing them up'. In Madagascan waters, however, a more advanced species of barnacle had worked out a parallax technique for using the position of a vision in two barnacles' visual fields to derive a corresponding position for a third. But though this was often called the 'distance', no barnacle really believed that visions existed in a three-dimensional world.

'Man,' observed Haldane, 'is after all only a little freer than a barnacle. Our bodily and mental activities are fairly rigidly confined to those which have had survival value to our ancestors during the last few million generations.' Anticipating ideas about evolved psychology that sprang up towards the end of the century, he observed that people think in two different modes, one for dealing with other people and another for inanimate objects. 'We are pretty nearly incapable of any other types of thought. And so we regard an electron as a thing, and God as a person, and are surprised to find ourselves entangled in quantum mechanics and the Athanasian Creed.' Maynard Smith experienced an access of comfort from the currents of reason, mathematics and atheism that intermingled in the parable. 'It was very moving to find that I wasn't alone in the world.'

Another book that influenced him greatly was *Last and First Men,* by Olaf Stapledon. Devoid equally of characters and deities, it is an epic history of human progress through technologically guided evolution, across astronomical expanses of time, from the viewpoint of the superior beings who succeed humankind. John came across the book in the public library at Minehead, in the West Country county of Somerset. So did a boy called

Arthur Clarke. 'I can still visualize the very shelf on which I found it,' Arthur C. Clarke recalled in his autobiography, testifying that it 'changed my whole outlook on the Universe and has influenced much of my writing ever since'. The distinguished evolutionary biologist and the celebrated science-fiction author got their boyhood revelations not just from the same book but the same copy of it.

John had a Minehead library ticket because his grandfather owned a home in the village of Exford, twelve miles away. Exmoor became his personal landscape, defining for him what countryside should be. When he moved to the Sussex Downs in middle life, it took him some time to appreciate the ecstatic simplicity of a green hill's roll under a lark-shimmering blue sky. His aesthetic ecology demanded a land shaped by water polishing through Old Red Sandstone; heather and streams instead of grass and chalk.

The area was the setting for a family passion which 'was also our religion, to the extent that the first hymn in church on the first Sunday of the stag-hunting season was always "As pants the hart for cooling streams, when heated in the chase".' Once, when quite young, and in all innocence, John asked his mother to show him the place in the Bible where Jesus went stag-hunting. Although on that occasion field sports caused a spat between them, as his mother wrongly suspected him of mockery, the thing that brought them closest together was their love of horses. John adored his pony, Vixen. He also developed a deep bond with his grandfather's groom, Fred Hain, who grew to be 'the nearest thing I had to a father'.

John became an accomplished rider, learned to show-jump and warmed to the thrill of the chase. A pony was also a companion for a lonely boy. As he reflected in later life, lonely children are often drawn to animals and natural history. But nature does not simply fill a social vacuum. It catches the eye; it poses questions; it is a continuous background source of curiosity and of delight. Those for whom this is true are natural historians, whether they enjoy encyclopaedic knowledge or simply the impulse to ask questions about the instances of life they detect around them. It was certainly always true for Maynard Smith, who even as a toddler would stare 'in wild surmise at animals of all kinds'.

The ones which first made a lasting impression upon him were extinct. As a child in Wimpole Street, he could hardly have avoided jaunts across

Regents Park to the zoo, but the visits that he would remember were to the Natural History Museum in South Kensington. In those days, before injection-moulded toys and computer-generated images, a passion for dinosaurs was an eccentricity; and as Maynard Smith once pointed out, it was still an eccentricity when Stephen Jay Gould was a child in New York. Maynard Smith suggested that the two of them might have come to hold different views on evolution if he had stayed true to fossils and Gould had watched birds in the country. As he pointed out, birdwatchers almost invariably assume that if a bird is doing something, there must be a reason for it. 'Fossils have a romance of their own, but they don't do much. If watching birds makes one an adaptationist, studying fossils often has the opposite effect.'

When John moved to the country, at the age of eight, his attention was drawn by the living creatures around him, especially birds. An aunt gave him and Valerie a guidebook to birds, in which he immersed himself, but he was not given any personal guidance or encouragement by an adult. He collected butterflies, as boys used to do, and kept frog spawn in spring, as children still do. John was also captivated by imaginary animals. The adventure stories he most enjoyed – Ernest Seton Thompson's *Two Little Savages*, or Jack London's *White Fang* – involved animals and life in the wilds. When he first visited the United States, in the mid-1950s, he was transported back to his childhood by the kingbirds and woodchucks.

Natural history became a question of philosophy when John plunged into his teenage ideological crisis. His housemaster at Eton tried to shore up his crumbling religious faith with natural theology, arguing that the features of living creatures revealed divine design. John became aware, from Haldane and his other reading, that there was another explanation. 'I saw it as a choice: you either believed in God or you believed in Darwin; you couldn't do both. And the choice was an easy one to make.'

This leap out of faith was not forced on him by the Church of England, which took Darwinism in its accommodating stride. Possibly his line was hardened by his mother's attitude, for she perceived evolution as a threatening idea. Doubtless the black-and-white vision of the adolescent played a part, but he maintained his position through an adulthood devoted to intellectual reflection. He avoided public controversy, at one point describing himself as an agnostic, and collegial confrontation: David Lack once asked him to take part in one of his attempts to mediate between evolution and Christianity, being unable to think of any other atheistical evolutionist who would be patient and courteous with his Christian colleagues. But Maynard Smith's stance anticipated that which later became Richard Dawkins's passion.

He and Dawkins were not the only ones. As he observed in his article about dinosaurs, 'the path that starts with the argument from design goes on to see that the main problem for any theory of evolution is to explain adaptation, and concludes by seeing natural selection as the major cause of evolutionary change, is a common one. It accurately describes my own intellectual development as a boy, and I think it is widespread among evolutionary biologists: in England and America, at least, it is surprising how many of them are lapsed Christians.'

After her husband's death, Isobel Maynard Smith set about ensuring that her son would still follow the course through childhood that had been envisaged for him. That was to culminate in Cambridge, as had her father's and those of most of his male relatives. She entertained no such ambitions for her daughter and was determined that she should not go on to higher education, despite the aptitude Valerie had shown at school. Instead of graduating from university or medical school, Valerie's allotted course involved 'coming out' as a debutante, a rite of passage identifying her as a marriageable young woman whose future would duly be secured by a suitable husband. Isobel Maynard Smith's discrimination against her daughter illustrates, more clearly than the case of Naomi Mitchison, one of the reasons why the principal figures in this story are all male.

Valerie did eventually earn a diploma from Liverpool University after the war, during which she spent two years as an army officer in Palestine, seconded to the Royal Electrical and Mechanical Engineers, and rose to the rank of captain. Her career diverged further from her brother's thereafter: while his religious faith had imploded long ago, hers now deepened and she became a parish worker – the nearest a woman could get to the priesthood in those days – for the Church of England.

John was able to assert his own influence over his course in life at a much earlier age. Frederick Pitman had two ambitions for his grandson. One was that John should repeat his success at rowing, but though John was fit, he was never large enough. The other was that, as he had shown competence with numbers and was Frederick's closest male descendant, he should go into the family firm. When John was about fifteen, however, he realised that, whatever he was going to do in life, he was not going to be a stockbroker. Having grown up with the assumption that money would always be available, he had no interest in pursuing it further.

He announced his decision as the family sat around the Sunday lunch table at Scarletts one day. What, his grandfather asked in the following silence, was he going to do then? John had not considered that question. But he knew that he had to say something, quickly. Having recently heard a lecture at school from an engineer who had been in charge of building the Sydney Harbour Bridge, he came up with an answer. The idea stuck, and in due course he was awarded a place to read engineering at Trinity College, Cambridge. It proved to be an excellent training in how to apply maths to material problems.

In the summer of 1938, after John finished at Eton, the Maynard Smiths crossed the Channel and travelled in an arc that took them from the cold embers of the last war to the crucible of the next. Isobel had wanted to visit the battlefields of the Western Front, where she and their father had met. At Ypres, John was distressed at the sight of the names of the dead covering the great Menin Gate in their legions and the sound of the Last Post at sunset.

From Belgium they travelled on to Berlin in their Hillman Minx. On the way they stopped at Cologne and went to see the cathedral. Their guide casually made an anti-Semitic remark in his perfect English, the first of many such comments John was to hear from Germans he met: these disturbed him more than the outward manifestations of the Nazi project. The incident was not the only ominous element of the journey. Isobel let her daughter do the driving, which could only mean that she was ill.

For John and Valerie, Berlin was two or three weeks sailing on the Wannsee and evenings in pubs with their cousins. Then their uncle, Noel Mason-MacFarlane, set off on a mysterious business trip. He took John with him, bowling through the Reich in his Rolls-Royce, down south to Austria and Czechoslovakia. 'Mason-Mac' was Britain's military attaché in Berlin. Quite what he was up to on his tour, which covered the front on which Hitler was then concentrating his expansionist ambitions, John never discovered. But he received an education in politics and the affairs of the world as they drove, arguing as they sped down the autobahns whose construction was one of the Reich's strategic priorities. And his uncle also arranged that he saw Hitler in action, taking him to see the *Führer* address an open-air rally outside Berlin.

John had left Eton with vague leanings towards socialism and pacifist sympathies. His mother would not speak of her time in the war, but that very silence made him realise that her experience had been terrible. Like many of his contemporaries, he inclined to pacifism as a result of what his parents and their generation had gone through, but he could not have discussed it with his mother. His uncle Noel was the foil and guide he needed. Colonel Mason-MacFarlane believed that Britain and its allies should meet the Nazi threat in kind. In March 1939, after watching the Nazis seize the Czech portion of Czechoslovakia, he wrote a memorandum arguing for a pre-emptive attack on Germany. He did not persuade his government, but in the summer of 1938, he persuaded his nephew that Nazism could not be resisted passively. 'I didn't like to admit it at the time,' Maynard Smith recalled, 'but he convinced me that we were going to have to fight.'

Thus it was that a High Tory steered John Maynard Smith towards the Communist Party. As the summer of 1938 turned to autumn, the British prime minister Neville Chamberlain met Hitler in Munich and returned home to proclaim 'peace in our time', Hitler took over the Sudeten region of Czechoslovakia, and Maynard Smith went up to Cambridge. There he entered a politicised society whose overwhelming preoccupation was Fascism and how to oppose it. Inevitably, the high ground was held by the faction that seemed most resolute and cogent in its opposition to Hitler, Franco and Mussolini. 'I came back to England and found that the one group who really appeared to be clear about what it was all about were the Communists.' Within a few months, he had joined the Party.

Later, to John's and general astonishment, Mason-Mac also moved to the left. In 1945, with the general election impending, he phoned his nephew to ask for his help. Noel, now a Lieutenant-General and a knight, had decided to stand for Parliament in the Labour interest. But he wasn't entirely sure what a trade union was, and summoned his communist nephew for a tutorial on the Labour movement. John spent a couple of days returning the political favour his uncle had bestowed on him in a different world. Mason-Mac took the seat of North Paddington from Brendan Bracken, a close associate of Churchill's, but was forced by illness to resign it the following year.

Back in 1939, the warnings John and Valerie had received in Germany proved gravely justified. Their mother died; the war began. But for John, that year was also the one in which he exchanged isolation for a community full of young, politically awakened intellectuals like himself; one in which ideas, through the Party, were connected to action, and intellectuals became part of a worldwide movement.

And there were girls. 'Mind you, they kept them in this sort of paddock, Girton; you had to be really keen.' Girton, one of two women's colleges, was a couple of miles removed from the centre of the city, though that was the least of the obstacles between Cambridge's female students and the university. The number of women students was restricted to a quota of 500, so as to maintain a sex ratio of one to ten, and the university refused in any case to accept them as members. They earned degrees but were not awarded them – though when Cambridge finally did reconcile itself to the opposite sex, in 1948, it conferred degrees retrospectively.

Political activity provided a welcome opportunity for male and female students to spend time together, and one of the attractions of the Cambridge University Socialist Club was that it contained large contingents from the women's colleges, unlike many of the other student societies. It was at a Communist Party camp, at Easter 1939, that John and Sheila Matthew first became aware of each other. She was able to visit John in his rooms at Trinity College up to the hour of ten o'clock. Once she overstayed and had to be smuggled out, disguised in one of the academic gowns which male undergraduates were obliged to wear, monkishly, when out after dark. On the other hand, a backhanded advantage of the university's discrimination against women was that Girton students were not subject to the authority of the Proctors, the colleges' security force.

Academic work was low on John's list of priorities, especially after his first year. In 'Red Cambridge', under the shadow of war, it was easy for a young man not to concentrate on engineering studies. This was not what the Party ordered, according to the historian Eric Hobsbawm, who had graduated the term before Maynard Smith entered the university.

Hobsbawm recalls in his autobiography that communist students were exhorted to 'be as much to the fore on the academic front as the political'.

Maynard Smith, however, failed to uphold the principle of struggle on two fronts. Instead, he organised the Communist Party in Cambridge, becoming secretary of its 100-strong branch, and also became secretary of the Socialist Club, ten times larger and pretty much as red. In the latter capacity, he once persuaded Haldane to address a meeting. The day before, Haldane sent a telegram saying, 'Not coming unless train back that night guaranteed.' Not having met Haldane, Maynard Smith lied that a train would be available, then waited until the audience's applause and some hastily plied pints of beer put Haldane in a good humour before putting it to him that he had been coerced into meeting his commitment. This was the first occasion on which Maynard Smith showed that he was capable of standing up to Haldane, an ability that would prove valuable in the forging of their friendship. Nonetheless, Maynard Smith was relieved that Haldane took the incident in good part and then forgot it.

Sheila had also been propelled far to the left by force of events, having been apolitical before the shock of Munich, and likewise became involved in student political organisation. For a time she ran the University Labour Federation, which brought together student socialist societies. Two years older and an academic year ahead, she completed her course in 1940 and went on to spend much of the summer of the Blitz working in London. In January 1941, she and John married.

John had tried to join the Army when the war broke out, disregarding the Party leadership's contortions over the issue. He was told that his eyesight was a liability but his engineering skills were an asset, and he should finish his degree. On graduation, in 1941, he was directed to Armstrong Whitworth, an aircraft manufacturer based in Coventry. Sheila joined him the following year, working in the wind-tunnel section. By then, however, he had become convinced that the company was incapable of designing a useful plane, and eventually he persuaded some visiting civil servants to reassign him. They sent him south to Miles Aircraft, near Reading and the familiar ground of Scarletts.

Here Maynard Smith worked as a stressman, doing the calculations that ensured an aircraft would survive in the air. Sheila obtained a job with the company, working on calculations in the stress office too. John found the work rewarding in itself, though the responsibility was onerous, as were the seventy-hour weeks. The experience taught him to trust models, a lesson that would become fundamental to his work as a scientist. Simplification was possible and safe: one could assume that air was incompressible and still make calculations that would ensure the survival of the aircraft and its crew. If patently false assumptions like this, refuted by the pneumatic tyres on the plane's wheels and its crew's inflatable lifejackets, could produce sound results in the real world, models could be used with confidence in theoretical science. At the same time, and for obvious reasons, Maynard Smith formed the valuable habit of not making mistakes in computations.

His work was not, however, much of a contribution to the war effort. Miles had little to add to the basic trainers it had already produced for the RAF. After D-Day, it was apparent that no aircraft then being designed would be ready before the war ended. Maynard Smith spent the last year of the war working on a small transport aircraft, the Merchantman, which had been conceived as a flying horsebox.

With the end of hostilities, the prospects looked unpromising for the aviation industry in general and Miles in particular. By now he and Sheila had started their family; their first son, Anthony, was born in 1944, and their daughter Carol in 1946. John decided to quit the industry. Once again, his eyesight influenced his decision. He would never be able to fly aeroplanes himself, and so he never grew to love them.

More than that, he wanted to go beyond engineering. For a time, he considered rocketry. The technological advances of the war had brought space within reach, and the intellectual demands of the enterprise would be enough for the keenest mind. But even so, he felt that, absorbing as the engineering problems were in themselves, the questions they raised were not deep enough. He wanted to be a scientist.

What kind of scientist was another matter. Chemistry was out: he did not warm to it at all. He considered physics, having already taught himself the basics of quantum theory and the special theory of relativity. But he knew from his studies that although he could understand it, given sufficient effort, he would never be able to innovate in it; nor was he competent enough with equipment to make a good experimental physicist. Biology was easier and harmonised with his love of natural history.

He wrote to an old Cambridge friend and comrade, Patricia Clarke, telling her that he was thinking of going into biology. What kind, he asked, didn't involve chemistry? Clarke, a biochemistry graduate who went on to become a microbial geneticist, suggested he try genetics. She had heard good reports of University College in London, and Haldane was there, which clinched it for Maynard Smith.

So, in October 1947, Haldane received a 'Dear Comrade' letter from Luckmore Drive in Reading (actually quite a typical address for his comradely correspondents). Although the Communist Party was conventional in its deference to academic rank – it had separate branches at Cambridge for undergraduates and faculty – its style of address allowed a young graduate to petition a professor 'fraternally' rather than as an obedient servant. 'As an explanation of the "comrade",' Maynard Smith wrote, 'I am at present secretary of the Reading Branch of the Party – a fact for which you are partly responsible.' He stated his intention to leave engineering for biology, asked for Haldane's advice, hinted at a meeting and mentioned the possibility of working as a lab assistant.

Perhaps it was the clarity of the young man's expression, or the tone of confidence it created, or simply that J. B. S. was in a good mood that morning; whatever the reason, Haldane replied almost immediately, and positively. Maynard Smith wrote back with what, in retrospect, reads as a synopsis of what would distinguish him as a scientist. He told Haldane that 'my interest is mainly in evolution and in genetics. My main existing qualification is that I am a competent mathematician, and in so far as I have shown any ability as an engineer, it has been in expressing physical problems in terms of mathematics. I read recently Huxley's "Evolution, the new synthesis", and there seemed to be plenty of scope for a mathematical approach to the subject of natural selection, the origin of species, and so on.'

He also demonstrated the typical English evolutionist's enthusiasm for spinning hypotheses off from amateur natural history. Noting his interest in birdwatching, he added a parenthetical speculation that different songs may have been selected in chiffchaffs and willow warblers, which are indistinguishably nondescript in appearance, to prevent crossbreeding between them.

This letter, with its evolutionary ideas framed by communist salutations, represented a balance in Maynard Smith's life which he knew could not hold. The decision to become a scientist involved more than a change of career. At Cambridge he had been involved in politics to the exclusion of other intellectual activities; when he was designing aeroplanes, that had occupied his mind as well as his time; and if he went into science, that would now become his exclusive preoccupation. 'I knew that science would absorb me ... if I became a scientist, that was the end of politics, as far as practical activity was concerned. So I was in fact deciding to abandon political activity. And I felt deeply guilty about that.'

Yet although he agonised, he had also made up his mind. He always found it hard to sleep on decisions, even ones as momentous as changing his career or getting married: 'I know what I'm going to do and I do it.' In 1948, the Maynard Smiths moved to Golders Green in North London. Here they stayed and raised their children, the third of whom, Julian, was born in 1949.

These were grim years in a country that had been prostrated by the war, rationing, the Austerity programme and the worst winter of the century. But the privations did not oppress the Maynard Smiths too much. 'It was rather grey, but the kids were young and fun, and we were basically very happy people.' They were also sustained by the happy combination of a source of income and a modest attitude towards it. John inherited sufficient money from his mother and grandfather to be able to make decisions without having to worry greatly about their effect on the family's finances. Unlike most young couples, they could afford to spend three years without earnings while he went to college and she stayed at home with their children. They had security and were content without extravagance; indeed, they would have been uncomfortable with it, for they were of a generation for whom thrift has been a lifelong watchword.

John's small group of fellow zoology undergraduates – there were only nine in his year – were a mixture of school-leavers and war veterans. Aubrey Manning, who became John's best friend, found himself sat next to a former RAF navigator twice his age. For Manning, the most exciting thing in zoology was ethology, the field study of animal behaviour, which was emerging under the leadership of Niko Tinbergen and Konrad Lorenz. At first Maynard Smith was suspicious of this view of animals, for which his engineering background had not prepared him, but he was gradually converted.

Ethology was largely an extracurricular pursuit at UC. It appealed to bright undergraduates, who enjoyed knowing something new which their teachers (apart from Helen Spurway) had yet to grasp. 'The standard text-book on behavior . . . was an account of how flatworms, maggots, and other invertebrates orient to light and other stimuli. As an ex-engineer, I found it a pleasure: the animals were behaving like robots that I could have designed myself. The lectures were given by G. P. Wells (son of H. G.). His favorite animal was the lugworm, *Arenicola*, whose complex 20-min cycle of feeding and defecating he had worked out . . .'

Zoology was a matter of comparative anatomy. 'It seemed to me then, as it still does,' recalled Maynard Smith, 'that the obvious need, once Darwin had published the *Origin of Species*, was to understand heredity, and not to do more anatomy. This was obvious to Darwin himself . . . Sadly, it was not obvious to T. H. Huxley, nor to those responsible for training biologists in the English-speaking world, so that, a hundred years later, students were still being exposed to a course in nineteenth century anatomy.' When D. M. S. Watson, who taught them zoology, remarked to them that crocodiles had done 'damn-all since the Cretaceous', there was a hint of the pot calling the kettle black.

After graduation, Manning went on to Oxford to study under Tinbergen, as did another friend, David Blest. Maynard Smith had spoken there about bird flight, a transitional topic between aircraft engineering and biology, at one of an annual series of ornithological meetings that David Lack organised for undergraduates. Lack arranged for his paper to appear in Penguin's *New Biology* paperback series – a welcome success in the face of frustrations he experienced trying to get papers on animal locomotion published – and encouraged him to apply to Oxford too. But Maynard Smith felt that he would be at a disadvantage in the field because of his poor eyesight. In any case, ethology had not displaced his enthusiasm for evolution and genetics. He decided to remain with Haldane at University College. 'I thought, "Well, I just won't be very good at it. I'd better do the sums."'

Precious few biologists were prepared to do those. When Haldane gave a course of lectures on population biology, he started off with a full house, but the attendance dwindled as the equations rolled on, until at the end there were just four people in the audience: John and Sheila Maynard

Smith, Lionel Penrose, Fisher's successor as Galton Professor, and Cedric Smith, who succeeded Haldane in the Biometry chair. Sums put the Maynard Smiths in rather exclusive company.

In the event, however, John did very little mathematics until Haldane went to India: 'It's not that he actively discouraged me, but he was so bloody clever that if a problem came up when we were talking, he would solve it.' Haldane had formed a decent opinion of Maynard Smith's abilities as an undergraduate and anticipated that he would be largely self-propelled as a researcher. 'He has so many ideas of his own that he will, perhaps, be difficult to fit into a laboratory; but I am willing to take the risk,' Haldane wrote in a letter supporting a grant application, three months before Maynard Smith took his final exams. His main weakness, J. B. S. added, was that he was 'said to be rather clumsy at fine work such as dissection; but this is offset by his capacity for making apparatus'. With his unusual qualifications, particularly his knowledge of maths and how to apply it to practical problems, the student was 'well worth backing'.

Maynard Smith became a fruit-fly experimentalist, working with Helen Spurway, who ran the laboratory, rather than Haldane. Prof was discouraged from going near the lab, because 'He was just very clumsy. He dropped things. Helen was quite different. Helen was a marvellous observer.' Maynard Smith learnt much from her, and also from a fellow student, Jean Clarke, with whom he collaborated for many years. Luckily, he turned out to be 'quite a good farmer' – an apt term in a fly lab, with its rotting fruit and ranks of milk bottles. He kept his flies alive, which not all his colleagues could.

Maynard Smith took a job as an assistant lecturer in zoology, under Peter Medawar, and Sheila began to work part-time in the Galton Laboratory, doing statistical calculations in human genetics. By the time they left UC, in 1965, Lionel Penrose had succeeded in changing his job title to Galton Professor of Human Genetics, instead of Eugenics. Proud to declare that, during his tenure, the Chair of Eugenics had not been held by a eugenist, Penrose finally emerged the victor in the half-century of struggle over the purpose of studying human heredity.

Haldane's own ideological struggle, over Lysenko, reached its climax round about the time Maynard Smith went back to college. They did not discuss the matter. Although J. B. S. was slightly less aloof from undergraduates than other members of the faculty, socially the two groups were separate castes. Nor were the barriers lowered within the Party, and in any case Maynard Smith was little more than a sleeping member after he moved to London.

Once he ceased to be active in the Party, he began to reflect upon it, and inactivity grew into alienation. He was shocked by the Lysenko affair; not by Lysenkoism itself, but by the fact that the Party's Central Committee had imposed its line upon the scientific community. And on this matter he had to accept that it was a fact. British communists could dismiss the reports about the *Gulag* as propaganda and could persuade themselves that their comrades in the East were building 'new democracies' with their purges and puppets. 'Bulgaria Is Optimistic', proclaimed the *Daily Worker*; its science columnist, Haldane, a keen conference delegate, suggested Budapest might be the 'gayest place in Europe'. But Maynard Smith read about the Lysenko affair in a report issued by the Soviet authorities themselves: the account of the 1948 meeting of the Lenin Academy of Agricultural Sciences. He understood genetics and therefore realised that the Lysenkoites did not. '[I]f the central committee of the Soviet communist party could be wrong about that, what else could they be wrong about?' he wondered. 'It was the crack in the dyke.'

The weakness was structural. Maynard Smith had been a committed Party member, but he had never been in a position to live a comprehensively Marxist life. Unlike intellectuals in the arts and humanities, he worked in a domain where Marxism had to stand back and defer to expert knowledge. Sociologists or historians might be convinced that their entire discipline could be contained within the greater Marxist philosophy, but there was no such thing as Marxist engineering. Truth or falsity were not matters for debate or edict. Either the sums were right and the plane stayed in the air, or they were wrong and the wings broke off. Although Maynard Smith, like Haldane, believed that Marxist theory could assist biologists in their work, his own working life had so far been spent in one of the few domains to which Marxism had no pretensions.

Nor had his commitment ever been subjected to the kind of moral ordeals by which Central Committees hardened their cadres, or broke them. He was never the kind of communist for whom 'the test of his devotion to the cause was the readiness to defend the indefensible', in the historian Eric Hobsbawm's words. 'It was . . . the constant challenge: "Test me some more: as a bolshevik I have no breaking point."' The kind of communists Hobsbawm calls 'bolshevik' – authentic, unconditional, total – were obliged to accept that Moscow was always right, no matter how far it contradicted their observations, their beliefs or themselves. True communists had to be ready to believe one thing on Monday and its opposite on Tuesday, should the line change. Yet when the war broke out and the Comintern ruled against it, standing the international communist movement's previous position on its head, Maynard Smith had applied to join the Army. How did that square with the Party line? 'I don't recall asking them,' he answered, sixty years on, with a chuckle that sprang from the serenity of age but probably did not misrepresent the impulses of his youth. As a young man Maynard Smith was a Marxist and a communist, but he was never a Bolshevik.

After the war, the main significance of his Party membership was that it gave him membership of a community. The Communist Party of Great Britain entered a decline in 1945 from which it never recovered, though the rot was slowed by the social and personal support which came with belonging. Communist affiliation offered a network of contacts, a high-minded freemasonry, which remained healthy as ideological commitments sickened. It was natural that the Maynard Smiths should contact the local branch when they moved from Reading to North London. Party branches were Marxist parishes.

Losing faith was one thing but renouncing it was another, until the Soviet Union itself committed a public act of such monstrous perfidy that members at last felt released from their obligations. The Party's decline itself made resigning harder. 'It's very hard to leave a beleaguered group of people,' Maynard Smith observed, looking back: 'You feel like a rat leaving a sinking ship.' The internal degradation of the Party as an organisation of disciplined believers only really became apparent in 1956. John and Sheila Maynard Smith were part of the exodus that followed the Soviet invasion of Hungary.

Like most British ex-communists, they had lost faith in the Party rather than in their ideals, and they remained on the left in their sympathies. Britain in the 1950s offered a featherbed to a falling communist. The 1945

Labour government had inaugurated the 'Welfare State', with a publicly owned health service at its core, as well as nationalising the railways and the heavy primary industries, coal and steel. Although the Conservatives were in office from 1951, they did not attempt to dismantle the new social-democratic order. Labour would return to power some time, offering the prospect of a British road to socialism, to coin the CPGB's phrase, upon whose final destination comrades could differ according to their political temper. Those who still hankered after the hammer and sickle might allay their uncertainties with the subtle assumption, prevalent among British communists, of their national superiority over the barbarian Russians. Haldane played on this sentiment when he remarked that a socialist Britain 'would no more resemble the Soviet Union than the Church of England resembles the Russian Orthodox Church'. Most were content with the modest sense of fairness and progress in which British social democracy took pride. They also had confidence in the assumption, shared by many conservatives as well as socialists, that history was moving towards the left. The future belonged to the state, the market to the past. Planning and welfare were the dominant themes in western Europe, while Soviet efforts in concrete on the ground, and then rockets in space, made the command economy look like a proposition to be reckoned with. As Maynard Smith approached middle age, the apparent course of history offered a suitable reconciliation between his left-wing sentiments and his desire for a quiet life.

Although he had been 'disgusted' by those among his comrades who told him what to think about Lysenko, despite their ignorance of genetics, Maynard Smith had not been so hostile to Lysenkoist ideas themselves. In 1948, the year in which the controversy reached its peak and he began his zoology degree course, he thought that 'Marxism was a good guide to scientific practice'. He had yet to realise that he would have to choose between the one and the other.

As a Marxist, he expected development to take place dialectically, in nature, or thought, or history. Agents or forces acted upon each other, in dialogue or struggle. Among the UC zoology students' teachers was Hans Grüneberg, a German geneticist for whom Haldane had provided a haven from the Nazis. He was fond of the orthodox slogan of the day, 'Genes Control Development'. This was a challenge to a Marxist who would expect that if genes influenced development, development should in turn influence genes. One day, before Grüneberg arrived for a lecture, Maynard Smith drew a caricature of him on the blackboard as the driver of a horse-drawn carriage, brandishing a whip, and underneath it wrote the slogan that grated on Maynard Smith's Marxist sensibilities.

At one stage, he thought his flies might help him extend orthodox science into the territory the Lysenkoites had claimed. His early experimental work was based on inbreeding and the many forms of damage it does to flies. Among its effects, he found, was an inability to cope with high temperatures, which in outbred flies is affected by the temperatures at which they are raised. It occurred to him that as an adaptation which presumably affected all the cells of the organism, this could be an ideal system in which to look for Lamarckian effects. He spent six months looking but was not greatly surprised by his failure to find any.

Gradually, not dialectically, he came round to Grüneberg's position and accepted that there is 'something deeply undialectical' about genes. In due course he came to appreciate the prescience shown by Weismann, who became his second favourite evolutionist after Darwin. Once the structure of DNA had been elucidated, it was possible to phrase the dogma in molecular terms: information can pass from DNA to proteins but not from proteins to DNA. When teaching, though, he always drew students' attention to the exceptions to the rule that nucleic acids have a monopoly on inheritance. The main one is cultural inheritance, whereby the lessons an animal learns in life may be transmitted to its offspring. There are also one or two examples of physiological Lamarckian inheritance, notably changes that occur in flax which has been given large quantities of fertiliser, and that then persist for several generations in plants raised without fertiliser.

In this, as in his research, Maynard Smith followed the geneticist William Bateson's dictum: 'Treasure your exceptions'. The few anomalies demonstrate that Lamarckian mechanisms are possible but also that they are very rare. So the dogma is true, but in imparting it to students, Maynard Smith was at pains to accompany it both with exceptions and explanation. A dogma should have a reason behind it, and adaptation must be the reason behind a biological dogma. The changes that organisms undergo in life are usually caused by injury, illness or age. As these are generally harmful, no mechanism has evolved to pass them on down the generations.

Another investigation with heterodox leanings had positive results and proved to be ahead of its time. One of the many failures suffered by inbred flies is that of their eggs to hatch. Maynard Smith wanted to find out whether this was because the eggs were defective or because they had not been fertilised. Spurway's laboratory used *Drosophila subobscura*, a species which is common in the wild in Europe. These flies are convenient for mating studies because they do not mate until after a courtship dance and so need to be able to see what they are doing; the experimenter can prevent them from jumping the gun by keeping them in the dark. Maynard Smith sorted a hundred flies into male and female pairs, each in a small glass tube, which he placed under a black cloth. When he was ready, he brought out the tubes and watched. All the outbred pairs mated within about ten minutes, but an hour later, the inbred males were still trying, and not getting anywhere.

The courtship dance turned to be a test of the males' ability to keep up with the females. A female would make rapid side-stepping movements; the male had to remain facing her. If he failed, the female would not mate with him. (Males had altogether looser criteria and would attempt to copulate with a blob of wax if it was moved in roughly the right way.)

Maynard Smith took lasting pride in having made the first clear demonstration of how females select mates. At the time, however, he failed to persuade his friends at Oxford of his interpretation. The ethologists' world was dominated by the concept of instincts, which were universal properties of a species. 'Consequently they were not interested in differences between individuals. And if two animals behaved differently, it was because they had different motivation or drive. One animal was hungry, the other wasn't, so they behaved differently.' Ethologists did not consider genetic causes for differences within the species; 'it was not their thing. And their attitudes towards my experiments . . . was that the male wasn't motivated.' One of the Oxford group, Margaret Bastock, had drawn this conclusion from her own studies, having observed that wild-type *Drosophila melanogaster* females did not mate with yellow mutant males. 'I said to them, "Look, I've watched this bloody male, he's been trying to mate with this female for an hour; he gets desperate in the end and tries to jump straight on and gets kicked off. There's no way you can say this male isn't motivated!'" If the doubters had seen it for themselves they might have been convinced, but Maynard Smith's efforts to film the hapless suitors were unsuccessful. The lights needed were so hot that the flies wilted altogether.

University College has an obtuse flair for gloom and convolution. Like the chambers and corridors of some vast battleship, its rooms often seem to be below the surface even if they are not. Its parquet and panelling are easily overlooked: its underlying grandeur is subordinated to the practical demands of intellectual inquiry. This was an appropriate habitat for Haldane, with his classical woodwork and caterpillar-tracked algebra. His Department of Biometry, along with Peter Medawar's Department of Zoology, was installed in what used to be the warehouse of a department store, the ground floor of which was said to be occupied entirely by lavatories; these had to be numerous, being segregated by caste as well as sex.

Like a ship, the place nurtured camaraderie. Comic verse, still in fashion, was one of its expressions; Maynard Smith was one of the versifiers. Haldane also enjoyed using the occasional theatrical vulgarity to step briefly around the ladder of rank. He made a point of not using the staff lavatory – an egalitarian gesture not matched by his routine treatment of secretaries and other subordinates – and so had the opportunity to inform undergraduates that he preferred to wash his hands before urinating, rather than afterwards, since he was confident of his aim but not so sure about the carcinogens which he might have on his fingers.

Such gestures can, of course, also serve to show who is in charge. On another much-recounted occasion, the Haldanes set out to give Maynard Smith and a woman postgraduate a lift home after a session in the Marlborough pub, a traditional fixture after the students finished their final exams, had continued into the small hours at their flat below Parliament Hill Fields. Smoke began to fill the decrepit car: after some time this was drawn to Prof's attention. He delegated Maynard Smith, as an engineer, to investigate: it turned out that some of the carpet had fallen through the floor onto the transmission shaft and had caught fire. 'The ladies will go and stand behind yonder lamp-post,' Haldane commanded, then turned to the younger man and told him: 'Smith: The method of

Pantagruel!' Haldane's Rabelaisian humour would not have been complete without a reference.

It helped that Maynard Smith fell naturally into a conversational style of scholarly debate salted with soldierly vernacular; that he had a gift for conversation, an ability to listen and the self-confidence to stand up for himself. He had what it took to get on with J. B. S. They also had a series of similar passages in their personal stories, from Scottish descent through Eton to Cambridge communism. But what really mattered was that Maynard Smith 'found Haldane's mind immediately sympathetic'. Both of them were puzzle-solvers, as Maynard Smith puts it; both thought mathematically because therein lay their intuitions, not because they were obliged to; both put clarity and directness first when they wrote. 'Today I find it hard to distinguish resemblances between us that arose by independent convergence, and those that arose because I have copied him,' Maynard Smith wrote, more than thirty years after he graduated from UC.

Haldane in his turn appreciated Maynard Smith's mind. Indeed, he appreciated both the Maynard Smiths' minds: he once told John, in a postscript to a letter, that he would send a collection of some of his papers when they were published, as John and Sheila were among the rare people who understood them. And the Haldanes also appreciated John's qualities of character, as they demonstrated in July 1956, when each wrote out a will on a single piece of paper. Each left everything to the other, and in the event that the other died first, to John Maynard Smith, whom they would trust to dispose of their property according to their wishes.

Haldane, of course, had no children to inherit what he possessed, and he felt this lack deeply. Maynard Smith barely knew his father, who had died when John was eight. Was J. B. S. the father and John Maynard Smith the son the other never had? The Haldanes' wills cannot help but point to the possibility. Maynard Smith agrees that his relationship with Haldane was filial, but not that Haldane was a father figure. This was not one of those instances in which childless adults take under their wing a young person who still needs some bringing up. Maynard Smith was in his thirties, with a family of his own. Nor did he lack for accomplishment and confidence: these were, after all, necessary qualities for becoming close to Haldane in the first place.

Although Haldane came to regard Maynard Smith as probably his closest friend at UC, the latter recalled that the relationship was 'surprisingly impersonal in some ways', as required by collegial and public school convention. 'The affection was real on both sides . . . but not often expressed . . . We never got beyond calling one another "Smith" and "Prof".'

Maynard Smith wept when Haldane left Britain, and he wept when Haldane died. And ever afterwards he would weep again when he leafed through Haldane's letters or when he recollected the day that he drove Haldane to the airport for his last departure to India. It was snowing as they crossed Hampstead Heath. Without thinking, John stopped the car when they reached the Whitestone Pond. They got out and looked at the London park in winter. 'He said, "I'm afraid I'll never see this again." And I said, "No, I guess you won't, Prof."'

'And then he said to me, "I'd like you to say goodbye to Sheila for me. I'd like you to tell her how much I love and admire her."' He had been staying with the Maynard Smiths after his discharge from hospital, where he had undergone surgery for cancer. Sheila had cooked his meals; he had done Julian's Greek homework for him. But he could not say such a thing to Sheila herself, nor put his feelings in writing to John. When Haldane learned that his cancer was terminal, in 1964, he wrote to Maynard Smith immediately. But even that letter began 'Dear Smith' and ended 'Yours sincerely, J. B. S. Haldane'.

10

Puzzles and Games

In 1965, Maynard Smith was invited to become the first Dean, or head, of the School of Biological Sciences at the new University of Sussex. Seeing an end to the frustration of teaching a degree that still 'could have been run by Thomas Henry Huxley', he accepted the job, exchanging comparative anatomy for evolution, titles for forenames and the Euston Road for the South Downs.

Sussex was fresh air and an open canvas. Like the ancient colonists whose earthworks still rumple the carpet of the hilltops, the Maynard Smiths settled themselves on high ground, on a ridge overlooking a village near the campus. They found a bungalow set upon a generous apron of land facing south, ideal for enjoying the variation of plants under domestication; over the years, their garden became a showpiece.

At the university a heady atmosphere of scholarly idealism was brewing, in which exchange between disciplines was a cardinal virtue. It urged communication where UC had insisted on compartmentalisation. The Gower Street dreadnought still divided biology up into departments of zoology, botany, biochemistry and genetics. Maynard Smith went to Biols, as his School at Sussex was known, because he 'wanted to break down the divisions between the different branches of biology. I thought that biologists ought to be trained across the board, from whole organisms to biochemistry.'

As well as the grime of London, Maynard Smith left behind the flies. His new administrative responsibilities sat ill with the routines of *Drosophila* 'farming', and so he shifted from experiments to theory. In the early stages of his career he had been deterred from theoretical work by a couple of rejected papers on animal locomotion and the proximity of Haldane's intellect – 'Why do theory when Haldane's sitting in the room next door?' After Haldane went to India, Maynard Smith ventured more into theoretical work. As he settled into his professorial role, he had the circumstances and the confidence to make his own contribution to evolutionary theory.

Although his approach to problems resembled his mentor's, he chose them on a different basis. Haldane saw natural selection as a fascinating puzzle, which he would take out of its box every so often until the end of his life. But for him it was one of a range of intellectual challenges, enjoying no particular priority among them. By contrast, adaptation raised almost every question that Maynard Smith sought to answer. For him, adaptation 'is *the* problem that a biologist has to explain . . . If you're a competent naturalist, the one thing that hits you in the face about everything you're seeing is adaptation.'

There are, however, exceptions, and these are to be treasured. 'My own research interests tend to have concentrated precisely on those things that at first sight are not adaptive. Because it's a puzzle. You don't study things you understand; you study things that don't make sense. At least, I think you should.'

The first evolutionary anomaly that he examined was the most obvious one. 'At first sight, ageing is something that an animal shouldn't do. It can't increase its fitness, that's for sure, so why does it do it? I think the thing that attracted me to the subject was partly that it was a puzzle from that point of view; there was a contradiction between what the animal was doing and what natural selection should tend to make it do.'

His investigations were set in train by the arrival at UC of an old college friend from his Cambridge days. Alex Comfort later became a household name, or at least a bedroom one, as the author of *The Joy of Sex*, but he made his scientific name as a gerontologist. Comfort wanted to investigate the effects of age in *Drosophila*; Maynard Smith and his colleague Jean Clarke, decided that 'there was no way that a fly looked after by Alex Comfort would live for more than a week', and so they had better do the experiment themselves. Maynard Smith applied the technique to his inbreeding studies, finding that outbred flies lived about twice as long as inbred ones, and then began to get interested in the causes of ageing.

The University College zoologists were given their cue by the departmental head, Peter Medawar, whose inaugural lecture was the first robust Darwinian statement on why living things should grow old. Wallace and Weismann had both suggested that individuals died for the good of the group, reproducing and then clearing themselves out of the way of their young. Such a sacrifice would seem to be superfluous, though, for organisms rarely survive long enough in the wild to die of old age. Reproduction declines with age because survival does, and so, therefore, does the importance of genes. A gene whose harmful effects were not exerted until late in life would escape selection pressure against it. If it had beneficial effects earlier in life, it would be favoured despite the damage it did later on.

These principles, later developed mathematically by Bill Hamilton, became the basis of evolutionary thinking about age and decline. Medawar encouraged Maynard Smith to pursue the subject, though they did not discuss it: unlike many scientists, Medawar tended not to talk about science beyond what the job required.

At the time, many of those interested in the problem were struck by the fact that different parts of an organism tend to fail at the same stage in its life. They were tempted to suppose that a single process underlay the unravelling. Maynard Smith came to doubt this. As he and the American evolutionist George Williams realised, different systems could deteriorate for different reasons, but natural selection would synchronise their failure. If one cause of senescence acted faster than others, it would relax the selection pressure against genes which sped up slower causes, while itself being under selective pressure to slow down; gradually all would be brought into line. As long as there were other contenders, natural selection would not allow a single mechanism to control the process of ageing.

Economically, the logic could hardly be simpler: 'There's no point in making a heart that lasts for fifty years if you're going to die at the age of three.' There remained the question of the various processes that caused different systems to fail, but these were increasingly biochemical issues and so outside Maynard Smith's sphere of interest. He was not unmoved by internal processes, though. While at UC he developed a sideline concerning how patterns, such as stripes and segments, form in organisms; and he has consistently emphasised the importance of developmental processes. Although adaptation was '*the* problem' he had to explain, it was not the only problem he was interested in. As an orthodox Darwinian he is disarmingly pluralist.

When Haldane was in University College Hospital being treated for cancer, Maynard Smith visited him daily. He brought Prof detective mysteries and science fiction until about a week after Haldane's operation, at which point Haldane asked, 'Smith, why don't you bring me something sensible to read?' Maynard Smith went down the road to Dillon's Bookshop, where he found a book by a naturalist named Vero Wynne-Edwards, entitled *Animal Dispersion in Relation to Social Behaviour*. At 650 pages it was substantial enough for Prof and obviously packed with natural history, so Maynard Smith bought it without inspecting its arguments.

A couple of days later, he returned to find J. B. S. sitting up in bed with the book. 'He said, "Smith, do you know what this book says?" I said, "Not really." He said, "Well, there are these blackcock, you see, and the males are all strutting around, and every so often a female comes along, and one of them mates with her. And they've got this stick, and every time they mate with a female, they cut a little notch in it. And when they've cut twelve notches, if another female comes along, they say, 'Now, ladies, enough is enough!'"'

Haldane's mockery was widely echoed – though he was sufficiently impressed by Wynne-Edwards's 'wonderful series of facts' to support his election to the Royal Society – and the book became the text against which modern Darwinism defined itself. Besides the reactions from British scientists, George Williams's book *Adaptation and Natural Selection* was effectively a response to it, although Williams had nearly finished his manuscript by the time he saw *Animal Dispersion*.

Wynne-Edwards had made explicit the assumption, held tacitly by many of his fellow naturalists, that animals act for the good of the species. Leks are gatherings at which blackcocks, male black grouse, gather before dawn and stake out territories that they defend with leaps, sallies and postures. The latter, sustained by the 'most virile' specimens for two hours at a stretch, show off the male's splendid lyre-shaped tail. Meanwhile, females, known as greyhens, observe and then take their pick of the males. To awed birdwatchers, it sometimes looks like a fairy vision of a medieval tournament; and to Wynne-Edwards, it seemed as though the knights held true to a chivalric code of self-denial. Even when the 'master-cock' was temporarily incapacitated by the females' 'incessant demands', his subordinates could be deterred from taking his place by the 'restraint of the system'. J. B. S.'s notches parodied Wynne-Edwards's suggestion that males would undertake a roughly constant number of matings and then decline further offers. Wynne-Edwards believed that a lek 'could conceivably be a collective operation' in which individuals forewent opportunities to reproduce in order to keep the population under control. A sceptic would ask what was in it for them, and so would natural selection.

Nearly ten years before, in 1955, Haldane had sketched a hypothetical circumstance in which a gene might spread despite inducing its bearers to act against their own interests. His example concerned a gene that encouraged somebody to jump into a river to save a child. If the children saved were closely related, they would be likely to carry the gene themselves, and so it might be favoured even if it sometimes sent its bearers to their deaths.

Haldane made his observations in an informal article and did not develop them. That burden was assumed by Bill Hamilton, then a young graduate student who had failed to find a comfortable niche at Cambridge and failed to find one at the London School of Economics or University College either. Working mainly in his bedsit – and sometimes at Waterloo Station, just to have people around him – he struggled with his ideas in bunkered isolation, until in 1963, his first paper was published in *American Naturalist*. It was a brief summary of a much longer paper that he had sent to the *Journal of Theoretical Biology*. This eventually appeared the following year in two parts, at the suggestion of John Maynard Smith, one of its referees.

While Maynard Smith 'did not at the time follow the mathematical details of Hamilton's paper', he was persuaded that he 'was on to something' by the wide range of cases to which he applied his theory. 'At the time, however, I was more interested in Wynne-Edwards than Hamilton. To understand this, one must know that the central problem of ecology . . . seemed to many of us to be the regulation of population numbers.' *Animal Dispersion*, which had come out in 1962, was beginning to provoke questions among evolutionarily-minded naturalists. At Oxford, a healthy respect for natural selection had grown up in Niko Tinbergen's zoology department, thanks to the influence of Fisher's lieutenants and

Tinbergen's own guiding precepts. Puzzled both by Wynne-Edwards's book and the enthusiasm with which it had been received by biologists, David Lack telephoned Maynard Smith, asking him to come to Oxford to discuss it. Lack, Maynard Smith, Tinbergen and Arthur Cain spent an evening talking over the problem. Having recently read Hamilton's paper, Maynard Smith told the others that if they were going to attack *Animal Dispersion*, they should distinguish Hamilton's promising idea from Wynne-Edwards's misguided one. A new name was needed: out of the meeting came the term 'kin selection'.

He introduced the new expression to published science in a letter to *Nature* entitled 'Group Selection and Kin Selection', which appeared in 1964. Group selection, arising from competition between groups of members of a species, rather than individuals, was how Wynne-Edwards believed social behaviour evolved. Kin selection, 'the evolution of characteristics which favour the survival of close relatives of the affected individual', was what Haldane and Hamilton had realised was really going on.

Maynard Smith challenged Wynne-Edwards with a mathematical model, which emphasised the severe conditions that would have to be met before animals would forego issue while other members of the species carried on breeding. Group selection was a tenuously special case, but individual selection was inexorable. Anti-social elements would always appear: group selection models had to show why these corrosive mutations would not multiply regardless of the group's interests. Natural selection has neither foresight nor a sense of greater good.

He learnt this at the outset. When he unconsciously assumed the greater good in one of his early undergraduate essays at University College, Haldane jotted in the margin 'Pangloss' Theorem': evolution acts for the best in the best of all possible worlds. The comment might also have been scribbled upon the column Haldane had written for the *Daily Worker* not long before, in which he made the least of the selective role of conflicts between members of the same species and described contests between males as a 'perversion' of evolution.

Although Konrad Lorenz had been a cult enthusiasm among the UC zoology students, Maynard Smith had felt even then that something was not quite right in Lorenz's accounts of animal conflicts. Lorenz described how contests between animals were often limited to ritual displays, discriminating winners from losers with a minimum of damage to either. The semblance of enlightenment encouraged the idea that these patterns of behaviour had evolved for the good of the species.

Maynard Smith also learned two other theorems from Haldane. One was Aunt Jobiska's theorem, taken from Edward Lear's nonsense poem 'The Pobble Who Has No Toes': 'It's a fact the whole world knows.' The other was the Bellman's theorem, derived from Lewis Carroll's 'The Hunting of the Snark': 'What I tell you three times is true.' These, he was assured, were sufficient to do the whole of science.

In the light of the earlier discussion of Fisher and his theorem, there would seem to be a case for adding to this trio the comment on fitness that serves as an epigraph to the discussion of Haldane. Richard Dawkins eventually provided clarification, however. He distinguished between several different meanings of the word. There was the kind of fitness that Wallace and Darwin understood, an informal quality, similar to and overlapping with the everyday athletic sense of the word, which people knew when they saw it. 'Classical fitness' was a measure of an individual's success in producing offspring that themselves survived to reproductive age. Population geneticists would apply this criterion to particular genetic configurations, usually at single sites in the genome. Then there was Bill Hamilton's inclusive fitness, embracing an individual's effect on the reproductive success of relatives; and there was also the relatives' effect on the individual's reproduction to consider. Dawkins took the title for his discussion from 'The Hunting of the Snark': 'An Agony in Five Fits'.

A contest with rules is a game, and the essential feature of a game is that 'the best strategy to adopt depends on what others are doing'. Twenty years later, in 1970, and after five years as Dean at Sussex, Maynard Smith was given three months' sabbatical leave. He filled it with a stint at the University of Chicago and decided that while there he would return to the problem of contests among animals. An idea proposed by the wandering American scholar George Price, the man who made sense of Fisher's Fundamental Theorem, prompted Maynard Smith to investigate whether a tool of neoclassical economics could be adapted to represent the dynamics between animals.

Price, who had much in common with Hamilton in his isolation, had come to London in 1967, after a varied career that had taken him from the University of Chicago, where he trained in chemistry, to the Manhattan Project, which produced the first atomic bombs, to science journalism. Supporting himself from funds acquired in a divorce settlement and an insurance payout for injury sustained during an operation for thyroid cancer, he passed his days in scientific libraries and the exploration of Darwinian theory. He came across Hamilton's 1964 papers and was inspired by them to produce his own formula describing the action of natural selection. A correspondence and a friendship with Hamilton ensued. Price also wrote a paper on fights between animals, which he submitted to *Nature*. Maynard Smith was asked to review it. Though it was too long for *Nature*, he was impressed by Price's basic idea, which was that animals stabilise their contests not for the sake of the species but for that of their own skins. When they avoid escalating fights, it is to avoid retaliation.

Maynard Smith wondered if the idea of retaliation could be formalised. In Chicago, he learnt the basics of game theory, an analytical framework developed by John von Neumann and Oskar Morgenstern in the 1940s to model the process of making decisions that are influenced by the decisions of others. He was not the first to think of evolutionary processes as games. Fisher had implicitly treated sex ratios as games – though this only became clear to Maynard Smith subsequently – in which the value of producing one sex as offspring is enhanced to the extent that other parents produce the other sex. In the early 1960s, Richard Lewontin had attempted to apply game theory to biological problems but deemed the exercise a failure. Closer to home, in 1967, Bill Hamilton had published a paper which closed with an explicit discussion of sex ratios as games.

Again, however, Maynard Smith did not appreciate this until later. At the time, he did not read to the end of the paper. This was not untypical of him: the tendency was encouraged by the combination of poor eyesight and a vivid mathematical imagination. The problem comes first, then the solution and then the literature. 'Only when I've more or less done something, and I start thinking, "Well, this actually has come out; I ought to write it up," do I start trying to find out what other people have said on the subject.'

In Chicago, he formalised the idea of retaliation using game theory. Back home, when he came to write it up, he realised that he had to quote Price. In order to do that, he had to contact him, which he eventually achieved by getting Price's central London address from *Nature*, going round and banging on the door. As Price had not published his idea, Maynard Smith persuaded him that the paper should appear under both their names.

Nature ran 'The Logic of Animal Conflict' in November 1973. It pointed out that, given the benefits that accrue to the winners in contests between male animals, natural selection might in this arena be expected to be red in tooth and claw. Instead, however, selection often seemed to have gone to considerable lengths to limit the damage in these contests. Arabian oryxes do not quite bend over backwards to avoid hurting each other, but they do have to kneel down in order to tussle using their long and back-ward-curving horns. Many species of snake will wrestle among them-selves, but refrain from using their fangs. Mule deer bucks 'refuse to strike "foul blows"', declining to attack when their opponents expose the unpro-tected sides of their bodies.

Sceptical that such traits and behaviours could be produced by group selection, Maynard Smith and Price set out to show how they could be produced by individual selective advantage. They calculated pay-offs in simulated contests between players using five different strategies: Hawk, which invariably uses dangerous tactics; Mouse, which never does; Bully, which uses dangerous tactics against cautious ones, and vice versa; Retaliator, which tends to meet force with the same degree of force; and Prober-Retaliator, which occasionally probes restrained opponents with unrestrained attacks, pressing them if it does not provoke retaliation. Hawk represented 'total war', the rest 'limited war'.

The criterion of success for a player was that it should operate, in Maynard Smith's most influential phrase, an 'evolutionarily stable strat-egy', or ESS. This was a strategy which, if practised by nearly all members of a population, could not be supplanted by any other strategy. Although a mutant with a different strategy might occasionally appear, it would not spread.

By setting the average pay-offs out in tables and comparing them, it could be seen that total war was not evolutionarily stable. Mouse and Bully both did better against Hawk than Hawk did against itself; a population of Hawks could thus be 'invaded' by a Mouse or Bully mutant. Conversely, a Mouse or Bully population could be taken over by Hawks; Retaliator, however, was an ESS.

Among real animals, there might be no such 'pure' ESS. Instead, the stable system would be a 'mixed' strategy, in which a population comprised individuals employing different strategies or in which individuals themselves adopted different strategies on different occasions. Either way, the proportion of instances in which each strategy was used would remain stable. Individual evolutionary advantage could limit war, though retaliation, as Price had recognised, was needed to guarantee stability.

The lesson has lasted, though Maynard Smith came to feel that he and Price had not done a very good job. Other workers showed that there was an alternative ESS they had missed. But when the political scientist Robert Axelrod conducted a famous series of games from which 'tit for tat' – start by co-operating, then copy your opponent's previous move – emerged as the best strategy, Maynard Smith felt that he knew this already. 'Tit for tat' was another name for 'retaliator'. 'On the other hand,' he acknowledges, Axelrod 'made it vivid in a way that perhaps we didn't.' Axelrod made a splash with a paper published by the American journal *Science* in 1981, together with his co-author, Bill Hamilton.

The Hawk–Mouse game was renamed too, becoming known as the Hawk–Dove game. That was what Maynard Smith called it in the first place, working in Chicago during the Vietnam War, and those were the names that got as far as *Nature*'s proofs. Then Price asked to withdraw his name from the paper, because he now felt that as the word 'dove' was identified with the Holy Spirit, its use in this context would be blasphemous. Maynard Smith met his objection by suggesting 'mouse' as a substitute.

This was not Price's first reservation about their choice of words. In February 1973, he had written to his collaborator about the use of the word 'evolve'. Pointing out that he believed in divine creation, he had altered 'what strategy will evolve under natural selection' to 'what strategy will be favoured under individual selection'. There was no problem about 'evolutionary stability', however, as belief in creation was compatible with belief in evolution. Quite how Price had decided where to draw the line between divine and material processes is mysterious, but it is clear that, as he went on, he felt obliged to render ever more to the Lord. In earlier discussions, he himself had suggested using the word 'dove'.

Selection Revealed

Price had spent much of his life as a resolute atheist; his belief, conflicting with his wife's Catholicism, had contributed to the breakdown of his marriage. In the spring of 1970, however, he began to dwell upon a series of incidents that had recently happened to him. Calculating the odds against them, he became convinced that they were so improbable that divine intervention must have lain behind them. On 7 June 1970, he opened the floodgates of faith. He ran through the streets of London near his flat and into the first church he found, where he knelt down and prayed.

Price had secured an academic niche at University College's Galton Laboratory, having impressed the biostatistician Cedric Smith with what has become known as the Price equation. This formula, a new means to analyse natural selection, was 'very interesting, very pretty' and like nothing Smith had seen before. Now Price combined his science with a new line of work in biblical exegesis, producing a new chronology for Easter in which the traditional Holy Week was extended to twelve days. Impressed by Price's 'Sherlock Holmes mind' and attention to detail, Bill Hamilton found it a 'gripping tale'. Hamilton's own agnosticism, and his Darwinism, did not stop him appreciating a new version of the greatest story ever told.

For his part Price continued to balance his faith and his evolutionary science, but as his precarious distinction between 'evolve' and 'be favoured' suggests, it was not a stable arrangement. The difficulty of finding a diplomatic form of words was a symptom of a greater struggle, not between the idea of evolution and the doctrines of Christianity, but over how Price believed God wanted him to spend his time on Earth. At the end of the summer of 1972, he underwent what he saw as a test of his vocation. He explained to Maynard Smith that for some time he had known that he would not be able to go on living a conventional life, with an ordinary job and an ordinary flat, but he had resisted the realisation. 'Wishful

thinking kept me supposing that it was not really going to happen to me –
or at least not in the extreme way that it seemed always to happen in the
accounts I had read by missionaries and others who had themselves lived
"the life of faith".'

In those accounts, he continued ruefully, God would always supply the
necessary cheque just before the moment of disaster. He had calculated
that his deliverance would arrive around 20 September. 'However, it
appears that God's standards of what constitutes "disaster" are on a different scale from mine. Furthermore, it appears that His standards are
more accurate than mine . . .' A month later, Price was still hanging on, but
he looked forward 'eagerly' to the imminent meeting of God's standards of
disaster, once his last 15p was gone.

He spent it, but the Lord did not provide. Maynard Smith challenged
him to admit that he had been wrong, but Price defiantly replied that he
still had a tin of baked beans in the fridge . . . and his Barclaycard, a device
St Matthew did not envisage when he reported the words 'Take therefore
no thought for the morrow' in the passage that had impelled Price's drive
to poverty: 'Therefore I say unto you, Take no thought for your life, what
ye shall eat, or what ye shall drink, nor yet for your body, what ye shall put
on . . .'

After these comic touches, Price ventured towards tragedy. His surgery
for thyroid cancer had left him dependent on artificial supplies of the hor-
mone thyroxine. At times of desperation, he told Bill Hamilton, he would
sometimes stop taking this medicine as a way to test God's wishes for him.
On one such occasion he was taken to hospital, where a doctor recognised
signs of thyroid deficiency and restored the medication without telling
him; he duly took it as a sign that God wanted him to carry on. He underwent a second revelatory crisis in February 1973, in which he became
seized with the conviction that his duty was to other people rather than to
scripture. Henceforth the precept by which he would live his life was the
one set down in Luke 6:30: 'Give to every man that asketh of thee; and of
him that taketh away thy goods ask not again.'

The consequences of his freelance mission were predictable. At the
extremity of altruism, he was a dove in a world of hawks. Or rather, he was
trying to be a pure dove in a world that cannot be taken over by dovish-
ness, in which an individual trying to practise Christian virtue must

embed it in a mixed strategy. Price had seen the need for retaliation, and now he renounced it.

As a voluntary worker he was a breathtaking force. The manager of an old people's home recalled how on Christmas Eve in 1973 he descended upon them like an 'angel', stayed up with her wrapping presents, and in the morning fed and dressed all twenty-one residents after she overslept. But hawkishness was taking its toll. He had given up his flat in June and his remaining possessions shortly thereafter. This inevitably drew his charitable work across the threshold of University College, where he was now sleeping in his office. One angry drunk, whose wife Price had been sheltering from his aggression, repeatedly showed up and threw his weight around, on one occasion urinating over the steps of the Genetics Department. Price remarked to his daughter that making the front cover of *Nature*, with the 'Animal Conflict' paper, should compensate for the fouling of the front entrance to the building. But the poor and disordered drove him away from his academic haven nonetheless. So did a disillusionment with theoretical mathematical genetics, which he felt 'wasn't very relevant to human problems'. He thought of going into economics; he ended up in a communal (and, at the time, quite famous) squat in Tolmers Square, on the other side of the Euston Road.

Towards the end of 1974, he began to retrace his steps. 'Jesus wants me to do less about helping others and give more attention to sorting out my own problems,' he told Hamilton. He had formed an attachment to a woman who lived in the squat and had started to accumulate possessions again; he told his brother that he was contemplating marriage, had abandoned his attempts to help those hardest to help and had moderated his interpretation of Christian duty. Hamilton encouraged him to return to science full-time; he also received encouragement in the form of letters from the influential American geneticists Richard Lewontin and James Crow, both of whom expressed their regret that they had been slow to appreciate the significance of his work.

But this new life never succeeded in replacing the quest that had driven him to the edge of material existence or the depression through which it churned. He stayed with the Hamiltons before Christmas 1974 and was due to visit them again after the holiday. Over that most testing of seasons, he despaired finally. On 5 January, he was found dead in his room, having snipped through his carotid artery with a pair of nail scissors. Hamilton's name was found on copies of recent letters, and so the police asked him to take care of Price's few effects. He found a room with a bare bulb and broken windows patched with brown paper, a mattress, a chair, a table and some ammunition boxes (these were available at a local military surplus shop and were useful for storage). Price had retained a few clothes, his papers, his typewriter and two volumes of Proust. 'As I tidied what was worth taking into the suitcase, his dried blood crackled on the linoleum under my shoes: a basically tidy man, he had chosen to die on the open floor, not on his bed.'

Price's short suicide note spoke of depression induced by the difficulties he experienced, especially in trying to practise charity, and the feeling that he was a burden on his friends. The inquest raised the possibility that his judgement had been affected by his health, for there was evidence that he had lapsed from taking his thyroxine again.

His funeral service was held on secular premises, his Christian fervour being outweighed, as far as the Church of England was concerned, by the manner of his death. It was, however, attended by the priest from the church he had attended, All Souls, which is next door to the BBC's Broadcasting House. Also present were Hamilton, Maynard Smith and several unkempt figures who had evidently appreciated Price's efforts to bring them true Christian charity. Afterwards the priest offered the scientists his own explanation of Price's fate. The trouble was, the cleric observed, that George Price had taken his Christianity too seriously. 'I think that he felt that what was good enough for St Paul was good enough for him,' Hamilton replied.

Hamilton also believed that his own early papers, on how natural selection could promote altruism on the basis of shared genes, might have precipitated Price's long religious agony in the first place. 'By suggesting to him that life evolved purely by natural selection would not be nearly as benign as he had previously supposed, the papers seem to have had a profound effect on him. Could this limited nepotistic altruism be the best, the most "humane", that evolution could achieve? If so the prospect for humanity seemed stark.' Having satisfied himself that Hamilton had got it more or less right, Price became depressed. A week or so later, the Holy Spirit descended upon him.

This interpretation, which was taken up by Andrew Brown in his book *The Darwin Wars*, is appealing despite its bleakness, for it proposes a clear, and indeed causal, relationship between Price's evolutionary thought and his religious faith. It depends upon the timing, with the conversion following a matter of days after the completion of the mathematical investigation. But it appears that Hamilton was mistaken about this. He later provided his correspondence with Price to James Schwartz, who wrote an account of Price's life for the journal *Lingua Franca*. According to Schwartz's record of the correspondence, Price wrote to Hamilton, asking for a reprint of 'The Genetical Evolution of Social Behaviour', in March 1968. In the summer he wrote to tell Hamilton of his equation, a 'more transparent' formulation of the main result in the 'Genetical Evolution' papers. His conversion, which Schwartz dates with a quote from Price, did not take place until nearly two years later.

It remains possible that Price was impelled to accept Christ because he had become convinced that human nature was incapable of true virtue without divine assistance. His pursuit of altruism certainly looks like an attempt to prove that we are capable of rising above natural selection. But he lived with the implications of kin selection for two years before becoming a Christian, and another two before abandoning a relatively conventional way of life. Even then, he continued to work on evolutionary theory, collaborating with two outstanding but godless evolutionists apparently without any difficulty more fundamental than the one that was settled by the adoption of the word 'mouse'.

Indeed, he seemed to feel that God had assisted him in his work. Like Alfred Russel Wallace, he appeared reluctant to take credit for his greatest insight. His equation seemed to everyone else to have come from nowhere. As Hamilton observed, it owed nothing to any previous selection theory. Price himself considered it a miracle. It was 'ludicrous', he told Hamilton, to suppose that somebody who had previously known nothing of statistics could have discovered the simple but transparent formula that had eluded population geneticists ever since Fisher. He must therefore have been chosen to bring the news of this truth about natural selection, a mystery among mysteries.

There is no such simple formula to explain the man who sailed over on the *Queen Elizabeth* to learn about natural selection in its heartland, improved upon the work of the great English selectionists Fisher and Hamilton, and found the Lord there too; a Word higher than numbers.

At first, John Maynard Smith didn't 'think there was much mileage' in the idea of evolutionarily stable strategies. In Chicago, he set stability conditions as a problem for the graduate students he was teaching. Most of them managed to work out the answers; it was a straightforward enough procedure: 'One felt nothing important could be that easy.' The great thing about it, as far as Maynard Smith was concerned, was that it showed that George Price's speculative ideas about retaliation really did work.

Then he went down to Austin, Texas, to give a seminar. By that time, he was thinking about the next stage in the hawk–dove scenario: the war of attrition. Limiting the damage in a contest will tend to encourage a contest without limits. A confrontation in which the contestants merely threaten each other will drag on until attrition wears one of them down to the point of capitulation. In the long run there are no winners, though: Maynard Smith worked out that the expected average pay-off is zero.

If humans were playing such a game, Maynard Smith thought, they would toss for it. Tossing a coin is a means of making a symmetrical situation asymmetric. Among other species, the obvious asymmetry to apply would be occupancy of a territory. Maynard Smith had hit upon the 'bourgeois' strategy: play Hawk if you are an owner and Dove if you are an interloper. What the sums seemed to say, he told his audience in Texas, was that animals ought to respect ownership. But he didn't suppose they really did. After all, how could they?

A young lecturer called Larry Gilbert stood up and told him how. Gilbert had done his Ph.D. fieldwork in California, studying 'hilltopping' among swallowtail butterflies. Male swallowtails occupy hilltops, where females fly up to mate with them. There are more males than hilltops, so unsuccessful ones have to settle for territories on the slopes, where the females appear less ready to tarry. Occasionally a male flies up to a hilltop where another is already in residence: the two spiral round each other for a few moments, and the intruder departs. Gilbert tested what would happen when the asymmetry of ownership was removed. He 'let one butterfly have the hilltop on Mondays, Wednesdays and Fridays, and the other one have it on Tuesdays, Thursdays and Saturdays', keeping them in the dark on their days off. After two weeks, he released both of them on the hilltop. They engaged in a protracted spiral flight, in which each damaged the other.

'I sat there absolutely mesmerised,' Maynard Smith recalled. 'I think it was at that moment that I thought, "Well, maybe I'm on to something."' The ESS idea could be applied to a whole range of contests, not just the situation Price had raised. Gilbert's was only the first of a number of cases in which nature appeared to have gone out of its way to confirm Maynard Smith's predictions. Its sublime conformity, combined with Gilbert's low publication profile, led Maynard Smith's Sussex colleagues to refer to Gilbert as 'John's imaginary biologist'. Eventually Maynard Smith succeeded in proving his existence by producing him in person.

That organic textbook, the countryside around Oxford, provided an example very similar to that of the Californian swallowtails. Speckled wood butterflies are as familiar a sight along English woodland paths as cabbage whites on garden vegetable patches. Their chocolate and cream colour schemes are stylised reflections of the dappled shade that they frequent; a speckled wood territory is a patch of sunlight. The Oxford biologist Nick Davies found that in Wytham Woods, as on the Californian hilltops, an intruder and an occupier would engage in a brief spiral flight, and the intruder would go away. In Sweden, however, speckled woods proved to be a more truculent breed, less willing to conform to textbook standards. When occupiers left their patches and returned to find squatters, they invariably drove them away. Davies suggested that the Swedish butterflies were more combative because warm sunny patches were scarcer on the ground in Sweden than in England, making them more valuable and therefore more worth fighting over. He had netted his males during the memorably long hot summer of 1976; in subsequent cooler summers, he had found that the butterflies in Wytham Woods contested their patches longer.

Maynard Smith explored some questions arising from evolutionary game theory with another British biologist, Geoff Parker. One of these was why animals should have bourgeois values. 'Geoff was a good socialist in those days,' Maynard Smith recalled; Parker wanted to know why the convention was that the owner wins rather than the intruder. The answer turned out to be that if the convention favours the intruder, it turns the owner into a new intruder and so is a recipe for constant turmoil: the new intruder will win its next contest, creating another dispossessed intruder, and so on. Nature offers a supporting example in the spider *Oecibus civitas*. At first sight this species appears impeccably bourgeois, gathering together to form exclusive estates in which each spider has its own web and hiding hole. If one is driven out of its hole, however, it may scuttle into another, displacing the occupant, which in turn runs off to another hole; the ensuing domino effect may uproot most of the group.

Parker himself had identified the key elements of a war of attrition among male dungflies, although there was no actual fighting. The attrition involved the length of time a male was prepared to hang around a cowpat waiting for females to arrive at it. His returns would diminish as the cowpat grew stale and attracted fewer females, but his pay-off would depend on what other males did. If the others did not stay at the cowpat very long, it would be worth remaining, because there would be no other competition for any females that did arrive. If others stayed, on the other hand, he should go. As it turned out, the number of matings expected for loiterers was the same as that for leavers, showing that an ESS had been established. This was one of many demonstrations, in species ranging from butterflies to baboons, of the underlying principle that 'whenever the best strategy for an individual depends on what others are doing, the strategy actually adopted will be an ESS'.

Evolutionary game theory became Maynard Smith's most distinctive and celebrated contribution to evolutionary thought. Having set the ball rolling, though, he found it outrunning him. 'It all got too mathematical for me,' he confesses.

He also steered clear of attempts by economists to get what they doubtless saw as their ball back. There are, according to theorists, formal similarities between classical and evolutionary games. The ESS, for example, can be seen as a form of 'Nash equilibrium': named after the mathematician John Nash, this refers to a situation in which players have adopted a set of strategies that offer an individual player no chance of benefiting from a change of strategy. Nevertheless, Maynard Smith saw the two forms of game theory as processes with a shared notation but different logic: neoclassical economics is a matter of rational choices; biology is a matter of dynamics.

*

Neoclassical economics sat uncomfortably with his political instincts, too. He had been mildly embarrassed by the irony of going to Chicago, the nest of neoliberalism, and splicing elements of neoclassical economic code into biology. In doing so, however, he was furthering a long British tradition of exchange between economics and the natural sciences. Karl Marx, who welcomed Darwin's *Origin of Species* as the basis in natural science for his theory of class struggle, nonetheless remarked 'how Darwin recognises among beasts and plants his English society with its labour, competition, opening up of new markets, "inventions", and the Malthusian "struggle for existence".' The influence of Adam Smith's 'invisible hand', leading individuals to promote the greater good by pursuing their own interests, is also easy to detect in the idea of adaptation by natural selection. And behind Smith stands the shadow of Isaac Newton, according to a study of the 'genealogy' of natural selection by David Depew and Bruce Weber. Classical economists drew on Newtonian concepts; in drawing on Smith and Malthus, Darwin drew upon Newton, one of the highest sources of authority and conceptual power in British science.

Darwin was able to recognise his English society all the more easily because of his British intellectual culture, which was based on the individualism most clearly evident in Adam Smith's view of economics. Individualism worked for British evolutionists, as Maynard Smith implicitly reaffirmed when he went to America and came back with a set of games borrowed from Smith's intellectual descendants.

He ran into another tangle of ideology and biology when he encountered Edward O. Wilson's book *Sociobiology: The New Synthesis* in 1975. Most of it was concerned with insects, but he turned first to the chapters in which Wilson attempted to demonstrate the value of applying the same biological considerations to human social behaviour as to ant societies.

Discussing it with his colleagues over a Friday evening drink in the Swan, the pub over the hill behind Biols that served as their licensed common room, he found that his initial reaction differed sharply from theirs. The graduate students mostly welcomed it for putting the evolution of social behaviour on the map. Maynard Smith regarded it as an 'absolute disaster', realising that its *démarche* into social science would turn its subject into a political debate in which the science would be submerged. He also found Wilson's discussion of human sociobiology 'half-baked', which added to his dismay.

Nevertheless, his reviews of Wilson's books were even in temper and judgement. In her history of a quarter-century's controversies over socio-biology, *Defenders of the Truth*, Ullica Segerstråle picks him out as one of only a few players with a foot in both camps – and a 'strong commitment to both fairness and communication'. His most trenchant criticisms of Wilson were delivered in a review of *Genes, Mind and Culture*, a book Wilson co-wrote with Charles Lumsden. They were strong because they addressed mathematics, not matters of opinion. Maynard Smith had noted that the initial reviews of the book had passed judgement without examin-ing the models of cultural evolution on which its arguments rested, and therefore 'spent several months trying to understand the maths'. Other authors would have deemed this concentration on mathematics sufficient guarantee against bias, but Maynard Smith struck up a reviewing alliance with an anthropologist, Neil Warren, to balance any prejudices he might bring to the subject as a biologist.

Even then, he was 'still coming to terms with Marxism'. The difficulty was not fundamental, nor had it ever been, as Haldane had shown with his insistence on the inequality of man and its compatibility with commu-nism. Only a couple of years after Maynard Smith quit the Party, the blurb underneath his picture on the back of his book *The Theory of Evolution* (high forehead, thick swatch of hair swept to the side, between his teeth the pipe that was an obligatory accessory for a scientist on a Pelican paper-back in those days) had declared his interest in 'the social consequences of the fact that all men are not created equal, although they may be equally valuable if given the right opportunities': sociobiology *avant la lettre*. After that came years of experience with the idea of kin selection; but at the back of his mind was still the Marxist precept that being determines con-sciousness. Neither pole was satisfactory: there was more to morality than kin selection, and more to human nature than a blank slate upon which the external world may write what it pleases. 'I tend to find myself disagreeing most strongly with whichever side I talked to last,' he observed as the debates simmered along.

In the 1990s, a new form of human sociobiology emerged, calling itself evolutionary psychology. It differed from its predecessor in one major respect concerning adaptation. The first wave of human sociobiologists had sought evidence that people behave so as to maximise the number of their surviving children. Its success outside traditional societies was limited and was overshadowed in the modern world of artificial contraception. Evolutionary psychologists resolved this incongruity by proposing that adaptations should be sought in the mind rather than in behaviour. They argued that human psychology had evolved in response to the conditions of life a hundred thousand years ago and often produced very different results in conditions that had largely arisen during the last hundred years.

Maynard Smith found himself more in sympathy with the evolutionary psychologists than he had with the earlier sociobiologists, 'but quite why isn't obvious to me'. It was not the suggestion of an adaptive lag between evolved psychology and current environments, although he regarded the idea as a sensible one. He had earlier been impressed by Mildred Dickemann's study of dowries in India, which indicated that people did in fact arrange their affairs so as to maximise the number of their children who survived to adulthood; along with work by William Irons, it made him warm to sociobiology. He was disappointed by the dearth of similar data in evolutionary psychology, which seemed largely content to confine its output to ideas. But he was pleased to find that the evolutionary psychologists did not display the 'naive insistence that everything is to be explained in simple genetic terms' that he had encountered in Wilson's argument.

He did not, then, see a fundamental difference between the kind of human sociobiology that looks for ongoing efforts to maximise reproductive success and the kind that seeks to describe the adaptations which supported those efforts in ancient times. 'On the other hand I think I'm different, and consequently have reacted more sympathetically to this current wave who call themselves evolutionary psychologists.' Over the years, some of the dyes in his ideological fabric had faded.

'I start with a problem, which is usually a problem about the world; it's a fact about animals or plants that puzzles me. Some animal is doing what the theory shouldn't let it do – at first sight the simple version of the theory would predict that it did one thing, and it does something else. If I get anywhere with the problem, I tend to start making simple little models.'

The model is 'only half the battle'. After that comes intuition, and after that the idea is put into words. Doing it the other way round would be like building the walls before the foundations. This is Maynard Smith's way of tackling a problem in biology, and follows in Haldane's footsteps. Intuition is valuable in the first place to himself, enabling him to understand how the modelled effect works. Once put into words, it is in a form that can be readily shared. Therein lies one of John Maynard Smith's most distinctive gifts: his flair for making sense of biological ideas and enabling others to grasp them. A very great part of his influence as a scientist arises from the happy combination of a mathematical intellect and a love of conversation.

In trying to follow the ideas of others, however, he relies on maths; reviewing books by Richard Dawkins, he remarked with some surprise that he had no difficulty following them, even though they contained not a single line of mathematics. When he first started out in biology and was writing papers on animal locomotion, he faced the difficulty that many of his fellow biologists were effectively innumerate. One paper, which he retrospectively claimed as possibly the first in biology to treat optimisation mathematically, included the equation $dw/dj=0$. 'The editor, offended by this attempt to sully a respectable biological journal with mathematics, asked, "Why don't you cancel the d's?"' – not recognising that the equation was a differential one, in which the d's are not numbers.

Over the subsequent half century, much of biology came to speak Maynard Smith's language. He did, however, encounter a pocket of resistance. Amotz Zahavi, an Israeli naturalist, proposed in 1975 that animal signals were based upon what he called the Handicap Principle. A wolf begins to close on a gazelle; the latter springs vertically in the air, several times, instead of making off horizontally as fast as it can. It is demonstrating that it is so fit that it can afford to waste time and energy without endangering itself. Underlying this ostentatious display is the principle that 'in order to be effective, signals have to be reliable; in order to be reliable, signals have to be costly'. The peacock maintains his tail not despite the burden it imposes on him but because of it.

Zahavi insisted that, although his theory was about costs, he was under no obligation to calculate them. He preferred to watch birds and apply his intuition to what he observed. The superiority of mathematics was just snobbery – 'If it's in words, it's intuition; if it's in symbols, it's science.' Zahavi is a reactionary from the backwoods of natural history, setting a granite face on his belief that neo-Darwinism can be a romantic pursuit.

Maynard Smith, of course, took the view that, in order for the theory to be considered reliable, the costs would have to be demonstrated by calculation. He tried to represent Zahavi's argument in a model, but the results did not support the Handicap Principle. Zahavi came to Sussex and the two of them held a summit conference at the Maynard Smiths' house. It was, John recalled, one of the worst weekends of his life. Neither appeared to grasp a word the other said. Afterwards, Sheila decreed that Zahavi was not to cross their threshold again, not because of his behaviour, but because of the mood he had put her husband in. John himself was left inclined to dismiss the Handicap Principle.

Other analysts saw more potential in the idea (including Maynard Smith's student Andrew Pomiankowski). In 1990, Alan Grafen published a paper which persuaded Maynard Smith that there might be something in it after all. Crucially, Grafen treated costs in relative rather than absolute terms. The price of a gold bracelet may be the same to a top footballer and a humble fan, but the real cost to the richer man is far lower. Maynard Smith had not incorporated this effect into his own model, because Zahavi had not included it in his account.

Maynard Smith was impressed by Grafen's treatment but daunted by the maths. He realised that if he found Grafen's mathematics hard to grasp, it would leave many other people entirely at a loss. After spending much of a holiday in Sweden pacing round an island as he tried to devise a more accessible version, he came up with what he dubbed the Sir Philip Sidney game. It was named after the sixteenth-century poet who is best remembered for the line of prose he spoke after he had been hit by a Spanish musket-ball on the Dutch battlefield of Zutphen. As he raised a water bottle to his lips, Sir Philip saw a mortally wounded soldier casting his eyes longingly at it. He passed the bottle to the soldier, saying, 'Thy necessity is yet greater than mine.'

Maynard Smith adapted this moral example for the purpose of evolutionary instruction. To make it credible, it required inclusive fitness; the two wounded men should be brothers. What was needed was a reliable signal to confirm that the second man's need really was greater than Sir Philip's. Having specified the conditions algebraically, Maynard Smith confirmed that there were indeed circumstances in which signals had to be costly in order to be reliable.

Meanwhile, the importance of costs in signalling was becoming widely accepted, not least through the influence of work by Richard Dawkins and John Krebs. Signals between animals, they argued, tended to be a manipulative activity rather than a co-operative one, for it was so often in the interests of one animal to deceive another. They described the possibility of signalling 'arms races', as efforts to deceive would provoke increasing 'sales resistance' from the receivers of the signals. Signals given during competition – over resources such as territory or access to potential mates – would tend to be loud, literally or metaphorically, and a loud signal is a costly one. If co-operation could be established, however, the co-operators could signal to each other in cheap 'conspiratorial whispers'. The lesson of the debates over group selection was being followed through: in the evolution of behaviour, mutual benefit is not a sufficient explanation for anything.

When Maynard Smith returned to the subject of animal communication, about ten years later, he felt no further obligation to make his adversary's case for him. Zahavi's handicap theory had successfully colonised the field – for the wrong reasons, as far as Maynard Smith was concerned. Naturalists nowadays felt under an obligation to apply a theory to their work, and they hoped that a single theory would cover it; being uncomfortable with mathematics, they hoped that Zahavi's would do.

Maynard Smith was there to tell them that life is not that simple. One of his central themes was that there are many circumstances in which signals can be reliable without being costly. As in the other major areas of biology he had investigated, he had reached the conclusion that there was no single – and consequently easy – answer.

He had helped to define modern Darwinism by criticising Wynne-Edwards's ideas about the power of natural selection to act on groups and by introducing the term 'kin selection' to distinguish Hamilton's mechanism from it. But Maynard Smith was left with a nagging doubt. If evolutionists rejected group selection as the basis of social behaviour, could they accept it as the basis of sex? Even Fisher had regarded sex as the one major phenomenon that might best be explained by its advantages to populations rather than individuals, and his view had prevailed as an assumption among evolutionary biologists.

Having rather lost interest in death, Maynard Smith became increasingly concerned with sex. The more he thought about it, the more he realised how hard it was to square with natural selection. But it was no more intuitively obvious to biologists than to anybody else that the means of reproduction for most complex organisms should pose a problem for a theory centred upon reproductive success. Maynard Smith's main contribution to the problem of sex lay in pointing out to his colleagues that there is a problem.

It arises from the imbalance by which the sexes are defined. Sex itself is the exchange of genetic material between organisms. Among creatures which consist only of single cells, there is a kind of gender division. A '+' cell can fuse only with a '−' cell, and vice versa. They are mirror images of each other. In more complex organisms, the two classes of reproductive cells differ in size. One class is small, specialised for mobility, and the other large, in order to store resources. Small gametes are male, and large ones female; they likewise define the individuals that produce them.

Males are thus the sex which by definition tends to contribute less to offspring. The tendency is counterbalanced in species within which males assist in the care of the young. But broadly speaking, producing males incurs a cost. The difficulty is at its starkest in organisms – cod, for example – in which males do not contribute anything to the offspring beyond fertilisation. If a mutation were to arise in a female cod that allowed her to reproduce without needing her eggs to be fertilised, she would have twice as many daughters as an ordinary sexually reproducing female. Her descendants would all carry the gene for asexual reproduction and would rapidly increase their share of the population. Unhampered by the 'twofold cost of sex', the virgin mutants would take over.

They might take over more than their own gene pool, too. Species in which asexual reproduction appears to have replaced sex include many of those runaway successes of hedge and garden, blackberries and dandelions. Being able to spread rapidly, they are powerful colonisers. While sexually reproducing dandelions still flourish in regions of southern

Europe, northern Europe is dominated by asexual lines, which retain the apparatus of their sexual ancestry in their flamboyant but superfluous flowers.

On evolutionary timescales, though, they may be a flash in the pan. Abandoning sex is like quitting a steady job to play the stock market. Lineages that go clonal may strike it rich, but they tend not to last long. Doing without males is physiologically feasible for a wide range of organisms, including lizards, but not evolutionarily sustainable. After an initial boom, asexually reproducing populations are liable to be replaced by ones with the conventional sexual lifestyle. The pattern is indicated by the incidence of asexual reproduction, which occurs in species, or genera, but hardly ever dominates families or orders of organisms.

This, as Maynard Smith came to acknowledge, is a process in which selection does appear to be acting on populations, as distinct from individuals. George Williams was less inclined to tolerate group selection – in Maynard Smith's opinion, he 'is the person who really forced us to face up to it' – and pointed out that sex must have short-term advantages for individuals in order to withstand competition from the asexual option. It must certainly have had immediate advantages for the very first organisms that practised it, for otherwise it could not have become established. The problem of sex is a daunting compound of adaptive questions: its advantages for populations and its benefits for individuals; how it is maintained and how it arose in the first place. So, as Maynard Smith asked in the *Journal of Theoretical Biology* in 1971, 'What Use is Sex?'

It might, as Fisher and Muller had suggested forty years previously, be useful for combining beneficial mutations. If a mutation arises in a sexually reproducing individual and another one in a different individual, sexual combination may bring the two together in a common descendant. In an asexual population, no individuals would carry both mutations until each had occurred in the same lineage. Sex might therefore be a way to enable organisms to evolve quicker. That could be particularly useful for organisms which needed to keep up with rapidly changing environmental conditions. But in other circumstances, sex could be a disruptive force. A combination of genes in an organism that reproduces is by definition a successful one; by recombining genes in the offspring, sex will tend to break up successful teams.

Another use for sex might be to avoid 'Muller's ratchet', by which harmful mutations inexorably accumulate. Within a hypothetical population, individuals will have varying numbers of moderately harmful mutations. Some may have none, but at some stage a generation will appear in which there are no such optimal individuals. If there are still individuals with only one harmful mutation, they will represent the new optimum, and the ratchet will have moved up a notch. Without sex to halt it, it will continue to rise.

Then there is Maynard Smith's gearbox, a metaphor for the possible role of sex in neutralising mutations that lacks the steely edge of Muller's ratchet. Sex could produce a fit individual by combining sound components from flawed parents, like a garage in which a roadworthy car is assembled from one with a working engine but a worn-out gearbox and a second with a functional gearbox but an unserviceable engine. The objection to this is 'Yes, madam, but what if it had my beauty and your brains?', George Bernard Shaw's reply to the actress who suggested they have a child on the assumption that nature would choose the best from each of them. Maynard Smith, incidentally, read Shaw avidly as a boy, but grew up to be just the kind of 'Neo-Darwinian' that the playwright and advocate of 'Creative Evolution' abhorred.

The maths backed the metaphor: the ability of sex to combine favourable mutations could be very good for populations, and sexual populations would lose harmful mutations quicker than asexual ones. Possibly the ability to evolve more quickly, or to clear undesirable mutations efficiently, might also be good for individuals. But the models have proved less successful in grasping the point of sex for the single organism. Williams suggested that its advantage at the level of the individual lay in its ability to shuffle the cards and deal a range of genetic hands: variety would be an asset in an unpredictable environment. Maynard Smith's analysis concluded that, for this to be the explanation, the environment would have to be as unpredictable as a jumping bean. He suggested instead that sex might come into its own when two strains of an organism, adapted to somewhat different conditions, both began to colonise a new environment: the ability to hybridise would make the process of adaptation thousands of times quicker.

The engine and gearbox came in useful, many years later, for a scenario illustrating how sex might have first arisen. Sexual reproduction is based upon the ability to double and halve the number of chromosomes in a cell, which is called diploid if it has two sets and haploid if it has only one. Ancient cells, Maynard Smith's collaborator Eörs Szathmáry argued, were not built to withstand damage from the 'free radical' ions which oxygen kindles. With two sets of chromosomes, damage in one series could be checked and repaired by reference to the second.

There may be advantages to having only a single set of chromosomes, though, such as faster growth or a lower load of mutations. If so, an organism might get the best of both states by evolving a life cycle that swung between the two. A haploid cell could double its chromosomes to become diploid on its own. But if this process was replaced by the fusion of two haploid cells, damaged elements in one could be replaced by sound ones from the other. The benefits would be felt more reliably if the cells were genetically different, so a division into + and − would be favoured, bringing sex into being.

As the investigations stimulated by Maynard Smith's question have unfolded, theories of sex have resolved into two themes. One, the clearance of mutations, implies that the purpose of sex is maintenance; the other, the speeding of evolution, suggests that sex is for fresh adaptation. To put it another way, it is either to make up for the deterioration of the genome or to make up for the deterioration of the environment.

The deleterious mutation hypothesis was developed in large measure by the Russian biologist Alexey Kondrashov, whose interest in the evolution of sex was stimulated (before his emigration to the United States) by Maynard Smith's book of that name. Mutation clearance becomes credible as an explanation if organisms undergo more than one deleterious mutation per individual in each generation. The evidence on this score has yet to settle. One of Maynard Smith's Sussex colleagues, Adam Eyre-Walker, has calculated that humans have about two such mutations each per generation. But he and his co-worker Peter Keightley also found that this rate was a couple of orders of magnitude above those of *Drosophila*, while mutation rates in chickens and mice were also less than one. The longer a species takes to complete a generation, the more time there is for mutations to occur.

Rapid evolutionary response presumes that environments are in sufficient flux to require it. An environment in such a state of constant flux must be one which consists largely of other organisms. According to the 'Red Queen' view of evolution, selection is driven by the pressure of competition with surrounding organisms, which are themselves constantly evolving. The most dynamic, and selectively challenging, of these competitors are parasites. Maynard Smith was among those who became persuaded that parasites were likely to have been a driving force in the evolution of sex.

On this he agreed with Bill Hamilton, but in their agreement the difference in their thought was highlighted. For Hamilton, the selective role of parasites was a uniquely powerful explanatory idea, which came to dominate the latter part of his intellectual life. He believed that with it he had answered Maynard Smith's question. But even after thirty years, with all the computing power and genetic data that could now be brought to bear, Maynard Smith himself still saw it as the puzzle of puzzles. 'We don't really understand it,' he says. 'It's just too hard for us.'

He no longer suspected, as he once had, that the question might not be answerable within a Darwinian framework. But what makes it so difficult is that the ordinary Darwinian framework of individual selection does not cover it. Whereas the problems of animal behaviour, for example, can be addressed by considering the fitness of individuals and that which they share with their kin, sex demands 'a whole slew of answers' about the effects of selection at different levels. Since sex became a problem for biologists, they have become aware that, as well as individuals and populations, there is 'a great bewildering mass' of self-replicating entities within the genome with mutually conflicting interests to consider as well.

All the while, underfoot, the dandelions added insult to the gardening evolutionist's uncertainty. Nothing a gardener can do will stop the dandelions underfoot from sticking two vegetable fingers up to sexual reproduction. And each one that escapes the hoe long enough to flower, despite having no use for insects, defies adaptationism with a gratuitous gesture.

As their careers progress, many scientists exchange knowledge for power, or at least have power thrust upon them. They complain of their administrative responsibilities and savour the taste of political influence. John Maynard Smith, however, simply carried on as he had started.

His academic career had begun when Peter Medawar bumped into him in a University College corridor and offered him a job. Unlike today's endlessly assessed and bureaucratically tormented academics, he was able to wear his obligations outside research relatively lightly. This was not always appreciated by postgraduate students seeking supervision, and deprived Biols of a source of political support behind the scenes. But he made up for it by omitting to retire.

He and Sheila never collaborated on major scientific problems. They wrote just one joint paper, though naturally they talked science, and John would often confirm that 'Sheila's checked the sums'. But he felt that research collaborations are very like marriages and are liable to unravel in similar ways. 'To try and bring both off in one relationship – I think it would be terribly hard.'

Instead, he took up the subject Sheila had worked on at Sussex, microbial genetics, where she left off. Through the 1990s he devoted much of his time to bacteria. This was modern molecular biology, driven by the torrents of data that the technology now generated. Maynard Smith's role was largely to develop statistical methods for analysing the data, though it was a question of adaptation that drew him into the work – antibiotic resistance, a form of evolution in action that humankind cannot afford to ignore. As he and his colleagues have pointed out, bacterial evolution is not hampered by the barriers that divide other forms of life into discrete species. Although bacterial types are named as if they assorted tidily into genera and species, they exchange genetic material on a much broader basis. While any two bacteria will probably not exchange genes by recombining their chromosomes if their genetic sequences differ by more than about 20 per cent, they may be joined by intermediates into a 'sexual continuum' that spans the bacterial world. There are no bacterial species, only bacteria.

Maynard Smith contemplated vistas like these, 'major transitions' in evolution, animal communication, human language and a huge range of other problems that came his way in his collegial life. Many of these he tackled in collaborative studies, providing valuable support and encouragement for younger colleagues. Into his eighties and the twenty-first century, he still went into work every day; he looked much the same as always, his grey hair swept back as if by a hand abstracted in thought, and exactly how a child would imagine a kindly old scientist should look. His manner of speech owed nothing to his years, apart from the gentle hints in his accent of the class into which he had been born. Much of the time he resembled the students, in fleece, hiking trousers and trainers, and took a similarly nonchalant attitude to status and grooming with his small Rover car. He was a presiding genius who embodied the spirit of the school.

His influence was recognised further afield, including Stockholm, where in 1999 he shared the Crafoord Prize with Ernst Mayr and George Williams, and Kyoto, where he received the Kyoto Prize in 2001. Both these awards are regarded as devices to fill the gaps in the Nobel Awards' coverage, which does not extend into biology beyond physiology and medicine.

But his influence was best appreciated outside formal proceedings: at lunchtime, in the Swan, or at conferences, where he would go and sit with young researchers whose work interested him, genially and generously encouraging them to make the best of their cases. They had the pleasure of appreciating the third of his great gifts: for conversation, as much a part of his science as his skill in maths and his love of natural history.

Animals play games; one species of lizard, it now transpires, plays the stone–paper–scissors game. Children play it like rolling dice: two downward shakes of the fist, and on the third, a choice of gestures: two fingers outstretched stands for scissors, a flat palm for paper, and a fist still clenched for stone. Scissors cut paper, paper wraps stone, stone blunts scissors. Each wins against one and loses against the other, and so it is among side-blotched lizards.

Among these reptiles, which are formally known as *Uta stansburiana* and live on the Coast Range of California, males come in three colour morphs. Males marked with orange blotches on their throats are aggressive, extremely dominant and mate with many females in the large territories they hold; they have testosterone levels to match. Blue-throated males are less dominant and less polygynous; they hold smaller territories, enabling them to guard their mates more closely. The third class of males has a yellow throat marking, resembling that of females. Yellow-throated males are furtive and do not draw attention to themselves by perching on rocks, unlike the other morphs. They are what are known as 'sneakers', a term adopted as a polite compromise after Maynard Smith's unsuccessful bid to get the expression 'sneaky fucker' into the evolutionary game literature. They do not hold territories or guard mates, but attempt to mate when other males are not looking.

This strategy is effective against orange-throats, whose territories are too big for them to guard all the females within them. If a yellow-throat does run into an orange-throat, it makes a head-bobbing gesture similar to that made by a female signalling that it does not wish to mate. This fools orange-throats, but doesn't wash with blue-throats, whose judgement is presumably less clouded by testosterone. Nor is the sneaker strategy effective against blue-throats, who do guard their mates. Blue-throats, however, are defeated by the orange-throats' aggression. Orange beats blue, blue beats yellow, yellow beats orange.

The result is a cycle, lasting four or five years, in which the three morphs enjoy successive phases of ascendancy. Orange-throats invade blue-throats' territories and breed in their place. As the numbers of orange-throats increase, though, they provide increasing opportunities to the yellow-throated sneakers, which thus replace the orange-throats. Now the blue-throats have their chance to expand, since their mate-guarding strategy trumps the sneakers. This sets the stage for the orange-throats' return; and so on indefinitely.

Maynard Smith saw that such a system could evolve and outlined it in *Evolution and the Theory of Games*, years before the American field biologists Barry Sinervo and Curtis Lively discovered it among the lizards. ('Curt and I just looked at each other and we said, "Dude! This is the rock–paper–scissors game!"') A natural theologian might conclude that *Uta stansburiana* was placed on this Earth to demonstrate the truth of evolutionary theory by a Creator who shared John Maynard Smith's sense of humour.

BILL HAMILTON

'I am a child of the receding wave of the Romantic Movement and as such I still hanker for miracles.'
  William D. Hamilton, 1996

11

The Sting of Altruism

The Hamilton family, according to the novelist Alasdair Gray, is 'as far as possible, a self-supporting republic'. Its territory, though small, contains crops, manufacturing facilities, defensive structures and a mine. Behind its cloak of woods and contours, it maintains its traditions, its values and its proud scientific heritage. A motorway now cuts it off from its hinterland, but though the noise hangs in the air, the trees shrug off the intrusion.

Bettina Hamilton, a doctor, and Archibald Hamilton, an engineer, settled here in 1938. Both were from New Zealand and had found their way to Kent by way of the Middle East. Archibald had built a road through what is now Iraqi Kurdistan and was held in high regard by Kurds from the region for decades afterwards. He then joined the British Army and was posted to Cairo. Here, on an island in the Nile, William Donald Hamilton was born in 1936.

Army and colonial life disagreed with Archibald Hamilton, so the family came to England, where he set up as a civil engineer specialising in bridge design. His greatest success was the Callender–Hamilton prefabricated steel bridge, used by the Army during the war and still in production today. It served the Hamiltons as it did its users, providing austere but robust support.

The family found a place to settle at a spot rejoicing in the name of Badgers Mount, on the edge of the North Downs in the county of Kent. The house was new, scaled for suburbs but placed in country which was still rural and enfolded enough to ignore London looming just above it. Soon after, the skies above Kent became the *Luftwaffe*'s highway to the capital, and the south-eastern corner of Britain began to shimmer in the national mind's eye, a vision of what was most precious and most vulnerable on the island. When the Royal Air Force pilots looked down at the lanes and harvests, intimate and orderly, they saw what they were fighting for. The Spitfires patrolled above Arcadia.

After abandoning an attempt to return to New Zealand, the Hamiltons saw the war through at Badgers Mount. They dug air-raid shelters, taking cover in them during the Blitz and the flying bomb campaign. The sandy soil lent itself to the purpose. When the family received an addition, it was easy for Bettina to scrape out an extra shelf for the new baby. Finding room in the house was not so simple. By the end of the war there were five children, and eventually six. Bill was obliged to sleep where he could.

Archibald commanded a unit of Home Guard volunteers, men who were too old or otherwise ineligible for proper military service. He applied his engineering skills with gusto, making explosives according to formulae he had developed for blasting tunnels in Kurdistan and stockpiling them in the garden. Some of the material was used in improvised demolition charges and 'sticky' bombs, which the Home Guardsmen tested on a nearby golf course. In his memoirs Archibald boasted that his unit had come through his munitions programme unscathed. He omitted to mention that his explosives nearly claimed the life of his eldest son.

Bill and his sister Mary were the senior children, born before the war and somewhat separate from the others, who all came after the watershed of 1939. Bill's boyhood was one of treehouses and bird's-nesting, of wandering barefoot along woodland lanes with insect net in hand and chasing clouded yellow butterflies through fields of red clover. Like much else about him, it really belonged to the world that ended when the war was declared.

He pursued his insects in the way that he pursued everything that mattered to him in his life as a naturalist and a scientist: with intensity, stamina and no regard for risk. 'Stone-turning – that, as it now occurs to me, is a trait that might almost define the compulsive juvenile entomologist,' he reflected nearly fifty years later. 'He is a turner-over of junk in waste places, a puller of loose bark from rotting logs. You never know what you might find: the spilled rice confusion of pupae of an ant nest, the sinister dark and yet glorious iridescence of a ground beetle.'

Or one of his father's explosives dumps. Pulling a flint from a bank one day – it was 1949, and he was twelve – he discovered a cache of rusty tins crammed into a rabbit burrow. His father relieved him of them, but Bill noted where they had been placed, in the large shed which Archibald

Hamilton, a keen inventor, used as a workshop. Together with a friend, Bill set about making a small bomb of his own. He filled a cartridge case with gunpowder and put the open end in a vice to pinch it shut. When he tightened the screw, the cartridge exploded. He ran into the house, drenched in blood, and collapsed in the hall. After weeks in hospital, locally and in London, he was left with a scarred torso, brass shrapnel fragments in his lungs, and the ends missing from three of his fingers.

Risk runs through the Hamiltons as high-wire brilliance runs through the Huxleys. So do the intellectual currents which Archibald and Bettina brought together. One son followed his father directly into engineering; two of their daughters became doctors, like their mother; another became an agricultural botanist. Bill shared Bettina's enthusiasm for natural history and Archibald's aptitude for maths. It was this combination of talents that made him the scientist he was. He was a genius as a naturalist, to match any of his Victorian predecessors, and his mathematical abilities were robust enough to meet the most exacting demands of twentieth-century evolutionary biology.

He was also animated by a powerful expressive spirit that runs through the Hamilton family, instilling in him literary ambitions and leading his elder sister to study art before turning to medicine. The pattern can be seen in the next generation too. One of his daughters, Helen, is an ecologist, and another, Ruth, has obtained a doctorate in biology; the third, Rowena, has studied art.

The shed is still there, equipped to light-industrial standards, and in the middle is the workbench with the vice at which Bill nearly killed himself. So is the croquet lawn that Bettina cleared and levelled after the war, once the land was no longer required for food production. Deeper into the territory, half hidden among ferns and foxgloves, is a derelict flint cottage, built by the children. Elsewhere on the edge of the woods, which the family added to their territory as a buffer, is a pit dug as a mine by Robert, the brother who became an engineer. The Hamiltons were enthusiastically practical, and often enthusiastic far beyond practicality.

At the edge of the land, with the hills of the North Downs across the fields behind, stands a Nissen hut, a standard wartime design in which sheets of corrugated iron are bent into a low tunnel. Inside, the end of the hut has been faced with flints, with a number of gaps filled by coloured glass. This is a shrine to Alex, the last-born of the children, who was killed in a climbing accident at the age of nineteen. Bill was away when it was built, but he found his own remarkable way of commemorating his brother, who had paid the price of risk that he had escaped. He took over Alex's bicycle, using it around Oxford till the end of his own life. The speed and recklessness with which he rode it became part of his legend.

Another hut stands in the woods, this one a modern prefabricated cabin. Much of its space is filled by a water craft, formerly Alex's, in the form of a cabin on top of two pontoons. These were originally aircraft drop-tanks, taken from the large quantity of surplus of which Archibald Hamilton relieved the military after the war, confident that it would come in useful. Bill put the cabin up, anticipating that he could use it as a hide-out in his retirement. He left a handprint in the concrete of the floor, his distinctively abbreviated signature.

After his death in 2000, some of his belongings were taken to the family house. In the sitting room, where the children used to do their homework, is a seasoned old leather car seat. Bill salvaged it from a Vauxhall that had reached the end of its road in Hamilton hands, and used it as furniture. He called it the 'kin selection chair', because he was sitting on it when he thought of the idea upon which his scientific impact is based. On the walls hang a couple of cases displaying specimens from his collection of Brazilian insects, one of beetles and one of butterflies. He liked to arrange his butterflies in arcs and angles, making them look more like fireworks and less like tissue soldiers on parade.

On a summer's day, it is evident that the republic has annexed a little patch of Arcadia. The garden and its surroundings are the southern English countryside in miniature, abundant and intimate, managed but tangled; always promising another path to follow, another tree to climb, another stone to turn. A hammock is stretched between two trees in a little grove near the workshop. Close by the house is the hedge of laurel that Bill used as his stock of poison, placing crumpled leaves in the killing jar which he carried with him on his collecting expeditions.

The house itself still stands above the decades that have passed since it was built, largely indifferent to the luxuries that have stifled the upright spirits of almost all its contemporaries. True to its traditions and eloquent

about them, practical and Romantic in the same breath, the Hamiltons'
home lacks the gentlemanly grandeur of Darwin's house at Downe, a few
miles away, but in imagination it is as rich.

War surplus material usually came from auctions, but occasionally it
descended from the sky. In the woods where he sought out sticks suitable
for his insect nets, Bill came across a length of steel cable which he used to
make the frames across which the silk nets were stretched. It had formerly
tethered a barrage balloon, one of thousands raised as obstacles to enemy
aircraft, which had been cut loose during an air raid. The nets fitted into
the frame of Bill's bicycle, which he used to extend his collecting range.
He liked to cycle to the hills in the garden's background – now cut off by
the motorway – which contained more of the downland species that
inspired him. Sometimes he stayed out overnight, sleeping under hedges.
  He was guided by books his mother gave him or which he obtained
from second-hand bookshops. These 'praised collecting as an end in
itself, treated it almost as an art'; persuaded by them, he began to collect
the books themselves, notably ones by the nineteenth-century French
entomologist Jean Henri Fabre. Then, in a bookshop in Sevenoaks, where
he attended a prep school, he found himself confronted with E. B. Ford's
book *Butterflies*. This was the first in Collins's successful 'New Naturalist'
series, launched the year the war ended in the conviction that it was time
for naturalists to get out of doors and see how living creatures lived.
  'Mohammed II captured Constantinople on May 29th 1453, when the
Middle Ages which, it might be said, began on Christmas Day in the year
800, came to an end.' With his opening sentence, Ford made it clear that
his horizons were far broader than the shades of distinction between one
butterfly and the next. He began by recapitulating the history of butterfly
collecting in Britain, starting with the Renaissance. Then, having set butterfly collecting in historical context, he devoted the rest of the book to its
scientific context. Inside its neo-Romantic wrapper – a caterpillar and
swallowtails in the foreground, a tiny windmill at the water's edge behind
– the book offered a stiff course in genetics and ecology, rather than insects
in rows and inventories of traits.
  Ford anticipated the maxim given some time later by the American evolutionist Theodosius Dobzhansky that nothing in biology makes sense except

263

in the light of evolution. 'It has always appeared to me that evolution is the key-note of biological study and research; consequently . . . I have allowed that point of view somewhat to influence the construction of the book.' Naturally enough, the book was also influenced by his own selectionist point of view and his experimental interest in measuring selection's effects.

Having paid tribute to the old naturalists who had instituted the British tradition of butterfly-collecting, Ford encouraged his readers to become new naturalists; scientific auxiliaries who could conduct studies on the effects of selection. He suggested that, for example, those who caught large numbers of the Chalk-hill Blue 'merely to fill their cabinets with curios' might usefully undertake release and recapture experiments upon normal specimens and variants. He recommended that they read a simple book on statistical methods, if necessary, in order to analyse their results.

Leafing through *Butterflies* in the bookshop, Bill Hamilton sensed 'a possibility of some ambivalence or heresy' towards his collector's ideals. Despite his doubts, though, he developed a longing for Ford's book, which he would pick up every time he went into the bookshop. After a year (by which time it had sold 20,000 copies, despite its relatively high price of eighteen shillings) his parents bought it for him as a birthday present. He was ready for Ford's message. The hints about Darwinism his mother had dropped now developed into a fascination with evolution and a respect for the power of natural selection. Indirectly, this was the beginning of Ronald Fisher's influence upon him. Bill unconsciously followed in Fisher's footsteps when he chose the *Origin of Species* as a school prize.

It was not until he discovered Fisher's own works, at Cambridge, that he properly understood Ford's 'mysterious genetics'. In the meantime, it took him about five years to grasp mysteries such as the ratio between heterozygotes and homozygotes – individuals with one copy of a particular gene variant and those with two – in cross-bred offspring. Encouraged by Ford, who entitled one of his chapters 'Practical Genetics', he embarked on breeding experiments, 'but I found Ford had made it sound too easy'. After two years, Bill had failed even to reveal any genes from the original peppered form from among the local melanic population of *Biston betularia*.

He had more or less given up collecting by the time he left Tonbridge, a venerable and nearby Kent public school, and was called up for his compulsory National Service. To his great disappointment, the Army considered the injuries he had sustained from the explosion and declined to post him abroad. His stint as a military bureaucrat had one significant consequence for his scientific development, though. He was stationed in Hampshire, where he was able to visit his Aunt Prue. Defying Ford's legendary misogyny, Prudence Jackson was a naturalist and a collector. She was both fond of beetles and serious about their study, showing Bill how a committed collector worked.

After his two-year stint in the Army, he worked for a time at the East Malling Research Station, which had been set up by the fruit growers of Kent to put the 'Garden of England' on a scientific footing. When he went up to Cambridge, he continued what Ford's book had started. He read Genetics, entering the Department just after Fisher retired as its head. Coincidentally, he found himself in Fisher's old college, St John's, and it was from the college library that he obtained Fisher's *Genetical Theory of Natural Selection*.

He wanted something to make up for the limited treatment given to evolution by his zoology lecturer. In the *Genetical Theory*, he got more than he bargained for. He saluted it on the jacket of an edition issued in 1999: 'This is a book which . . . I weighed as of equal importance to the entire rest of my undergraduate Cambridge BA course and, through the time I spent on it, I think it notched down my degree.' (He graduated with an upper second.) 'Most chapters took me weeks, some months; even Kafka whom I read at the same time couldn't depress me like Fisher could on, say, the subject of charity, nor excite me like his theory of civilisation. Terrify was even the word in some topics and it still is, so deep has been the change from all I was thinking before.'

It was the latter part of the book, dealing with eugenics, which first hooked him. Fisher's mathematical reasoning was 'rather beyond me', he told his sister Mary. They corresponded using postcards, which were a medium for sharing their interest in art, and which Bill developed into a singular graphic form. He would cram them with ingeniously arranged text, which might only leave a space smaller than the stamp for the address. Their delivery speaks volumes for the Post Office's sense of duty, and its sense of humour. In at least one example, Bill arranged the text in a grid pattern, using colour to create a kind of cursive plaid. The motive was not so much economy as privacy. Bill and Mary liked to feel, as youthful intellectuals sometimes do, that their deeper ideas were exclusive and secret.

Already, Bill had learned that some of his deeper ideas tended to get a cool reception in the outside world. When he encountered the *Genetical Theory*, he announced to Mary that he had 'discovered a grand new source of arguments'. These concerned 'our old topic, the decline of civilisations. I now know why they decline, and how to stop them, and that after having read only two chapters . . . Though written in a very mild and erudite manner it is intensely provocative. There are many echoes of my old opinions (which I never really abandoned, merely stopped thumping because I couldn't face the unpopularity they caused.)' He kept his counsel for another forty years.

His comments suggest that his eugenicist leanings developed independently from his interest in Darwinism. At any rate, the two enthusiasms were not integrated until he read Fisher. Thanks to Fisher, Hamilton came to believe that civilisation depends on natural selection.

Although the professor and the undergraduate might have been cheered to find that each had maintained the eugenicist faith in the face of contemporary opinion and recent history, Hamilton never became a disciple. On the few occasions that they met, Fisher did not deign to take much interest in him or make any effort to put the young man at his ease. Bill reported to Mary how he and some colleagues had 'with trepidation' gone to ask Fisher about a statistical question. 'It was teatime and he was chatting with some students, carpet slippered, white haired, senile . . . He is urbane, almost supercilious, everything he says has profound weight – I begin to dislike him, he must be laughing at us. He took my problem a little testily – what is all this about? – and grasped it immediately. I expected him to answer my question at once, from his immense experience, and I suspect he could have done so; but no . . .'

Fisher's status as Hamilton's intellectual hero survived their personal contact. If not Fisher and Hamilton against the world, it was them against the people who were teaching Hamilton biology. Hamilton found that his lecturers either appeared not to have heard of Fisher or disapproved of him if they had. They were also rather indifferent towards natural selection, and so were not concerned that it might conflict with the good of the species. Taking Fisher instead of his teachers as his guide, Hamilton set out to investigate how altruism could be reconciled with natural selection.

His first 'algebraic attack' on the problem was directed at the model for the selection of altruism which Haldane had published in 1932, in his

Causes of Evolution. This was an analytical cul-de-sac, exploring the possibility of selective competition acting between 'tribes', some of which had become enriched with genes for altruism and some of which had not. Hamilton found Haldane's algebra 'strangely irrelevant' and the model implausible. John Maynard Smith later came to the conclusion that the reason Haldane failed to establish the basis of altruism was that, despite having vital insights into the problem, he had been asking the wrong question. Haldane had been thinking about Christian saints and war heroes who won the Victoria Cross. He should have been thinking about ants and wasps. 'Most biologists are now persuaded that relatedness is at least highly relevant; but we would not have reached that conclusion if our central concern had been to explain the behaviour of Christian martyrs.'

Haldane had grasped the essential principle that 'in so far as it makes for the survival of one's descendants and near relations, altruistic behaviour is a kind of Darwinian fitness . . .' He had returned to this point more recently, and this time his aim was true. In a Penguin *New Biology* article he pointed out, using the hypothetical example of saving a child from drowning, that genes which induced altruistic behaviour would be favoured in proportion to the degree of relatedness between benefactor and beneficiary. Hamilton's understanding of altruism, and his theory of the evolution of social behaviour, also arose from this insight.

In his memoirs, Hamilton wrote that he had read Haldane's *New Biology* paper but had forgotten it, which was why he had made Haldane's earlier treatment his target. 'One reads and forgets,' he observed; but on the question of where credit for the evolutionary theory of altruism was due, he found it far easier to forget than to forgive.

Hamilton approached the altruism problem in a style that proved characteristic. Although proof had to be mathematical, any source of insight was welcome. He looked to fiction and to his own family for indications as to how kinship was valued, as well as to population genetics. And he looked to the Department of Social Anthropology, thinking that a course in that subject might teach him about how different cultures saw kinship. The Department rejected his application, and his own Department of Genetics also showed no enthusiasm for the idea of combining genetics with social anthropology. He thereupon decided to leave Cambridge after completing his degree.

This was the first of many felt rebuffs from academics and their institutions. The next came from Moray House, a teacher-training college in Edinburgh. With the precedents of Fisher and Lack in mind, he thought that working as a teacher might secure him an income while leaving him enough time to pursue his ideas. Moray House, however, told him that a genetics degree would only qualify him to teach biology in junior schools. Though he imagined that this might be a rewarding role, Hamilton took the response as a snub to genetics and to himself. He soon broke off negotiations and decided that he would rather be a carpenter instead. Surviving examples of his handiwork suggest that he would have been very good at it. His performance as a lecturer suggests that he would have been as bad a schoolteacher as Fisher.

He was accepted as a postgraduate student at University College's Galton Laboratory, but Lionel Penrose refused to sponsor his study of the altruism problem, adding his doubts over whether it was a problem at all. Hamilton thought that people who reacted in this way suspected he 'might be a sinister new sucker budding from the roots of the recently felled tree of Fascism'. He was certainly a new shoot on the stump of eugenics, whose local shrubbery Penrose had been trying to root out ever since he was appointed professor of it.

Those whose acquaintance with him was tenuous might well have wondered about the ideology beneath the algebra. But those who knew him better saw almost no politics in him at all, beyond a conventional belief in 'Queen and Country', and in later years, a keen admiration for Margaret Thatcher. He wrote a novel – an adventure story in which a scientist stumbles upon a gateway to another world – but found that its thousand dense pages were a barrier to publication. When he sampled the work of Alasdair Gray, who had been suggested as an editorial guide, he found he didn't care for its socialist politics. That, however, was a belated discovery. As young men, he and Gray had discussed human nature and the cruel strains within it. Hamilton considered that these must be evolved adaptations, whereas Gray tended to think that they arose from social structures. But although their differences fell along familiar lines, they did not identify each other as ideological antagonists. Gray formed little impression of his friend's political views.

Hamilton appeared apolitical because he did not take part in the rest of the world's political conversations. His politics were contained within his biology. Fisher was just about the only person who would really have understood them, but by the time they met, the old eugenicist and the young one had decided to keep their views to themselves. After the Third Reich, the civilised world ascribed sinister motives to those who prophesied the decline of civilisations.

Eventually he ended up with a couple of grants and an affiliation with the London School of Economics to go with his uneasy lodgement at the Galton Laboratory. Instead of building on these connections, he fell into a life of scholarly vagrancy. He rented a bedsit in Chiswick, six miles away, and spent his days among book stacks, making the most of the long opening hours at Senate House and the Holborn public library. Afterwards, to stave off being alone, he would take his notes to Waterloo Station and work surrounded by the late-night traffic there.

For journeys of two miles or less, he went on foot. Saving money was the justification; the real reason was an attempt to drum up 'elemental forces' with his footsteps, to discover the Arcadian vestiges in the city by walking it as he had walked the paths around his home. 'Even a lonely child crying on the street did not tug my heart as hard as a bracken fern when I saw it, for example, in the valley of the stream once known as the Fleet . . .'

By 1964, though, he was travelling different roads in different style, ploughing the ruts of a primitive Amazonian highway atop an old American jeep. Hamilton had achieved his rite of passage as an evolutionary naturalist, following Wallace's trail from temperate England to tropical Brazil. Unlike Wallace, however, he did not look to the forest to make his name. His theory was assembled, if not polished or debugged, and in the course of publication. He went to the Amazon in search of supplementary detail, to explore in bees and wasps some ideas about social insects that he was working into his major statement. Hamilton was used to veil and gloves, having helped his mother with her beehives, but they proved inadequate defence against the boiling swarm which erupted one day when he gave a farmer a hand to open a packing-case hive. These were 'killer bees', derived from the African strains that his host, Warwick Kerr, had introduced to the Americas eight years before. Hightailing it out of there in his jeep, enveloped in venomous insects, he got off more lightly than on the later occasion in which he tunnelled into the middle of an abandoned termite mound to reach a wasps' nest; the occupants left him incapacitated for two days.

Characteristically, Hamilton failed to obtain the LSE authorities' permission to go, and they had to be persuaded to have him back. Publication had not gone smoothly, either. John Maynard Smith, refereeing for the *Journal of Theoretical Biology*, recommended that his paper should be split into two, and *Nature* rejected an abstract of his ideas. It was accepted, however, by *American Naturalist*. In three pages, Hamilton indicated the principles of sociobiology and introduced the idea of looking at natural selection from a gene's point of view.

At the heart of it was the tricky business of fitness, left unfinished by Hamilton's predecessors. Although he was willing to examine selection at the level of the gene, what he really wanted to do was to firm it up at the level of the individual. The first was the key to the second. Hamilton extended the idea of individual fitness to include the effect of an individual's actions on the fitness of relatives. An individual's fitness is a measure of its ability to reproduce its genes. Since it shares genes with its relatives, helping them to produce more offspring is an indirect way to reproduce the genes they share by common descent. The closer the relative, the more genes they have in common, and so the more significant it is to the individual's 'inclusive fitness'.

Shared genes resolved the problem of altruism. According to 'Hamilton's rule', a gene which encouraged its bearer to help other organisms would be favoured by selection if the costs to the benefactor were less than the benefits to the recipients, devalued according to their degree of relatedness to the benefactor. 'To put the matter more vividly,' Hamilton observed, echoing Haldane's remarks, 'an animal acting on this principle would sacrifice its life if it could thereby save more than two brothers, but not for less.'

Hamilton saw this as a universal principle but wanted a striking example with which to face the sceptics who doubted that altruism was a problem. This was where the bees and wasps came in. The most obvious instances of biologically institutionalised altruism are the 'eusocial' insect species – ants, termites, many wasps and some bees – in which the sterile masses work to assist the tiny reproductive minority. Hamilton realised that such a division of labour could be favoured by a peculiar asymmetry in inheritance between the sexes, known as haplodiploidy. Under this mode of inheritance, males are descended from unfertilised eggs and so have just one set of chromosomes, while females grow from fertilised eggs and have two sets. As a result, sisters share a full complement of their father's genes, as well as half of their mother's. This leaves them sharing three quarters of their genes, whereas they only have half of their genes in common with their daughters. They might further their genetic interests more effectively by helping their mother to produce sisters than by producing offspring of their own. Or as Richard Dawkins put it, provoking his readers to rise to the Darwinian challenge, 'this might well predispose a female to farm her own mother as an efficient sister-making machine'.

The significance of these asymmetries in relatedness has been debated extensively since. It cannot be the only explanation for eusociality, as termites have sterile castes but inherit their genes in the usual way. Nor can it be the whole of the explanation for haplodiploid species, whose females are related by a quarter to their brothers. If females were to divide their attentions equally between their siblings, they would be improving the fitness of relatives with whom they shared half their genes overall. The degree of relatedness would thus be the same as that to their offspring, and so there would be no advantage in helping siblings – unless there were more sisters than brothers, or females were able to discriminate in favour of their sisters. And even if they did, Fisher's sex-ratio argument would raise its head. According to Fisher, if a population invests more in females than males, the value of females drops correspondingly. 'Thus the first female to stay home and look after her sisters . . . would indeed benefit,' reason John Maynard Smith and Eörs Szathmáry, 'but once the trait was common in the population, the advantage would disappear.' Theorists have suggested that the difficulties could be resolved if different broods, raised in different seasons or under different circumstances, had different sex ratios; but the issue remains 'among the most difficult in population genetics'.

Those who questioned Hamilton's examples were standing on his shoulders. It took a long time for his colleagues to absorb his ideas and apply them: Dawkins produced a graph, showing how often the 1964 double paper was cited, which does not begin to rise steeply until ten years later. Thereafter, he observed, kin selection turned into a bandwagon and provoked a backlash. Much of this, he argued, was based on misunderstandings: he listed twelve, admitting that he had 'fallen for some of them in my time'. Some were errors to which only biologists would be prone, such as the widespread apprehension that kin selection 'is a special, complex kind of natural selection, to be invoked only when "individual selection" proves inadequate'. Others had a wider prevalence. One was the idea that organisms had to be mathematicians in order to practice kin selection. It was exemplified by the anthropologist Marshall Sahlins, who objected that hunters and gatherers do not generally have counting systems that go beyond three, and added, 'I refrain from comment on the even greater problem of how animals are supposed to figure out that $r \ldots = 1/8$.' 'A snail shell is an exquisite logarithmic spiral,' riposted Dawkins, 'but where does the snail keep its log tables . . .?'

Another expressed the widespread objection to the idea of genes 'for' complex behaviour, such as altruism. Dawkins once took part in a debate about sociobiology together with John Maynard Smith, who suggested that one might have a gene for tying shoelaces. 'The air was thick with the unmistakable sound of worst suspicions being gleefully confirmed.' Maynard Smith's point, however, was that a gene 'for' a trait is simply one which affects that trait. When such a gene arose, it would influence complex behaviours which had already evolved. A gene for altruism might be one which reoriented parental care towards siblings. For instance, if a bird has an evolved rule of thumb that amounts to 'feed anything that squawks inside your nest', it will apply the rule to siblings if a genetic change induces it to remain in the nest until after its parents' next brood has hatched. Altruism might be less obvious, though. A gene that gave a lion bad teeth might be altruistic in effect if it impeded its gnawing and allowed its kin to eat more of a kill. Taking his cue from Fisher's argument that almost all traits would fall one side or the other of neutrality, Dawkins suggested that most genes might be classifiable as altruistic or selfish.

Hamilton had paved the way for Dawkins to campaign for a view of life in which selection acted upon the gene. His own view became less exclusive through George Price's influence. Although the real power lay in the lowest levels, he was ready to see selection as a process that could have effects of different strengths at different levels, gene, individual or group. Elliott Sober and David Sloan Wilson, who argue that group selection has encouraged the evolution of human altruism, have pointed out that

Hamilton's modified views rendered the original opposition between his kin selection and Wynne-Edwards's group selection out of date – though few of his colleagues noticed. 'The majority of evolutionary biologists not only continued to believe that the HMS *Kin Selection* was afloat as an alternative to group selection, but they even imagined that Captain Hamilton was still at the helm.'

As well as disappointing Dawkins, his perspective dismayed a number of his listeners when he applied it to humans at a symposium held in Oxford in 1973. The anthropologist Sherwood Washburn, whom he had quoted by way of dedication, denounced it as 'reductionist, racist and ridiculous'. Hamilton discussed a population comprising small, inbreeding colonies. Within them, individuals would be closely related, encouraging 'genuine communism of behaviour'; but at their boundaries, the sharp drop in relatedness might promote hostility between neighbouring groups. Behaviour resembling warfare occurred among chimpanzees and other primates: perhaps the formation of war parties among males had become adaptive deep in the human evolutionary lineage. And perhaps it was not such a bad thing, selecting for intelligence or diverting human energies from the over-exploitation of other targets – 'Maybe if the mammoth-hunters had attacked each other more and the mammoths less they could be mammoth-hunters still.' But like Haldane, who had told his *Daily Worker* readers that sexual selection for size, through combat between males, might lead to extinction, Hamilton observed that 'Arms and armour seem to weigh one down in the end.' He offered this caution in case his remarks seemed like a 'paean to fascism'.

Like Haldane, too, he maintained pre-war assumptions about race and innate psychological differences, although his interest in the matter was passing. Haldane had once opined that England might benefit from the genes of 'talented Asiatic races'; Hamilton observed that genes for 'self-sacrificial daring', introduced by conquering pastoralists, might 'revitalize' a conquered people. (As Hamilton noted, the author Douglas Adams had almost the same idea in *The Hitch-Hiker's Guide to the Galaxy*, concerning a bulldozer driver with genes derived from the Golden Horde. Nobody protested about that, complained Hamilton, oblivious to irony.) Later, however, he added a new chapter to his narrative. As ancient groups developed different skills, they became more interesting to their neighbours, for each might have something the other wanted. Through exchange, *Homo economicus* evolved, and natural selection turned against the extremes of nepotism. Being nice to strangers became adaptive, and so did genuinely liking them: 'It pays.'

As biologists grew used to taking the gene's point of view, life began to look profoundly different. Having appreciated that shared genes were the basis for the evolution of co-operation, researchers began to recognise the immense potential for conflict that genetic asymmetries implied. The relationship between a mother and her unborn child might turn into a struggle over resources. Genes from one parent might struggle with genes from the other for influence over different regions of a developing organism. The genome came to look less like an orderly set of instructions and more like a 'parliament of genes'; or, in Hamilton's words, 'a company boardroom, a theatre for a power struggle of egotists and factions'.

For Hamilton, this came as a considerable personal relief. Genetic reductionism led him to see what many in the humanities learned from psychoanalytic theory and literary criticism: that the self is a fiction of coherence imposed upon constitutionally mixed feelings. '. . . I need not be so ashamed of my self-pity! I was an ambassador ordered abroad by some fragile coalition, a bearer of conflicting orders from the uneasy masters of a divided empire . . . Given my realization of an eternal disquiet within, couldn't I feel better about my own inability to be consistent in what I was doing, about my indecision in matters ranging from daily trivialities up to the very nature of right and wrong?' It would be beside the point to ask why genetic conflict, which is now taken to be part of the universal genomic condition, would make him less decisive than anybody else. The connections he made between his understanding of genetics and his psyche were emotional rather than logical, and all the stronger for it.

At the same time, one of his most cherished internal contradictions was that, despite having deduced a selfish gene behind every altruistic act, he still liked to imagine that his own actions and those of his friends were 'above all that, subject to far more mysterious laws'. He honoured George Price's quest to practise genuine altruism, noting the contrast between Price's desire to help the wretched of the London streets with his own preference of sympathy for a struggling basement fern.

*

Hamilton had not been all alone in London. There was a girlfriend, some-one who had known him all his life; but while he was in Brazil she ended the relationship. Possessed with doubt that he would ever marry or have children of his own, he offered to help pay for the education of two chil-dren, Romilda and Godofredo Nunes Dias, whom he had met in the for-est. With five siblings, he had plenty of potential as an uncle, but inclusive fitness was insufficient consolation. By seeking out the needs of distant others, he was doing one of the few things he could be confident that he had not evolved to do.

Back home, he got out of the city and into the Berkshire green belt, tak-ing a post at the Imperial College Field Station near Ascot. While there, he proved himself wrong about his personal prospects. In 1967, he married Christine Friess, whom he had met through his sister Janet. Christine, who qualified as a dentist the same year, moved into the flat above a garage which Bill shared with Jiři Úlehla, a visiting Czech colleague. Úlehla used to say that Bill and Christine were quite alike. They both spoke softly and thought slowly.

The following year he returned to Brazil, on a German cargo boat, and took Christine with him. They worked together, making forays along for-est trails in search of wasps' nests: paper lanterns, up to four feet long, hanging from trees that might be a hundred feet high and sometimes might have to be felled. At ground level they would be pestered by tiny sweat bees, the size of gnats; deterring them with smoke, Christine nearly got hooked on cigarettes.

When they went back to England, they brought the children Godofredo and Romilda with them – or rather Christine did, Bill having gone on ahead to prepare his Imperial College teaching course. The pre-vious November, Bill's youngest brother, Alex, had been killed in a climb-ing accident. It was suggested to Bill that the Brazilian children might be a comforting distraction for his grief-stricken parents, while Godofredo and Romilda themselves, now aged eight and thirteen, could benefit from a European education. The children stayed in Britain for about five years, living at Badgers Mount for about a year, and then with Bill and Christine until Romilda was eighteen. When Bill and Christine themselves returned to Amazonia, in 1975, they took with them the first two of their own three daughters.

12

Under the Bark

In Brazil and Berkshire alike, Hamilton applied himself to his dual *métier* of field natural history and theoretical modelling. The theme of inclusive fitness, with particular reference to the sex ratios it favoured under various balances of relatedness, could be pursued by feeding paper tape into primitive computers or prising bark off logs. Truffling into rotten wood in Silwood Park, close to Imperial's Field Station, took him back to his inquisitive boyhood, spent turning over stones to expose the street life of the segmented and the slimy. As an adult, armed with a binocular microscope, his investigations convinced him that the damp intimacy of rotting wood had been the making of arthropod life. It was under bark, he came to believe, that circumstances had conspired to favour the combination of sociality and sterility in termites and ants. And he relished the microscopic monstrosities he found, as bizarre in the Home Counties as the Amazon: a mite that 'balloons its body to be a gigantic watery play pen for sex-wise incestuous infants'; a midge that gives birth by exploding; beetle larvae that 'lie in soft cradles quilted with living food'; beetles half a millimetre long, with longer sperms coiled inside them. These were Hamilton's creatures.

None were more seethingly Hamiltonian than the fig wasps. These tiny insects, the length of a comma or two, pollinate fig trees and use the fruits as nests for their young. Hamilton reassured readers that figs from the supermarket might not contain any wasps, though the best varieties should. Noting that wild figs would once have contained hundreds of wasps each, he waded enthusiastically into an atavistic trope about the benefits of this extra protein, evoking ancient times when 'fig-tree fruiting was certainly a cause for celebration for forest wildlife and our ancestors must have whooped and brachiated' – swung from branch to branch – 'towards the fruiting crowns just as our great ape cousins and most monkeys do today'.

The protein lacing and the demands of these manoeuvres might, he suggested, have favoured the brain expansion that set our lineage apart.

Life inside a fig was like life under bark: concentration and enclosure made for intense relationships. Broadly speaking, intimate containment should often favour altruism, for it tends to keep closely related individuals close together. But the fig wasps' sexual arrangements led to close proximity between unrelated males; many had evolved savage cutlass jaws with which to fight for their individual interests. In Brazil, Hamilton itemised the casualties from a single fig: three live but maimed, a couple of dying ones and nearly fifty corpses. Only two males were alive and in one piece; though the toll from this fig was unusually high, one tree's fruiting would probably entail the deaths of several million wasps in combat. 'Their fighting looks at once vicious and cautious – cowardly would be the word except that, on reflection, this seems unfair in a situation that can only be likened in human terms to a darkened room full of jostling people among whom, or else lurking in cupboards and recesses which open on all sides, are a dozen or so maniacal homicides armed with knives.' In the lab, potent Brazilian coffee added to the understandably nervous insects' apprehension: they would scuttle for cover if jarred by the caffeine-induced tremors in the hairs of the brush Bill used to move them. Back home, acting on a tip-off, he observed fighting between male ants of an unusual species. They had colonised the drains of a hospital; he posed as a drain cleaner in order to collect his specimens.

Closeness and dispersal became twin themes to which he returned throughout his career. 'Viscous' populations, ones which stuck together, would on the whole be more inclined to altruism than ones whose members dispersed far and wide. Sticking together is not the same as flocking together, though. In a paper called 'Geometry for the Selfish Herd', Hamilton tried to formalise the idea that herds or flocks result from the attempts of individuals to minimise the distance between themselves and predators. This was an example of the kind of inquiry that Maynard Smith called puzzle-solving. Though the term was not really his style, Hamilton was puzzle-minded too. One example of his handiwork is a knotty wooden conundrum, which he devised to tease his relatives' spatial skills.

Although the Selfish Herd had an amusing aspect to it, the biological puzzles Hamilton chose to tackle were serious ones. Hamilton furthered

Fisher's intellectual tradition in his theoretical work, but the Oxford evolutionist Alan Grafen considers that their projects were significantly different. Fisher wanted to formalise evolutionary theory, Grafen observes, and created a framework in which to express Darwinism in terms of Mendelism. This added rigour to existing knowledge, rather than extending it. Hamilton learned from Fisher that it was possible to formalise, but he started from problems which he wanted to solve. His novelty was that he applied Fisher's framework to biologically important problems.

One such problem was dispersal, which he rated as an organism's third priority after survival and reproduction: in a study he conducted with Robert May, they found that it was always necessary, even if conditions at the destination were never better than at the point of departure. In the mid-1990s, dispersal provided a constructive resolution to an argument he had with James Lovelock, the originator of the Gaia hypothesis, that life acts to maintain the conditions for its survival. Like any orthodox evolutionist, Hamilton was fundamentally sceptical about the idea of all living things acting as one, but his dissident sympathies encouraged him from dismissing it out of hand. He followed up the suggestion made by Lovelock and his colleagues that dimethyl sulphide, a gas produced by marine algae, might help to stabilise the climate by lifting the earthly element of sulphur into the sky. The warmer the waters, the more gas the algae would generate; airborne, the sulphur would react with oxygen to form solid sulphate particles, which would seed the formation of clouds, which would cool the planet below; the algae would subside and send up less cloud-seeding sulphur. Dimethyl sulphide was also, in Lovelock's words, 'Gaia's way of ensuring a proper balance between the sulphur in the sea and on the land'. This kind of talk curled orthodox Darwinians' toes. Natural selection was a valid metaphor; natural regulation was a mystical conceit. For Gaians, the question was how the biosphere managed its climate and its sulphur budget; for Darwinians, the question was how algae improved their fitness by methylating sulphides.

Working with Tim Lenton, a young researcher who had published an article on 'Gaia and Natural Selection' in *Nature*, Hamilton set his speculative powers to work. He noted that algae make dimethyl sulphide from a precursor which has antifreeze properties, yet many of these algae are tropical. Perhaps, he suggested, they were sometimes lofted high into the air. Waves and currents were not very good at dispersing algae, but the frothing 'white-caps' concentrated microbial cells and might serve to spray them into the air; maybe the skies offered an escape to seas richer in nutrients. Dimethyl sulphide could help them reach the skies, for as water condenses around sulphate particles, forming clouds, it releases heat and creates an updraft. Certain bacteria contain chemicals that encourage the formation of ice, which could cause clouds to rain: it was possible to imagine 'team' efforts in which algae and bacteria collaborated on their dispersal strategy. But it was as hard as ever to see what principles might underlie the emergence of life-like processes in a system that did not replicate itself. Lovelock, Hamilton observed to Lenton, was like Lamarck: he had recognised a phenomenon but not explained it. Gaia theory, he implied, had yet to find its Darwin.

Nor did he aspire to the role. Gaia was one of a number of topics that he hoped to pursue, but his career was divided into two grand themes. The first half, lasting to around 1980, was dominated by the concept of inclusive fitness and the exploration of its implications; the second, which he pursued in Oxford from 1984, by the idea that sex evolved to counter the advantage enjoyed by parasites through their ability to evolve faster than their hosts. Each has a volume of his collected papers, *Narrow Roads of Gene Land*, loosely devoted to it.

The title is a homage to *Narrow Roads of Oku*, by the seventeenth-century Japanese traveller Matsuo Basho. Hamilton had the idea that his papers might correspond to Basho's poems and his introductory essays to his prose. The first volume was celebrated as a unique venture in scientific biography; the second greeted with an embarrassed silence. Hamilton saw Volume 2 as his intellectual testament, and he felt obliged to say what he had hitherto only hinted at.

His death in 2000 left his editors with a thousand pages' worth of text and a remarkable dilemma. The book was as he wanted it, but he surely would have accepted major changes had he lived. The limited sales prospects for such a sprawling and necessarily expensive tome would have been pointed out to him; the essays would have been shortened and tightened. In the process, it seems reasonable to suppose, the editors would have persuaded him to lose remarks such as the suggestion that Europe's Jews could have avoided persecution by limiting their population growth.

In the end, the editors decided, quite properly, that without him they could not choose what to cut and what to keep. They passed the whole text, guided not only by their editorial integrity but also by the mystique that had accumulated around Hamilton. His was the story of the genius whose insights nobody grasped for years; his thoughts must be left intact lest fresh gems be swept ignorantly away. This editorial reverence seems to have extended even to passages rooted in Hamilton's psyche rather than his science. But therein lies the text's richness. It demands to be read like literary fiction, for the sake of its complications and contradictions, rather than in spite of them. The essays are at their most revealing where their flaws are most obtrusive. They showed a man whose feelings remained as keen as his imagination throughout his life. No matter how many laurels were heaped upon him – election to the Royal Society, promotion at Oxford to a professorship, the Kyoto and Crafoord Prizes – he still smarted when a paper was rejected, and kept his grudges raw. Most revealing of all is an essay he wrote about his greatest fear, behind which lay a grievance that he had nursed for nearly four decades.

In 1972, George Price wrote a painstakingly worded letter to John Maynard Smith, telling him that Hamilton felt aggrieved over the manner in which he had refereed his 1964 paper on the evolution of social behaviour. Maynard Smith's suggestion that the paper be split into two had delayed its publication by nine months. During that time, Maynard Smith sent *Nature* his letter about kin selection, thus getting the phrase into print for the first time.

In his reply, Maynard Smith expressed his distress and agreed that he might be 'partly at fault'. Two other referees had already criticised Hamilton's paper, he explained, and it had seemed to him that this could only be because they had failed to understand it. Splitting the paper, he had thought, would make its arguments easier to follow. He accepted that he should have cited Hamilton's forthcoming paper in his letter to *Nature*, while pointing out that he had cited Hamilton's published paper on altruism. 'I don't think Bill Hamilton feels too badly about things now,' he remarked.

His confidence would have been supported by a cordial letter which Hamilton wrote to him that same day, commenting on a manuscript. But it was misplaced. Four years later, Hamilton's resentment was stirred by a review Maynard Smith wrote for *New Scientist* magazine of Edward O. Wilson's book *Sociobiology*. 'I first heard the idea in the now-demolished Orange Tree off the Euston Road,' Maynard Smith recalled. 'J. B. S. Haldane, who had been calculating on the back of an envelope for some minutes, announced that he was prepared to lay down his life for eight cousins or two brothers. This remark contained the essence of an idea which W. D. Hamilton . . . was later to generalise.'

Hamilton doubted the provenance of the anecdote. Rehearsing his complaints about the lack of interest Haldane's former colleagues had shown in his ideas when he was at UC, he suggested that Maynard Smith might have got the phrase from him and then attached it in his memory to Haldane. He acknowledged Haldane's remarks in *New Biology*, but denied that they were close enough to support the story.

His suspicions, and hackles, were also raised by the image of the back of the envelope. As he pointed out, he had spent two years and reams of paper on the problem. Maynard Smith's anecdote must have seemed to trivialise his efforts. At the same time, he acknowledged that he might be taking it a little too personally. He admitted that he had felt disappointed when he read Fisher's brief allusion to the matter in the *Genetical Theory* chapter on mimicry and realised that his idea was not entirely original. 'Traces of a proprietory [*sic*] feeling appear to remain in me!'

Naomi Mitchison affirmed that Haldane 'was constantly writing things on the backs of envelopes in the Orange Tree. I sometimes suggested a notebook: but no. He had probably been brooding over it at other times and getting the mathematics clear.' His published remarks were certainly not as epigrammatic or as precise. In the *New Biology* example, the value of a cousin's life was not an eighth of one's own, but merely 'very slight'. Somebody else had already mentioned altruism and the magic number in the same breath, however, and in print too: 'A is the eldest son, and stays at home; his brother B goes to the wars; then so long as A has some eight children, it does not matter, genetically, if B gets killed, or dies childless, there will be nephews to fill his place.' Fisher got there first, not in the *Genetical Theory*, but in the paper based on his address to the undergraduate eugenicists of Cambridge in 1912.

Maynard Smith summed the matter up in his own response: 'It is clear that Haldane understood the principle of kin selection before Hamilton.

Nevertheless, I have no doubt that the credit for the idea should go to Hamilton. What matters in science is not merely to understand an idea, but to see its relevance and to work out its consequences. Haldane did refer to ants and bees, but he did not develop the argument. It was left to Hamilton to show how the evolution of animal societies can be understood in terms of this idea. Hamilton, and not Haldane, became the intellectual father of sociobiology.' Alfred Russel Wallace would have applauded. As he had insisted, in awarding precedence to Darwin over natural selection, it was not the idea that counted, but what the thinker did with it.

Maynard Smith added that he had 'come to regard Hamilton as the most original and creative person working on evolution theory'. But Hamilton did not consider that new tributes cancelled out old wrongs. He brooded and began letters to Maynard Smith that he did not finish. Then, in October 1977, he found the occasion. He wrote to Maynard Smith, declining an invitation to attend a symposium. One reason was that he could not think of anything fresh to say. The other was that he did not believe the Orange Tree anecdote. 'This means that while I continue to have considerable respect for your versatility as a scientist and for your contribution in making our common field of interest advance as rapidly as it has, I am unable to respect you as a person.' Either Maynard Smith was 'some kind of amnesiac capable of uncon[s]ciously fabricating an anecdote harmful to the reputation of a fellow scientist' or he was capable of fabricating it consciously 'to avoid the discomfort of admitting intellectual indebtedness to a younger man'.

Hamilton acknowledged that Maynard Smith had praised his work subsequently, though adding 'more highly than it deserves' made this read like a further imputation of dishonesty. And, searching his feelings, he found from 'an inward accounting that surprises even me, that the one thing does not all balance the other'. He reiterated that he had spent several 'very miserable years' trying to prove the principle which, according to the anecdote, Haldane had announced in the pub. Since he doubted the story, 'I continue to resent it extremely, almost like the theft of a child'.

Once, at the Galton Laboratory, Cedric Smith had introduced him to Maynard Smith, who had failed to show any interest when told that Hamilton was working on altruism: '... so that I at once wrote you off as yet another failed hope of encouragement in a research ambition which even I at the time was half persuaded must be due to a mental aberration peculiar to myself'. Admittedly, his opinion of Maynard Smith ran counter to those of many of his colleagues, 'and I think most regard it as odd of me to be resentful towards someone who promotes my work and reputation as energetically as you do'. People reading newspaper accounts of child custody disputes, he observed, 'can be amazed at the apparently destructive irrationality of the behaviour involved, whereas people actually involved in such struggles themselves understand this behaviour very easily'.

Personal reputations should come a poor second to scientific progress, he affirmed, but 'I am ashamed that in practice I find myself much more selfish than my ideal'. This concluding observation encapsulates the remarkable character of the letter, animated as it is by Hamilton's intense 'inward accounting' between ethics and emotions. Just as students are enjoined to 'show your working' in their answers to maths problems – though to little effect in Ronald Fisher's case – he felt obliged to show his emotional working.

When Hamilton wrote that even if evidence could be found to give the anecdote provenance, he would still have considered it 'not quite gentlemanly' of Maynard Smith not to have told him about it earlier, he was referring without irony to a code of honour which both men shared. His insistent introspection, glimpsed even in a few lines to *New Scientist*, anticipated a culture of excavated and professed emotion quite contrary to the ethos that the two scientists absorbed at their public schools. Hamilton was behind the times in his ideology but ahead of it in his intimacy with his feelings.

Maynard Smith replied that he was grateful to Hamilton for writing 'with such honesty' on a subject about which he had 'some feelings of guilt'. These feelings were strongest about his failure to help Hamilton when the latter was a graduate student. 'I ask you to believe that this was stupidity, not malice, on my part.' He did not recall the meeting at which they had been introduced, and he had not recognised Hamilton's promise. That could have been because Hamilton might 'not have been very articulate'; it was certainly, and most importantly, because at that time Maynard Smith 'did *not* see the evolution of altruism as an important problem'.

He was 'quite certain' that he had not invented the eight cousins anecdote, and he had sufficient support in Haldane's *New Biology* article.

Haldane could have made the remark, and written the observation, without seeing that the situation became more complicated as the gene spread through the population. It was Hamilton who had worked the problem through, and Hamilton who should receive the credit for the theory of inclusive fitness.

Conversely, Maynard Smith felt he deserved credit for seeing the generality of the idea of an evolutionarily stable strategy, although now that Hamilton had raised the issue of citation, Maynard Smith felt he should acknowledge his failure to cite Hamilton's idea of an 'unbeatable strategy' in the paper on ESSs he wrote with George Price. He told Hamilton that he had read the 1967 paper 'Extraordinary Sex Ratios' – but not that he had failed to finish it – 'and the idea is basically the same'.

There were, he agreed, other early instances in which he had been remiss about citation. 'I know it looks a bit as if I have given you credit only when I had to, because the rest of the world was doing so, but not in the early days when it would have helped. If so, it is because, like others, I was slow to see the full significance of what you were doing.'

'I do not ask you to think that I have always behaved well,' Maynard Smith concluded, '– only that I am not more dishonourable than most men.' His letter makes it easy to concur. The major credits have become assigned as he suggested: inclusive fitness to Hamilton, evolutionary game theory to Maynard Smith. Hamilton's accusation and Maynard Smith's response compel attention less for what they have to say about the complicated paternity of the ideas at issue than for what they show about the characters of their authors. Much of it is to their credit. Both place integrity above priority: it is more important for each of them to behave correctly than to be first. Both are civil, regretful and distressed that they find themselves in this position. Maynard Smith expresses his understanding of Hamilton's feelings; Hamilton is generous enough to place his complaints in the context of feelings he wishes he did not have and is not bound by his code of conduct to share.

Nevertheless, the grievance was not dispelled by its airing. As the years went by, Fisher's leading intellectual descendant and Haldane's reproduced the mistrustful distance that their mentors had maintained. If they found themselves at the same party, separate clusters would form around each. Late in the day there was an exception – which Maynard Smith remarked upon to their hostess, Helena Cronin – when they met after a lecture given at the London School of Economics by Robert Trivers in 1998.

Bill Hamilton was in a relaxed mood that evening, though. He introduced Trivers's talk with a reminiscence about how Trivers, then an undergraduate, had impressed him with his ideas about how long relationships encourage reciprocity. When Trivers had still not published it after a couple of years, 'I began to think of pinching it for myself.' He refrained from comment on the theme of the lecture, which was entitled 'A Logic for Self-Deception'.

Hamilton's sense of humour did not extend to Maynard Smith, though. He kept his resentment smouldering and let it show in some of his last words. In his essay 'The Hospitals Are Coming', he recalled question time at a Nobel Conference, one of a series held not in Stockholm but at a boarding school in northern Wisconsin with a remarkable gift for luring eminent speakers – and, on this occasion, getting Hamilton and Maynard Smith on stage together. 'Just how much damage has modern medicine inflicted on the genetic reserves of humans,' a member of the audience demanded to know, 'by its attempts to keep genetically unfit individuals alive and producing children?'

'Speaking as someone who would be blind and useless in a hunter-gatherer society without my spectacles,' replied Maynard Smith, 'I'm extremely glad that people are keeping people like me alive and even allowing us to reproduce.'

'I'm all in favour of keeping John Maynard Smith alive,' Hamilton responded; but by the end of his essay, his commitment looked questionable. He went on to voice his concern about the results of improved treatments for people with genetic defects. These could create a population in which everybody carried several lethal genes that required constant medication. In the event of some calamity which disrupted the medical system, the whole population would be at mortal risk.

Maynard Smith suggested that technology might provide solutions at the same time that it created the problem. Instead of waiting for defective genes to express themselves, medicine would develop the capacity to turn bad genes into good ones. 'Maybe I am too optimistic, but I see that as a sensible response to your idea.'

The two scientists' shared understanding of natural selection placed them close to each other, despite their differing political outlooks. Maynard Smith did not challenge the premise that medical treatment would relax selection and thus allow harmful mutations to accumulate. From left of centre, he immediately looked to eugenics, and used the word in the same breath as 'optimistic' and 'sensible' – a juxtaposition that would disturb many, if not most, of those who read the same papers and voted for the same parties as he did. (He put it plainly a few years after Hamilton wrote his essay, according to the magazine *New Scientist*: 'Eugenics is a dirty word, but I don't think it should be . . .') Although his optimism referred to his confidence in technology, it rested more upon his confidence in common sense and goodwill. His answer implied that eugenic engineering could be a straightforwardly technical issue, based on a consensus about which genes were good and which were bad.

Hamilton did not applaud Maynard Smith's response. Nor did he protest that the ethical issues were weightier than Maynard Smith had acknowledged, though in his essay he remarked sharply that Professor Maynard Smith 'needs to say how we are to deal' with public reaction against the idea of tampering with nature. He suggested that a 'more open-minded' attitude towards research on early human embryos might assist the development of the techniques which Maynard Smith had foreseen. 'Some may decide,' he added, 'that such research is even less desirable than going along with old-fashioned natural selection.' When he expanded his argument in the essay, it became clear what this meant. Hamilton believed that instead of allowing human embryos to die in the course of research, it would better for the human species to let newborn babies die.

He had hinted at his dystopian vision of a hospitalised humanity in the first volume of *Narrow Roads*, and now he showed his working in relentless detail. This was what he had to say to society. It would not make him popular, but it was his duty as a scientist. He made this point in a strikingly pessimistic example, with an undertow of melancholy aggression. If the Royal Society bought him a telescope, using the public's money, he would be obliged to tell the world if through it he saw an asteroid heading for Earth, 'even if I think death is inevitable for us all and actually the best thing'.

Other scientists shirked this duty for the sake of popularity. They were, he said, 'demagogues'. He explained that the 'public loves and obeys demagogues; indeed that's what being a demagogue means – a persuasive person'. This definition is misleading but revealing. 'Demagogue' comes from *demos*, the people, and *agogos*, leading: it means a leader who plays upon popular prejudices. Hamilton defines the target of his opprobrium not as somebody who exploits prejudice, but simply as someone who is persuasive. Besides Maynard Smith, he also mentions Steve Jones, but his animus against UCL's Galton Professor of Genetics is not personal. As he fails to declare his interest, omitting to mention his grievances against Maynard Smith in either volume of *Narrow Roads*, his memoirs leave their readers without the context to his complaints. Unlike his private letter, his published essay does him little credit in this matter. Behind the protestations of duty can be discerned the sullen resentment of the boy in the corner towards the boy at the heart of the party.

In their different reactions, Maynard Smith and Hamilton remained true to their respective prophets. Haldane had noted the possibility that mutations might accumulate, but it did not prey on his mind. Hermann Muller took up the idea in the 1940s, introducing the term 'genetic load' to denote the burden of harmful mutations that would accumulate in the human species as it derogated from the laws of natural selection. Even he, however, was more concerned about the mutational effects of radiation. It fell to Hamilton to respond with Fisherian eugenic alarm.

He was particularly exercised about the Caesarean section, which he saw as an endorsement of androgyny. Women, he felt, were being encouraged to become as narrow-hipped as the opposite sex, 'in a spirit of a need to "catch up" with men in an Olympic record book'. As he freely admitted, he was something of a caveman in this aspect of his attitude towards women. 'I am a primitive, I think: I was once told that I look like the last of the Neanderthals: perhaps because of this streak, I find I don't even want to be part of a culture that considers it normal to have babies by Caesarean section.' He accepted that women should be permitted Caesareans in order to save their lives, but suggested that the state should then discourage them from having any more children. Whereas in such cases the state would attempt to do nature's work for it, in others it would step back and let nature take its course. Hamilton argued that severely handicapped infants should be killed. That was what sex was all about.

The two rival theories of the evolution of sex differ over whether its purpose is to keep ahead of parasites or to get rid of harmful mutations. But they agree, Hamilton pointed out, that sexual species can dispose of bad mutations more efficiently than asexual ones. Without sex, as Haldane was the first to observe, mutations are isolated: to maintain fitness, the rule must be 'one mutation, one death'. In sexual species, bad mutations may be combined in a single individual so that several can be eliminated for the same price. Hamilton put 'several at a time' in italics, and wished he could underline it twice. 'These defectives, I insist, *it is the evolved function of the sexual process to eliminate.*'

This was for the best, for parents, for siblings, for future generations and for the child itself. He offered an example from his own family: the next child his mother bore after him. Jimmy survived only a day or two because of an obstructed bowel. Hamilton recalled that his mother spoke little of her lost son, and when she did, she would observe that his loss had allowed her to give more to the others.

Every time Jimmy's name appears in the discussion, it is in inverted commas. That, Hamilton explained, was how it was bracketed in his memory, 'and I think of the commas as being my mother's too'. He assumed that his mother shared his feeling that Jimmy did not truly merit a name, and that she said little about the dead infant because there was little to be said. Nowadays, he thought, Jimmy might easily have been saved by an operation, but he was sure that although his mother was a doctor, she would 'never have allowed it if she could have prevented it'.

Bettina Hamilton's last born, Alex, died in his first week at university. Bill testified that 'everything I can remember about his personality I have preserved fiercely ever since the accident'. The risks he took riding Alex's bicycle round Oxford were in the spirit of daring that he remembered in his brother, and the risks he took in leaving it unlocked were taken in honour of the trusting nature that had lost Alex an earlier bicycle to a thief. Like George Price, Alex underwent a modest canonisation. Bill Hamilton stood in awe of Price's attempts to rise above human nature and take others with him through his heroic altruism; he cherished Alex's memory as an exemplar of trust. Yet the moral of both these lives was that generosity can have fatal consequences. Alex fell to his death in the wake of the less experienced climber to whom he was joined by a rope.

Excessive trust, Bill reflected, also contributed to the death of his family's dog, Freya, who tried to follow him across a busy road and was run over. He cried more for her than he had for Alex, and he wrote more about her too – three pages for Freya, less than a page on Alex, a couple of paragraphs about Jimmy. There is nothing unusual about the distribution of his feelings. Companion animals often enjoy an emotional privilege over human friends or relatives through no design of their own or of their keepers; Freya was a constant presence and a 'fourth child', whereas Alex had barely reached school age when Bill left home for university. But the more poignant Hamilton's recollections became, the more sharply they highlighted the weaknesses of feelings as a guide to ethics. He was more ready to imagine his dog's state of mind than the emotions behind his mother's silence.

His readiness to contemplate the killing of kin is also striking. As well as contending that his mother would have avoided life-saving surgery, even though he had just presumed that the procedure would be easy, he imagined himself on Robinson Crusoe's island, where he 'would indeed with my own hands kill a defective baby'. Some forty years earlier, discussing the human psyche with Alasdair Gray, he had taken the line that violent fantasies had an adaptive basis. This might seem to be a case in point.

Evolutionary psychologists would agree that adaptive strains may influence parents' actions in such circumstances, but they do not see the matter quite so starkly. One of the best-known and most highly regarded bodies of work to emerge from evolutionary psychology is summarised by Martin Daly and Margo Wilson in their book *Homicide*. They relate the killing of infants by mothers to a process of attachment between mother and baby which is somewhat conditional, entailing an initial 'assessment phase'. Usually this leads swiftly to a bond, but not always: the prospects for a happy outcome may be sapped if the mother cannot imagine a happy life for the two of them. In circumstances without the possibility of medical intervention, an absence of attachment might make less painful the decision to permit a handicapped infant's death, which might be in the mother's Darwinian interests.

Hamilton was certainly aware of Daly and Wilson's work, which is often treated as an honourable exception by people who are otherwise cautious or sceptical about evolutionary psychology. It could have given a Darwinian underpinning to his argument from personal emotion, yet he does not mention it. By contrast, in his remarks on the fate of the European Jews, he cited a book by an author on the fringe of the field, Kevin MacDonald, who depicted anti-Semitism as a 'reaction to the presence of Judaism as a highly successful group evolutionary strategy', a 'mirror image' of its target. MacDonald's theses, a Jewish-conspiracy theory in which Judaism itself is the conspiracy and natural selection the principal conspirator, are marginal ideologically, attracting accusations of anti-Semitism, and theoretically, being an exercise in group selectionism. Hamilton himself criticised the book, but on neither of these grounds: his complaint was that it failed to address the issue of population growth, which he considered fundamental. His attention to MacDonald contrasts remarkably with his inattention to Daly and Wilson. It is as if he became too wrapped up in his own feelings to notice them.

The image of a desert island recurred later in the essay, not as a predicament but an ideal. Caesarean sections, he argued, imperil our birthright: 'nothing less than the right to be free, a pair in paradise, forming their own island, giving birth naturally'. No setting for this conventional romantic image could be more incongruous than an essay about genetic degeneration. An isolated breeding population of a single pair is the acme of dysgenesis, creating a stagnant gene pool in which bad mutations do their worst.

By this stage, Hamilton continued, 'it should now be clear why over the years of my working life I have been slowly developing a paranoia for hospitals'. That working life was made possible by the hospital treatment which saved him from the consequences of playing with explosives. As he grew older, he saw the hospital buildings spreading, the medical dramas filling the television schedules, the pills filling up the bathroom cabinet; and for him the hospitals came to represent the inexorable modern menace that others see in immigrants or surveillance cameras.

It was certainly clear that he was possessed by this fear and that he felt compelled to make it public despite the hostility it would provoke. But it was not actually clear why the paranoia had grown to this extent. And the dystopian vision itself remained obscure. The 'Planetary Hospital' had much in common with the great totalitarian dystopias of the middle twentieth century: humans reduced to cogs in a global machine, or 'mites within its bowels', dominated by the technology they had created. Each of our lines, he warned, will become 'gradually enslaved through its physical and mental incompetence'. Within about five hundred years, 'we will have become ciphers and be without choice'.

What he did not explain was why such a fate would ensue from medical intervention. Kidney patients remain individuals however long they are obliged to spend connected to dialysis machines. Nor does mental incompetence accompany their physical dependency. But Hamilton insisted that the consequences of evading natural selection would be final. Either sociopolitical catastrophe would cause the technology to collapse, leaving a genetically degenerate population at nature's mercy, or the technology would prevail and destroy the human soul.

His scientific vision was dominated by the selective power of parasites, and he recognised the help that the globalised economy provided in distributing them round the world, yet he did not appear to consider that they might be nature's retort to the Planetary Hospital. His prophecies relied on italics and inverted commas more than on data or calculations. Yet they were presented as imminent. In two generations, he predicted, everybody would see what he was talking about.

Nobody rushed to echo the lone voice when the essay was published. Geneticists and evolutionary biologists recognise genetic load as a possible problem, in theory, but not as a concern. One of the few to have discussed it publicly is James Crow, a doyen of American genetics, who has raised the question of whether mutation rates pose a risk to human health. Like Hamilton, he anticipated that war or famine might send humankind back to the Stone Age, along with the additional burden of mutations that had occurred since and had not been removed by selection. The accumulation of mutations was a problem, he concluded. It was anything but urgent, though, unlike pressing matters such as global warming and population growth. The timescale was fifty to a hundred generations, 'which cautions us against advocating any precipitate action'.

Hamilton's great fear grew not from his understanding of science but of nature. Herein lay the most fundamental difference between him and John Maynard Smith. As a youth, Maynard Smith's evolutionary vision had been inspired by Olaf Stapledon's fantasies about how humanity might transform its own nature through technology. The young Bill Hamilton had also been excited by the idea of improving humanity, through eugenic design, but as he grew older, Stapledon's brave new worlds became

Hamilton's idea of hell. He believed that defying nature was both futile and wrong. If one was not fit as nature demanded, life was not worth living. His death, a catastrophic event following tropical exertions that would have been beyond many people a third of his age, was consistent with this view.

Bill Hamilton once introduced a lecture by Simon Baron-Cohen, who has developed an evolutionary perspective on the nature of autism. In a spectral voice that sounded affectless rather than deadpan, Hamilton remarked that he would be interested to hear the talk, as his mother had suggested that he himself might be autistic. She was not the only person close to him whose mind had been crossed by similar thoughts.

In the preface to the second volume of his collected papers, he deemed himself 'an irresponsible child, almost idiot savant'. Ten thousand miles from home, he would be more excited to note a similarity between an Amazonian flower and one he knew from the Kentish hills than by encountering a fellow countryman in a riverside bar. He would rather talk to a local man about varieties of strychnine vine, and might talk to him for weeks before thinking to ask whether the man was married or had children. He simply did not share the priorities of most of his fellow human beings. It was 'a trait approaching to autism about what most regard as the higher attributes of our own species'.

He turned it into a selling point. In this limited vision, he suggested, there was a rare clarity: 'some kinds of autists, unaffected by all the propaganda they have failed to hear' may 'see further into the true shapes that underlie social phenomena'. Equipped with his unique understanding of how social behaviour evolved, he was 'a person who . . . believes he understands the human species in many ways better than anyone and yet who manifestly doesn't understand in any practical way how the human world works – neither how he himself fits in and nor, it seems, the conventions limiting what he is allowed to discuss'. By identifying himself as an idiot savant, he laid claim to a holy fool's licence.

His ethical considerations on issues such as abortion were informed by rivalries between sibling plants rather than contests between human brothers, which were 'culture-infected and therefore vastly more complicated than what I understand'. But he used such observations to construct an identity as a narrator as complicated as anything a critic might be required to tease out of a literary novel, questioning his own reliability and then obliquely answering his own questions, while proposing on the off-beat that his reliability might be uniquely high. In remarking upon his failure to ask about wives and children, he made it clear that he understood why this mattered: not for the sake of etiquette, but because people want to talk about their dearest relationships. His references to autism were embedded in expressions of concern for how his readers would react to the truths he was constitutionally obliged to tell. He might not empathise, but he cared.

Autism comes readily to mind nowadays. Conceived as a disorder occurring across a broad spectrum of intensity, it is widely understood to centre on limitations in the ability to relate to people, often accompanied by a fascination with objects. The idea has lodged that autism is an excessive concentration of traits which are widespread in, and to some extent characterise, male psychology. Whatever the truth of this belief, Hamilton and individuals close to him were drawn to it as a means to understand how his mind worked. He relied upon analysis instead of intuition to understand human relations, and so he needed to insist that these could be satisfactorily interpreted using the same tools that worked for any other species, by turning relationships into data. His encyclopaedic capacities as a naturalist also spoke to the stereotype, while his early isolation looked consistent with it.

Perhaps the most telling of the resonances, however, is the moment in the 'Hospitals' essay where he faces his bereaved mother's silence and sees his own feelings. Under the modern explanatory concept of autism, this looks like a failure to recognise the existence of emotions not one's own, though in Freud's day, the word would have been 'narcissism'. Here he considered that introspection sufficed and did not look to sociobiology, his customary guide to understanding how people work. If he had, it would have steered him around his error, for one of the core principles of evolutionary psychology is that women and men invest asymmetrically in reproduction, and so are likely to have different feelings about it. Disregarding this insight, he based his judgement upon the assumption which also underlay his dystopian warnings: that on the question of what made life worth living, what went for him went for the world.

Yet these are all chords, not the symphony. Several people close to him thought that he had qualities reminiscent of autism, but the greater point is precisely that they were close to him. Even in his youthful loneliness he had at least one serious relationship; later he married and had a family, which remained together for many years; latterly, he formed another serious relationship, which he was in at the time of his death. He was not short of love nor companionship. Although his was the kind of personality with which only a minority can connect, the life he led brought him into contact with plenty of people who became fast friends and many more whose acquaintance with him instilled lasting affection. His social skills did not fare well in the hubbub of a crowded room or in the space between a lectern and an audience; they were utterly inadequate faced with the glassy artifices of an Oxford college dinner, but they had a quiet strength.

Had he been a young man, he would have cut a recognisable figure with his isolation, insecurities and resentments, his scuffed sense of his own genius, his defiant belief that he possessed unique insights into the human condition, his self-absorption and his drive to express himself in images far outside the common stock. His sense of personal drama was classical in scale. In a São Paulo bookshop he read Aeschylus and wept at Apollo's warning to Orestes, identifying with the protagonist whose fate was to be pursued and tormented by the Furies.

At the last, though, when his most awful thoughts were finally published, the Furies were silent. So was almost everybody else; the book received few notices. His peers lifted the bark, and lowered it hastily back down. Bill Hamilton ended his publication career as he had started it, with a text that was too long, too challenging and too idiosyncratic for his colleagues to take. But unlike that first paper, and plenty of others throughout his working life, it was issued by its intended publisher without alteration. That was fitting as well as proper.

Congo, Amazon, Wytham

Ed Hooper's quest was a story written for Bill Hamilton. It involved both hospitals and parasites, and blamed the former for the latter. Hooper came to suspect that HIV had been transferred to humans through the use of material from chimpanzees for the manufacture of polio vaccines in Congo during the 1950s. Many scientists would have kept their distance from a researcher without qualifications in the relevant disciplines, but in his foreword to Hooper's book, Hamilton saluted the author's success in teaching himself virology, genetics and evolution. Like Hamilton in the early days, Hooper had struggled to build up a controversial thesis in the face of establishment hostility and disdain. Like Hamilton, too, he had run the risks of the tropics in pursuit of the evidence he needed. Hamilton saw Hooper's OPV (oral polio vaccine) hypothesis as more than a hypothesis. It was a matter of scientific integrity and Truth with a capital 'T'.

In 1999, Hooper and Hamilton went to Congo together, mingling with the soldiers of several different armies in the streets of Kisangani. While Hooper worked journalistically, investigating the history of a camp where vaccines had been produced, Hamilton collected faecal samples from the pet chimpanzees that turned out to be common in the suburbs. These were to be tested for chimpanzee simian immunodeficiency virus, the putative precursor of HIV.

Hamilton also wanted samples from wild chimpanzees, which might be descended from those which had been around the camp during the polio trials, and he decided to return for them the following year. Having fallen ill on the first trip, he felt he needed capable companions, not for his own sake, but for the samples'. A team of two or three people, with field skills, stood a better chance of bringing the stools home.

He recruited a young doctoral student, Mike Worobey, who was in the Zoology Department at Oxford as a Rhodes scholar. Worobey was eminently well qualified for the task, combining theoretical skills in virology with experience in fighting forest fires, by rappelling down to them from helicopters, which he gained during student vacations in his native Canada. He in turn approached a friend from home, Jeff Joy. A fellow firefighter, Joy had also become a biologist and had developed techniques for climbing to parts of trees that were particularly difficult to reach. Worobey and Joy were attracted by the prospect of working with Hamilton, whom they held in awe, but were sceptical about the OPV hypothesis. Hamilton didn't mind scepticism. It was the sight of a loner up against an establishment that stirred his sense of fairness.

They left Heathrow for Congo on 3 January 2000, just after the world celebrated the new millennium. In Entebbe, still as near as passenger airliners got to Kisangani, Hamilton paid a diamond dealer $300 for seats in a small turboprop plane that took them the rest of the way. The King Air made its final approach as near to the vertical as it could safely manage, in the way that transport aircraft do where airports are oases surrounded by the threat of ground fire.

Kisangani itself was in a state of rough and ready peace, enforced by the Rwandan troops who dominated the city. A few weeks after Hamilton and Hooper's visit, fighting had broken out between the Rwandans and their former Ugandan allies, causing most of the city's inhabitants to flee into the jungle. The Rwandans won, but the Ugandan forces remained in the area after a ceasefire was agreed. Six months after Hamilton's second visit, hostilities erupted again.

Hamilton and his companions installed themselves in the Palm Beach Hotel, where they noted with interest the bullet trajectory revealed by the holes in the window, curtain and wall of their room. The *pax Rwandana* made their arrangements simpler, since the occupation force had rendered the local bureaucracy impotent. Médecins Sans Frontières aid workers arranged for them to meet Commander Frank, a senior Rwandan officer, who satisfied himself that they were innocuous. After about a week, they received a letter of assistance from the civilian governor and headed out towards the forest in a Toyota Land Cruiser.

They stopped at a village beside the mile-wide Congo river and then moved on a few kilometres to a settlement where their interpreter's sister, José, arranged for local hunters to act as guides. After a ten-hour trek, the scientists found themselves in a remote clearing in which a small dwelling had been built and some crops planted. The guides had not taken them to the chimpanzees but to rendezvous with the hunter who, unlike them, was capable of finding the apes. He lived here with his family, subsisting mainly by catching catfish from streams, smoking them and taking them to market. In the jungle the hunters would cook catfish up with chanterelle mushrooms in a pot, eating it for breakfast, lunch and dinner.

The guides spent a couple of days drinking palm wine and smoking marijuana, assuring the scientists that there were no chimpanzees around. Then, to the scientists' relief, the group moved into the forest and got to work. The hunters would listen for the apes' calls, track the chimpanzees for up to forty kilometres, wait overnight and then collect the faeces and urine from beneath the chimps' roosts in the morning. Joy's tree-climbing equipment was never needed.

While waiting for the hunters to return, Hamilton made his own forays into the jungle with his machete. He was in his element and delighted to be there. He met the challenges of heat and hiking as surely as his companions less than half his age.

For their part, Worobey and Joy were similarly delighted to be a captive audience for this most encyclopaedic of naturalists. They found him never at a loss for a taxonomic classification or a spirited hypothesis. When he saw male vervet monkeys, their scrotums debonair in shades of sky blue, he speculated that the colouring was an 'honest indicator' of resistance to parasites: the males burdened with the fewest parasites would be the bluest. When he walked through a village, he would name each species of plant they passed, although he had only been there briefly once before. 'I don't know why I fill my head with all this garbage,' he remarked after identifying a particularly obscure specimen. The younger men never felt that they were expected to sit at the master's feet.

Worobey had to cut the seminar short. On the first day, he got a thorn stuck in his hand, which became infected and steadily more painful. At the camp, he was more or less immobile, and so nobody realised just how serious the infection was. He began to realise his predicament as he hiked back, carrying the first batch of samples, through vines, mud, water and his own fever. His guide, one of the inexpert hunters, brought them out of the forest in the wrong spot. Each village exercised rights over surrounding tracts of forest, and the party did not have permission to be in the area. Worobey was too ill to do anything but sit on the ground, surrounded by villagers, a couple of whom were drunk and became threatening. Fortunately, the strong and subtle José showed up in the village and rescued Mike from an increasingly ugly situation.

He got a ride back to Kisangani, where a Red Cross nurse examined his hand and pondered whether to amputate the thumb. The moment when the nurse casually let his patient know what he was doing was the moment when Worobey fully comprehended the risks he had run. It was a Hamiltonian lesson. They had worried about war, but parasites were the greater menace.

His thumb was spared and the thorn extracted, but the Médecins Sans Frontières doctor was alarmed by the infection. Worobey was treated with antibiotics and remained at the MSF house, along with the samples, which were stored in the freezer. Hamilton and Joy returned to Kisangani two days later. In all, the team obtained about thirty samples from up to twenty individual chimpanzees.

On 25 January, Worobey had recuperated enough to join the others at the Palm Beach Hotel, where they drank Fanta with Commander Frank and discussed the Rwandan genocide. Now, however, Hamilton was becoming ill. They thought it might be malaria. The disease came readily to mind here. 'If a place could feel like malaria, it seems to me this is what it would feel like,' observed another western visitor to Kisangani, sandbagged by the heat and humidity.

The next day, Hamilton told the others that he had a terrible headache. Worobey and Joy realised that this was serious: Hamilton's extraordinary toughness and tolerance to pain had been impressed on them in the forest. They obtained anti-malarial medicine from a pharmacy and decided to get out of Kisangani on the first available flight. The mood at the airport was tense, sharpened by rumours of an attack on the city by Congolese government forces, and the scientists were beset by officials hustling them for money. Hamilton was on the upswing of the fever cycle. He lay on top of their pile of luggage, sweating and shaking, but not complaining.

After several hours, they managed to get on a flight to Kigali, the Rwandan capital, by which time Hamilton's fever had abated. When they reached Entebbe, though, his condition worsened again. A doctor diagnosed *falciparum*, the most lethal species of malarial parasite, but the medicine he gave him seemed to quell the disease. As they passed through the airport at Nairobi, Hamilton pointed out some acacia trees on the horizon. Ants lived on acacias, shaping the living trees around them, both in Africa and South America. He had been wondering for some years whether the associations between the insects and the trees had evolved separately on each continent or dated back to the time when the two land masses were joined. If he had been feeling better, he said, they could have spent their three hours' transit break in Nairobi collecting ants.

By the time they landed at Heathrow, he seemed to be consolidating his recovery. The next day, he went to University College Hospital, where he was tested for malaria. While waiting for the test results he collapsed, suffering a massive haemorrhage, and became unconscious. For six weeks his loved ones and friends visited his bedside, talking to him and reading him his favourite poems by A. E. Housman. Some of his fellow scientists prayed for his recovery to a God they did not believe in. He died on 7 March 2000, without regaining consciousness.

The post-mortem investigation found the probable site of the haemorrhage, an ulcer in the gut, near an artery. It appeared typical of the kind of ulcer which is caused by anti-inflammatory drugs, such as ibuprofen or aspirin. There were open bottles of both medicines in Hamilton's baggage. A scenario suggested itself: he had taken aspirin or ibuprofen to relieve the headache and other symptoms of his malaria; one of the tablets got stuck to the wall of his gut and corroded it away.

By the time he collapsed, the malaria was gone, according to the results of the tests in London; massive injections of quinine had cleared the parasites from his blood. But the disease could have been prevented instead of cured. Worobey and Joy took prophylactic medicines against malaria; Hamilton did not. The reason, Worobey understood, was that Hamilton believed he was immune after all his time in Brazil. Such a belief, implicitly assuming that the malarial parasites of the Amazon were identical to those of the Congo, seems remarkably insouciant in an evolutionary biologist who gave pride of theoretical place to parasites and their ability to out-adapt their hosts.

Perhaps his suspicion of organised medicine was at work; perhaps it had been subverting his health for some time, if the ulcer had developed before the expedition. Perhaps it was the rough practicality of an old tropical hand. Peter Henderson, his companion on many of his Amazonian expeditions, observes that tropical veterans do not take prophylactic antimalarials because of the harm they can cause in both the short and the long term. Henderson has lost many friends among field biologists who have chosen to work in the tropics. Their life expectancy aligns itself with that of the region in which they spend their time: they are vulnerable to infections, accidents and other humans.

If anybody appreciated parasites, Hamilton did, and nobody who flew into Kisangani at the end of the 1990s could have failed to appreciate the hazards arising from the presence of at least two rival armies. Nobody was better placed to know the risks than he was. The question is, why did he choose to run them? How did he come to decide that the potential benefits outweighed the potential hazards?

Some of his colleagues seemed to feel that he had wanted an excuse to get back into the field. Robert May, the President of the Royal Society, said as much at the Royal Society meeting on the origins of HIV, posthumously sponsored by Hamilton. But Hamilton did not need to drop in to a war zone for that. He could always return to the Amazon, and had wanted to do so one more time before he retired: he had continued to maintain a research connection there, in the flooded forests of the Mamirauá nature reserve. Amazonia is not a place where a naturalist runs out of species to study.

The expedition certainly did not demand Hamilton's special gifts or skills. In the event the scientists did not even make use of Jeff Joy's specialist tree techniques: local men conducted the collecting forays. It was a dirty job which somebody else could perfectly well have done. Nor was it a matter of personally undertaking to get Ed Hooper the evidence he needed. They fell out during the first Kisangani trip and had little contact with each other afterwards, though they had made progress in healing the rift by the time Hamilton returned to Congo. Yet if he had brought back samples that supported the hypothesis, he would only have got credit for a supporting role. As in so many aspects of his later career, Hamilton was acting contrary to professorial type. Instead of sitting at a desk and adding his name to subordinates' papers, gathering incremental credit without incremental effort, he sat in a tent and packed shit into bottles. In the event, the samples offered no support for the OPV hypothesis, which was pronounced dead in *Nature* after tests on stored samples of polio vaccine found that they had been made using tissue from rhesus monkeys, not chimpanzees.

If he felt a personal obligation, it was to the idea that he had elected to champion. He was supporting not just a solitary and embattled investigator but an idea that he felt was undeservedly oppressed and unrecognised – as had been his own first idea about altruism, which was like a child to him. And Bill Hamilton took pride in doing things himself. In this he was true to his family's tradition, as he was in taking the risk and marking it down. His calculations were influenced by his horror of a life dependent on hospitals. His personal instincts told him that it was better to quit while ahead, and die as nature intended, than to linger into disability and senility.

He was mindful of death and had long anticipated his final curtain. It made an unannounced entrance, hyperbolic but otherwise outside the normal idiom of book-jacket 'shouts', in his comments on the back cover of the 1999 edition of Fisher's *Genetical Theory*: 'By the time of my ultimate graduation, will I have understood all that is true in this book and will I get a First? I doubt it.' Fisher himself believed in a supreme External Examiner to mark the most final of finals. Hamilton's colleagues generally did not, and awarded him honorary degrees instead. Robert Trivers called him 'one of the greatest evolutionary theorists since Darwin'; Richard Dawkins proposed him as 'a good candidate for the title of most distinguished Darwinian since Darwin'.

Some years earlier, in a lyrical flourish of the dispersal trope that played throughout his thought, he had revealed detailed plans for his departure. They concluded the article which began with him turning stones and cycling through the lanes around Badgers Mount. The piece goes on to identify his own youthful emotions upon finding a colony of the Adonis Blue butterfly one evening among juniper bushes on a hillside near his home with Alfred Russel Wallace's near-swoon upon capturing a birdwing butterfly in the Moluccas. Hamilton finishes by taking his readers with him to the forest floor in Brazil – without warning them to leave their aesthetic sensibilities behind. He watches a dead chicken begin to heave and then burst open at the neck. A beetle the size of a golf ball emerges, smeared with innards and carrying a ball of flesh, which he presents to a female that emerges from the soil and disappears back underground with the remains. The naturalist returns in the cold rain to the reserve's canteen to eat chicken, too, and wonder about 'the mysteries of the forest undertakers', who sometimes team up to bury a carcass whole. He looks forward to when he is old and all the beetles' secrets are known; when it will be easy to attract them across great distances using 'foetid chemicals', and outlines his plan to have his body laid out in a Brazilian forest, where the *Coprophanaeus* beetle will feed upon him and bury him:

> Later, in their children, reared with care by the horned parents out of fist-sized balls moulded from my flesh, I will escape. No worm for me, or sordid fly: rearranged and multiple, I will at last buzz from the soil like bees from a nest – indeed, buzz louder than bees, almost like a swarm of motor bikes. I shall be borne, beetle by flying beetle, out into the Brazilian wilderness beneath the stars, carried under those beautiful and un-fused elytra which we will all hold over our backs. So, finally, I too will shine like a violet ground beetle under a stone.

Resurrection and assumption, into nature instead of heaven; dung-beetles become the vehicles in which the 'I' carries on. Fantasies about immortality are no more the preserve of believers than are fantasies about flying. But choosing to indulge one in public suggests at least a relaxed attitude to the question of the hereafter. 'I sometimes fantasise that if I studied religions seriously I might end up a Ba'hai,' he observed in a letter, noting that 'they seem to have a generally kindly approach'.

He had little religious baggage of his own: religion had been one of the things Archibald Hamilton warned his children against. Practised with absence of zeal, Church of England rites were agreeably familiar and unobjectionable. They were in the background of Bill's family life, too, for his father-in-law was a priest. Bill did not mind that his wife went to church occasionally or that his daughters sang in the choir.

If he had been an atheist, he would have said so. He called himself an agnostic, and he did not seem patently the kind of agnostic who is an atheist in all but name. If you didn't know better, you might almost imagine that he was a man who could gaze at a sunset and see divinity beyond it.

He was laid to rest not on the Amazonian forest floor but in a small cemetery on the edge of Wytham Woods, a short walk from the cottage in which he had lived. Luisa Bozzi, his companion, promised him that 'from here you will reach again your beloved forests. You will live not only in a beetle, but in billions of spores of fungi and algae. Brought by the wind higher up into the troposphere, all of you will form the clouds, and wandering across the oceans, will fall down and fly up again and again; till eventually a drop of rain will join you to the water of the flooded forest of the Amazon.'

His grave was marked by a disc of limestone, which he had found in a local quarry while searching for fossils, and within a few months by a tangle of plants, untidy and quite apt, as if the motley species had gathered in tribute to the naturalist who had known them all so well.

'While the rest of us speak and think in single notes, he thought in chords.' – Robert Trivers on Bill Hamilton.

RICHARD DAWKINS

'We reach out in our search for meaning, until we suddenly realise it is we who actually provide the purpose in a universe which otherwise would have none.'
  Richard Dawkins, 2004

13

What Genes Want

Each of the evolutionists in this series has their emblematic creatures. Wallace has his birds of paradise. Fisher can be represented by the scarlet tiger moth, whose colours he hoisted in his transatlantic war against Sewall Wright. Haldane's should be guinea pigs, because he did his first genetic studies on them and because he was so ready to make a guinea pig of himself. Maynard Smith might be assigned the fruit flies on which he spent his first ten years as a biologist, but the game-playing lizards of California would be more fitting heraldic supporters. For Hamilton wasps are the natural choice. And Richard Dawkins has his biomorphs. Unlike the others, they undoubtedly have a creator. Dawkins brought them into being himself.

His biomorphs manifested as images on a computer screen, evolved forms with a remarkably biological quality in their geometry. Dawkins wrote the software which generated them and was their selective agent – 'With a wild surmise, I began to breed, generation after generation, from whichever child looked most like an insect . . . I still cannot conceal from you my feeling of exultation as I first watched these exquisite creatures emerging before my eyes . . . I couldn't eat, and that night "my" insects swarmed behind my eyelids as I tried to sleep.'

This was Dawkins's fieldwork, and his natural habitat. He was an alumnus of the Oxford school, but he was never inclined to search Wytham Woods for a moth or snail case study of his own. As an undergraduate he treated zoology as an approach to philosophy, and it was as philosophy that he took up evolution ten years or so later. His was a universal Darwinism, in which abstraction rose above nature. But it remained local too, for it never left Oxford.

*

Clinton Richard Dawkins was born in 1941, in Nairobi, and was taken two years later to Nyasaland (now Malawi), where his family lived until he was nearly eight. His father was an agricultural officer in the colonial civil service, applying knowledge acquired studying botany at Oxford, and then applying it directly in Oxfordshire, after he inherited a farm near Chipping Norton from a distant cousin. Twenty miles from Oxford, it remained Richard's home throughout his boyhood, although he was sent to boarding school and so lived on the farm only in the holidays. He would be taken for walks upon which his father would advise him of the Latin names of the wayside plants and the taxonomic relationships between them, but neither the information nor the flora and fauna, English or African, inspired him.

Nor did he seem inspired as a pupil at Oundle, the public school he attended later in England. His father's biological interests combined with the inspirational efforts of his biology teacher, Ioan Thomas, to influence him in his sixth-form subject choices, but his preferences were not marked. Acquaintance with the theory of evolution had a corrosive effect on his already shaky religious faith by providing an alternative to the argument from design, but he did not discover a scientific calling instead. Though the school did not regard him as promising Oxbridge material, his family had a tradition to uphold. Around a dozen of them, including his father and grandfather, had been Balliol men. Thomas agreed to give him extra tuition, while warning him that Balliol might be a bit high for him to aim. But Dawkins secured a place and read zoology.

It was not until his second year that his capacity for fascination was unlocked. In those days the Oxford tutorial system was based on perfect ratios: one tutor to one student, one essay on one topic, once a week. Sent to the library to read up on a subject narrow enough for him to cover the whole of the literature, each week he found himself 'a kind of world authority' on a different detail of nature. Knowledge was authority to tell the tutor what was what. 'I really loved that, and I think it was that experience that made me really take to the idea of an academic life.'

He was transported by concentration too. Sleeping the topic and dreaming it, 'it almost became like a mystical experience' that gave him 'an almost poetic affinity' for the corner of zoology in question. The transcendent elements were those which mattered to him. 'I almost thrust the facts to one side and went straight for the ideas.' The bigger the idea, the more he was absorbed by it. He turned zoological essays into lofty, 'probably a bit pretentious', philosophical inquiries. One of his tutors, Arthur Cain, positively encouraged his philosophising.

Much of his intellectual exploration was conducted within his essays. Around the turn of the 1960s, students had yet to become conspicuously political, though Oxford provided ample opportunities to sample establishment politics rather as one might attend a classical concert: 'You could go and hear cabinet ministers any week you liked, and I used to do a fair bit of that.' It was not a matter of conviction, though, and even his animus against religion, inflamed at school, had dimmed into indifference. As for other interests, he didn't play sports, and he was 'too shy' to tackle the barriers the university placed around its small complement of female students.

He soon found that 'if you wrote an essay . . . which suggested that something was too trivial to count in natural selection, you got jumped on'. The precept came down from E. B. Ford and pervaded the department. 'It really became quite locally heretical, though it wasn't in the rest of the world, to ever talk about anything being neutral, or too insignificant to count. Selection was the great god, and selection was thought to be powerful enough to drive evolution to just about any lengths.'

This is indeed Richard Dawkins talking, not Richard Lewontin. Thanks to Ford (though he never gave him tutorials) Dawkins was intellectually formed in a uniquely selectionist atmosphere. Selection was the one god he did not see fit to reject. He absorbed the new orthodoxy and went on to become its leading promulgator. But even he found Cain's pronouncements 'on the perfection of animals' too heady to take neat. He spent an evening with Cain arguing about them over a pub supper. Nevertheless, he was impressed by the trenchancy of Cain's paper, which 'hit me in the solar plexus' when he heard it as a lecture. It was an early lesson in the power of Darwinian advocacy.

If anyone deserved to have supreme confidence in adaptation, it was Cain. Half a century on, his work with Philip Sheppard on snails remains the keystone of what is arguably the solidest and most substantial analysis of evolution in action. Cain and Sheppard demonstrated that features previously considered neutral were adaptively significant; subsequent studies identified further selective pressures and shed light upon when they did not operate, as well as when they did. The snails vindicated Ford's view of evolution more comprehensively and decisively than his own scarlet tiger moths, or Bernard Kettlewell's peppered moths. At the time, though, those industrialised insects represented frontiers that selectionists were pushing ever further back. With selection pressures undergoing double-digit inflation, Oxford was bullish.

The moths, butterflies and snails were joined by gulls and sticklebacks, the most celebrated objects of Niko Tinbergen's attention and popular choices of study for his graduate students. Dawkins sees Tinbergen as a lifelong selectionist, who found his natural habitat when he came to Oxford. He notes a 'rather shocking' anecdote of Tinbergen's about how, as a student at Leiden in the 1920s, he was firmly told off by his professor for suggesting that the reason birds flock more densely when attacked by a predator might have something to do with survival value. Dawkins was impressed by the 'ruthlessly mechanistic attitude to animal behaviour' Tinbergen displayed in his undergraduate lectures. 'I was particularly taken with two phrases of his – "behaviour machinery", and "equipment for survival".' They remained latent in his imagination until he wrote *The Selfish Gene*, for which he condensed them into the phrase 'survival machine'. (According to Tinbergen's biographer Hans Kruuk, Tinbergen learned to regard animals as objects from the Inuit hunters among whom he spent a year in Greenland as a young man. If that is so, Dawkins may claim Arctic intellectual ancestry – which, for critics of his mechanistic view of life, might make a change from the usual white European suspects.)

In 1963, the year after Dawkins graduated, Tinbergen set out the terms of ethological inquiry into animal behaviour. Ethologists could ask how a behaviour evolved within a lineage and how it developed within an individual animal. They could ask about its proximate causes, the events within the body and outside it that were involved in its occurrence, and they could also ask about its ultimate causes, its function and its survival value. Dawkins identified himself as a functional ethologist, meaning that he was concerned with ultimate adaptive causes. By the time he reached Oxford, he considers, these had also become Tinbergen's principal concern. Oxford's field genetics and field behavioural studies converged on the theme of selection.

Dawkins did not go out into the field himself, though. Wags would later suggest that he had tried it once but retreated when he encountered a wasp. He became one of Tinbergen's graduate students – 'We felt ourselves members of a privileged elite, an Athens of ethology' – having enjoyed the unusual benefit of half a term's tutorials from the ethologist. Up to that point, he had been considering postgraduate studies in biochemistry.

At first, the questions he asked were about the development of behaviour in chicks, but after about a year, he became intrigued by the question of what actually went on in the chicks' heads when they chose to do one thing rather than another. Instead of investigating it neurophysiologically, he developed a mathematical model of choice. Tinbergen remained his official supervisor but was unable to offer the mathematical expertise he needed. That came from Tinbergen's deputy Mike Cullen, to whose intellectual generosity, given at the expense of his own publication record, Dawkins pays fulsome tribute.

Dawkins rates his own mathematical abilities as 'pretty poor'. He is confident that he has a basic mathematical intuition, and he can do algebra, but he has trouble with calculus. Like the zoologist Solly Zuckerman, he is inclined to hum his way through formulae when he encounters them in a scientific paper. But among the unmathematical ethologists, he acquired a reputation for numeracy. It boosted his confidence and encouraged him to approach computer terminals without the fear they generally inspired in those early mainframe days.

Computers were not the only transformative scientific resources that he adopted early. One day, Cullen brought Bill Hamilton's 1964 papers to the Animal Behaviour group's discussion club. Dawkins shared Cullen's excitement, and expressed some of it not long after, when in 1965 he deputised for Tinbergen on an animal behaviour course. He felt a touch of guilt at devoting two of the lectures to Hamilton, for it was a radical departure from Tinbergen's treatment of animal behaviour. Excitement won out, though, and stimulated the first fanfares of the rhetorical style in which his radical Darwinism would be constituted. Diffident at first, he showed his notes about immortal genes leaping down the generations to Cullen, who gave his images the thumbs-up.

Through reading Hamilton, Dawkins had glimpsed the gene's-eye view of life. *The Selfish Gene* can be read as a development of George Williams's

Adaptation and Natural Selection, the manifesto of gene-centred evolutionary theory, but Dawkins worked out his ideas upon the basis of the inspiration he got from his compatriot. 'I was immediately inspired by Hamilton, and I think by Williams a bit later, but by then I'd got my own thoughts thoroughly in order and so almost didn't need Williams.' The process might have been simpler had he worked from Williams, though, for the American's commitment to the gene's-eye view was stronger than Hamilton's.

Dawkins did not at first see how selfish genes were, or how contingent the behaviour of animals was upon self-interest. Looking reflexively to the Church of England when in need of a metaphor, he began his first lecture on animal communication by quoting a prayer for absent friends, 'bound together by the unseen chains of Thy love'. While the Oxford animal behaviourists had grasped that an animal does not act for the good of the species if it is not acting for its own good as well, they still saw animals' interactions with each other through a rosy glow of mutualism instead of the web of manipulation and deceit that animal behaviourists now behold. Dawkins did not really appreciate how different a Hamiltonian vision of nature was from Tinbergen's until he had written *The Selfish Gene* in the mid-1970s.

He finished his doctorate, married a colleague, Marian Stamp, and accepted an offer to go and teach in California. Richard and Marian thought that Berkeley would be a stimulating environment, but they did not realise just how stimulating the Berkeley air had become until they arrived in 1967. They became involved in the political movements that seized the campus, marching against the Vietnam War and licking envelopes for the liberal candidate Eugene McCarthy in the Democratic presidential primary contests. For the first and only time in Dawkins's career, science was overshadowed by politics. It was also the first and only period of his career that he spent away from Oxford.

He was swept some way towards the left, and the tide did not bring him all the way back when it receded (back in England, he always voted Labour or for the Liberals in their various incarnations). But he was never in danger of freaking out. He never tried drugs – 'rather disappointingly nobody ever offered me any!'

After a couple of years, they had come to feel that 'heady though it was, it was not a very productive way to spend your life'. Tinbergen made him an offer too good to miss, and he returned to Oxford as a lecturer in zoology. Marian Stamp Dawkins had remained a doctoral student of Tinbergen's while in California; she has also continued her career at Oxford, achieving distinction in the fields of animal psychology and animal welfare. She and Richard collaborated, and published together, on the theory of decision-making.

In the mid-1970s, Richard spent a year working on a paper about hierarchical organisation, which completed the systems chapter of his scientific life. He now had an opportunity to complete a book he had started during a hiatus which had arisen in 1972, when strikes cut electricity supplies and the government cut the working week to three days. The selectionism that he had absorbed as a student was about to come to the boil. In 1976, *The Selfish Gene* was published, and Richard Dawkins finally found his calling.

Back in 1972, he referred to the two embryonic chapters as his 'bestseller', but he did not anticipate the truth in his jest. Nor did he see it as especially radical. 'I just thought of it as being a rhetorical exposition of what we'd known ever since Fisher.' For Dawkins, as well as his readers, however, it took the exposition to reveal the radical truth in what evolutionists already knew.

The ferment was not just in Dawkins's own mind. Between the blackouts of 1972 and the sabbatical of 1975, biologists were introduced to Maynard Smith's evolutionary games, and they began to take more notice of Hamilton. In the United States, Robert Trivers also emerged as a potent source of insight into behaviour and the genetic interests underlying it: he explored how co-operation could be sustained between unrelated individuals through reciprocity, developed Fisher's sex-ratio argument into a hypothesis about how parents would be expected to allocate investment in offspring of different sexes, and considered the possibility that there might be conflicts of genetic interest between parents and offspring. Nowadays, talk of investment and interests is as ubiquitous in evolutionary literature as it is in the newspapers, but back then there was a place for a text that crystallised the new view of life. Although Dawkins was modest in his prefatory claims about the value of *The Selfish Gene* to experts, he recognised his significance more clearly later. 'I do declare myself not to be a populariser. I now think that what I would like to claim for myself is that I changed the way biologists think about biology.'

He had rewritten the rules of scientific discourse by admitting the public. Before *The Selfish Gene*, there was formal scientific literature, for internal circulation only, and there were popularisations in which experts simplified accepted ideas for public consumption. *The Selfish Gene* overruled this division. It articulated ideas which were not yet fully accepted or appreciated among scientists and which came as a cumulative revelation to its author in the process of writing it.

Today it is recognisable as the prototype for what John Brockman, patron of scientific thinking and literary agent for scientific thinkers, would twenty years later proclaim as the 'Third Culture': scientists conduct public conversations with each other, 'and the public gets to look over their shoulder'. But *The Selfish Gene* was not written with the condescension evident in this remark. Dawkins wanted to inspire the public to share what had now become his passion. Lay readers were the ones he had uppermost in mind when he conceived the book, and he put the public first in all but one of its successors. If he had not written *The Selfish Gene* in a way that any willing and able reader could comprehend, it would not have transformed the way that his colleagues look at evolution.

He intended *The Selfish Gene* in part as an antidote to the greater-goodism he heard in BBC nature documentaries, and as a belated counterblast to similar assumptions in popular books by Konrad Lorenz and Robert Ardrey. These authors influenced his style in that he felt that their rich rhetoric needed to be matched. As important as the imagery, however, was the openness of the language. By minimising the jargon, Dawkins made modern evolutionary theory into public intellectual property. He enabled scholars across the faculties, and the intelligentsia at large, to join him in turning biology into philosophy. The whole book, from the title onwards, invited a debate about values.

Conceptually radical, visibly universal in its relevance, and 'gripping', as its author had intended, it became a beacon for biology departments. 'The world must be full of people who are biologists today rather than physicists because of Dawkins,' observed John Maynard Smith. Distinguishing between popularisation and contributions to original thought in a form that can be generally understood, he compared it to David Lack's *Life of the Robin*. Having failed to conform to the pattern in which a youthful enthusiasm for natural history was institutionalised as a university biology course, though, Dawkins provided a source of inspiration that rendered natural history unnecessary. This was not before time, for Hamiltonian childhoods of bird's-nesting and bicycling down country lanes had by then vanished beneath a carpet of motorways and television.

His interest in computers was also more in tune with the technophilic outlook of a younger generation. In his own life it occupied the place that specimen collections commanded in the lives of amateur naturalists, though the purpose of hunting bugs was to remove them rather than to amass them. It was also an exercise in practical skills that he was not applying in orthodox laboratory work. And it was at once a private and a social activity, suited to a simultaneously private and social personality. 'Every day you're having to struggle, and suddenly the thing you're working on works, and then something neat appears . . . and you rush into the next room and say, "Come and look at this!"' Emerging from his code into the glow of hacker 'social approval', he found that neat stuff is not just its own reward. He found a natural niche in the computing community, and later a natural constituency, which welcomed as one of its own a thinker for whom life 'is just bytes and bytes and bytes of digital information'.

Computer code is an implacably selfish form of digital information, though, and Dawkins was left with the uneasy feeling that he had failed to resist its demands with sufficient resolve. He ended up with a string of major programming projects under his belt, including the Dawkins Organ, a software-based device for recording observations about animal behaviour using a keyboard, a program for translating from one computer language into another, a program to imitate cricket song, and the 'nadir' of his compulsion, a word-processing program he developed to write *The Blind Watchmaker*, on the pretext that the word processor supplied with the Apple II computer was inadequate. 'If you add them up, that's actually a lot of time wasted in a career. It's quite surprising in a way that I managed to write six books.'

*

The Selfish Gene introduced Dawkins's distinguishing idea: that what natural selection acts upon is the gene, which is what replicates, not the individual, which is a vehicle for the replicating genes. It combined Tinbergen's mechanistic ruthlessness with clarion rhetoric rich enough to leave Lorenz lost for words. 'We are survival machines – robot vehicles blindly programmed to preserve the selfish molecules known as genes. This is a truth which still fills me with astonishment.'

It also introduced the word 'meme' to the language, denoting a piece of cultural information that replicates, and signifying that Darwinian selection is a process universally applicable to replicating information, living or otherwise. The point was subsequently illustrated by the way in which the phrase 'lumbering robots' achieved replication throughout commentaries on Richard Dawkins. Many commentators have failed to appreciate that Dawkins sounds exultant not because he sees us as machines, but because he sees us as human nonetheless.

His next book, *The Extended Phenotype*, was the only one he addressed directly to his scientific peers, and indeed urged upon them – 'if you never read anything else of mine, please at least read *this*'. It placed the key concepts of its predecessor before them, taking the opportunity to answer accumulated criticisms, and offered not a new theory but 'a new way of seeing biological facts'. He considered the last four chapters to contain 'the best candidate for the title "innovative" that I have to offer'. This was his discussion of the idea that 'the replicator should be thought of as having *extended* phenotypic effects, consisting of all its effects on the world at large' – including artefacts or other organisms – 'not just its effects on the individual body in which it happens to be sitting'. Having based his first book on the assumption that 'if adaptations are to be treated as "for the good of" something, that something is the gene', Dawkins was now mounting an attempt 'to free the selfish gene from the individual organism which has been its conceptual prison'.

One of the jailers of this Bastille was Bill Hamilton, who found himself cast in the role of the revolutionary deemed insufficiently radical by his disciple. Although Dawkins never wavered in his admiration for Hamilton, he felt that the idea of inclusive fitness was an obstacle to seeing biological facts through the gene's eye. Inclusive fitness was about the selection of genes, but it complicated the issue by trying to fit into biology's existing frame of reference. 'Before Hamilton's revolution, our world was peopled by individual organisms working single-mindedly to keep themselves alive and to have children. In those days it was natural to measure success in this undertaking at the level of the individual organism. Hamilton changed all that but unfortunately, instead of following his ideas through to their logical conclusion and sweeping the organism from its pedestal . . . he exerted his genius in devising a means of rescuing the individual.'

John Maynard Smith sympathised. He thought that Hamilton had been trying to rescue Fisher's Fundamental Theorem, and agreed that this had made matters more complicated. Inclusive fitness was 'a swine to calculate'. It was a lot easier to ask, 'If I was a gene, what would I do?'

William Paley, the eighteenth-century theologian, famously opened his book *Natural Theology* by observing that if he came across a watch lying on the ground and asked how it came to be there, he should be forced to conclude from its intricacy and precision that it must have had a maker. It had been designed; since the works of nature showed just as much evidence of contrivance and design, they too must have had a Designer. This was the 'argument from design' that evolutionists took over, leaving its theistic roots showing in the personification of nature implicit in 'natural selection'. Dawkins rendered it explicit in the title of his next book, *The Blind Watchmaker*. Naturalistic explanations of nature were to have a suite of images to match anything in the supernatural armoury.

Dawkins now proclaimed Darwinism a 'universal truth'. Speculating that visitors from Andromeda would appreciate humankind's understanding of evolution but would be uninterested in the 'parochial' issues of psychological and social phenomena addressed in the arts, he implied that evolutionary biology was a higher form of knowledge. It was also aesthetically superior. 'There is more poetry in Mitochondrial Eve than in her mythological namesake,' he declared in *River out of Eden*, referring to the common human ancestor indicated by comparative DNA analysis. He began *Climbing Mount Improbable* by relating how he had heard a literary lecture about figs, which had considered them as symbol, as text and as pretty much anything except figs. It was, he gave the reader to understand, an effete and pretentious performance, but his point was not about style.

Dawkins objected in principle, insisting that the biological story of figs was richer and better. In due course he told it, recounting Hamilton's researches and demonstrating the appreciation of natural history that he had developed in maturity. Hamilton also saw poetry in biology, comparing his scientific papers to Basho's poems, but he did not treat scientific literature as a higher form than the artistic kind, for which he seemed to have a profound emotional and cognitive need. He wanted to join it, whereas Dawkins wanted to beat it.

If Darwinism was a universal truth, it had a particular value for Dawkins. It gave him a defence against the charge of practising armchair science, to which many biologists were hostile, as he had 'been made painfully aware'. Universal truths did not have to be verified throughout the universe, and perhaps not even beyond the armchair. 'We should scarcely attack Euclid because he did not sally forth with ruler and protractor to measure a statistical sample of triangular and circular objects in the field or the laboratory.' Universal Darwinist arguments could substantially reduce 'prior uncertainty about life all over the universe', but did not require visits to other planets. Offering a deal to 'empirically minded, white-coated, or gum-booted biologists', he undertook 'not to forget that Darwin's own triumph, for all that it *could* have been launched from any armchair in the universe, was in fact the spin-off of a five-year circumnavigation of this particular planet'. Nevertheless, he implied, his science was none the worse for being done in the manner of philosophy.

He was readier to show empirical evidence due humility when not responding to pressure from his peers. In *River out of Eden*, he reflected on the temptation to assume purpose rather than just presuming it. One of ethology's most celebrated research projects was the one in which Karl von Frisch discovered that it was possible to determine the location of food from the 'waggle-dance' performed by bees. The dance thus looked as though it had been designed for the purpose of guidance. Subsequently, however, this interpretation was challenged by the revisionist claim that, although the dance contained the information, the bees did not read it. The question had to be settled by experiments, which confirmed that the bees were reading the guidance information. Dawkins recalled that he had been 'openly derisive' when he first read the sceptical case. 'And this was not a good thing to be', even though the argument turned out to be wrong.

'My derision was based entirely on the "good design" assumption . . . The dance was so complicated, so richly contrived, so finely tuned to its apparent purpose of informing other bees of the distance and direction of food. This fine tuning could not have come about,' in his view and that of many other Darwinian biologists, 'other than by natural selection . . . In a way, we fell into the same trap as creationists do when they contemplate the wonder of life.' He had been so confident that even if he had been ingenious enough to think up the decisive experiment, he 'would not have bothered to do it'.

The note of triumph was dominant in his writings, though, and with it exaltation. Though that ruthlessly mechanistic sentence about 'robot vehicles' is more frequently replicated than the sentence about truth and astonishment which follows it, the latter is just as important. He harped on wonder, and on the theme that science is its true fount. The wonder he felt in contemplating nature was equal in depth and intensity to mystical or romantic transports. There was nothing to be gained outside reason.

In 1995, his unique position as a public intellectual was institutionalised in the Charles Simonyi Chair for the Public Understanding of Science. For Dawkins, fretting over the time he had spent making contributions to the computing community, this was a spectacular vindication of the hacker faith that if you spread neat stuff around, neat stuff will come back to you in return. Simonyi is a computer scientist who had accumulated stock-option wealth through his senior position ('Chief Architect') at Microsoft and had become a Dawkins fan. He endowed the chair in order to allow Dawkins to continue in the same vein. The professor was installed in the Oxford University Museum, where Thomas Huxley had seen the Lord deliver Bishop Wilberforce into his hands and where the Christian Darwinist David Lack had conjured the ghosts of 'reverend scientists'.

When Lack and his wife climbed the museum's tower to observe the swifts, it was an exclusive privilege and a demanding exercise. Today, the birds are on worldwide show via webcam. Dawkins belongs both to the old Oxford towers and the new world of networks. Unlike some of his colleagues, who would no more frequent a chat-room than E. B. Ford would patronise a fish-and-chip van ('I would not have believed it possible that there could be so much wickedness in the world,' Ford sighed upon first beholding one), Dawkins is at home on-line, where the exclusivity of the Oxford tutorial is replaced by the familiarity of talk radio. When he feels slighted he answers back – 'The answer to your rather patronising question is no, I had a liberal upbringing and was never oppressed by religion.' He seems to lack the assumption of dominance that true media adepts enjoy.

Nor has he assumed power along with fame, unlike his friend and colleague John Krebs, who has acquired a knighthood and administrative office as the head of the Food Standards Agency. In this respect, between his two great predecessors as leading public communicators of biology, he took after Haldane rather than Thomas Huxley. His status has always been attended by a degree of uncertainty, arising from the opinions of those among his peers who, because he has published relatively little for their consideration alone, do not regard him as an evolutionist's evolutionist. He was not elected to the Royal Society until 2001.

Dawkins is nothing if not Oxford, though. There is a certain resemblance to Ford, in the precision of speech and thought, the attention to detail, the polished presentation and the attentiveness to effect. But you would never catch Dawkins talking about the 'wickedness' of a fish-and-chip van. Ford took Oxford aesthetic standards to the point of parody, using irony to make his own intolerance tolerable. Dawkins has no place for irony, and little for amusement. His mind is lawyerly: he seeks to establish a single truth, not to qualify it or play tricks with it. As far as he is concerned, there is only one way of looking at things. When his six-year-old daughter Juliet (from his second marriage, to Eve Barham) suggested to him that flowers were 'to make the world pretty, and to help the bees make honey for us', he set her straight. He also tried to dislodge Father Christmas from her six-year-old mind, using arguments based on physics, to little effect.

His occasional references to his daughter in his public rhetoric throw into relief his personal defensiveness, which has successfully defied the efforts of a procession of interviewers to get him to talk about himself. When Juliet was ten he wrote her an open letter, 'Good and Bad Reasons for Believing', an argument about the superiority of rationally established truth over the religious dogma to which she had been exposed. In a new preface, he explains that he had thought about writing it but was 'shy to give' the advice until asked by John Brockman to contribute to a collection of advice to young persons. Although, or more probably because, the person and the subject were as dear to him as they could be, the letter was no more personal than a speech to a school assembly. Yet when he learned of the sudden death of his friend Douglas Adams, the comic science-fiction writer, the 'keening lament' he wrote came straight from the heart and appeared on the front page of the *Guardian* within a couple of days. Released by the duty to pay tribute to a friend, his powers of emotional expression proved themselves in the most public of ways.

Like many individuals who are drawn to public expression, he is shy. Face to face, his manner is assiduously courteous, using custom to compensate for mixed social feelings and creating a line of defence which is conciliatory rather than antagonistic. Behind the veil drawn by his shyness, Dawkins seems highly attuned to the media and his profile in them. He is an authentic celebrity, his widely noted good looks set off to best effect by grooming and trimmings chosen with a stylish eye. And he enjoys the luxury that comes with celebrity, in the splendid house (a few minutes' walk from the site of the Haldane pile in North Oxford) which he shares with his third wife, Lalla Ward.

He also makes the most of the platforms that are always available to him. Journalists know that he is good for a quote (More single-religion schools? 'Positively evil') and editors can rely on him for rapid-response opinion pieces ('Dangerous nonsense': the idea of life after death, 15 September 2001). If he has anything else to say, he sends a letter. His politics are conducted similarly to his science. They are based on principles, and just as universal Darwinism does not require visits to other planets, they do not require personal experience of the countries in question. The view from Oxford is sufficiently clear.

They are also nothing if not morally impassioned. Dawkins's political comment conveys a sense of right and wrong which is as categorical as his atheism. He seems as certain about the moral basis of his opinions as he is about his scientific reasoning, and to the extent that certainty is a matter of feeling, he is. The impression is enhanced by the absence of reflection in his work about the basis of morality in a godless universe. Dawkins takes right and wrong as given, but has very little to say about the nature of the giver.

Morality is a given in his own thinking, not because he has worked it out through reason, but because his mental atmosphere is electric with moral sentiments. When he perceives unfairness, he feels it intensely. 'If I feel that somebody has been unjustly treated – overlooked for promotion or something of that sort – I have sleepless nights.' The manner in which George W. Bush became President of the United States, by the decision of the Supreme Court, is the kind of 'injustice' which gives him 'an almost visceral pain'. A visceral pain, however, is a gut feeling; and as Dawkins advised Tony Blair, the British Prime Minister, one should try not to think with one's gut.

Although he has always been drawn through science to philosophy, he has not devoted very much effort to placing his moral sentiments on a philosophical footing. Instead, his moral compass works much the same as those that guide so many of his fellow Britons, for whom God is an optional or an accessory presence at most. Having rejected religion, he adopted a practical utilitarianism, assessing actions on the basis of the sum of good or harm that they were likely to do. A distinctive weighting was added to his calculations by the childhood influence of his mother, who had strong feelings about the treatment of animals (to the annoyance of the local fox hunt, which had to abandon its pursuits when it reached the walls of the family farm). Dawkins also cites the effect of the Dr Dolittle series of children's books, which 'definitely instils a very strong recognition of the double standards by which we in our human ethics favour the human species as opposed to others'.

'Double standards' is the crucial term in this remark. Rather than trying to develop a comprehensive moral philosophy, he has sought to underpin his moral sentiments by homing in on logical inconsistencies. What informs his sentiments is 'a hatred of inconsistency and double standards'. This hatred is a vital strategic asset, because it takes the fight to the enemy. Rather than pronouncing that one position is right and another wrong, Dawkins prefers to play an adversary's inconsistent positions against each other – 'Well, if you think this is wrong, how can you possibly say this is right and be consistent? You can't have it both ways.' He is forced on to the attack because he is ultimately unable to match his opponents' certainties, not being certain that absolute rights and wrongs exist. Yet for all practical and polemical purposes, he packs a powerful two-hander – of logical certainty and moral conviction. The latter does not stand up to the same scrutiny as the former, but it is at least as strong. Where possible, Dawkins makes the most of his command of logic; where he cannot make his logic run, he has his moral passions to sustain him. The combined effect is dazzling.

As well as being unable to settle the question of the validity of moral sentiments – untruths and cruelty *feel* wrong, but why, actually, *are* they wrong? – Dawkins is hesitant in exploring the roots of such feelings. 'I suppose you could make a Darwinian case . . .' he begins, but decides against it, after a pause: 'No, that's quite hard . . . Certainly I would say the sort of society in which I wish to live is the kind of society in which people don't cheat and lie, and where everybody pays their taxes. I could imagine myself moving to a society in which people only refrain from stealing because they're frightened of being caught, people only pay their taxes because they're frightened of being caught, people lie all the time and have no sense that the truth is something valuable. If I imagine myself into such a society, I think I would be very unhappy, and so I think it is worth work-ing to protect society against degenerating into that.' Having balked at applying the theory of natural selection, Dawkins turns to introspection and personal feelings. Though his ideas about a good society would strike a consensus chord, unlike Hamilton's essay on genetic degeneration, the intellectual reflexes are the same. Both men look to their own psychologies rather than to evolutionary psychology.

A number of evolutionary thinkers have suggested that moral sentiments are instincts, that as our distant ancestors developed increasingly complex societies, it became adaptive for them to have feelings about right and wrong, and so such emotions have become components of our evolved psy-chology. Leda Cosmides, one of the founders of the evolutionary psychol-ogy movement which emerged in the 1990s, has devised ingenious experiments which she adduces in support of this hypothesis. People have trouble solving puzzles in which they have to detect breaches of if–then rules, such as 'if the sunset is red, tomorrow will be sunny'. About three quarters usually fail – but Cosmides found that around three quarters get the answer right when breaches imply cheating. When the rule is 'if you tidy your room, you may have an ice-cream', most people can see how to check whether the child is honouring the deal. Cosmides concludes that the mind contains systems adapted to detect cheats. Dawkins admires the ingenuity of her experiments and considers them 'deeply interesting', but notes that the conclusions remain controversial. In principle he does not doubt that, since 'we are evolved beings, it ought to be positively surprising if evolutionary psychology didn't help us to understand society.' Nevertheless, it is a project he would rather leave to others, while he concentrates on the human capacity to rise above human nature.

He thus remains more or less where he was at the end of the original edition of *The Selfish Gene*, when he hailed our species' unique ability to 'rebel against the tyranny of the selfish replicators'. Human sociobiology has moved on a long way since then, accumulating a substantial body of work discussing how co-operation may be established within, rather than despite, an evolutionary context. As Dawkins himself put it in a chapter added to a later edition describing some of this work, 'even with selfish genes at the helm, nice guys can finish first'. Yet he turns to Maynard Smith's idea of evolutionarily stable strategies, the kind in which players may co-operate or they may defect, to express his fears about the fragility of decency. He worries that although a society may achieve a co-operative strategy in which people value the truth and pay their taxes for the common good – an Enlightenment ESS, it could be called – 'there's an ever-present threat of a sudden degeneration and swing to the other ESS, of "always defect".'

How can an Enlightenment ESS arise in the first place, though? Taking the long view, beyond Dawkins's perspective, the answer is irresistible. In the struggle to suppress cheating and maximise co-operation, humanity's greatest invention was religion. Without it, cheating could only be controlled by punishing the offender after the event. When collective morality was personified and accorded supernatural powers, beliefs became the main agents of control, preventing defection and reducing the need for punishment. This fundamental transition was surely the basis of human culture, and of progress, which eventually enabled some thinkers to work out reasons to behave well even in the absence of gods to fear.

Whether or not they see it as a force for good, various evolutionary thinkers (including Maynard Smith, in a co-authored book on animal signals) have supposed that religious behaviour is adaptive. When Dawkins looks at religion, though, the first thing he sees is parasites. In his most memorable comments on the subject, he depicted religious ideas as 'viruses' that take advantage of young children's openness to information, which he located in an evolved predisposition to absorb their people's culture. He had in mind his own daughter, then aged six, who was receiving religious instruction from a Catholic nun. This was personal: a longer view, or a good word for religion, was unthinkable.

The alternative to the Enlightenment ESS might be labelled Barbarism, but another name comes to Dawkins's mind. 'I suppose it's because I'm so conscious of the fact that the human species has this rather precarious position,' he reflects, 'of being perhaps the only non-Darwinian species, as far as our own ethics and the way we run our own society are concerned. It is continuously vulnerable to what I would see as degeneration to naked, raw Darwinism – a kind of Thatcherite society, which I see as closer to Darwinism.

'I think what I feel is that human society has over centuries painfully weaned itself away from naked Darwinism, painfully built up a delicate, gossamer structure of trust and co-operation and, well, just plain niceness. Because I know and understand Darwinism, I see the threat lurking there just below the surface, ready to pull us down again.'

Critics of sociobiology like Steven Rose used to claim that the science was biased, an ideological bid to make conservative free-market ideology seem like laws of nature. For Dawkins, the awful truth is that the science is unbiased, the universe is pitiless, and Mother Nature is a discarnate Margaret Thatcher. Without a deity, Dawkins is left to assume that goodness can only be created by humankind, and he has a profound sense that humans create much of what is good and precious when they cease to act like Darwinian beings.

At the same time, his sense of moral order seems to be reflected in the sense of order that underlies his writings on evolution. Stephen Jay Gould looked into the fossil record and saw the luck of the cosmic draw. Dawkins agrees that the universe is fundamentally meaningless: 'The universe we observe has precisely the properties we should expect if there is, at bottom, no design, no purpose, no evil and no good, nothing but blind pitiless indifference.' Unlike Gould, though, he minimises the role of chance in the fate of evolved designs. The only place for randomness is in the variations from which nature selects. Like Fisher, Dawkins seems to value natural selection as a force that generates order; lacking Fisher's faith in God, he sees it as an only begetter. Natural selection may be blind and pitiless, but it introduces design into the universe. It is the first cause of meaning.

14

The Meaning of Sunset

J. B. S. Haldane was deaf to music. He made a gesture of his disability, instructing John Maynard Smith to tell him when the National Anthem was being played, so that he could refuse to stand up. Maynard Smith is, however, unable to appreciate music himself. Alfred Russel Wallace and Bill Hamilton lacked musical ears too. It would be too much of a stretch to imagine a chorus from this quartet or a link between their shared musical limitation and the way their scientific minds have worked. There must be a reason for everything, but everything does not have to be a reason.

The broader picture is clear. Between them the six evolutionists in this series encompass a glorious wealth of talents and knowledge, most of which can be resolved into the two dimensions of natural history and mathematics. At one end of the spectrum is Wallace, who never felt that the absence of any mathematical skills had impeded his evolutionary studies and whose understanding derived entirely from natural history. At the other is Fisher, more at home in the sea of numerical relations than on the land of language. Like Maynard Smith, Fisher is a natural historian frustrated by poor eyesight. Haldane and Dawkins are not instinctive natural historians but show due appreciation of animals. Hamilton is both maths and natural history, the latter second to none.

They also divide into dimensions of clarity and opacity, with Maynard Smith and Dawkins at the clear end, and Fisher and Hamilton at the other. The distinction is also that between public and private. Maynard Smith's peers and juniors alike value his flair for constructive simplification, which oils the wheels of scientific inquiry for himself and for his colleagues. Dawkins has written books that not only won him public celebrity but also shaped the outlook of a younger generation of evolutionary biologists. The two men differ in style. Dawkins is shy and essayistic; he likes to develop his arguments in writing and at length. Maynard Smith is gregarious and conversational; he makes many of his insights available as remarks. He has a preference for domesticated metaphors, like his suggestion that sex may be comparable to building a car from one with a worn-out engine and one with a broken gearbox, whereas Hamilton's arguments take their examples from nature and seethe with tiny monsters. Richard Dawkins turns the same body of theory into fencing displays and glittering argument.

Each man responded in his special way to the idea of natural selection; their responses may in turn seem to reflect on the idea itself. It cannot be denied that all of these scientists are men or that it looks as though, to adapt Fisher's observation, natural selection is a mechanism for generating a high degree of eccentricity. But should one think the worse of evolutionary theory because large parts of its canon were written by odd white males?

The sex ratio of 6:0 may be egregious by today's standards but was entirely normal for the periods in which these thinkers were formed. When Maynard Smith went up to Cambridge in the late 1930s, only one in ten of the entire student population was female. Today, women earn more than half the biological science degrees awarded in Britain, both at first and postgraduate levels. Within biology, they take more than half the genetics degrees, which would suggest that they are not put off by the idea of evolution or its analytical methods. There is nothing in the subject matter to suggest that evolutionary theory will not achieve a suitably Fisherian 1:1 sex ratio – though even if other factors do not impede women's progress in biology, it may take till the middle of the century, and a long march through the institutions, to achieve the power shift that will have taken place once half the professors of evolutionary biology are women.

As and when the sex ratio evens up, the questions that evolutionary biology asks will probably also alter. It was surely not coincidental that Darwinism finally embraced Darwin's idea of female choice, as the agent of sexual selection, during the upsurge of feminism in the 1970s and 1980s. Instead of undermining the Darwinian paradigm, female involvement and feminist influence consolidated it.

The suggestion of endemic eccentricity can be answered in three words: John Maynard Smith. But if his example, so eminently sensible and well adjusted, does not counterbalance the extremes of mood and opinion shown elsewhere, there are other possibilities to consider. One is that radical ideas need uncommon personalities. Another is that somebody who entertains radical ideas in one domain is likely to adhere to them in another. All six of these evolutionists have combined bold thinking about natural selection with unorthodox ideologies: spiritualism or campaigning atheism, communism or eugenic conservatism.

In this respect they show the benefits of living in a culture distinguished by continuity and accommodation. If Haldane and Maynard Smith had spent the early 1950s in America, they might have had to undergo McCarthyist inquisition about their Communist Party memberships and might have lost their jobs. If they had been in Russia, they would surely have been dismissed from their posts because of their Mendel–Morganist convictions. At University College, they were left undisturbed with their log tables and fruit flies. For Fisher, the great ideological conflict of the twentieth century meant sparring at High Table with a Marxist fellow don. Richard Dawkins enjoys a public status in Britain that might be difficult for him to attain in the United States, where professions of faith are almost universal.

Americans are also much readier than Britons to believe that the words of the Bible are literally true. Nearly half of all Americans believe that Creation took place as the Bible says it did, and God placed humans on Earth within the last ten thousand years. Another 40 per cent believe humankind evolved from other species over millions of years, under divine guidance, while only one in ten believes that the human species evolved naturally, without any help from God. In Britain, fewer people profess to believe in some kind of God, and fewer than one in ten take the Bible literally. Whereas Creationism is a powerful ideological force in the United States, in Britain it has so far achieved little more than a small bridgehead in the secondary-school system.

The British situation represents the durability of the Victorian settlement between natural and supernatural accounts of the living world. After British evolutionists took over natural theology and replaced its chief executive, it carried on working smoothly under the new management. The Church of England seemed almost relieved not to have to take scripture literally, and secured its continuing influence by diffusing itself into a nimbus of moral sentiments as close and persistent as the island's cloud cover. God became optional, but his values lingered on.

Today, the active fault lines of the settlement are visible in public resistance to sociobiology and unease about what genes should be said to do. By and large, liberal culture on both sides of the Atlantic would prefer not to entertain the accounts of human behaviour that evolutionary psychologists have been advancing since the 1990s. Ian McEwan's novel *Enduring Love* alludes to kin selection and game theory in its opening scene, in which unrelated bystanders abandon their efforts to restrain a runaway balloon; but it is an isolated example of a cultural work by a major figure which is informed by a sympathetic understanding of evolutionary psychology. People remain reluctant to accept that qualities which make humans special have evolved by natural selection.

They are supported in their resistance by the prominence won by critics of evolutionary orthodoxy, whose views combine to give the impression that they balance those of the mainstream. This is a source of continuing frustration to orthodox evolutionists like Maynard Smith and Dawkins, for whom the late Stephen Jay Gould became an increasingly irksome *bête noire*. There once was a time when Gould was ready to hail Maynard Smith as 'the world's kindest man and also the most brilliant and celebrated of committed adaptationists', but by the mid-1990s, relations between them had deteriorated beyond repair. 'Because of the excellence of his essays,' observed Maynard Smith, 'he has come to be seen by non-biologists as the pre-eminent evolutionary theorist. In contrast, the evolutionary biologists with whom I have discussed his work tend to see him as a man whose ideas are so confused as to be hardly worth bothering with . . .' This comment, undoubtedly true and representative of opinion as it was, allowed Maynard Smith to avoid confronting Gould directly. He did, however, indicate the reason for his vexation: that Gould was 'giving non-biologists a largely false picture of the state of evolutionary theory'.

The objection is fair. Evolutionary theory now looks like life, tangled, dauntingly complicated, and diverse. Nowadays voices can be heard speaking up for group selection or dismissing the Fisher–Haldane–Wright 'synthesis' as an obstacle to progress. William Provine, the latter revisionist, rejects the concept of natural selection while he is at it. 'Natural selection does nothing,' he snorts, comparing it to archaic scientific fictions like phlogiston or the ether. His objection, however, is the old one, that nature is not a person. The process described by the phrase is not in question, and the very diversity of evolutionary theory, which has allowed reservations and exceptions to be presented as major challenges, is founded upon the study of adaptive processes. Natural selection is no longer assumed to be the major evolutionary force at all levels of living organisation, now that neutral evolution at the molecular level is understood. Molecular biologists do not assume that natural selection is responsible for the changes they observe. But biologists looking at the forms of organisms and their behaviour still do, for natural selection is still the only known mechanism of adaptive change, and the evolutionary research program remains an adaptationist program.

Part of the trouble with Gould, for orthodox evolutionists, was that he was a palaeontologist, upholding the fossil-hunters' tradition of awkwardness. His fellow critic Richard Lewontin, by contrast, is a geneticist who commands great respect among his peers for his theoretical work. Loosely speaking, it could be said that orthodox evolutionists regard Gould as simply muddled, whereas their objection to Lewontin is that he is excessively rigorous. Like Gould, Lewontin has enjoyed a privileged position as a public authority on evolutionary theory – though Maynard Smith's contributions to the *London* and *New York Review of Books* have offset the monopoly significantly.

Maynard Smith presented an alternative, not an antithesis. With his sympathies still on the left, and seen to be so, he confounds the assumption that reductionism and sociobiology lie on the right. He treats the Marxist influences on the thinking of Lewontin and Gould as philosophical error rather than ideological evil. His concern for fairness and his genial manner have combined to produce a public persona that is statesmanlike, gracious and not altogether unlike that of Nelson Mandela. Some scientists' public reflections on biology and society are compelling; others' are reassuring; his, exceptionally, are both. He makes it clear that one may do reductionist science, or apply sociobiology to humans, or talk of genes for this or that, without endangering one's values or diminishing life's richness.

Like Fisher and Dawkins, Maynard Smith refutes the canard that the

British do not care for philosophy. He may, however, affirm the continental prejudice that the British idea of philosophy lacks depth. Maynard Smith once recalled how Ernst Mayr put him in his place, when he wondered whether the dialectics in the biologist Richard Goldschmidt's writing betrayed Marxist convictions, by reminding Maynard Smith 'that only illiterate Anglo-Saxons have to get their dialectics from Marx and Engels: he and Goldschmidt had been raised on a diet of Hegel'. (So was Haldane, but then he was a Celt.) Other observers may mistrust the British neo-Darwinians' robust confidence in metaphor and common sense. Maynard Smith, however, is comfortable with metaphor because for him it is secondary to mathematical thought, upon which his confidence rests.

Richard Dawkins is unlikely ever to be accused of statesmanship. As America brought its might to bear on Iraq in the second Bush presidency, he was provoked into a series of remarks that seemed to put him back in touch with his late-1960s Berkeley youth. 'Please commission an opinion poll asking the electorate the following simple question – which would you prefer: regime change in Baghdad, or regime change in Washington?' Haldane could not have put it better himself. Dawkins's anti-imperialist indignation underlines that as a public communicator of science, he belongs in Haldane's polemical tradition rather than the Huxleyan establishment.

Each of the contemporary evolutionists in this series also defied the ultra-Darwinian stereotype in their attitudes towards the application of evolutionary theory to human behaviour. Hamilton, Dawkins and Maynard Smith have all declared themselves to be sociobiologists, yet have all displayed a degree of reserve about evolutionary psychology. In Hamilton's case, revealed by his preference for introspection in his essay on the 'Planetary Hospital', it seems to have been because he wanted to be a novelist. For Dawkins, it is because he wants humans to be special. For Maynard Smith, it is because he is a biologist.

All of them have been sobered by their contemplation of how behaviour evolves. Most of them have decided that the universe is without pity and indifferent. None, however, has fallen into nihilism; each offers an example, which may be measured according to its observers' values and its own coherence, of how to live in truth in a world that no longer needs God's truth to explain it. Though they could discard the creeds they were taught, they were constituted by their values. None of the evolutionists in these stories ever doubted they knew right from wrong, or wanted for a sense of purpose.

'The tints of the decaying leaves in an American forest are described by every one as gorgeous; yet no one supposes that these tints are of the least advantage to the trees.' Charles Darwin, *The Descent of Man*

One of Bill Hamilton's last bold ideas, published a year after his death, was that the colours of autumn leaves are signals urging insects to go and pick on somebody else. Having previously suggested that the bright colours of birds' plumage might be a signal of good health, indicating the ability to resist parasites, Hamilton conjectured that the same message might be broadcast in autumn leaves. One tree may manage to stage a more spectacular display than another, thereby inducing potential insect parasites to choose its more pallid rival.

This is a deal between parties with opposing interests in which both sides' interests are served. The tree will not have to expend any more resources in resisting attack, and may avoid hazards such as viral infection which might follow in the wake of even brief insect forays. The insects avoid a struggle they may well lose, and are directed towards hosts that they will find easier to colonise.

Before Hamilton and the other neo-Darwinians, naturalists would have been content with an argument resting merely on benefits. Now the method concentrates equally, if not more, upon costs. Hamilton and his collaborator, Sam Brown, adduced evidence that aphids take a heavy toll on trees that they infest. Lime and oak saplings often weigh less at the end of the year, after aphid depredation, than they did at the beginning. Sycamores spread like grass writ large, but their marching palisades would be far thicker if not for aphids. It has been calculated that without aphids to check them, sycamores would lay down nearly three times as much wood in the course of a growing season.

The living colour also looks extravagant to our eyes. It would surely be very expensive to stage such a show by any artificial means. For Darwin, such a comparison would be merely coincidental. The same could be said of a sunset, after all. A sunset upon a tree, just before it boards itself up for winter, must surely be a by-product of physiology rather than an adaptation. Darwin saw animal spectacle differently, arguing that gorgeous plumage in male birds was the product of female choice. Wallace countered this by maintaining that spectacular colours arose from a superabundance of energy, that they were a by-product of physiology. When it came to trees, Darwin sounded more like Wallace.

Birdwatchers, as Maynard Smith points out, can't seem to help feeling that there must be a reason for whatever they see a bird doing. Hamilton, with his all-seeing naturalist's eye, extended this intuition to trees. And from his neo-Darwinian perspective, what looked like an extravagant display might well be an extravagant display. He realised that autumn's red shift could be an instance of Zahavi's Handicap Principle. Fisher had suggested that extravagances like the peacock's tail had evolved because meeting female tastes outweighed the costs of keeping up appearances; Zahavi argued that the costs were the point, honestly signalling fitness through waste. When a gazelle springs up and down instead of fleeing a wolf, showing that it has energy to waste, it is telling the wolf to go and pick on somebody else. This is to their mutual advantage. The gazelle's risk of losing its life is reduced, and the wolf's chances of hunting success are increased.

Zahavi detected this principle at work in a breathtaking range of animal species, but it fell to Hamilton to discern it in trees. To make the case, he and Brown had to demonstrate that autumn colours might be costly. They noted that much of the pigment that produces the display is lost when the leaves fall. In the Norway maple, for instance, nearly all of the green chlorophyll is reabsorbed as the leaves prepare to be shed, but no more than half of the yellow carotenoid pigment is recovered. The green is recycled; the red and yellow are largely wasted. And some trees synthesise pigments specially for the season.

Hamilton and Brown predicted that the more species of aphids that beset a species of tree, the more gorgeous would be its display. They tested the idea by going through field guides and grading different tree species' autumn colours according to the descriptions given. A tendency to yellow was found to go with a greater range of parasite species, while a tendency to red was associated with threats from aphids which exclusively patronised the species in question. These colours were interpreted as markers of 'defensive commitment'.

Trees signal to aphids their commitment; aphids make their choices accordingly. This is what comes of assuming a purpose: reason reinvents a world lost with childhood, in which trees talk and the woods are full of activities that are beyond the scope of human senses. Darwinism is blamed for taking meaning from the world by making divine purpose optional. But Darwinism in much of its practice is a project to populate the world with meaning, by identifying it in as many aspects of life as possible.

Richard Dawkins saw spring in Hamilton's autumn too. In his eulogy at the New College memorial service, he referred to the idea as an example of 'that youthful inventiveness that seemed, if anything, to increase as Bill grew older'. Each autumn, the trees of Wytham Woods will unfold their banner behind Hamilton's grave, and lower it. If you require meaning, look around.

Notes

Abbreviations

BMC SA: BioMed Central Science Archive, www.biomedcentral.com/sciencearchive;
video recordings – over five hours – of John Maynard Smith interviewed by Richard
Dawkins in 1997.

HA: Haldane Archive, National Library of Scotland.

HP: Haldane Papers, University College London Library.

Reasons for Everything

AIMS AND ACKNOWLEDGEMENTS

'"ultra-Darwinians"': Gould (1997).

'. . . a study of . . . to settle contests': Maynard Smith and Harper (1988).

'"especially indignant . . . if they chose"': Darwin (2003), 99.

'. . . pitiless and indifferent, in Dawkins's words . . .': Dawkins (1995), 96, 133.

1. SENSES OF PURPOSE

'"Darwin's dangerous idea"': Dennett (1995).

'. . . traditional interpretations of the Bible . . .': Repcheck (2003), ch. 2.

'. . . general acceptance . . . common ancestors. . .': Mayr (2002), 94–6.

'. . . blended away . . . Ronald Fisher explained the problem . . .': Fisher (1930), ch. 2;
Ridley (1997), A4.

'. . . Fleeming Jenkin . . .': Gayon (1998), ch. 3; Gould (1991), 340–53.

'Mendel . . . and his work were sufficiently known. . .': Tudge (2000). See also Henig
(2000).

'"People from Aristotle . . . than their successors"': Cain (1964).

'"ultra-Darwinians"': Romanes (1897).

'" . . . the main but not exclusive means . . ."' Darwin (1859), 6.

'"Great is the power of steady misrepresentation"': Darwin (1902), 395.

'should have read *On the Origin of Species by Means of Natural Selection and All Sorts of
Other Things*': Young (1998b).

'"I am convinced . . . natural selection"': Darwin (1909a), 92.

'... Gould took up the term ...': Gould (1997).

'"British hang-up"': Brockman (1995), 54.

'Nor ... Michael Ruse ... discover potential mates': Ruse (1999), 203.

'... a soft spot for hopeful monsters': 'A Short Way to Corn', Gould (1985).

'... issued a manifesto against adaptationism ...': Gould and Lewontin (1979).

'" ... a British pastime"': Lewontin (1972).

'Arthur Cain, still nettled ...': Cain (1979).

'"There were no real field naturalists ... dissecting room"': Bowler (1992), 108–9.

'The historian of science David L. Hull observes...': 'History of Evolutionary Thought', in Pagel (2002), vol. 1, E-7.

'... Peter Bowler argues ...': 'Scientific Attitudes to Darwinism in Britain and America', in Kohn (1985).

'American naturalists ... into the world': Numbers (1998), ch. 1.

'"along certain beneficial lines"': Darwin (1875), 428.

'"intellectual aristocracy"': in Plumb (1955).

'"thought of God"': Ben Waggoner 'Louis Agassiz (1807–1873)', www.ucmp.berkeley.edu /history/agassiz.html

'American geneticists ... experimental work which persuaded Mendelians ...': Provine (2001), 108–29.

'"hardening"': Grene (1983), ch. 4.

'Perhaps the two ... their own mentors': This suggestion is from Jonathan Hodge.

'"Because of the accident ... British know better"': Maynard Smith (1986), 126–7.

'"I never met ... naive adaptationist"': Maynard Smith (1991).

'"mystery of mysteries"': Darwin (1998), 3.

'... Ernst Mayr ... German birdwatcher ...': Mayr (1993); Jared Diamond in Mayr (2002), vii–ix; Michael Shermer and Frank J. Sulloway, www.stephenjaygould.org/library/mayr_interview.html; 'The Grand Old Man of Evolution'; 'Ernst Mayr: What Evolution Is', www.edge.org/3rd_culture/mayr/mayr_index.html

'"Theories of Evolution ... better adapted"': Fisher (1936b).

'" ... it is *the* problem that a biologist has to explain ..."': interview, 26 June 2002.

'"adaptationist program ... test *if* they do"': Lewontin (1979).

'"genteel"': Lewontin (1974), 30.

'"All sorts of different people ... an engine-driver"': James Fisher (1945).

'Darwin learned much ... they were hardly ...': Browne (1995), 521–5.

'Natural theologians ... assemblages of adaptations ...': Radick (2003).

'"daily and hourly scrutinising ... each organic being"': Darwin (1998), 70.

'"most deeply ... A dog might as well speculate on the mind of Newton"': Darwin, letter to Asa Gray, 22 May 1860, Francis Darwin (1887), ii, 312.

'Haldane ... atheist ranks': Haldane, 'What I Believe', script of BBC Home Service broadcast, 17 June 1947, HP Box 20.

'"immediately sympathetic"': Maynard Smith, 'In Haldane's Footsteps', in Dewsbury (1985).

'"present on every page"': Maynard Smith and Szathmáry (1997), xiv.

'. . . a photo of Haldane . . .': lecturing, in front of blackboard, with arms folded; reproduced on several web pages, including www.marxists.org/archive/haldane/

''' . . . Gorki's Tolstoy. . .''': W. D. Hamilton in a postcard to his sister Mary Bliss, 1959, read by her at his memorial service, 1 July 2000. The typescript, 'Memoir of My Brother's Youth', was kindly provided by Dr Bliss.

'"Our mathematics may impress zoologists . . ."': Haldane (1964).

'"if you can't stand algebra . . ."'Maynard Smith (1998a), ix.

'Haldane made the point . . .': Haldane (1955).

'. . . genetic conflict . . .': Maynard Smith and Szathmáry (1997), ch. 8.

'. . . the smiling faces of children furiously kicking one another . . .': Partridge and Hurst (1998).

'"entities . . . larger whole after it"': Maynard Smith and Szathmáry (1997), 4.

Alfred Russel Wallace

2. MALTHUS, MALARIA AND THE MALAY ARCHIPELAGO

'his "Sarawak Law"': Wallace (1855).

'Malthus's "Principles of Population"': Malthus (1798).

'"friction upon the specially prepared match"': Marchant (1916), i, 116.

'which had impressed . . . Leicester's town library': Wallace (1905), i, 232.

'"there suddenly flashed . . ."': Wallace, quoted in Brooks (1984), 181. Wallace wrote five accounts of this incident: all are quoted in McKinney (1972), while Brooks (1984) discusses versions written in 1903 and 1905.

'"would necessarily *improve*. . ."': Wallace (1905), i, 362.

'"The more I thought . . ."': Wallace, quoted in Brooks (1984), 181.

'"How extremely stupid not to have thought of that!"': e.g. Irvine (1956), 82.

'Huxley displayed such acuity . . . years younger': Wallace (1905), i, 324.

'their inordinate fondness for beetles': Fisher, R. C. (1988); 'A Special Fondness for Beetles', Gould (1996). The provenance of the quote remains unclear.

'"Now it is . . . problem of species"': Marchant (1916), 115.

'Samuel Stevens . . . stick to collecting': Wallace (1905), i, 355.

'"had none of . . . the species-man"': *ibid.*, 116.

'"Then at once . . . effect of this. . ."': Wallace (1905), i, 362.

'"I never saw . . ."': Charles Darwin, 18 June 1858, in Darwin (1887), ii, 116.

'"at once struck"', '"Here, then . . . briefest sketch of it"': Darwin (2003), 57.

'"So all my originality . . ."': Charles Darwin, 18 June 1858, in Darwin (1887), ii, 116.

'. . . the paper Wallace had sent him': Wallace (1858).

''' . . . the moon to Darwin's sun"': Irvine (1956), 64.

'"reveals that he wrote . . ."': Hamilton (2001), 584.

'Darwin recognised . . . individuals or groups': Malcolm Jay Kottler, 'Charles Darwin and Alfred Russel Wallace: Two Decades of Debate over Natural Selection', in Kohn (1985), 371–9.

'"Natural Selection is supreme"': Wallace (1889a), 444.

"'some of my critics . . .'": Wallace (1905), ii, 22.

'. . . fourteen thousand miles . . .': Beddall (1969), 143.

"'central and controlling incident'": Wallace (1905), i, 336.

"'the character . . . himself'": Wallace (1905), i, 89.

'*contra* Malthus': Robert Owen, 'An Address to the Inhabitants of New Lanark', in Arblaster and Lukes (1971).

"'the more picturesque and impassioned'": Wallace (1905), i, 78.

"'I therefore thoroughly agreed with Mr Dale Owen's conclusion . . .'": Wallace (1905), i, 88–9.

"'unjust, unwise, and cruel'": Wallace (1905), i, 158.

"'robbery'": e.g. Wallace (1905), i, 152.

"'The Welshman . . . good enough for him'": Wallace (1905), i, 207.

"'The single window . . .'": Wallace (1905), i, 211.

"'Had my father . . . '": Wallace (1905), i, 197.

"'that beautiful little instrument . . .'": Wallace (1905), i, 110.

"'first introduction to . . . the mystery of nature'"; "'and as one after another. . .'": Wallace (1905), i, 192.

"'too delicate and beautiful . . .'": Wallace (1905), i, 194.

"'Our own weeds . . .'": Marchant (1916), i, 86–7.

'The son . . . an enthusiastic entomologist': Beddall (1969), 17.

"'Whenever . . . the sound of a trumpet'": Fisher, R. C. (1988).

'nothing doing at Neath': Wallace (1905), i, 229.

"'an almost trackless labyrinth'": Wallace (1905), i, 231.

'he struggled to reconcile the two': Durant (1979).

"'new bible of natural law'": Secord (2000), 73.

"'When I touched . . . the ecstasy of adoration'": Wallace (1905), i, 262.

'In Darwin's case . . .': Browne (1995), 461–2.

"'I do not consider . . . applied when collected'": Wallace (1905), i, 254.

"'spurious, glib eloquence'": Secord (2000), 501.

"'overwhelming numbers . . . origin of species'": Wallace (1905), i, 256–7.

"'hot moist mouldy air'": Bates (1892), 3–4.

"'whose last country ramble . . .'": *ibid.*, 5.

"'The weather was not so hot . . .'": Wallace (1889b), 3.

"'The few sounds . . . unable to explain'": Bates (1892), 35–6.

"'The poor little animal . . .'": Wallace (1889b), 29.

"'the most powerful and dangerous animal . . .'": *ibid.*, 166.

"'tame Indians'", "'absolute uncontaminated savages'": Wallace (1905), i, 288.

"'hardly make oneself believe . . . fellow-creatures'": Darwin (1905), 210.

"'the difference, between savage and civilised man'", "'greater than between a wild and domesticated animal'": *ibid.*, 201; Browne (1995), 243.

'. . . moved to verse': Wallace (1889b), 176–80.

'. . . sleeping by his side for four nights . . .': Ernest Clodd, in Bates (1892), xxvi.

"'I'm afraid the ship's on fire . . .'": Wallace (1889b), 271; (1905), 303.

"'a kind of apathy . . .'": Wallace (1889b), 272.

"'almost foolish'": Wallace (1905), i, 303.

" . . . liquid flame'": Wallace (1889b), 275.

'. . . valuable contact in Sir James Brooke . . .': Raby (2001), 67.

"'two conflicting races . . .'": Wallace (1905), i, 346.

"'wholesale murder'": Wallace (1905), i, 347.

"'vivid impression'": Wallace (1905), i, 354.

"'every species . . . allied species'": Wallace (1855).

'Patrick Matthew . . .': Gould (1985), 336–7, 345–6.

"'One day something . . . "': Wallace (1905), i, 361.

"'And at the conclusion . . . unprovided for'": Malthus (1798),14–15.

"'the constant . . . tyrannic lords'", "'the constant . . . among savages'": Malthus (1798), 21.

"'exact boundary-line'": Wallace (1869), 299.

'. . . James Moore . . . "Saxons" dominated "Celts"': James Moore, 'Wallace's Malthusian Moment: The Common Context Revisited', in Lightman (1997).

"'Of the accidental . . . more vigorous neighbours'": Gould (1985), 343–4.

'one of the most celebrated of the Spice Islands': according to Wallace, quoted in McKinney (1972), 137.

'But his records . . . prestigious venue': McKinney (1972), 131–7.

"'I do honestly . . . a new philosophy . . .'": Marchant (1916), i, 73.

"'his name should . . . no further go!!!'": Wallace (1905), i, 372–3.

"'I have for many years . . . totally ignorant'": *ibid.*, ii, 221.

'He judged himself . . . then before me . . .': Wallace (1905), i, 225–6.

"'been marked by . . . on which they bear'": Brent (1981), 416.

"'On the Habits of the Orang-Utan of Borneo'": Wallace (1856).

3. Natural and Supernatural Selection

"'I am engaged . . . peace and happiness'": Wallace (1905), i, 368.

"'Fine specimens . . . rest of the day . . .'" Wallace (1869), 318.

"'My first crew . . . food and water'": *ibid.*, 507.

'. . . the quest for the birds of paradise. . .': e.g. 'Narrative of Search After Birds of Paradise', in Wallace (1905), 387–94, www.wku.edu/~smithch/wallace/S067.htm

'*tædium vitae*': Marchant (1916), i, 72.

"'elasticity and freshness . . . a pleasure'", "'to cut short . . . banishment'": Marchant (1916), i, 79.

'. . . nearly £100': Wallace (1869), 513, says £100; Raby (2001), 161–2, says £92, and gives further financial details.

'Huxleys' house . . . at his ease': Wallace (1905), ii, 34.

"'a most beautiful . . . natural selection'", "'bright dresses'", "'Heliconide dress'", "'many small steps of variation and selection'": Bates (1862). See also Gayon (1998), ch. 6.

'. . . noted Wallace. . .': 'Mimicry, and Other Protective Resemblances Among Animals', in Wallace (1871).

"'fully occupied . . . social enjoyments'", "'the cultivated minds . . . Women of the Future'": Wallace (1890).

'. . . a King Bird of Paradise . . .': Wallace (1869), 414.

'"We may give . . . Mr Darwin"': Cronin (1993), 146.

'"Heaven protect . . . your argument"': Marchant (1916), i, 170.

'"I grieve . . . understand each other"': *ibid.*, i, 189.

'"it has made . . . half mad"': *ibid.*, i, 166.

'"utterly shattered"': 'On Our Knowledge of the Causes of the Phenomena of Organic Nature', in Huxley (1893), aleph0.clarku.edu/huxley/CE2/Phen.html

'"Objector-General"': Darwin and Seward (1903), i, 274.

'. . . an orphan baby. . .': Wallace (1905), i, 343–5; (1869), 50–4.

'Malthus had made a sharp impression on Darwin. . .': Vorzimmer (1969), Herbert (1971), Radick (2003).

'"Light will be thrown . . ."': Darwin (1998), 394.

'"question of questions . . . we are tending . . . "': 'On the Relations of Man to the Lower Animals' (1861), in Huxley (1894), 77, aleph0.clarku.edu/huxley/CE7/RelM-L-A.html

'"if by an advocate . . . he cannot convince"': *ibid.*, 150–1.

'. . . the Confederates were at work . . .': Moore (1994), 326.

'. . . a disdainful review . . .': Anon. (1863). The author was Charles Carter Blake, a leading figure in the Anthropological Society.

'. . . how natural selection might have shaped humanity': Wallace (1864).

'. . . and he told Wallace he would not cross its threshold . . .': Raby (2001), 176.

'"disgustingly coarse"', '" . . . every kind of debauchery"': Wallace (1889b), 157.

'"hardly help a shudder"', '" . . . Frei Jozé's fertile brain"': *ibid.*, 225.

'"The white men in our Colonies . . ."': Wallace (1900), ii, 113; www.wku.edu/~smithch/wallace/S113.htm

'"moderate flogging"': Wallace (1889b), 82.

'"In fact . . . family of children"': *ibid.*, 82–3.

'"Can it be right . . . attributes of man"': *ibid.*, 83.

'"I could not . . . European supervision"': Wallace (1905), i, 288.

'"civilised man . . . appreciate and enjoy"': Wallace (1869), 415.

'"A warlike and energetic people . . ."': *ibid.*, 548.

'"The more I see . . . on the whole . . ."': Wallace (1905), i, 432–3.

'"as much brains as average Europeans"', Wallace (1871), 338; www.wku.edu/%7Esmithch/wallace/S165.htm

'"as pure a love of truth as the most moral among civilized men"': *ibid.*, 341.

'"could only have . . . a philosopher"': *ibid.*, 356.

'"rigid law . . . its action"': Wallace (1889), 469.

'warned Darwin': Malcolm Jay Kottler, 'Charles Darwin and Alfred Russel Wallace: Two Decades of Debate over Natural Selection', in Kohn (1985), 420.

'"I hope you . . . my child"': Marchant (1916), i, 241.

'"No"': *ibid.*, 240.

'"I differ grievously . . . regard to Man"': *ibid.*, 243.

'"I can quite comprehend . . . mental hallucination . . ."': *ibid.*, 243–4.

'"contribution to the natural history of the island"': Wallace (1869), 156.

'He first took . . . wheeled up to her': Wallace (1896), 127–44.

'The movement had arisen from that of mesmerism . . .': Crabtree (1993), 229–35.

'"It may be all true . . . any other"': Marchant (1916), ii, 187.

'"Witch *Sabbat*"': Desmond (1994), 192.

'. . . he was later offered solace . . .': Raby (2001), 212–3.

'"utter sceptic"': Wallace (1896), 132.

'"the intervention . . . spiritual man"': Wallace (1871), 360.

'"What is there . . . easiest way?"': *ibid.*, 342.

'"even an Australian . . . baskets and nets"': Huxley (1893), 175, alepho.clarku.edu/huxley/CE2/DarC.html

'"every time . . . man of science . . ."': *ibid.*, 175–6.

'"seemed to see the whole effect"': Wallace (1905), i, 362.

'Wallace urged it upon Darwin . . .': Wallace, letter to Darwin, 2 July 1866, Marchant (1916), i, 170–4; Young (1998b).

'"must be the select of their generation"': *ibid.*, 124.

'"If left to operate . . . away the degraded"': Taylor (1992), 88.

'"continuity"', '" . . . guiding intelligences . . ."': Wallace (1871), 360; www.wku.edu/~smithch/wallace/S716note.htm

'. . . he attended a séance . . .': Raby (2001), 240–1.

'. . . Wallace had applied . . .': *ibid.*, 180.

'Hooker was derisive . . . "lost caste terribly" . . . was mollified . . .': *ibid.*, 223–5.

'"Give the people . . . scientific priestcraft"': Rockell (1912).

'"the last of the great Victorians"': *ibid.*

Ronald Aylmer Fisher

'Natural selection is a mechanism. . .': quoted by Julian Huxley in Huxley, Hardy and Ford (1954).

4. NATURAL NOBILITY

'The lectures that Ronald Aylmer Fisher gave to his fellow undergraduate eugenicists . . .': 'Mendelism and Biometry', 'Social Selection', in Bennett (1983), ch. 2.

'"eclipse of Darwinism"': Huxley (1942), 22–8.

'. . . and published them twenty-five years later . . .': Fisher (1936a).

'"One of the great . . . 'theory of gases' tells me"': Bennett (1983), 56–7.

'"to infect others with a similar passion"': *ibid.*, 58.

'"mind viruses"': Dawkins (1993).

'" . . . a thirty-toof"': Box (1978), 13.

'"horses, tennis courts, and boats"': Box (1978), 6.

'"cold and insensitive"', '"Their communication . . . feelings of others"': *ibid.*, 10.

'"scattered her memorials through his life"', '"plump little"', '"unquestioning adherence"': *ibid.*, 8.

'"their love made an *intellectual* hothouse"', '"When he was . . . on the floor"': *ibid.*, 10.

'"top-heavy . . . his stance"': *ibid.*, 19.

'. . . a vogue for Nietzsche . . .': Thatcher (1970), 20.

'"What man is . . . can be bettered"': Fisher (1914).

'. . . no more than Nietzsche would have expected . . .': Thatcher (1970).

'. . . a side-effect of evolution . . .': Gould (1993), 321–2.

'Nietzsche had reflected upon Darwin . . .': Maudemarie Clark, 'Nietzsche, Friedrich (1844–1900)', in Craig (1998).

'"I am afraid . . . then disappear"': Mazumdar (1992), 97–8.

'"a rather extreme kind of Socialist"', Haldane (1932a), 131; letter to Fisher, 29 April 1930, Bennett (1983), 209.

'"Judgements of human excellence . . . take their value"': Fisher (1915).

'"She . . . felt the need . . . life's work in him . . ."': Box (1978), 43.

'Fisher's understanding of sexual selection . . . unfit to fight the next great war': Bartley (1994).

'"great body of men . . . patriotism"': Box (1978), 54.

5. IN THE SIXTH DAY

'"I suspect . . . pundit in turn"': letter, 18 September 1943, Bennett (1983), 265.

'. . . he developed his vision of evolution': see especially Fisher (1922a).

'"a leap in the dark"': Fisher (1922b).

'. . . the metaphor of a microscope's focus': Fisher (1930), 40–1.

'"extremely minute"': *ibid.*, 118.

'"The fate of those . . . determine their drift"': Fisher (1929).

'If one selective intensity was a fifty-thousandth . . .': *ibid.*

'. . . ratio of males to females . . .': Fisher (1930), 141–3.

'. . . his slit-trench style . . .': Hamilton (1996), 131.

'As Hamilton explained . . . stabilises at 1:1': Hamilton (1996), 143.

'"almost any I have written"', '"it helped sex-ratio theory . . ."': Hamilton (1996), 132.

'. . . he thought that peoples exposed longest to civilisation would have undergone strong selection against feticidal tendencies': Fisher (1922c); (1930), 201–2.

'"those who are most willing to murder their offspring . . ."': Fisher (1922c).

'"the more severe will be the selection . . ."': *ibid.*

'It came to him . . .': Edwards (1994).

'John Turner . . . has argued . . .': John Turner, 'Fisher's Evolutionary Faith and the Challenge of Mimicry', in Dawkins and Ridley (1985).

'. . . he observed in a radio talk . . .': Fisher (1947).

'"the primary elements . . . reality divinely guided"', '" . . . your letter by its conundrums . . ."': letters, 22 January and 3 February 1947, Bennett (1983), 262.

'"like the result of a game of chance . . ."': Fisher (1950).

'. . . indeterminacy . . .': M. J. S. Hodge, 'Biology and Philosophy (Including Ideology): A Study of Fisher and Wright', in Sarkar (1992), 256–9; Turner, *op. cit.*

'"at all times . . . an instant earlier"': Hodge, *op. cit.*

'Fisher's formulation . . . slow itself down': Depew and Weber (1995), 251.

'...share his opinion...': One who does is Grafen (2003).

'"either false or trivial"': BMC SA 3/52.

'"However regrettable . . . "': Peter O'Donald, unpublished commentary for students.

"'the principle of Natural Selection . . . patrons of his establishment'": Fisher (1930), 37.

"'the function of natural selection . . .'": Turner, *op. cit.*

"'picturesquely'": Fisher (1936b); Edwards (1994).

'Wright's exposition . . . was certainly ambiguous': Provine (1986), 307–17. See also Turner (1987).

"'total population on the planet'": letter to Wright, 13 August 1929, Bennett (1983), 273.

'. . . Corrado Gini . . .': Gini's ideological and scientific views, as well as his involvement with the Fascist regime, are discussed extensively in Ipsen (1996).

"'was able to befriend . . . almost destitute'": Box (1978), 420.

"'one of the most dangerous Nazi activists of the Third Reich'": Proctor (1988), 307. See also Trunk (2003).

"'eliminated through the racial–political measures of recent years'", "'foreign racial elements'": *ibid.*, 211.

'*Persilschein* . . .', "'very good term'": Müller-Hill (1988), 84.

"'Slight, bearded, eloquent, reactionary, and quirkish'": Norman T. Gridgeman in Gillespie (1972), 8.

"' . . . a natural biological variation . . .'": Committee on Homosexual Offences and Prostitution (1957).

"'because Jesus Christ would have signed it'": Bryan Clarke (1995); Hooper (2002), 233. Miriam Rothschild is the source in each, but in the first her quote refers to the report and in the second to a petition.

"'See what you made me do'": Box (1978), 11.

"' . . . replaced by some mirage his wife called God'": *ibid.*, 395.

"'He needed friends imperiously'": *ibid.*, 11.

The Oxford School

6. MOUNTING PRESSURES

Scarlet Tigers

"'a smallish man . . . like a snake's'": Box (1978), 181.

"'delighted to join me . . .'": Mayr and Provine (1980), 335.

"'fastidious old bachelor'": interview, 26 February 2001.

"'conditioned by his expectations'": Hooper (2002), 236.

"'my friend the Pope'": Bryan Clarke (1995).

"'How is your pussy?'" Hooper (2002), 174.

"'clean his palate'": *ibid.*, 99.

"'So even as a child . . .'": Bryan Clarke (1995).

"'always avoided . . . before our minds'": Ford (1977), 13.

"'dancing haze'", "'a great outburst . . .'": Ford (1981), 74.

"'genetics into the field'": Mayr and Provine (1980), 338.

"'fatal'": Fisher and Ford (1947).

"'general good'": Fisher (1941).
"'According to William Provine . . .'": Provine (1986), 436; 'Great Snail Debate', *ibid.*,
    437–49.

A Million Snails

'Philip Sheppard arrived . . . excavated soil': Cyril Clarke (1977). See also John R. G.
    Turner, 'Sheppard, Philip Macdonald', in Holmes (1990).
"'They didn't even dream of doing any actual work . . .'": Provine (1986), 439.
"'decided then and there'", "'wholly neutral'": Cain, *ibid.*, 441.
'They surveyed snails . . .': Cain and Sheppard (1950, 1954).
"'all situations supposedly caused by drift should be reinvestigated'": Cain and
    Sheppard (1950).
'. . . field studies he had begun during the war . . . small populations': Gayon (1998),
    362–4.
'the all-pervading influence of natural selection . . .': Provine (1986), 452.
'. . . Lamotte found that bandless snails seemed to do better . . .': Lamotte (1959).
'Cain acknowledged that random processes . . .': Cain (1964).
'. . . where previously isolated populations have met': Davison and Clarke (2000).
"'a body . . . except man'": Jones, Leith and Rawlings (1977).

Peppered Moths

"'pointing at the chandeliers . . .'": Hooper (2002), 132.
"'the chimney of the world'": Marcus (1974), 46.
'. . . Heslop Harrison . . .': Sabbagh (1999).
"'looks as if dipped in ink'": Ford (1981), 89.
'He was also sceptical . . . melanic heterozygotes might be physiologically superior': Ford
    (1937).
'. . . Tinbergen was unusual among Oxford lecturers in using slides': Richard Dawkins,
    interview, 26 February 2001.
'. . . around Liverpool . . .': Clarke and Sheppard (1966).
'. . . less than ten per cent at the end of it': Cook *et al.* (1999).
'. . . Majerus, who bought Ford's *Moths* . . . four weeks later': Majerus (1998), v.
'. . . reviewed in *Nature* by . . . Jerry Coyne . . .': Coyne (1998).
"'certain'": Sargent *et al.* (1998).
"'all of us . . . natural selection'": Coyne (2000).
"'I have caught" . . . "they be convinced'": 'The Peppered Moth Controversy', Darwin
    Day Lecture, organised by the British Humanist Association, London School of
    Economics, 12 February 2004.
For a recent view on the strength of natural selection, see Conner (2001).

Wings and Prayer

"'one species had been taken and modified for different ends'": Darwin (1905), 373–4.
"' . . . clean, clear Darwinian ideas . . .'": interview, 26 June 2002.
"'zoological imagination'": Lack (1973).
"'offset by . . . European settlers'": Lack (1968), 1.

"'no evidence . . . adaptive significance'": quoted in Weiner (1994), 54–5.

"'but was so put off . . . from pacifism'": Lack (1973).

'He thought . . . same region': Lack (1968), 62; Gause (1934).

'By 1960 . . . were adaptive': Lack (1968), iii.

'Cormorants . . .': Lack (1945).

"'aerial plankton'": Alister C. Hardy (1973), obituary appreciation of David Lack, *Ibis*, 115, 436.

"'essentially depended on the full acceptance of natural selection'": Lack (1973).

'one of the last Fellows . . . an amateur', *ibid.*

"'And as they sang . . . circling swifts'": Lack (1956), 16. See also Lack (1961).

J. B. S. Haldane

"'Fitness is a bugger'": quoted by Maynard Smith, interview, 26 June 2002.

7. LOOSE CANNON

"'Twins, my god, twins!'": Mitchison (1975), 45.

'. . . named two of them after Bateson and Punnett . . .': Mitchison in Dronamraju (1968), 302.

"'Reduplication in Mice'": Haldane, Sprunt and Haldane (1915).

"'Oh, it's you'", "'It has always . . . shall wake up'": Clark (1968a), 42.

"'How you propose to give an account of my career beats me'": letter, 26 October 1959, HA Acc.9589/164.

"'dilute ginger beer . . .'": Pirie (1966).

'. . . his own rabbit . . .': 'On Being One's Own Rabbit', Haldane (1927).

"'the kind of scientist . . . in one's head'": Duncan & Weston-Smith (1977), 242.

"'Haldane's characteristic style . . . no further polishing'": James F. Crow, 'Sewall Wright's Place in Twentieth-Century Biology', in Sarkar (1992), 178.

"'I was bottle-washing . . . third of science'": HA 9589/165, transcript of 'self-obituary' recorded for BBC, 20 February 1964.

"' . . . the mechanical chap . . .'": Clark (1968a), 20.

"'had few French . . . *mein liebe Kollege*'": Mitchison (1975), 83.

"'My mater and I . . . again soon'": Mitchison (1973), 88; Werskey (1978), 55.

'. . . a draft autobiography . . .': HA Acc. 9589/166.

"'From an intellectual . . . and I did'": *ibid.*

"'the first case . . . Church of England'": Clark (1968a), 34.

"'love–hate'": Mitchison (1975), 61.

'. . . fellow scientist . . .': Mitchison (1973), 69.

"' . . . hobyah type of fairy . . .'": Mitchison (1975), 96.

"'swank'": HA 20564/20655, 36.

"'I am enjoying . . . does not like it'": *ibid.*, 30.

"'However . . . frighten me much'": *ibid.*, 32.

"'I can always start an artillery battle . . .'": *ibid.*, 82.

"'I find this . . . attacking so well'": *ibid.*, 38.

"'subaltern's war'": *ibid.*, 38.

"'less intellectual subordinates'": Clark (1968a), 38.

"'funking'": HA 20564/20655, 43.

"'I seem to remember . . . existing circumstances'": HA Acc. 9589/166.

"'one of the happiest months of my life'": *ibid.*

"'the best job ever'": HA 20564/20655, 59.

"' . . . the right sort of chaps'": transcript of 'Frankly Speaking', BBC interview, transmitted 22 June 1956, HA Acc. 9589/165.

"'jumped like a shot rabbit . . . by that name'": HA Acc. 9589/166.

'. . . cut through the fuse and take the detonator off . . .': HA 20564/20655, 68.

"'We must have a shot at cocaine some day'": letter from Charlotte Burghes, 4 November 1923, HA DEP 300.

"'A satisfactory theory . . . past transmutations'": Haldane (1924).

"'As far as . . . a different font'": Dawkins (1991), 374.

'. . . John Maynard Smith, who challenged Kimura . . .': Maynard Smith (1968). See also Ridley (1996a), ch. 7; Kimura and Ohta in Ridley (1997).

"'Through a blur . . . in the combat'": Haldane (1923), 1–2.

"'the centre of scientific interest'": *ibid.*, 10.

"'the greatest Jew since Jesus'": *ibid.*, 11.

"'has told us . . . will our descendants'": *ibid.*, 14.

'. . . the irrational streak his sister knew he shared . . .': Mitchison (1975), 96.

'. . . he told a correspondent – Frank Allaun . . .': letter, 9 June 1943, HP Box 10.

"'I dare say . . . one's privacy'": Clark (1968a), 111.

"'rather stupid . . . race of super-men . . .'": Haldane (1923), 57.

"'eugenic official . . . procurer'": *ibid.*, 41.

"'the greater fertility of the less desirable members of the population'": *ibid.*, 66–7.

"'mankind will be free in an altogether new sense'": *ibid.*, 68.

"'biological inventions'": *ibid.*, 42.

"'There is no . . . a perversion'": *ibid.*, 46.

"'radical indecency'": *ibid.*, 45.

"'altered the path . . . the Venus of Milo'": *ibid.*, 43.

"'the most romantic figure on earth'", "'a poor little scrubby underpaid man'": *ibid.*, 77.

"'It took a staphylococcus . . . deserve fascism'" : HA Acc.9589/166

"'I knew he'd object . . . accounting for them'": Julian Huxley (1970), 138.

"'uneducated'": Haldane (1925), 21.

"'Besides being wounded . . . septic shell-wound'": *ibid.*, 22.

"'Suddenly . . . in gas masks . . .'": *ibid.*, 47.

"'If I stated . . . to be found'": Haldane (1938), 144; Barkan (1992), 258–9.

"'but I should . . . whites over negroes'": Haldane (1938), 148.

"'I prefer that my country should be on the winning side'": Haldane (1925), 4.

"'some successor . . . on the moon'": Haldane (1925), 19.

"'This is my man!'": Charlotte Haldane (1949), 17.

"'teaching was J. B. S.'s supreme hobby . . .'": Charlotte Haldane (1949), 20.

'"that little devil of an Unborn"': letter from Charlotte Haldane, 9 April 1924, HA DEP 300.

'Naomi warned her that he wanted a child . . .': undated letter from Charlotte Haldane, 1924, HA DEP 300.

'"Could you manage 4 o'clock on Monday?"': letter from E. S. P. Haynes, 19 February 1925, HA DEP 300.

'. . . as Peter Medawar observed . . .': Clark (1968a), 9.

'"charade"': Clark (1968a), 45.

'Medawar and the poet Stephen Spender . . .': Medawar (1988),129; Spender (1985), 458.

'Charlotte herself claimed . . .': Adamson (1998), 62.

'"My pink pillar . . ."': letter from Charlotte Haldane, 6 August 1924, HA DEP 300.

'. . . the couple's denial served as part of Haldane's defence . . .': He showed the tribunal a copy of the *Times* report (21 October 1925, p. 5) which mentioned it.

'"Big, fat, bald, sensual, funny, grumpy, canine, pontifical"': letter from Charlotte Haldane, 4 September 1925, HA DEP 300.

'" . . . chains of brass, or better of tungsten . . ."': Haldane (1971), 72.

'"Well, if he is writing fairy-tales I suppose I had better do so too"': Adamson (1998), 69.

'"a handsome man . . . sense of humour"': Charlotte Haldane (1949), 42.

'"To him . . . science and scientists"': *ibid.*, 51.

'. . . their leading role in the measurement of natural selection . . .': Haldane (1929).

'. . . a quartet including . . . Chetverikov': as it was for Theodosius Dobzhansky, Mayr and Provine (1980), 234.

'"as full of bloody Communists as Cambridge"': Clark (1968a), 97.

'"turned dizzily . . . that was all"': Mitchison (1979), 62.

'she went straight to her brother': Benton (1990), 53–4.

'"I bit his arm; he twisted my wrist"': Mitchison (1979), 211–2.

'"with great courage . . . had been lost"': Mitchison (1979), 77.

'her scientific and her erotic passions were inseparable': HA DEP 300.

8. COMRADE PROF

'"In the application . . . worse than useless"': Haldane (1969), 43.

'"Till 1933 . . . Marxist philosophy"': Kunitz and Haycraft (1942), 597.

'. . . natural selection "negates" mutation . . .': Haldane (1937b).

'Sixty years on . . . dialectical thought': Shapiro (1993).

'"grimmer optimism"': Haldane (1937b).

'"violent discussions"': Haldane (1969), 133.

'. . . Hermann Muller . . . treated their scientists': Charlotte Haldane (1949), 318.

'" . . . impressed upon him with a rubber stamp"': letter to Julian Huxley, 9 March 1937, quoted in Paul (1983).

'. . . views prevalent among Russian evolutionists . . . *Mutual Aid*': Francesco M. Scudo and Michele Acanfora, 'Darwin and Russian Evolutionary Biology', in Kohn (1985); Depew and Weber (1995), 289–91; Kropotkin, Petr Alekseyeevich (1902), *Mutual Aid: A Factor of Evolution*, Heinemann, London; www.calresco.org/texts/mutaid.htm

"'rather mechanical'", "'beautifully dialectical theory'", "'. . . acceptance of Marxism
. . .'": Haldane (1969), 136–7.
"'arrests on the ground of scientific opinions are quite impossible'": letter, 23 June 1937,
HA MS.20534 /80.
"'test of the devotion . . . becomes important'": Haldane (1932a), 137.
"'The American negro is making trouble . . .'": Barkan (1992), 182.
"'So if you keep . . . future generations'": Haldane (1932a), 4.
"'little positive evidence'": Haldane (1938), 15.
"'one man is superior . . .'": Marx (1960), 17;
www.marxists.org/archive/marx/works/1875/gotha/ch01.htm
"'The formula . . . I agree with him'": HA MS.20609.
"'that nasty little lecher Herbert Morrison . . .'": letter to Naomi Mitchison, 25
December 1954, HA Acc.10720.
"'hard, small and very irregular'": Kalmus (1991), 85.
'. . . a Soviet military intelligence agent . . .': West (1999).
'. . . an intercepted message sent in September 1940 . . .': Venona document,
web.archive.org/web/20000929012018/http://www.nsa.gov/docs/venona/docs/
sept40/06_Sept_1940_R5_m1_p1.gif
"'were cossetted and privileged to an absurd degree'": Charlotte Haldane (1949), 255.
"'surprise and mental uneasiness'", "'. . . intellectually and emotionally incapable . . .'":
ibid., 258–9.
'He came fourth in the ballot . . .': 'The Communist Party 17th National Congress,
Shoreditch Town Hall, October 1944, Election of Executive Committee', HP Box 36.
"'our finest plant geneticist . . .'": Haldane (1940a), 82.
"'You simply couldn't . . . 12-times table'": Julian Huxley (1949), 103.
"'very remarkable examples . . . several respects'": Haldane (1940a), 83.
'. . . his antipathy to chromosomes . . .': Haldane (1940b).
'This would be . . . elaborated scientifically . . .': Haldane (1940a), 83.
"'Vavilov was shot about once a year . . .'": Haldane (1947), 212.
'. . . views might end up closer to Lysenko's': letter, 3 January 1945, HP Box 18.
"'refute false views on scientific grounds'": letter to J. R. Campbell, editor of *Daily
Worker*, 1 December 1949, HA Acc.9589/164.
"'Interventions . . . prominent feature'": draft letter to the *Guardian*, c. 1946, HA
MS.20548/157.
"'from the Eugenics point of view . . .'": letter replying to member of public, 8 August
1949, HP Box 17.
"'Recent controversies . . . present time'": letter, 22 June 1948, HA MS.20535/66.
'For several years . . . *Doklady*'s pages': Eric Ashby, 'Science Without Freedom?', *The
Listener*, 4 November 1948.
"'carefully laid trap'": Julian Huxley (1949), 34.
"'Morgano–Weismannite . . . Weismannite–Morganist ideology'": *ibid.*, 37–9.
"'The struggle . . . socialist agriculture'": A. G. Morton, 18 November 1948, 'The Present
Position in Biology', HP Box 18. See also Fyfe (1950).
"'absolute disagreement'", "'in the very strongest manner'": letter to Maurice Cornforth,

20 November 1948, HP Box 18.

'. . . a resignation letter . . .': HA MS.20546/200; Clark (1968a), 171–2.

'He wrote and circulated a statement . . .': 'Note by J. B. S. Haldane on the *Daily Worker* Educational Controversy', HP Box 15.

'Now, he proposed to transform the climate . . .': Joravsky (1970), 130–1, 141.

'95 per cent of the trees . . .': *ibid.*, 154.

'"A good Marxist . . . internal contradictions"': Haldane (1969), 141.

'. . . competition was inevitable as soon as a species became fairly dense': Haldane (1932b), 119.

'. . . one of his early *Daily Worker* columns . . .': 'Beyond Darwin', Haldane (1941b). See also Haldane (1937b).

'"without it . . . a fiction"', '"Natural selection . . . same species"', '"happens very rarely"': *Daily Worker*, 1 November 1948.

'. . . while accepting that intraspecific competition . . .': Haldane (1964), 354.

'. . . which were then published in *The Listener*': 9 December 1948.

'. . . in a Party journal . . .': Haldane (1949).

'"seriously exaggerated"': *The Listener*, 9 December 1948.

'Even the non-Mendelian changes . . . viruses or similar agents': Haldane (1940b).

'he still had a good word to say for Lysenko even at the end of his life': HA 9589/165, transcript of 'self-obituary' recorded for BBC, 20 February 1964.

'. . . public flak . . .': notably Langdon-Davies (1949).

'"We geneticists . . . slanders against us"': letter to Maurice Cornforth, 9 February 1949, HA Acc.9589/164.

'"because of Stalin's interference in science"': Clark (1968a), 186.

'According to one account, Haldane remained a member . . .', '"quit the Party . . . a flood"': Malcolm MacEwen, 'The Day the Party Had to Stop', in Miliband and Saville (1976).

'On 2 April . . . Agricultural Sciences': John Saville, 'The Twentieth Congress and the British Communist Party', *ibid.*

'"wish no longer . . . human race"', '"criminal state"': Clark (1968a), 209, 210.

'. . . chameleons in the garden': Helen Spurway, HA DEP 300.

'. . . Murdoch Mitchison's suggestion . . . cross holy men': interview, 27 September 2000.

'"one-storied 'ivory tower'"': Haldane (1964).

'"I was afraid Helen was going to kill herself . . ."': interview, 22 February 2000.

'Writing in 1968 . . .': HA DEP 300.

'. . . Lorenz . . . joined the Nazi party in 1938 . . .': Kalikow (1983).

'"annihilate the healthy nation"', '"racial idea as the basis of our state"': Nisbett (1976), 82–3.

'Haldane . . . tried to bring Lorenz to England in 1950': letter to John E. Harris, 26 October 1950, HP Box 18.

'Lorenz had written . . . presence of their peers': Kruuk (2003), 127–8.

'. . . Lehrman . . . critique of Lorenz's theories . . .': Lehrman (1953).

'. . . addressing the Royal Anthropological Institute in 1956 . . .': Haldane (1956).

'. . . the group photograph taken at the Paris conference . . .': reproduced in Clark (1968a) and Morris (1979).

'Ernst Mayr came to visit Haldane . . .': Futuyma and Antonovics (1992), 25.
"'A Defense of Beanbag Genetics'": Haldane (1964).
'John Maynard Smith . . . continued the defence . . .': Maynard Smith (1988), 13-14.
"' . . . me last shit'": BMC SA 2/42.
"'But I am very angry'": letter, 7 September 1964.

John Maynard Smith

'I think I was always an adaptationist . . .': interview, 22 February 2000.

9. BETTER DO THE SUMS

"'The Pitmans speak – to practically nobody'": Butler (1972), 20.
"'marvellous training'", "'What I am . . . wholly critical'": interview, 22 February 2000.
"'no good will come of mixing them up'": Haldane (1927), 277.
"'Man . . . million generations'": *ibid.*, 279.
"'We are pretty . . . Athanasian Creed'": *ibid.*, 280.
"'It was very moving to find that I wasn't alone in the world'": BMC SA 1/6.
"'I can still . . . writing ever since'": Clarke (1989), 29.
"'was also our religion . . . in the chase'": interview, 22 February 2000.
"'the nearest thing I had to a father'": interview, 3 June 2002.
"'in wild surmise at animals of all kinds'": interview, 21 October 1999.
"'Fossils have . . . opposite effect'": Maynard Smith (1991).
'. . . describing himself as an agnostic . . .': Maynard Smith, 'An Agnostic View of
    Evolution', in Ramsey (1965).
'David Lack once asked him to take part . . .': interview, 26 June 2002.
"'the path . . . lapsed Christians'": Maynard Smith (1991).
'In March 1939 . . . attack on Germany': Butler, 93-5.
"'I didn't like . . . have to fight'", "'I came back . . . the Communists'": interview, 21
    October 1999.
"'Mind you . . . really keen'": *ibid.*
'. . . one of the attractions of the Cambridge University Socialist Club . . . other student
    societies', 'be as much to the fore on the academic front as the political': Hobsbawm
    (2002), 117.
'. . . Cambridge's female students and the university . . .': Maddox (2002), 44-5.
'. . . assume that air was incompressible . . .': BMC SA 1/10.
"'As an explanation . . . are partly responsible'", "'my interest is . . . and so on'": letters to
    Haldane, 1 and 6 October 1947; HP Box 19.
"' . . . science would absorb me . . . guilty about that'", "'I know what I'm going to do and
    I do it'", "'It was rather grey . . . very happy people'": interview, 21 October 1999.
'. . . Maynard Smith was suspicious of this view of animals . . .': Maynard Smith (2001).
"'The standard textbook . . . had worked out'": Singh and Krimbas (1999), 632.
"'It seemed to me . . . nineteenth century anatomy'": Maynard Smith (1991).
"'damn-all since the Cretaceous'": Maynard Smith and Szathmáry (1999), 15.

'. . . his paper to appear in Penguin's *New Biology* . . .': Maynard Smith (1953).

'"I thought . . . do the sums"', '"It's not that . . . would solve it"': interview, 21 October 1999.

'. . . Haldane wrote in a letter . . .': to the Secretary of the Agricultural Research Council, 21 March 1951; HP Box 34.

'" . . . just very clumsy . . . marvellous observer"': interview, 26 October 1999.

'"quite a good farmer"': interview, 21 October 1999.

'. . . Penrose had succeeded . . . held by a eugenist . . .': Mazumdar (1992).

'"Bulgaria Is Optimistic"', '"gayest place in Europe"': *Daily Worker* 26 August, 27 September 1948.

'" . . . the central committee . . . crack in the dyke"': Maynard Smith, 'J. B. S. Haldane', in Sarkar (1992), 49.

'"the test of his devotion . . . breaking point"': Hobsbawm (2002), 140.

'"It's very hard . . . a sinking ship"': BMC SA 1/20.

'Like most British ex-communists . . .': Almond (1954), 358.

'" . . . Church of England resembles the Russian Orthodox Church"': letter to M. K. Elias, 2 June 1951, HP Box 18.

'"disgusted"', '"Marxism was a good guide to scientific practice"': Maynard Smith, 'J. B. S. Haldane', in Sarkar (1992), 49.

'He spent six months looking . . .' Maynard Smith (2000).

'"something deeply undialectical"': Maynard Smith, 'J. B. S. Haldane', in Sarkar (1992), 49.

'. . . second favourite . . .': BMC SA 6/112; Maynard Smith (1988), 13.

'Once the structure of DNA . . . down the generations': Maynard Smith (1998a), 8–12.

'Another investigation with heterodox leanings . . .': Maynard Smith (1956).

'"Consequently they were . . . male isn't motivated"': interview, 26 October 1999; Maynard Smith (1999), 634.

'. . . said to be occupied entirely by lavatories . . .': Medawar (1988), 122.

'. . . without a reference': Rabelais (1944), XVII, 51–2.

'"found Haldane's mind immediately sympathetic"', '"Today I find . . . I have copied him"': Maynard Smith, 'In Haldane's Footsteps', in Dewsbury (1985), 348.

'. . . Haldane came to regard Maynard Smith as probably his closest friend at UC . . .': letter to D. P. Basu, 13 May 1959, HA MS.20643/100.

'"surprisingly impersonal . . . 'Smith' and 'Prof'"': interview, 22 February 2000.

'"He said . . . admire her"': interview, 26 October 1999.

'. . . he wrote to Maynard Smith immediately': 7 September 1964.

10. PUZZLES AND GAMES

'"could have been run by Thomas Henry Huxley"', '"wanted to break down . . . organisms to biochemistry"': interview, 26 October 1999.

'"Why do theory when Haldane's sitting in the room next door?"': interview, 3 June 2002.

'"is *the* problem . . . I think you should"': interview, 26 June 2002.

'"At first sight . . . make it do"': interview, 3 June 2002.

"'there was no way ... than a week'": interview, 26 October 1999.

'Peter Medawar ... age and decline': M. R. Rose, 'The Evolution of Senescence', in Greenwood *et al.* (1985).

'At the time ... process of ageing': Maynard Smith (1962).

"'There's no point ... age of three'": interview, 26 October 1999.

'... emphasised the importance of developmental processes ...': Maynard Smith (1998b), Maynard Smith *et al.* (1985).

"'Smith, why don't ...'", "'He said, 'Smith ... enough is enough'": interview, 26 October 1999.

"'wonderful series of facts'": J. B. S. Haldane, letter to Michael Swann, 27 June 1964, HA MS.20546/164.

'... Williams had nearly finished his manuscript by the time he saw *Animal Dispersion* ...': Brockman (1995), 41.

"'most virile'", "'master-cock'", "'restraint of the system'", "'could conceivably be a collective operation'": Wynne-Edwards (1962), 212–6.

'... Haldane had sketched ...': Haldane (1955).

"'did not at the time follow ... population numbers'": Maynard Smith, 'In Haldane's Footsteps', in Dewsbury (1985), 351.

"'the evolution ... affected individual'": Maynard Smith (1964).

"'Pangloss' Theorem'": Dewsbury (1985), 351.

"'perversion'": *Daily Worker*, 1 November 1948.

'Richard Dawkins eventually provided clarification ...': Dawkins (1999).

"'the best strategy ...'": Maynard Smith (1988), 203.

'... in 1967, Hamilton had published a paper ...': 'Extraordinary Sex Ratios', Hamilton (1996).

'... he did not read to the end of the paper ...': interview, 26 October 1999.

"'Only when I've more or less done something ... other people have said on the subject'": interview, 3 May 2002.

'... had not done a very good job ...': Maynard Smith, 'In Haldane's Footsteps', in Dewsbury (1985), 352–3.

"'On the other hand ... perhaps we didn't'": interview, 3 June 2002.

'Axelrod ... paper published by ... *Science* in 1981 ...': Axelrod and Hamilton (1981); Hamilton (2001), ch. 4.

'... use of the word "evolve"': letter to John Maynard Smith, 12 February 1973.

'... he himself had suggested using the word "dove"': letter to John Maynard Smith, 20 April 1972.

Selection Revealed

"'very interesting, very pretty'": Schwartz (2000).

"'Sherlock Holmes mind'", "'gripping tale'": Hamilton (1996), 322.

"'Wishful thinking ...'", "'God's standards ...'", "'eagerly'": letter to John Maynard Smith, 19 October 1972, in Brown (1999), 4.

'... the words that had impelled Price's drive to poverty': Matthew 6:25–34.

'"angel"': Schwartz (2000).

'"wasn't very relevant to human problems"': curriculum vitae, reproduced in Frank (1995).

'"Jesus wants . . . own problems"': Schwartz (2000).

'"As I tidied . . . on his bed"': Hamilton (1996), 174.

'" . . . what was good enough for St Paul . . ."': John Maynard Smith, interview, 26 October 1999.

'"By suggesting . . . seemed stark"': Hamilton (1996), 320.

'As Hamilton observed . . .': *ibid.*, 172.

'. . . "ludicrous", he told Hamilton . . .': *ibid.*, 322–3.

'"think there was much mileage"': interview, 26 October 1999.

'"One felt nothing important could be that easy"': interview, 3 June 2002.

'" . . . Mondays, Wednesdays and Fridays . . ."': interview, 26 October 1999; Maynard Smith (1988), 214.

'"I sat there absolutely mesmerised"': interview, 26 October 1999.

'"John's imaginary biologist"': BMC SA 3/65.

'. . . Nick Davies found that in Wytham Woods . . .': Davies (1978).

'In Sweden . . . drove them away': Wickman and Wiklund (1983).

'Davies suggested that the Swedish butterflies . . .': Davies (1979).

'. . . some questions arising . . . Geoff Parker': Maynard Smith and Parker (1976). See also Ruse (1999), ch. 10.

'"Geoff was a good socialist in those days"': BMC SA 3/64

'. . . supporting example in the spider *Oecibus civitas* . . .': Maynard Smith (1982), 96.

'"whenever the best . . . be an ESS"': Maynard Smith (1988), 215.

'"It all got too mathematical for me"': interview, 26 October 1999.

'Karl Marx . . . Adam Smith's view of economics': Young (1998a), Radick (2003).

'And behind Smith . . . British science': Depew and Weber (1995), ch. 10.

'"absolute disaster"': interview, 26 June 2002.

'"half-baked"': Segerstråle (2000), 241.

'"strong commitment to both fairness and communication"': *ibid.*, 243.

'. . . a review of *Mind and Culture* . . .': John Maynard Smith and Neil Warren, 'Models of Genetic and Cultural Change', Maynard Smith (1988).

'"spent several months trying to understand the maths"': *ibid.*, 52.

'"still coming to terms with Marxism"': interview, 26 June 2002.

'" . . . disagreeing most strongly . . ."': Maynard Smith (1988), 51.

'"but quite why isn't obvious to me"': interview, 26 June 2002.

'"On the other hand I think I'm different . . ."': *ibid.*

'"I start with a problem . . . simple little models"': interview, 3 June 2002.

'"only half the battle"': Maynard Smith (1978), 111.

'. . . reviewing books by Richard Dawkins . . . line of mathematics': Maynard Smith (1988), 113.

'" . . . cancel the d's?"': Maynard Smith (1995).

'"in order . . . signals have to be costly"': Zahavi and Zahavi (1997), xiv.

'"If it's in words, it's intuition . . ."': Amotz Zahavi, comment made at workshop on 'Signs of Quality: The Handicap Principle in Biology, Economics and Culture',

hosted by University College London at London Zoo, 8 December 1999.
'Other analysts . . . Grafen published . . .': Pomiankowski (1987), Grafen (1990).
'. . . work by Richard Dawkins and John Krebs . . .': Krebs and Dawkins, 'Animal Signals: Mind-Reading and Manipulation', in Krebs and Davies (1984).
'"is the person who really forced us to face up to it"': interview, 3 June 2002.
'A combination of genes . . . break up successful teams': Barton and Charlesworth (1998).
'. . . gearbox . . .': Maynard Smith (1988), 166; interview, *the evolutionist*, 1999, cpnss.lse.ac.uk/darwin/evo/jms.htm
'"Neo-Darwinian"': Shaw (1945), ix.
'. . . how sex might have first arisen': Maynard Smith and Szathmáry (1997), ch. 9; (1999), 87–91.
'. . . Adam Eyre-Walker . . . two such mutations each per generation . . .': personal communication, Keightley and Eyre-Walker (2000). The rate given in the paper is 3, but the estimates have since been revised downwards.
'"We don't really . . . hard for us"', '"a whole slew of answers"', '"a great bewildering mass"': interview, 3 June 2002.
'"To try . . . terribly hard"': BMC SA 5/98.
'. . . bacterial evolution . . . discrete species': Maynard Smith, Feil and Smith (2000).
'"sexual continuum"': Maynard Smith and Szathmáry (1997), 166.
Maynard Smith (1996); Sinervo and Lively (1996); Sinervo (2000); Sinervo, Svensson, and Comendant (2000); Zamudio and Sinervo (2000); Barry Sinervo , 'Lizardland', www.biology.ucsc.edu/~barrylab/lizardland/game.html
'"Curt and I . . . rock–paper–scissors game!"': Steve Mirsky (1996), 'The Lizard Kings', *Scientific American*, 19 June.

Bill Hamilton

'"I am a child . . . for miracles"': Hamilton (1996), 3.

11. THE STING OF ALTRUISM

'Archibald had built a road . . .': Archibald Hamilton (1958).
'It served the Hamiltons . . .': Mary R. Bliss, 'In Memory of Bill Hamilton: Hazards of Modern Medicine', www.unifr.ch/biol/ecology/hamilton/hamilton/bliss.html
'wandering barefoot . . . red clover': Hamilton (2001), 125.
'"Stone-turning . . . ground beetle"': Hamilton (1992).
'"praised collecting . . . an art"': *ibid.*
'. . . Collins's successful "New Naturalist" series . . .': Marren (1995).
'"Mohammed II . . . to an end"': Ford (1945), 7.
'"It has always . . . construction of the book"': *ibid.*, 1.
'"merely to fill their cabinets with curios"': *ibid.*, 253.
'"a possibility of some ambivalence or heresy"': Hamilton (1992).
'"mysterious genetics"': *ibid.*
'"but I found . . . too easy"': *ibid.*

'"rather beyond me"', '"discovered a grand new source of arguments"', '"our old topic . . . unpopularity they caused"': undated postcard from W. D. Hamilton to his sister Mary Bliss, read by her at his memorial service, 1 July 2000.

'"with trepidation"', '"It was teatime . . . but no . . ."': undated postcard, 1959.

'intellectual hero . . . towards natural selection': Hamilton (1996), 21.

'"algebraic attack"', '"One reads and forgets"': Hamilton (1996), 22.

'. . . altruism which Haldane had published . . .': Haldane (1932b), 207–10.

'"strangely irrelevant"': 'Selection of Selfish and Altruistic Behaviour in Some Extreme Models', Hamilton (1996), 222.

'"Most biologists . . . Christian martyrs"': Maynard Smith, 'J. B. S. Haldane', in Sarkar (1992), 42–3.

'"in so far . . . Darwinian fitness . . ."': Haldane (1932b), 131.

'. . . Penguin *New Biology* article . . .': Haldane (1955).

'" . . . sinister new sucker . . . tree of Fascism"': Hamilton (1996), 4.

'"elemental forces"', '" . . . a bracken fern . . ."': *ibid.*, 12–13.

'. . . devalued . . .': Dawkins (2001).

'"To put the matter more vividly . . . not for less"': Hamilton (1996), 7.

'" . . . an efficient sister-making machine"': Dawkins (1989), 175.

'The significance of these asymmetries . . . in favour of their sisters': Trivers and Hare (1976).

'"Thus the first female . . . population genetics"': Maynard Smith and Szathmáry (1995), 265–7.

'. . . Dawkins produced a graph . . .': Dawkins (1989), 326.

'"fallen for some of them in my time"': Dawkins (1979).

'" . . . the unmistakable sound of worst suspicions being gleefully confirmed"': Dawkins (1982), 22.

'"feed anything that squawks inside your nest"': Dawkins (1979).

'. . . he was ready to see selection . . . at different levels': Hamilton (1996), 365.

'"The majority of evolutionary biologists . . . Captain Hamilton was still at the helm"': Sober and Wilson (1998), 78.

'"reductionist, racist and ridiculous"': *ibid.*, 317.

'"genuine communism of behaviour"': *ibid.*, 340.

'"Maybe if the mammoth-hunters . . ."', '"Arms and armour . . ."', '"paean to fascism"': *ibid.*, 345.

'"talented Asiatic races"': letter replying to member of public, 8 August 1949, HP Box 17.

'"self-sacrificial daring"', '"revitalize"': Hamilton (1996), 345.

'. . . Golden Horde . . . complained Hamilton, oblivious to irony': *ibid.*, 318.

'Later, however, he added a new chapter . . . "It pays"': Hamilton (2001), 356–9.

'"parliament of genes"', '"a company boardroom . . ."', '" . . . I need not be so ashamed . . . right and wrong"': Hamilton (1996), 133–4.

'" . . . subject to far more mysterious laws"': *ibid.*, 2.

12. UNDER THE BARK

'"balloons its body . . . living food"': *ibid.*, 388–9.

"'fig-tree fruiting . . . most monkeys do today'": *ibid.*, 424.

"'Their fighting . . . armed with knives'": *ibid.*, 441.

"'Geometry for the Selfish Herd'": Hamilton (1971); (1996), ch. 7.

'. . . dispersal, which he rated as an organism's third priority . . .': Hamilton and Lenton (1998).

'. . . a study he conducted with Robert May . . .': Hamilton and May (1977); Hamilton (1996), ch. 11.

"'Gaia's way . . .'": Lovelock (1987), 104.

'Working with Tim Lenton . . . did not replicate itself': Hamilton and Lenton (1998); Lynn Hunt, 'Send in the Clouds', *New Scientist*, 30 May 1998, 28–33; Hamilton, 'Cloud Cover' (letter), *New Scientist*, 27 June 1998, 52; reply by Lovelock, 'Don't Knock Gaia', *New Scientist*, 11 July 1998, 57.

'a letter to Maynard Smith': 19 October 1972.

'In his reply, Maynard Smith . . .': 24 October 1972.

"'I first heard . . . later to generalise'": 'Survival through Suicide', *New Scientist*, 28 August 1975, 496.

'. . . suggested that Maynard Smith might have got the phrase from him . . .': 'Haldane and Altruism', *New Scientist*, 1 July 1976, 40.

'. . . Fisher's brief allusion to the matter . . .': Fisher (1930), 159.

"'Traces of a proprietory feeling appear to remain in me!'": *New Scientist*, 22 July 1976, 195.

"'was constantly writing . . . getting the mathematics clear'": *New Scientist*, 5 August 1976, 300.

"'very slight'": Haldane (1955).

"'A is the . . . fill his place'": Fisher (1914).

"'It is clear . . . on evolution theory'": *New Scientist*, 29 July 1976, 247.

'He wrote to Maynard Smith . . .': 19 October 1977.

'Maynard Smith . . . wrote': 27 October 1977.

"'I began to think of pinching it for myself'": Darwin Seminar, London School of Economics, 9 December 1998 (LSE recording).

"'The Hospitals Are Coming'": Hamilton (2001).

"'Just how much . . . producing children'", "'Speaking as someone . . . us to reproduce'", "' . . . keeping John Maynard Smith alive'", "' . . . a sensible response to your idea'": *ibid.*, 456.

"'Eugenics is a dirty word . . .'" 'Games and Theories', *New Scientist*, 14 June 2003, 48–50.

"'needs to say how we are to deal'": Hamilton (2001), 458.

"'Some may decide . . . natural selection'": *ibid.*, 457.

'He had hinted . . . the first volume . . .': Hamilton (1996), 193.

"'even if I think . . . the best thing'": Hamilton (2001), 453.

"'public loves . . . a persuasive person'": *ibid.*, 467.

"'in a spirit . . . Olympic record book'": *ibid.*, 485.

"'I am a primitive . . . Caesarean section'": *ibid.*, 530.

'He accepted . . . more children': *ibid.*, 503–4, 531.

'"several at a time" ... underline it twice': *ibid.*, 472.

'"These defectives ... *eliminate*"': *ibid.*, 473.

'"and I think of the commas ..."', '"never have allowed it ..."', '"everything I can
remember ..."': *ibid.*, 478.

'"fourth child"', '" ... kill a defective baby"': *ibid.*, 481.

'"assessment phase"': Daly and Wilson (1988), 71–2.

'"reaction to the presence of Judaism ..."', '"mirror image"': Kevin MacDonald,
'Summary of *Separation and Its Discontents: Toward an Evolutionary Theory of Anti-
Semitism*'; www.csulb.edu/~kmacd/books.htm

'Hamilton himself criticised the book ...': Hamilton (2001), 280, n11.

'" ... a pair in paradise, forming their own island ..."', '" ... a paranoia for hospitals"',
'"Planetary Hospital"': *ibid.*, 488.

'"mites within its bowels"': *ibid.*, 489.

'"gradually enslaved ... without choice"': *ibid.*, 493.

'" ... any precipitate action"': Crow (1997).

'"...an irresponsible child ..."', '"a trait approaching to autism ..."', '"some kinds of
autists ... social phenomena"', '"a person who ... allowed to discuss"', '"culture-
infected ... what I understand"': Hamilton (2001), xxvii–xxxi

'"If a place ... would feel like"': Tom Bettag, 'Producer's Journal: Congo',
ABCNEWS.com, 7 September 2001,
abcnews.go.com/sections/nightline/DailyNews/TomNotebook_Congo.html

'Some of his fellow scientists prayed for his recovery, to a God they did not believe in':
Mary Bliss, 'Memoir of my Brother's Youth', read at his memorial service, 1 July 2000.

'... research connection ... Mamirauá ...': see Henderson, Hamilton and
Crampton (1998).

'pronounced dead ... not chimpanzees': Weiss (2001).

'"one of the greatest evolutionary theorists since Darwin"': obituary by Robert Trivers,
Nature, 404, 828, 20 April 2000.

'"a good candidate ... Darwinian since Darwin"': obituary by Richard Dawkins,
Independent (London), 10 March 2000.

'... upon capturing a bird-wing butterfly in the Moluccas': Hamilton refers to the 'Rajah
Brooke swallowtail in Borneo', but seems more likely to be alluding to the famous passage, from Wallace (1869), quoted here on page 61.

'"the mysteries of the forest undertakers"', '"foetid chemicals"': Hamilton (1992).

'"Later ... under a stone"': Hamilton (1992).

'"I sometimes fantasise ... generally kindly approach"': letter to John Hartung, posted
by Hartung to HBES-L (Human Behavior & Evolution Society email list), 10 June
1996.

'"from here ... the Amazon"':
www.unifr.ch/biol/ecology/hamilton/hamilton/bozzi1.html

'"While the rest ... thought in chords"': Trivers (2000).

Richard Dawkins

'We reach out in our search . . .': Dawkins (2004).

13. WHAT GENES WANT

'"With a wild surmise . . . tried to sleep"': Dawkins (1991), 73.

'Acquaintance with the theory . . . argument from design . . .': Thomas Sutcliffe, 'The Prophet of Reason', *Independent* (London), 5 July 2001.

'"a kind of world authority"'. . . '"too shy"': interview, 21 November 2000.

'"if you wrote an essay . . ."': interview, 26 February 2001.

'. . . anecdote of Tinbergen's . . .': Tinbergen (1963).

'"ruthlessly mechanistic" . . . "survival machine"': Dawkins, Halliday and Dawkins (1991), xii.

'According to Tinbergen's biographer . . . Greenland as a young man': Kruuk (2003), 63–4.

'. . . Tinbergen set out the terms . . .': Tinbergen (1963).

'" . . . an Athens of ethology"': Dawkins, Halliday and Dawkins (1991), xi.

'. . . Mike Cullen . . . fulsome tribute:' interview, 26 February 2001; John Krebs and Richard Dawkins, 'Mike Cullen' (obituary), *Guardian* (London), 10 April 2001.

'"pretty poor" . . . hum his way . . .': interview, 26 February 2001.

'"I was immediately inspired by Hamilton . . . almost didn't need Williams"': *ibid.*

'" . . . what we'd known ever since Fisher"': interview, 26 February 2001.

'"and the public gets to look over their shoulder"': Marek Kohn, 'Laboratories against the Literati', *Independent* (London), 24 March 2000. See also Brockman (1995).

'"gripping"': Dawkins (1989), v.

'"The world must be full . . . because of Dawkins"': Ian Parker, 'Richard Dawkins's Evolution', *New Yorker*, 6 September 1996.

'. . . he compared it to David Lack's *Life of the Robin*': Maynard Smith (1988), 105.

'"Every day you're having to struggle . . . social approval"': interview, 26 February 2001.

'" . . . bytes and bytes and bytes . . ."': Dawkins (1995), 19.

'"nadir", "If you add . . . six books"': interview, 26 February (2001).

'"We are survival . . . astonishment"': Dawkins (1989), v.

'"lumbering robots"': Dawkins (1989), 19.

'" . . . at least read *this*", "the best candidate . . ."': Dawkins (1999), viii.

'"a new way of seeing biological facts"': *ibid.*, 1.

'"the replicator . . . happens to be sitting"': *ibid.*, 4.

'"if adaptations . . . conceptual prison"': *ibid.*, vi.

'"Before Hamilton's revolution . . . rescuing the individual"': *ibid.*, 194.

'. . . Hamilton had been trying to rescue . . . "what would I do?"': BMC SA 3/51, 52.

'" . . . more poetry in Mitochondrial Eve . . ."': Dawkins (1995), xii.

'"been made painfully aware"', '"We should scarcely attack Euclid . . ."', '"prior uncertainty about life all over the universe"', '"empirically minded, white-coated . . ."': Richard Dawkins, 'Darwin Triumphant: Darwinism as a Universal Truth', in Robinson and Tiger (1991).

'"openly derisive . . . bothered to do it"': Dawkins (1995), 101–2.

"'robot vehicles'": Dawkins (1989), v.

"'. . . so much wickedness in the world'": Marren (1995), 102.

"'The answer to your rather patronising question . . .'": 'You Ask the Questions', *Independent* (London), 23 December 1998, *Wednesday Review*, 8, www.world-of-dawkins.com/Dawkins/Work/Interviews/independent_questions.htm

"'to make the world pretty . . .'": Dawkins (1996), 236.

"'shy to give'": Dawkins (2003), 241.

"'keening lament'": 'Lament for Douglas Adams', *Guardian* (London), 14 May 2001.

"'Positively evil'": Ben Russell, 'Dawkins Leads Atheist Revolt against "Evil" Church Schools', *Independent* (London), 24 February 2001.

"'Dangerous nonsense'": Richard Dawkins, 'Religion's Misguided Missiles', *Guardian* (London), 15 September 2001.

"'injustice'", "'an almost visceral pain'": interview, 1 August 2001.

'. . . as Dawkins advised Tony Blair . . . think with one's gut': Dawkins (2003), 29–30.

"'definitely instils a very strong recognition . . .'", "'. . . if you think this is wrong . . .'", "'I suppose you could make a Darwinian case . . .'": interview, 29 April 2003.

"'rebel against the tyranny of the selfish replicators'": Dawkins (1989), 201.

"'. . . nice guys can finish first'": *ibid.*, 233.

"'there's an ever-present threat . . . always defect'": interview, 29 April 2003.

'Taking the long view . . . one way or another:' Robin Dunbar, 'What's God Got to Do with It?', *New Scientist*, 14 June 2003, 38–9; John Maynard Smith and David Harper (2003), *Animal Signals*, Oxford University Press, Oxford.

"'viruses'": 'Viruses of the Mind', Dawkins (2003); www.world-of-dawkins.com/Dawkins/Work/Articles/1993-summervirusesofmind.htm

"'I suppose it's because . . . pull us down again'": interview, 29 April 2003.

"'The universe . . . pitiless indifference'": Dawkins (1995), 133.

14. THE MEANING OF SUNSET

'. . . women . . . take more than half the genetics degrees': www.set4women.gov.uk/set4women/statistics/tables/table_433.htm

'Nearly half of all Americans believe . . . take the Bible literally': George Bishop, 'Back to the Garden', *Public Perspective* May/June 2000, 21–3, www.ropercenter.uconn.edu/pubper/pdf/pp113b.pdf; University of Cincinnati Public Relations Office, 18 August 1998, 'University of Cincinnati Study Shows Americans Persist in Religious Worldview of Evolution', www.uc.edu/info-services/bishop.htm; MORI, 'Voting and the Influence of Religion', 23 June 2000, www.mori.com/digest/2000/c000623.shtml

"'the world's kindest man . . . committed adaptationists'": Gould, 'Fulfilling the Spandrels of World and Mind', in Selzer (1993).

"'Because of the excellence . . . state of evolutionary theory'": Maynard Smith (1995).

'. . . voices can be heard speaking up for group selection . . .': Wilson and Sober (1994), Sober and Wilson (1998).

"'Natural selection does nothing'": Provine (2001), 199.

'Natural selection is no longer assumed . . . behaviour still do . . .': Endler (1986), 239–41; Ridley (2003).

'"that only illiterate Anglo-Saxons . . . diet of Hegel"': Maynard Smith (1988), 35–6.

'"Please commission an opinion poll . . . regime change in Washington?"' Dawkins, letter to the *Guardian* (London), 18 February 2003.

'"The tints . . . to the trees"': Darwin (1909a), 403.

'One of Bill Hamilton's last bold ideas . . .': Hamilton and Brown (2001). See also Archetti (2000).

'Handicap Principle': Zahavi and Zahavi (1997).

'In his eulogy . . .': Hamilton (2001), xiv.

Bibliography

Adamson, Judith (1998), *Charlotte Haldane: Woman Writer in a Man's World*, Macmillan, Basingstoke.

Alexander, Richard D. (2000), 'William D. Hamilton Remembered', *Natural History*, June, 44–6.

Almond, Gabriel A. (1954), *The Appeals of Communism*, Princeton University Press, Princeton, NJ.

Anon. (1863), 'On the Relations of Man to the Inferior Animals', *Anthropological Society Review and Journal* (May), 107–17; alepho.clarku.edu/huxley/comm/ScPr/AnthrSocRev.html.

Arblaster, Anthony, and Lukes, Steven (1971), *The Good Society: A Book of Readings*, Methuen, London.

Archetti, Marco (2000), 'The Origin of Autumn Colours by Coevolution', *Journal of Theoretical Biology*, 205, 625–30.

Axelrod, Robert, and Hamilton, W. D. (1981), 'The Evolution of Co-operation', *Science*, 211, 1390–6.

Barkan, Elazar (1992), *The Retreat of Scientific Racism: Changing Concepts of Race in Britain and the United States between the World Wars*, Cambridge University Press, Cambridge.

Bartley, Mary M. (1994), 'Conflicts in Human Progress: Sexual Selection and the Fisherian "Runaway"', *British Journal for the History of Science*, 27, 177–96.

Barton, N. H., and Charlesworth, B. (1998), 'Why Sex and Recombination?', *Science*, 281, 1986–9.

Bates, Henry Walter (1862), 'Contributions to an Insect Fauna of the Amazon Valley. *Lepidoptera: Heliconidae*', *Transactions of the Linnean Society of London*, 23, 495–566.

Bates, Henry Walter (1892), *The Naturalist on the River Amazons*, John Murray, London.

Beddall, Barbara G. (1969), *Wallace and Bates in the Tropics: An Introduction to the Theory of Natural Selection*, Macmillan, London.

Bennett, J. H. (ed.) (1983), *Natural Selection, Heredity and Eugenics, Including Selected Correspondence of R. A. Fisher with Leonard Darwin and Others*, Clarendon, Oxford; www.library.adelaide.edu.au/digitised/fisher/natsel/index.html

Benton, Jill (1990), *Naomi Mitchison: A Century of Experiment in Life and Letters*, Pandora, London.

Bowler, Peter J. (1989), *Evolution: The History of an Idea*, University of California Press, Berkeley.

Bowler, Peter J. (1992), *The Eclipse of Darwinism: Anti-Darwinian Evolution Theories in the Decades around 1900*, John Hopkins University Press, Baltimore.

Box, Joan Fisher (1978), *Ronald A. Fisher: The Life of a Scientist*, John Wiley & Sons, New York.

Brent, Peter (1981), *Charles Darwin: 'A Man of Enlarged Curiosity'*, Heinemann, London.

Brockman, John (ed.) (1995), *The Third Culture: Beyond the Scientific Revolution*, Simon & Schuster, New York.

Brooks, John Langdon (1984), *Just Before the Origin: Alfred Russel Wallace's Theory of Evolution*, Columbia University Press, New York.

Brown, Andrew (1999), *The Darwin Wars*, Simon & Schuster, London.

Browne, Janet (1995), *Charles Darwin: Voyaging*, Jonathan Cape, London.

Browne, Janet (2002), *Charles Darwin: The Power of Place*, Jonathan Cape, London.

Butler, Ewan (1972), *Mason-Mac: The Life of Lieutenant-General Sir Noel Mason-Macfarlane*, Macmillan, London.

Cain, Arthur (1964), 'The Perfection of Animals', in Carthy, J. D. and Duddington, C. L. (eds), *Viewpoints in Biology*, Vol. 3, Butterworth, London; extract in Ridley (1997).

Cain, Arthur (1979), 'Introduction to General Discussion', *Proceedings of the Royal Society of London* B, 205, 599–604.

Cain, Arthur J., and Sheppard, Philip M. (1950), 'Selection in the Polymorphic Land Snail *Cepaea nemoralis*', *Heredity*, 4, 275–94.

Cain, Arthur J., and Sheppard, Philip M. (1954), 'Natural Selection in *Cepaea*', *Genetics*, 39, 89–116.

Chavot, Philippe (n.d.), 'Eléments d'Histoire de l'Ethologie en France: Analyse du Contexte National et International, 1948–1968', ecobio.univ-rennes1.fr/sfeca/histoire/historique-1948-1968.doc

Clark, Ronald (1968a), *J. B. S.: The Life and Work of J. B. S. Haldane*, Hodder & Stoughton, London.

Clark, Ronald W. (1968b), *The Huxleys*, Heinemann, London.

Clarke, Arthur C. (1989), *Astounding Days: A Science Fictional Autobiography*, Gollancz, London.

Clarke, Bryan C. (1995), 'Edmund Brisco Ford', *Biographical Memoirs of Fellows of the Royal Society*, 41, 145–68.

Clarke, Cyril (1977), 'Philip Macdonald Sheppard', *Biographical Memoirs of Fellows of the Royal Society*, 23, 465–500.

Clarke, C. A., and Sheppard, P. M. (1966), 'A Local Survey on the Distribution of the Industrial Melanic Forms in the Moth *Biston betularia* and Estimates of the Selective Values of these in an Industrial Environment', *Proceedings of the Royal Society of London* B, 165, 424–39.

Clutton-Brock, T. H. and Harvey, P. H. (1979), 'Comparison and Adaptation', *Proceedings of the Royal Society of London* B, 205, 547–65.

Committee on Homosexual Offences and Prostitution (1957), *Report of the Committee on*

Homosexual Offences and Prostitution, Parliamentary Papers, Cmnd 247, London.

Conner, Jeffrey K. (2001), 'How Strong Is Natural Selection?', *Trends in Ecology and Evolution*, 16, 215–7.

Cook, L. M., Dennis, R. L. H., and Mani, G. S. (1999), 'Melanic Morph Frequency in the Peppered Moth in the Manchester Area', *Proceedings of the Royal Society of London* B, 266, 293–7.

Coyne, Jerry A. (1998), 'Not Black and White', *Nature*, 396, 35–6.

Coyne, Jerry A. (2000), letter to *Pratt Tribune* (Kansas), December 6; pratttribune.com/articles/2002/12/06/news/export2264.txt

Crabtree, Adam (1993), *From Mesmer to Freud: Magnetic Sleep and the Roots of Psychological Healing*, Yale University Press, New Haven.

Craig, Edward (ed.) (1998), *Routledge Encyclopedia of Philosophy*, (CD-ROM), Routledge, London.

Cronin, Helena (1991), *The Ant and the Peacock: Altruism and Sexual Selection from Darwin to Today*, Cambridge University Press, Cambridge.

Crow, James F. (1997), 'The High Spontaneous Mutation Rate: Is It a Health Risk?' *Proceedings of the National Academy of Sciences*, 94, 8380–6.

Daly, Martin, and Wilson, Margo (1988), *Homicide*, Aldine de Gruyter, Hawthorne, NY.

Darwin, Charles (1875), *The Variation of Animals and Plants under Domestication*, ii, John Murray, London.

Darwin, Charles (1902), *The Origin of Species* (6th edn), John Murray, London.

Darwin, Charles (1905), *Voyage of the Beagle: Journal of Researches into the Geology and Natural History of the Various Countries Visited by H.M.S.* Beagle, Amalgamated Press, London.

Darwin, Charles (1909a), *The Descent of Man, and Selection in Relation to Sex*, John Murray, London.

Darwin, Charles (1909b), *The Foundations of the Origins of Species: Two Essays Written in 1842 and 1844*, Cambridge University Press, Cambridge.

Darwin, Charles (1998), *The Origin of Species* (2nd edn), Oxford University Press, Oxford.

Darwin, Charles (2003), *The Autobiography of Charles Darwin*, Icon, Duxford.

Darwin, Francis (ed.) (1887), *The Life and Letters of Charles Darwin*, John Murray, London; digital.library.upenn.edu/webbin/gutbook/lookup?num=2087

Darwin, Francis, and Seward, Albert C. (eds) (1903), *More Letters of Charles Darwin: A Record of his Work in a Series of Hitherto Unpublished Letters*, 2 vols, John Murray, London.

Davies, N. B. (1978), 'Territorial Defence in the Speckled Wood butterfly (*Pararge aegeria*): The Resident Always Wins', *Animal Behaviour*, 26, 138–47.

Davies, N. B. (1979), 'Game Theory and Territorial Behaviour in Speckled Wood Butterflies', *Animal Behaviour*, 27, 961–2.

Davison, Angus, and Clarke, Bryan (2000), 'History or Current Selection? A Molecular Analysis of "Area Effects" in the Land Snail *Cepaea nemoralis*', *Proceedings of the Royal Society of London* B, 267, 1399–405.

Dawkins, M. S., Halliday, T. R., and Dawkins, R. (eds) (1991), *The Tinbergen Legacy*,

Chapman & Hall, London.

Dawkins, Richard (1979), 'Twelve Misunderstandings of Kin Selection', *Zeitschrift für Tierpsychologie*, 51,184–200.

Dawkins, Richard (1989), *The Selfish Gene*, Oxford University Press, Oxford.

Dawkins, Richard (1991), *The Blind Watchmaker*, Penguin, London.

Dawkins, Richard (1993), 'Viruses of the Mind', *Free Inquiry*, 13, 34–41.

Dawkins, Richard (1995), *River out of Eden: A Darwinian View of Life*, Weidenfeld & Nicolson, London.

Dawkins, Richard (1999), *The Extended Phenotype*, Oxford University Press, Oxford.

Dawkins, Richard (2000) 'Forever Voyaging: The Genius of W. D. Hamilton, 1936–2000', *Times Literary Supplement*, 4 August 2000, 12–13.

Dawkins, Richard (2001), 'Survival of the Fittest What?', www.boxmind.com

Dawkins, Richard (2004), 'Why Are We Here?', Emblem/Mentorn production for Five (UK TV channel).

Dawkins, R., and Ridley, M. (eds) (1985), *Oxford Surveys in Evolutionary Biology* 2, Oxford University Press, Oxford.

Dennett, Daniel C. (1995), *Darwin's Dangerous Idea*, Allen Lane, London.

Depew, David J., and Weber, Bruce H. (1995), *Darwinism Evolving: Systems Dynamics and the Genealogy of Natural Selection*, MIT Press, Cambridge, MA.

Desmond, Adrian (1994), *Huxley: The Devil's Disciple*, Michael Joseph, London.

Dewsbury, Donald A. (ed.) (1985), *Leaders in the Study of Animal Behavior: Autobiographical Perspectives*, Bucknell University Press, Lewisburg, PA.

Dronamraju, Krishna R. (ed.) (1968), *Haldane and Modern Biology*, Johns Hopkins University Press, Baltimore.

Dronamraju, Krishna R. (ed.) (1995), *Haldane's* Daedalus *Revisited*, Oxford University Press, Oxford.

Duncan, Ronald, and Weston-Smith, Miranda (1977), *The Encyclopaedia of Ignorance*, Pergamon, Oxford.

Durant, John R. (1979), 'Scientific Naturalism and Social Reform in the Thought of Alfred Russel Wallace', *British Journal for the History of Science*, 12, 31–58.

Edwards, A. W. F. (1987), 'What Fisher Meant', *Nature*, 329, 10.

Edwards, A. W. F. (1990), 'R. A. Fisher, Twice Professor of Genetics: London and Cambridge', *Biometrics*, 46, 897–904.

Edwards, A. W. F. (1994), 'The Fundamental Theorem of Natural Selection', *Biological Reviews*, 69, 443–74.

Edwards, A. W. F., 'W. D. Hamilton's Darwinian Precursors', *Times Literary Supplement*, 6 December 1996, 17.

Edwards, A. W. F. (1998), 'Natural Selection and the Sex Ratio: Fisher's Sources', *American Naturalist*, 151, 564–9.

Edwards, A. W. F. (2000), 'The Genetical Theory of Natural Selection', *Genetics*, 154, 1419–26.

Edwards, A. W. F. (2001), 'Darwin and Mendel United: The Contributions of Fisher, Haldane and Wright up to 1932', in Reeve, Eric C. R. (ed.), *Encyclopedia of Genetics*, Fitzroy Dearborn, London.

Endler, John A. (1986), *Natural Selection in the Wild*, Princeton University Press, Princeton, NJ.

Farmeloe, Graham (ed.) (2002), *It Must Be Beautiful: Great Equations of Modern Science*, Granta, London.

Fisher, James (1945), *Watching Birds*, Penguin, Harmondsworth.

Fisher, Ronald A. (1914), 'Some Hopes of a Eugenist', *Eugenics Review*, 5, 309–15, *[Collected Papers]* CP3; www.library.adelaide.edu.au/digitised/fisher/3.pdf

Fisher, Ronald A. (1915), 'Evolution of Sexual Preference', *Eugenics Review*, 7, 184–92, CP6.

Fisher, Ronald A. (1918), 'The Correlation Between Relatives on the Supposition of Mendelian Inheritance', *Transactions of the Royal Society of Edinburgh*, 52: 399–433, CP9; www.library.adelaide.edu.au/digitised/fisher/9.pdf

Fisher, Ronald A. (1922a), 'On the Dominance Ratio', *Proceedings of the Royal Society of Edinburgh*, 42, 321–41, CP24; www.library.adelaide.edu.au/digitised/fisher/24.pdf

Fisher, Ronald A. (1922b), 'Darwinian Evolution of Mutations', *Eugenics Review*, 14, 31–4, CP26; www.library.adelaide.edu.au/digitised/fisher/26.pdf

Fisher, Ronald A. (1922c), 'The Evolution of the Conscience in Civilised Communities', *Eugenics Review*, 14, 190–3, CP28.

Fisher, Ronald A. (1929), 'The Evolution of Dominance; Reply to Professor Sewall Wright', *American Naturalist*, 63, 553–6, CP81; www.library.adelaide.edu.au/digitised/fisher/81.pdf

Fisher, Ronald A. (1934), 'Indeterminism and Natural Selection', *Philosophy of Science*, 1, 99–117, CP121; www.library.adelaide.edu.au/digitised/fisher/121.pdf

Fisher, Ronald A. (1936a), 'Has Mendel's Work Been Rediscovered?', *Annals of Science*, 1, 115–37, CP144; www.library.adelaide.edu.au/digitised/fisher/144.pdf

Fisher, Ronald A. (1936b), 'The Measurement of Selective Intensity', *Proceedings of the Royal Society of London* B, 121, 58–62, CP147; www.library.adelaide.edu.au/digitised/fisher/147.pdf

Fisher, Ronald A. (1941), 'Average Excess and Average Effect of a Gene Substitution', *Annals of Eugenics* 11, 53–63, CP185; www.library.adelaide.edu.au/digitised/fisher/185.pdf

Fisher, Ronald A. (1947), 'The Renaissance of Darwinism', *The Listener*, 37, 1001, 1009, CP217.

Fisher, Ronald A. (1950), *Creative Aspects of Natural Law: The Eddington Memorial Lecture*, Cambridge University Press, Cambridge, CP241; www.library.adelaide.edu.au/digitised/fisher/241.pdf

Fisher, Ronald A. (1971), ed. Bennett, J.H., *Collected Papers of Ronald A. Fisher, Volume I 1912–24*, University of Adelaide, Adelaide.

Fisher, Ronald A. (1999), *The Genetical Theory of Natural Selection: A Complete Variorum Edition*, Oxford University Press, Oxford.

Fisher, R. A., and Ford, E. B. (1947), 'The Spread of a Gene in Natural Conditions in a Colony of the Moth *Panaxia dominula* L.', *Heredity*, 1, 143–74, CP219; www.library.adelaide.edu.au/digitised/fisher/219.pdf

Fisher, R. C. (1988), 'An Inordinate Fondness for Beetles', *Biological Journal of the Linnean Society*, 35, 313-9.

Forbes, E. G. (ed.) (1978), *Human Implications of Scientific Advance: Proceedings of the XVth International Congress of the History of Science, Edinburgh, 10–15 August 1977*, Edinburgh University Press, Edinburgh.

Ford, E. B. (1937), 'Problems of Heredity in the Lepidoptera', *Biological Reviews*, 12, 461–503.

Ford, E. B. (1945), *Butterflies*, Collins, London.

Ford, E. B. (1981), *Taking Genetics into the Countryside*, Weidenfeld & Nicolson, London.

Frank, Steven A. (1995), 'George Price's Contributions to Evolutionary Genetics', *Journal of Theoretical Biology*, 175, 373–88.

Futuyma, Douglas, and Antonovics, Janis (eds) (1992), *Oxford Surveys in Evolutionary Biology*, 8, Oxford University Press, Oxford.

Fyfe, James (1950), *Lysenko Is Right*, Lawrence & Wishart, London.

Gause, George (1934), *The Struggle for Existence*, Williams and Wilkins, Baltimore; www.ggause.com/Contgau.htm

Gayon, Jean (1998), *Darwinism's Struggle for Survival: Heredity and the Hypothesis of Natural Selection*, Cambridge University Press, Cambridge.

Gillespie, Charles C. (ed.) (1972), *Dictionary of Scientific Biography*, vol. V, Charles Scribner's Sons, New York.

Glick, Thomas F. (ed.) (1974), *The Comparative Reception of Darwinism*, University of Texas Press, Austin, TX.

Gould, Stephen Jay (1985), *The Flamingo's Smile: Reflections in Natural History*, Penguin, Harmondsworth.

Gould, Stephen Jay (1991), *Bully for Brontosaurus: Reflections in Natural History*, Hutchinson Radius, London.

Gould, Stephen Jay (1993), *Eight Little Piggies: Reflections in Natural History*, Jonathan Cape, London.

Gould, Stephen Jay (1996), *Dinosaur in a Haystack: Reflections in Natural History*, Harmony, New York.

Gould, Stephen Jay (1997), 'Darwinian Fundamentalism', *New York Review of Books*, 12 June.

Gould, Stephen Jay, and Lewontin, Richard C. (1979), 'The Spandrels of San Marco and the Panglossian Paradigm: A Critique of the Adaptationist Programme', *Proceedings of the Royal Society of London* B, 205, 581–98.

Grafen, Alan (1985), 'Hamilton's Rule OK', *Nature*, 318, 310–1.

Grafen, Alan (1987), 'The Logic of Divisively Asymmetric Contests: Respect for Ownership and the Desperado Effect', *Animal Behaviour* 35, 462-7; users.ox.ac.uk/~grafen/cv/bourgeois.pdf

Grafen, Alan (1990), 'Biological Signals as Handicaps', *Journal of Theoretical Biology*, 144, 517–46.

Grafen, Alan (2000), 'W. D. Hamilton' (obituary), *Guardian* (London), 9 March 2000; www.guardian.co.uk/obituaries/story/0,3604,230968,00.html

Grafan, Alan (2003), 'Fisher the Evolutionary Biologist', *The Statistician*, 52, 319–29; users.ox.ac.uk/~grafen/cv/fisher.pdf

Grant, Bruce (1999), 'Fine Tuning the Peppered Moth Paradigm', *Evolution*, 53, 980–4; www.wm.edu/biology/melanism.pdf

Gray, John (2002), *Straw Dogs: Thoughts on Humans and Other Animals*, Granta, London.

Greenwood, P. J., Harvey, P. H., and Slatkin, M. (eds) (1985), *Evolution: Essays in Honour of John Maynard Smith*, Cambridge University Press, Cambridge.

Grene, Marjorie (ed.)(1983), *Dimensions of Darwinism: Themes and Counterthemes in Twentieth-Century Evolutionary Theory*, Cambridge University Press and Editions de la Maison des Sciences de l'Homme, Cambridge and Paris.

Haig, David, Pierce, Naomi E., and Wilson, Edward O. (2000), 'William Hamilton (1936–2000), *Science*, 287, 2438.

Haldane, Charlotte (1949), *Truth Will Out*, Weidenfeld & Nicolson, London.

Haldane, J. B. S. (1923), *Daedalus, or Science and the Future*, Kegan Paul, Trench, Trubner & Co, London.

Haldane, J. B. S. (1924), 'A Mathematical Theory of Natural and Artificial Selection, Part I', *Transactions of the Cambridge Philosophical Society*, 23, 19–41; in Ridley (1996b).

Haldane, J. B. S. (1925), *Callinicus: A Defence of Chemical Warfare*, Kegan Paul, Trench, Trubner, London.

Haldane, J. B. S. (1927), *Possible Worlds and Other Essays*, Chatto & Windus, London.

Haldane, J. B. S. (1929), 'Natural Selection', *Nature*, 124, 444.

Haldane, J. B. S. (1932a), *The Inequality of Man and Other Essays*, Chatto & Windus, London.

Haldane, J. B. S. (1932b), *The Causes of Evolution*, Longmans, Green, London.

Haldane, J. B. S. (1937a), 'The Effect of Variation on Fitness', *American Naturalist*, 71, 337–49.

Haldane, J. B. S. (1937b), 'A Dialectical Account of Evolution' *Science & Society*, 1, 473–86.

Haldane, J. B. S. (1938), *Heredity and Politics*, Allen & Unwin, London.

Haldane, J. B. S. (1940a), *Science in Peace and War*, Lawrence & Wishart, London.

Haldane, J. B. S. (1940b), 'Lysenko and Genetics', *Science and Society*, 4, 433–7.

Haldane, J. B. S. (1941a), *New Paths in Genetics*, Allen & Unwin, London.

Haldane, J. B. S. (1941b), *Science and Everyday Life*, Penguin, Harmondsworth.

Haldane, J. B. S. (1946), *A Banned Broadcast and Other Essays*, Chatto & Windus, London.

Haldane, J. B. S. (1947), *Science Advances*, Allen & Unwin, London.

Haldane, J. B. S. (1948), 'Biology and Marxism', *Modern Quarterly*, 3, 2–11.

Haldane, J. B. S. (1949), 'In Defence of Genetics', *Modern Quarterly*, 4, 194–202.

Haldane, J. B. S. (1955), 'Population Genetics', *New Biology*, 18, 34–51.

Haldane, J. B. S. (1956), 'The Argument from Animals to Men: An Examination of its Validity for Anthropology', *Journal of the Royal Anthropological Institute*, 86, 1–14.

Haldane, J. B. S. (1957), 'The Cost of Natural Selection', *Journal of Genetics*, 55, 511–24.

Haldane, J. B. S. (1964), 'A Defence of Beanbag Genetics', *Perspectives in Biology and Medicine*, 7, 343–59.

Haldane, J. B. S. (1969), *The Marxist Philosophy and the Sciences*, Books for Libraries Press, Freeport, NY.

Haldane, J. B. S. (1971), *My Friend Mr Leakey*, Cedric Chivers, Portway, Bath.

Haldane, J. B. S., Sprunt, A. D., and Haldane, N. M. (1915), 'Reduplication in Mice', *Journal of Genetics*, 5, 133–5.

Haldane, Louisa Kathleen (1961), *Friends and Kindred. Memoirs*, Faber & Faber, London.

Hamilton, Archibald Milne (1958), *Road through Kurdistan*, Faber & Faber, London.

Hamilton, W. D. (1971), 'Geometry for the Selfish Herd', *Journal of Theoretical Biology*, 31, 295–311.

Hamilton, W. D. (1992), 'No Stone Unturned: A Bug-Hunter's Life and Death', *Times Literary Supplement*, 11 September, 9–10.

Hamilton, W. D. (1996), *Narrow Roads of Gene Land: The Collected Papers of W. D. Hamilton, Volume 1: Evolution of Social Behaviour*, W. H. Freeman/Spektrum, Oxford.

Hamilton, W. D. (2000), 'In His Own Words' (interview with Frans Roes), *Natural History*, 46–7.

Hamilton, W. D. (2001), *Narrow Roads of Gene Land: The Collected Papers of W. D. Hamilton, Volume 2: The Evolution of Sex*, Oxford University Press, Oxford.

Hamilton, W. D., and Brown, S. P. (2001), 'Autumn Tree Colours as a Handicap Signal', *Proceedings of the Royal Society of London* B, 268 (1475), 1489–93.

Hamilton, W. D., and Lenton, T. M. (1998), 'Spora and Gaia: How Microbes Fly with their Clouds', *Ecology, Ethology and Evolution*, 10, 1–16.

Hamilton, W. D., and May, Robert M. (1977), 'Dispersal in Stable Habitats', *Nature*, 269, 578–81.

Henderson, P. A., Hamilton, W. D. and Crampton, W. G. R. (1998), 'Evolution and Diversity in Amazonian Floodplain Communities', in D. M. Newbery, H. H. T. Prins and N. D. Brown, *Dynamics of Tropical Communities: The 37th Symposium of the British Ecological Society London 1998*, Blackwell, Oxford.

Henig, Robin Marantz (2000), *A Monk and Two Peas: The Story of Gregor Mendel and the Discovery of Genetics*, Weidenfeld & Nicolson, London.

Herbert, Sandra (1971), 'Darwin, Malthus, and Selection', *Journal of the History of Biology*, 4, 155–227.

Hobsbawm, Eric (2002), *Interesting Times: A Twentieth-Century Life*, Allen Lane, London.

Holmes, Frederick L. (ed.) (1990), *Dictionary of Scientific Biography*, 18, Supplement II, Scribner's, New York.

Hooper, Edward (2000), *The River: A Journey back to the Source of HIV and AIDS*, Penguin, London.

Hooper, Judith (2002), *Of Moths and Men: Intrigue, Tragedy and the Peppered Moth*, Fourth Estate, London.

Huxley, Aldous (1923), *Antic Hay*, Chatto & Windus, London.

Huxley, Julian S. (1942), *Evolution: The Modern Synthesis*, Allen & Unwin, London.

Huxley, Julian (1949), *Soviet Genetics and World Science: Lysenko and the Meaning of Heredity*, Chatto & Windus, London.

Huxley, Julian S., Hardy, Alister C., and Ford, Edmund B. (eds) (1954), *Evolution as a Process*, Allen & Unwin, London.

Huxley, Julian (1970), *Memories*, Allen & Unwin, London.

Huxley, Thomas Henry (1893), *Darwiniana: Essays*, Macmillan, London.

Huxley, Thomas Henry (1894), *Man's Place in Nature*, Macmillan, London.

Ipsen, Carl (1996), *Dictating Demography: The Problem of Population in Fascist Italy*, Cambridge University Press, Cambridge.

Irvine, William (1956), *Apes, Angels and Victorians: A Joint Biography of Darwin and Huxley*, Readers Union, Weidenfeld & Nicolson, London.

Jones, S. J., Leith, B. H., and Rawlings, P. (1977), 'Polymorphism in *Cepaea*: A Problem with Too Many Solutions?', *Annual Review of Ecology and Systematics*, 8, 109–43.

Joravsky, David (1970), *The Lysenko Affair*, Harvard University Press, Cambridge, MA.

Kalikow, Theodora J. (1983), 'Konrad Lorenz's Ethological Theory: Explanation and Ideology, 1938–43', *Journal of the History of Biology*, 16, 39–73.

Kalmus, Hans (1991), *Odyssey of a Scientist: An Autobiography*, Weidenfeld & Nicolson, London.

Keightley, Peter D., and Eyre-Walker, Adam (2000), 'Deleterious Mutations and the Evolution of Sex', *Science*, 290, 331–3.

Keller, Evelyn Fox, and Lloyd, Elisabeth A. (1992), *Keywords in Evolutionary Biology*, Harvard University Press, Cambridge, MA.

Kohn, David (ed.) (1985), *The Darwinian Heritage*, Princeton University Press, Princeton, NJ.

Krebs, John R., and Davies, Nicholas B. (eds) (1984), *Behavioural Ecology: An Evolutionary Approach*, Blackwell, Oxford.

Kruuk, Hans (2003), *Niko's Nature: The Life of Niko Tinbergen and his Science of Animal Behaviour*, Oxford University Press, Oxford.

Kunitz, Stanley J., and Haycraft, Howard (1942), *Twentieth Century Authors: A Biographical Dictionary of Modern Literature*, H. W. Wilson, New York.

Lack, David (1943), *The Life of the Robin*, Witherby, London.

Lack, David (1945), 'The Ecology of Closely Related Species with Specific Reference to Cormorant (*Phalacrocorax carbo*) and Shag (*P. aristotelis*)', *Journal of Animal Ecology*, 14, 12–16.

Lack, David (1956), *Swifts in a Tower*, Methuen, London.

Lack, David (1961), *Evolutionary Theory and Christian Belief: The Unresolved Conflict*, Methuen, London.

Lack, David (1968), *Darwin's Finches: An Essay on the General Biological Theory of Evolution*, Peter Smith, Gloucester, Mass.

Lack, David (1973), 'My Life as an Amateur Ornithologist', *Ibis*, 115, 421–31.

Lamotte, Maxime (1959), 'Polymorphism of Natural Populations of *Cepaea nemoralis*', *Cold Spring Harbor Symposia on Quantitative Biology*, 24, 63–86.

Langdon-Davies, John (1949), *Russia Puts the Clock Back: A Study of Soviet Science and Some British Scientists*, Victor Gollancz, London.

Lehrman, Daniel D. (1953), 'A Critique of Konrad Lorenz's Theory of Instinctive Behavior', *Quarterly Review of Biology*, 28, 337–63.

Lenton, Timothy M. (1998), 'Gaia and Natural Selection', *Nature*, 394, 439–47.

Lewontin, Richard C. (1972), 'Testing the Theory of Natural Selection', *Nature*, 236, 181–2.

Lewontin, Richard C. (1974), *The Genetic Basis of Evolutionary Change*, Columbia

University Press, New York;
hrst.mit.edu/hrs/evolution/public/papers/lewontin1974/lewontin_gboec.html

Lewontin, Richard C. (1979), 'Sociobiology as an Adaptationist Program', *Behavioral Science*, 24, 5–14.

Lightman, Bernard (ed.) (1997), *Victorian Science in Context*, University of Chicago Press, Chicago.

Lovelock, James E. (1987), *Gaia: A New Look at Life on Earth*, Oxford University Press, Oxford.

Mackenzie, Donald A. (1981), *Statistics in Britain 1865–1930: The Social Construction of Scientific Knowledge*, Edinburgh University Press, Edinburgh.

Maddox, Brenda (2002), *Rosalind Franklin: The Dark Lady of DNA*, HarperCollins, London.

Majerus, Michael (1998), *Melanism: Evolution in Action*, Oxford University Press, Oxford.

Malthus, Thomas Robert (1798), 'An Essay on the Principle of Population', in Gribbin, John, and Coyne, Pat (eds) (1997), *Classics in Science,* vol. 1 (CD-ROM), Electric Book, London.

Marchant, James (1916), *Alfred Russel Wallace: Letters and Reminiscences*, 2 vols, Cassell, London.

Marcus, Steven (1974), *Engels, Manchester, and the Working Class*, Weidenfeld, London.

Marren, Peter (1995), *The New Naturalists*, HarperCollins, London.

Marx, Karl (1960), *Critique of the Gotha Programme*, Progress, Moscow.

Maynard Smith, John (1953), 'Birds as Aeroplanes', *New Biology,* 14, 64–81.

Maynard Smith, John (1956), 'Fertility, Mating Behaviour and Sexual Selection in *Drosophila subobscura*', *Journal of Genetics*, 54, 261–79.

Maynard Smith, John (1964), 'Group Selection and Kin Selection', *Nature*, 201, 1145–7.

Maynard Smith, John (1962), 'The Causes of Ageing', in Review Lectures on Senescence, *Proceedings of the Royal Society of London* B, 157, 115–27.

Maynard Smith, John (1958), *The Theory of Evolution*, Penguin, Harmondsworth, Middlesex.

Maynard Smith, John (1968), '"Haldane's Dilemma" and the Rate of Evolution', *Nature*, 219, 1114–6.

Maynard Smith, John (1971), 'What Use Is Sex?', *Journal of Theoretical Biology*, 30, 319–35.

Maynard Smith, John (1978), *The Evolution of Sex*, Cambridge University Press, Cambridge.

Maynard Smith, John (1982), *Evolution and the Theory of Games*, Cambridge University Press, Cambridge.

Maynard Smith, John (1986), *The Problems of Biology*, Oxford University Press, Oxford.

Maynard Smith, John (1988), *Games, Sex and Evolution*, Harvester Wheatsheaf, Hemel Hempstead.

Maynard Smith, John (1991), 'Dinosaur Dilemmas', *New York Review of Books*, 25 April.

Maynard Smith, John (1995), 'Genes, Memes, & Minds', *New York Review of Books*, 30 November.

Maynard Smith, John (1996), 'The Games Lizards Play', *Nature*, 380, 198–9.

Maynard Smith, John (1998a), *Evolutionary Genetics*, Oxford University Press, Oxford.

Maynard Smith, John (1998b), *Shaping Life: Genes, Embryos and Evolution*, Weidenfeld & Nicolson, London.

Maynard Smith, John (2000), 'The Concept of Information in Biology', *Philosophy of Science*, 67, 177–94.

Maynard Smith, John (2001), 'Cautionary Tales for Aspiring Species or The Beast's Book of Blunders', *Trends in Ecology & Evolution*, 16, 717–20.

Maynard Smith, John *et al.* (1985), 'Developmental Constraints and Evolution', *Quarterly Review of Biology*, 60, 265–87.

Maynard Smith, John, Feil, Edward J., and Smith, Noel H. (2000), 'Population Structure and Evolutionary Dynamics of Pathogenic Bacteria', *BioEssays*, 22, 1115–22.

Maynard Smith, John, and Harper, David G. C. (1988), 'The Evolution of Aggression: Can Selection Generate Variability?', *Philosophical Transactions of the Royal Society of London* B, 319, 557–70.

Maynard-Smith, John, and Parker, Geoffrey A. (1976), 'The Logic of Asymmetric Contests', *Animal Behaviour* 24, 159–75.

Maynard Smith, John, and Price, George R. (1973), 'The Logic of Animal Conflict', *Nature*, 246, 15–18.

Maynard Smith, John, and Szathmáry, Eörs (1997), *The Major Transitions in Evolution*, Oxford University Press, Oxford.

Maynard Smith, John, and Szathmáry, Eörs (1999), *The Origins of Life: From the Birth of Life to the Origin of Language*, Oxford University Press, Oxford.

Mayr, Ernst (1993), 'What Was the Evolutionary Synthesis?', *Trends in Ecology and Evolution*, 8, 31–4.

Mayr, Ernst (2002), *What Evolution Is*, Phoenix, London.

Mayr, Ernst, and Provine, William B. (eds) (1980), *The Evolutionary Synthesis: Perspectives on the Unification of Biology*, Harvard University Press, Cambridge, MA.

Mazumdar, Pauline M. H. (1992), *Eugenics, Human Genetics and Human Failings: The Eugenics Society, its Sources and its Critics in Britain*, Routledge, London.

McKinney, H. Lewis (1972), *Wallace and Natural Selection*, Yale University Press, New Haven.

Medawar, Peter (1988), *Memoir of a Thinking Radish*, Oxford University Press, Oxford.

Medvedev, Zhores A. (1969), *The Rise and Fall of T. D. Lysenko*, Columbia University Press, New York.

Miliband, Ralph, and Saville, John (1976), *The Socialist Register*, Merlin, London.

Mitchison, Naomi (1973), *Small Talk . . . Memories of an Edwardian Childhood*, The Bodley Head, London.

Mitchison, Naomi (1975), *All Change Here: Girlhood and Marriage*, The Bodley Head, London.

Mitchison, Naomi (1979), *You May Well Ask: A Memoir 1920–1940*, Gollancz, London.

Montagu, Ivor (1970), *The Youngest Son: Autobiographical Sketches*, Lawrence & Wishart, London.

Morris, Desmond (1979), *Animal Days*, Jonathan Cape, London.

Müller-Hill, Benno (1988), *Murderous Science: Elimination by Scientific Selection of*

Jews, Gypsies and Others in Germany, 1933–1945, Oxford University Press, Oxford.

Nisbett, Alec (1976), *Konrad Lorenz*, J. M. Dent, London.

Numbers, Ronald L. (1998), *Darwinism Comes to America*, Harvard University Press, Cambridge, MA.

Pagel, Mark (ed.) (2002), *Encyclopedia of Evolution*, Oxford University Press, Oxford.

Partridge, Linda, and Hurst, Laurence D. (1998), 'Sex and Conflict', *Science*, 281, 2003–8.

Paul, Diane B. (1983), 'A War on Two Fronts: J. B. S. Haldane and the Response to Lysenkoism in Britain', *Journal of the History of Biology*, 16, 1–37.

Pirie, N. W. (1966), 'John Burdon Sanderson Haldane 1892–1964', *Biographical Memoirs of Fellows of the Royal Society*, 12, 212–49.

Plumb, J. H. (ed.) (1955), *Studies in Social History: A Tribute to G. M. Trevelyan*, Longmans, Green, London.

Pomiankowski, Andrew (1987), 'The "Handicap Principle" Does Work – Sometimes', *Proceedings of the Royal Society of London* B, 231, 123–45.

Proctor, Robert N. (1988), *Racial Hygiene: Medicine under the Nazis*, Harvard University Press, Cambridge, MA.

Provine, William B. (1977), 'The Role of Mathematical Population Geneticists in the Evolutionary Synthesis of the 1930s and 1940s', in Coleman, William, and Limoges, Camille (eds), *Studies in History of Biology*, Vol. 1, Johns Hopkins University Press, Baltimore.

Provine, William B. (1986), *Sewall Wright and Evolutionary Biology*, University of Chicago Press, Chicago.

Provine, William B. (2001), *The Origins of Theoretical Population Genetics*, University of Chicago Press, Chicago.

Rabelais, Francis (1944), *The Five Books of Gargantua and Pantagruel in the Modern Translation of Jacques Le Clercq*, Modern Library, New York.

Raby, Peter (2001), *Alfred Russel Wallace: A Life*, Chatto & Windus, London.

Radick, Gregory (2003), 'Is the Theory of Natural Selection Independent of its History?', in Hodge, Jonathan, and Radick, Gregory (eds), *The Cambridge Companion to Darwin*, Cambridge University Press, Cambridge.

Ramsey, Ian T. (ed.) (1965), *Biology and Personality: Frontier Problems in Science, Philosophy and Religion*, Basil Blackwell, Oxford.

Repcheck, Jack (2003), *The Man Who Found Time: James Hutton and the Discovery of the Earth's Antiquity*, Simon & Schuster, London.

Ridley, Mark (1996a), *Evolution*, Blackwell, Oxford.

Ridley, Mark (1996b), *Evolution* (CD-ROM), Blackwell, Oxford.

Ridley, Mark (ed.) (1997), *Evolution*, Oxford University Press, Oxford.

Ridley, Mark (2003), 'Designer Darwinism' (review of *Darwin and Design: Does Evolution Have a Purpose?* by Michael Ruse), *Nature*, 423, 686.

Robinson, Michael H., and Tiger, Lionel (eds) (1991), *Man and Beast Revisited*, Smithsonian Institution Press, Washington.

Rockell, Frederick (1912), 'The Last of the Great Victorians: Special Interview with Dr. Alfred Russel Wallace', *Millgate Monthly*, August; www.wku.edu/~smithch/wallace/S750.htm

Romanes, George (1897), *Darwin, and After Darwin: An Exposition of the Darwinian Theory and a Discussion of Post-Darwinian Questions*, Longmans, Green, London.

Ruse, Michael (1999), *Mystery of Mysteries: Is Evolution a Social Construction?*, Harvard University Press, Cambridge, MA.

Sabbagh, Karl (1999), *A Rum Affair: How Botany's 'Piltdown Man' Was Unmasked*, Allen Lane, London.

Sargent T. D. *et al.* (1998), 'The "Classical" Explanation of Industrial Melanism: Assessing the Evidence', *Evolutionary Biology*, 30, 299–322.

Sarkar, Sahotra (ed.) (1992), *The Founders of Evolutionary Genetics: A Centenary Reappraisal*, Kluwer, Dordrecht.

Sarkar, Sahotra (2002), 'Evolutionary Theory in the 1920s: The Nature of the "Synthesis"', philsci-archive.pitt.edu/archive/00000722/

Schwartz, James (2000), 'Death of an Altruist', *Lingua Franca*, 10(5).

Schweber, Silvan S. (1977), 'The Origin of the *Origin* Revisited', *Journal of the History of Biology*, 10, 229–316.

Secord, James A. (2000), *Victorian Sensation: The Extraordinary Publication, Reception, and Secret Authorship of* Vestiges of the Natural History of Creation, University of Chicago Press, Chicago.

Seger, Jon, and Harvey, Paul (1980), 'The Evolution of the Genetical Theory of Social Behaviour', *New Scientist*, 87, 50–1.

Segerstråle, Ullica (2000), *Defenders of the Truth: The Battle for Science in the Sociobiology Debate and Beyond*, Oxford University Press, Oxford.

Selzer, Jack (ed.) (1993), *Understanding Scientific Prose*, University of Wisconsin Press, Madison.

Shapiro, Arthur M. (1993), 'Haldane, Marxism and the Conduct of Research', *Quarterly Review of Biology*, 68, 69–77.

Shaw, George Bernard (1945), *Back to Methuselah: A Metabiological Pentateuch*, Oxford University Press, Oxford.

Shermer, Michael (2002), *In Darwin's Shadow: The Life and Science of Alfred Russel Wallace: A Biographical Study on the Psychology of History*, Oxford University Press, Oxford.

Sinervo, B., and Lively, C. M. (1996), 'The Rock–Paper–Scissors Game and the Evolution of Alternative Male Strategies', *Nature*, 380, 240–3.

Sinervo, Barry *et al.* (2000), 'Testosterone, Endurance, and Darwinian Fitness: Natural and Sexual Selection on the Physiological Bases of Alternative Male Behaviors in Side-Blotched Lizards', *Hormones and Behavior*, 38, 222–33.

Sinervo, Barry, Svensson, Erik, and Comendant, Tosha (2000), 'Density Cycles and an Offspring Quantity and Quality Game Driven by Natural Selection Gradients', *Nature*, 406, 985–8.

Singh, R. S., and Krimbas, C. B. (eds) (1999), *Evolutionary Genetics: From Molecules to Morphology*, vol. 1, Cambridge University Press, Cambridge.

Sober, Elliott, and Wilson, David Sloan (1998), *Unto Others: The Evolution and Psychology of Unselfish Behavior*, Harvard University Press, Cambridge, MA.

Spurway, Helen (1952), 'Behold, My Child, the Nordic Dog', *British Journal for the Philosophy of Science*, 3, 265–72.

Stapledon, Olaf (1999), *Last and First Men*, Gollancz, London.

Sterelny, Kim (2001), *Dawkins vs. Gould: Survival of the Fittest*, Icon, Duxford.

Taylor, M. W. (1992), *Men versus the State: Herbert Spencer and Late Victorian Individualism*, Clarendon, Oxford.

Thatcher, David S. (1970), *Nietzsche in England, 1890-1914: The Growth of a Reputation*, University of Toronto Press, Toronto.

Tinbergen, Nikolaas (1963), 'On Aims and Methods in Ethology', *Zeitschrift für Tierpsychologie*, 20, 410–33.

Trivers, Robert (2000), 'Obituary: William Donald Hamilton (1936–2000)', *Nature*, 404, 828.

Trivers, Robert L., and Hare, Hope (1976), 'Haplodiploidy and the Evolution of the Social Insects', *Science*, 191, 249–63.

Trunk, Achim (2003), 'Zweihundert Blutproben aus Auschwitz: Ein Forschungsvorhaben zwischen Anthropologie und Biochemie (1943–1945)', preprint, Forschungsprogramm 'Geschichte der Kaiser-Wilhelm-Gesellschaft im Nationalsozialismus', www.mpiwg-berlin.mpg.de/KWG/Ergebnisse/Ergebnisse12.pdf

Tudge, Colin (2000), *In Mendel's Footnotes: An Introduction to the Science and Technologies of Genes and Genetics from the Nineteenth Century to the Twenty-Second*, Jonathan Cape, London.

Turner, John R. G. (1987), 'Random Genetic Drift, R. A. Fisher, and the Oxford School of Ecological Genetics', in Krüger, Lorenz, Gigerenzer, Gerd, and Morgan, Mary S. (eds), *The Probabilistic Revolution*, vol. 2, *Ideas in the Sciences*, MIT Press, Cambridge, MA.

Vorzimmer, P. (1969), 'Darwin, Malthus and Natural Selection', *Journal of the History of Ideas*, 30, 527–42.

Wallace, Alfred Russel (1855), 'On the Law Which Has Regulated the Introduction of New Species', *Annals and Magazine of Natural History* II, 16, 184–96; www.wku.edu/~smithch/wallace/S020.htm

Wallace, Alfred Russel (1856), 'On the Habits of the Orang-Utan of Borneo', *Annals and Magazine of Natural History* II, 18, 26–32; www.wku.edu/~smithch/wallace/S026.htm

Wallace, Alfred Russel (1858), 'On the Tendency of Varieties to Depart Indefinitely from the Original Type', in Darwin, Charles and Wallace, Alfred Russel, 'On the Tendency of Species to Form Varieties; and On the Perpetuation of Varieties and Species by Natural Means of Selection', *Journal of the Proceedings of the Linnean Society: Zoology*, 3(9): 53–62; www.wku.edu/~smithch/wallace/S043.htm

Wallace, Alfred Russel (1864), 'The Origin of Human Races and the Antiquity of Man Deduced from the Theory of "Natural Selection"', *Journal of the Anthropological Society of London*, 2, clvii–clxxxvii; www.wku.edu/~smithch/wallace/S093.htm

Wallace, Alfred Russel (1869), *The Malay Archipelago: The Land of the Orang-Utan, and the Bird of Paradise, A Narrative of Travel, with Studies of Man and Nature*, in Gribbin, John and Coyne, Pat (eds) (1997), *Classics in Science*, vol. 1 (CD-ROM), Electric Book, London.

Wallace, Alfred Russel (1871), *Contributions to the Theory of Natural Selection*, Macmillan, London.

Wallace, Alfred Russel (1889a), *Darwinism: An Exposition of the Theory of Natural Selection, With Some of Its Applications*, Macmillan, London.

Wallace, Alfred Russel (1889b), *A Narrative of Travels on the Amazon and Rio Negro*, Ward, Lock, London.

Wallace, Alfred Russel (1890), 'Human Selection', *Fortnightly Review*, 48, 325–37; www.wku.edu/~smithch/S427.htm

Wallace, Alfred Russel (1896), *Miracles and Modern Spiritualism*, George Redway, London.

Wallace, Alfred Russel (1900), *Studies, Scientific and Social*, 2 vols, Macmillan, London.

Wallace, Alfred Russel (1905), *My Life: A Record of Events and Opinions*, 2 vols, Dodd, Mead & Co., New York.

Weiner, Jonathan (1994), *The Beak of the Finch: Evolution in Real Time*, Jonathan Cape, London.

Weiss, Robin A. (2001), 'Polio Vaccines Exonerated', *Nature*, 410, 1035–6.

Werskey, Gary (1988), *The Visible College*, Free Association Press, London.

West, Nigel (1999), *Venona: The Greatest Secret of the Cold War*, HarperCollins, London.

Wickman, Per-Olof, and Wiklund, Christer (1983), 'Territorial Defence and its Seasonal Decline in the Speckled Wood Butterfly (*P. aegeria*)', *Animal Behaviour*, 31, 1206–16.

Williams, George C. (1966), *Adaptation and Natural Selection: A Critique of Some Current Evolutionary Thought*, Princeton University Press, Princeton, NJ.

Williams, George C. (2000), 'Some Thoughts on William D. Hamilton (1936–2000)', *Trends in Ecology and Evolution*, 15, 302.

Williams-Ellis, Amabel (1966), *Darwin's Moon: A Biography of Alfred Russel Wallace*, Blackie, London.

Wilson, David Sloan, and Sober, Elliott (1994), 'Reintroducing Group Selection to the Human Behavioral Sciences', *Behavioral and Brain Sciences*, 17, 585–654.

Wynne-Edwards, Vero C. (1962), *Animal Dispersion in Relation to Social Behaviour*, Oliver and Boyd, Edinburgh.

Yates, F., and Mather, K. (1963), 'Ronald Aylmer Fisher 1890–1962', *Biographical Memoirs of Fellows of the Royal Society of London*, 9, 9–120; www.library.adelaide.edu.au/digitised/fisher/raf.pdf

Young, Robert M. (1998a), 'Darwinian Evolution and Human History', human-nature.com/rmyoung/papers/paper95h.html

Young, Robert M. (1998b), 'Darwin's Metaphor: Does Nature Select?', human-nature.com/dm/chap4.html

Zahavi, Amotz, and Zahavi, Avishag (1997), *The Handicap Principle: A Missing Piece of Darwin's Puzzle*, Oxford University Press, Oxford.

Zamudio, Kelly R., and Sinervo, Barry (2000), 'Polygyny, Mate-Guarding, and Posthumous Fertilization as Alternative Male Mating Strategies', *Proceedings of the National Academy of Sciences, USA*, 97, 14427–32; www.pnas.org

Internet Resources

Many historical texts by evolutionists are available online. Notable sites include:

The Alfred Russel Wallace Page
www.wku.edu/~smithch/index1.htm

The Huxley File
alepho.clarku.edu/huxley/

Collected Papers of R.A. Fisher
www.library.adelaide.edu.au/digitised/fisher/index.html

Works by Darwin can be found at a number of sites, including Project Gutenberg,
promo.net/pg/

Author's website: www.marekkohn.tk

Index